Legislative Leviathan

California Series on Social Choice and Political Economy
Edited by Brian Barry (1981 to 1991), Robert H. Bates,
James S. Coleman (from 1992), and Samuel L. Popkin

1. *Markets and States in Tropical Africa: The Political Basis of Agricultural Policies,* by Robert H. Bates
2. *Political Economics,* by James E. Alt and K. Alec Chrystal
3. *Abortion and the Politics of Motherhood,* by Kristin Luker
4. *Hard Choices: How Women Decide about Work, Career, and Motherhood,* by Kathleen Gerson
5. *Regulatory Policy and the Social Sciences,* edited by Roger Noll
6. *Reactive Risk and Rational Action: Managing Moral Hazard in Insurance Contracts,* by Carol A. Heimer
7. *Post-Revolutionary Nicaragua: State, Class, and the Dilemmas of Agrarian Policy,* by Forrest D. Colburn
8. *Essays on the Political Economy of Rural Africa,* by Robert H. Bates
9. *Peasants and King in Burgundy: Agrarian Foundations of French Absolutism,* by Hilton L. Root
10. *The Causal Theory of Justice,* by Karol Edward Soltan
11. *Principles of Group Solidarity,* by Michael Hechter
12. *Political Survival: Politicians and Public Policy in Latin America,* by Barry Ames
13. *Of Rule and Revenue,* by Margaret Levi
14. *Toward a Political Economy of Development: A Rational Choice Perspective,* edited by Robert H. Bates
15. *Rainbow's End: Irish-Americans and the Dilemmas of Urban Machine Politics, 1840–1985,* by Steven P. Erie
16. *A Treatise on Social Justice, Volume 1: Theories of Justice,* by Brian Barry
17. *The Social Origins of Political Regionalism: France, 1849–1981,* by William Brustein
18. *Nested Games: Rational Choice in Comparative Politics,* by George Tsebelis
19. *Information and Organizations,* by Arthur L. Stinchcombe
20. *Political Argument,* by Brian Barry
21. *Women and the Economic Miracle: Gender and Work in Postwar Japan,* by Mary Brinton
22. *Choosing Justice,* by Norman Frohlich and Joe A. Oppenheimer
23. *Legislative Leviathan: Party Government in the House,* by Gary W. Cox and Mathew D. McCubbins

Legislative Leviathan

*Party Government
in the House*

Gary W. Cox and
Mathew D. McCubbins

UNIVERSITY OF CALIFORNIA PRESS
Berkeley · *Los Angeles* · *Oxford*

University of California Press
Berkeley and Los Angeles, California

University of California Press, Ltd.
Oxford, England

© 1993 by
The Regents of the University of California

Library of Congress Cataloging-in-Publication Data

Cox, Gary W.
  Legislative leviathan : party government in the House / Gary W.
Cox and Mathew D. McCubbins.

     p.   cm.—(California series on social choice and political
economy : 23)
  Includes bibliographical references (p.   ) and index.
  ISBN 0-520-07219-7 (alk. paper).—ISBN 0-520-07220-0 (pbk. : alk. paper)
  1. United States. Congress House—Committees.   2. United States,
Congress. House—Leadership.   3. United States. Congress. House—
Rules and practice.   4. Political parties—United States.
I. McCubbins, Mathew D. (Mathew Daniel), 1956–   . II. Title.
III. Series.
JK1429.C69   1993
328.73'0769—dc20   92-6802

Printed in the United States of America

9 8 7 6 5 4 3 2 1

To our wives, Diane Lin and Susan McCubbins

Contents

List of Figures   xi

List of Tables   xiii

Acknowledgments   xvii

Introduction   1
  1. The Weakness of Parties   2
  2. Committee Government   9
  3. Outline of the Book   14

PART ONE   THE AUTONOMY AND
DISTINCTIVENESS OF COMMITTEES   17

1. Self-Selection and the Subgovernment Thesis   19
  1. Self-Selection   21
  2. Constituency Interests and
    Assignment Requests   24
  3. Accommodation of Assignment Requests   27
  4. Accommodation of Transfer Requests   33
  5. The Routinization of the Assignment Process 40
  6. Norms in the Assignment Process   42
  7. Conclusion   43

2. The Seniority System in Congress 45

    1. Seniority in the Rayburn House:
       The Standard View 45
    2. Reconsidering the Standard View 47
    3. The Empirical Evidence 49
    4. Interpreting the Evidence 55
    5. Conclusion 58

3. Subgovernments and the Representativeness
   of Committees 60

    1. The Previous Literature 61
    2. Data and Methodology 69
    3. Results 73
    4. Conclusion 79

PART TWO   A THEORY OF PARTY
ORGANIZATION 83

4. Institutions as Solutions to Collective
   Dilemmas 85

    1. Collective Dilemmas 86
    2. Central Authority: The Basics 90
    3. Why Central Authority Is
       Sometimes Necessary 94
    4. Multiperiod Considerations 99
    5. Problems with Central Authority 103
    6. Conclusion 106

5. A Theory of Legislative Parties 107

    1. The Reelection Goal 109
    2. Reelection Maximizers and
       Electoral Inefficiencies 122
    3. Party Leadership 125
    4. Conclusion 134

PART THREE   PARTIES AS FLOOR VOTING
COALITIONS 137

6. On the Decline of Party Voting in Congress 139

    1. Party Voting: Trends in the 1980s 140
    2. Party Voting: Trends from 1910 to
       the 1970s 141

3. Party Agendas and Party Leadership Votes   145
4. Conclusion   154

PART FOUR   PARTIES AS PROCEDURAL
COALITIONS: COMMITTEE
APPOINTMENTS   159

7. Party Loyalty and Committee Assignments   163

1. Assignments to Control Committees   164
2. Party Loyalty and Transfers to
   House Committees   166
3. Assignment Success of Freshmen   183
4. Conclusion   186

8. Contingents and Parties   188

1. A Model of Partisan Selection   189
2. Which Committees' Contingents
   Will Be Representative?   191
3. Results   202
4. Conclusion   228

PART FIVE   PARTIES AS PROCEDURAL
COALITIONS: THE SCHEDULING POWER   231

9. The Majority Party and the
   Legislative Agenda   233

1. The Speaker's Collective Scheduling Problem   234
2. Limits on the Scheduling Power   237
3. Committee Agendas and the Speaker   241
4. Intercommittee Logrolls   248
5. Conclusion   251

10. Controlling the Legislative Agenda   253

1. The Majority Party and the
   Committee System   254
2. The Consequences of Structural Power:
   The Legislative Agenda   259
3. The Consequences of Structural Power: party control
   Public Policy   269
4. Comments on the Postwar House   270

Conclusion   275

Appendixes   279
    1. Uncompensated Seniority Violations,
       Eightieth through Hundredth Congresses   279
    2. A Model of the Speaker's Scheduling
       Preferences   283
    3. Unchallengeable and Challengeable Vetoes   287
    4. The Scheduling Power   290

References   295

Author Index   313

Subject Index   316

List of Figures

1. ASC Ratings, Ninety-seventh Congress   66
2. ADA Ratings, Ninety-seventh Congress   66
3. AFL-CIO COPE Ratings, Ninety-fifth Congress   68
4. A Standardization Game   88
5. A Prisoner's Dilemma   89
6. Average Leadership Support Scores on the Democratic Party Agenda, Seventy-third to Hundredth Congresses   149
7. Average Leadership Support Scores on the Republican Party Agenda, Seventy-third to Hundredth Congresses   150
8. Average Democratic Leadership Support Scores on Party Leadership Votes, Seventy-third to Hundredth Congresses   153
9. Average Republican Leadership Support Scores on Party Leadership Votes, Seventy-third to Hundredth Congresses   154
10. Average Leadership Support Scores on Party Leadership Votes, Northern and Southern Democrats, Seventy-third to Hundredth Congresses   155
11–22. Committee Leadership Support Scores, by Committee   264–65
23. Dissent from Committee Reports, by Party   272

List of Tables

1. Assignments and Requests of Democratic Freshmen, Eightieth to Hundredth Congresses   28
2. Assignments of Republican Freshmen, Eightieth to Hundredth Congresses   29
3. Assignment Success of Democratic Freshmen, Eighty-sixth to Ninetieth and Ninety-second to Ninety-seventh Congresses   31
4. Success of Democrats Requesting Transfer, Eighty-sixth to Ninetieth and Ninety-second to Ninety-seventh Congresses   35
5. Success of Democrats Requesting Transfer, by Committee Requested   36
6. Recruitment Patterns in Democratic Committee Transfers, Eighty-sixth to Ninetieth and Ninety-second to Ninety-seventh Congresses   37
7. Democratic Requests and Vacancies, Eighty-sixth to Ninety-seventh Congresses   39
8. Accommodation of Committee Requests of Democratic Freshmen Entering the Eighty-sixth to Ninetieth and Ninety-second to Ninety-seventh Congresses   41
9. Seniority Violations in the Eightieth to Hundredth Congresses   54
10. Geographical Unrepresentativeness on Committees in the House   64

11. Ideological Representativeness on Committees in the
House   70

12. Summary of Difference-of-Means Tests on ADA Scores
for House Committees, Eighty-sixth to Ninety-seventh
Congresses   75

13. Summary of Difference-of-Means Tests on ACA Scores
for House Committees, Eighty-sixth to Ninety-seventh
Congresses   76

14. Summary of Difference-of-Means Tests on Conservative
Coalition Scores for House Committees, Eighty-sixth to
Ninety-seventh Congresses   77

15. Summary of Difference-of-Medians Tests on NOMINATE
Rankings for House Committees, Eightieth to Hun-
dredth Congresses   80

16. Partisan Differences in Interelection Vote Swings, 1948–
88   114

17. Partisan Swings and Incumbent Candidates' Probabilities
of Victory   116

18. Northern Democratic Swings, Southern Democratic Victories, and Vice Versa   119

19. The Size of Party Agendas, Seventy-third to Hundredth
Congresses   148

20. Party Loyalty and Democratic Committee Transfers,
Eightieth to Hundredth Congresses   173

21. Party Loyalty and Republican Committee Transfers,
Eightieth to Hundredth Congresses   176

22. Democratic Transfers and Requests, Eighty-sixth to
Ninetieth and Ninety-second to Ninety-seventh Con-
gresses   177

23. Multinomial Analysis of Democratic Transfers and Requests, Eighty-sixth to Ninetieth and Ninety-second to
Ninety-seventh Congresses   182

24. Loyalty and First-Choice Assignments   184

25. Classification of Committees by Type of Externality   200

26. Summary of Difference-of-Means Tests on ADA Ratings
Between Democratic Committee Contingents and the
Party, Eighty-seventh to Ninety-seventh Congresses   204

27. Summary of Difference-of-Means Tests on ADA Ratings
Between Republican Committee Contingents and the
Party, Eighty-seventh to Ninety-seventh Congresses   205

28. Summary of Wilcoxon Difference-of-Medians Tests on
NOMINATE Ratings Between Democratic Committee

Contingents and the Party, Eightieth to Hundredth Congresses | 208

29. Summary of Wilcoxon Difference-of-Medians Tests on NOMINATE Ratings Between Republican Committee Contingents and the Party, Eightieth to Hundredth Congresses | 210

30. Summary of Quintile-based Chi-Squares on NOMINATE Ratings for Democratic Committee Contingents, Eightieth to Hundredth Congresses | 214

31. Summary of Quintile-based Chi-Squares on NOMINATE Ratings for Republican Committee Contingents, Eightieth to Hundredth Congresses | 216

32. Mean Absolute Difference (MAD) in Percent Voting Yes Between Committee and Noncommittee Democrats, Selected Congresses | 223

33. Democratic Realignment of Control Committees, Eightieth to Hundredth Congresses | 226

34. Republican Realignment of Control Committees, Eightieth to Hundredth Congresses | 227

35. Average Committee Support Scores, by Party | 267

36. Spatial Equilibria under Alternative Veto Specifications | 288

Acknowledgments

We thank the following people for their valuable and insightful, if not always heeded, comments: Joel Aberbach, Josh Cohen, Joe Cooper, Vince Crawford, John Ferejohn, Morris Fiorina, Gary Jacobson, Sam Kernell, Rod Kiewiet, Keith Krehbiel, Skip Lupia, Roger Noll, Bruce Oppenheimer, Nelson Polsby, Keith Poole, David Rohde, Frances Rosenbluth, Tom Schwartz, Ken Shepsle, Steve Smith, and Barry Weingast. We thank William Heller, Jonathan Katz, Diane Lin, Sharyn O'Halloran, and Brian Sala for their invaluable assistance. We thank Gary Jacobson, Rod Kiewiet, Garrison Nelson, Keith Poole, and Howard Rosenthal for sharing their data with us. We acknowledge the support of the NSF (grant # SES-8811022 and # SES-9022882) and UCSD. Finally, we thank our wives for their patience, love, and support, and our children—Dylan Cox, Colin McCubbins, and Kenny McCubbins—for their reasonably regular sleep habits, generally sweet dispositions, and consistently low bounce-weights.

Introduction

Congress is a collection of committees that come together periodically to approve one another's actions.
—Clem Miller, *Member of the House*

Scholars who compare political parties invariably conclude that American parties are much weaker than their European counterparts: they are much less cohesive on legislative votes; their influence over the flow of legislation is less complete; they control only a small fraction of campaign money; they exercise almost no control over nominations—the list could go on. Within the American context, observers have commonly concluded that parties influence legislators less than pressure groups, political action committees, or constituents do. Much of the literature of the past two decades, moreover, has been devoted to the thesis that American parties have been declining—both in the electoral and the legislative arenas.

If parties are so weak, then what are the organizing principles of American politics? The literature provides a ready stock of answers. In the electoral arena, it is the individual candidates who have the most powerful organizations, who collect the most money, and who define the course of electoral campaigns. In the legislative arena, it is above all the standing committees of Congress—and, in the last two decades, their subcommittees—that are the centers of power. The standard wisdom on the postwar Congress is that it has been an exercise first in "committee government," then in "subcommittee government." Party government usually has received mention only as something conspicuously absent.

This book reevaluates the role of parties and committees, and the interactions between them, in the post–World War II House of Repre-

1

sentatives. Our view is that parties in the House—especially the majority party—are a species of "legislative cartel." These cartels usurp the power, theoretically resident in the House, to make rules governing the structure and process of legislation. Possession of this rule-making power leads to two main consequences. First, the legislative process in general—and the committee system in particular—is stacked in favor of majority party interests. Second, because members of the majority party have all the structural advantages, the key players in most legislative deals are members of the majority party, and the majority party's central agreements are facilitated by cartel rules and policed by the cartel's leadership.

Just like members of other cartels, members of majority parties face continual incentives to "cheat" on the deals that have been struck. These incentives to cheat threaten both the existence of the cartel and the efficient operation of the relevant "market"—in this case, in legislative trades. The structure of the majority party and the structure that the majority party imposes on the House can be viewed as resolving or ameliorating members' incentives to cheat, thereby facilitating mutually beneficial trade.

It will take the rest of the book to explain fully what we mean when we describe parties as legislative cartels. The next section of this introduction considers some of the views of party against which we react and to which we look for inspiration or evidence. Section 2 then sets out the dominant "committee government" model. Finally, section 3 offers a road map to the rest of the book.

1. THE WEAKNESS OF PARTIES

The dominant theme in the literature on American parties in the past two decades, whether it deals with the electoral or the legislative arena, has been one of decline. The electoral side of the story is one of fewer voters casting straight-party ballots, fewer citizens willing to identify with any political party, a reduced role for party officials in the presidential nominating process, an increasing advantage for incumbents in House elections, and other signs of party decay (Wattenberg 1984; Crotty 1984). The trends are so large that some suggest that the future may hold "the evolution of a basically partyless electorate" (Crotty 1984, 276).

The legislative side of the story has gone hand in hand with the electoral.[1] Both studies of roll call voting and of party organization have furnished independent evidence of party decline. The roll call evidence (reviewed in detail in chapter 6) is marshaled primarily in studies published in the last two decades. The chief conclusion has been that levels of party voting in the House have declined, albeit unsteadily, since the revolt against Speaker Joseph Cannon in 1910. Studies of party organization also have noted a decline in the post-Cannon House, with the speakership weakened, the party caucuses largely quiescent, and each party's committee on committees (CC) operating within the confines of an inflexible seniority system that largely removed any opportunity for partisan tinkering with the leadership of the standing committees of the House.

The evidence on party organization did change considerably in the late 1960s and early 1970s as a wave of reform hit the House. Among other changes, the Democratic Caucus was reactivated, the speakership strengthened, and Democratic committee assignment duties transferred to a new, leadership-dominated Steering and Policy Committee. Nonetheless, the House in the 1970s also instituted reforms that greatly increased the status of subcommittees, and most congressional scholars have seen these "decentralizing" reforms as more than counterbalancing the increased powers of the party leadership (see, for example, Collie and Brady 1985, 275; Crotty 1984, 279; Shepsle and Weingast 1984, 354). The dominant interpretation of the 1970s reforms is that they served to convert a decentralized system of "committee government" into an even more decentralized system of "subcommittee government" (Davidson 1981b; Shepsle and Weingast 1984).

In the last few years high levels of party cohesion and an activist leadership have again motivated scholars to consider the notion of "party government." For example, Rohde (1991) discusses parties as conditionally active coalitions, taking action when there is widespread agreement. Kiewiet and McCubbins (1991) consider parties as procedural coalitions, arguing that the majority party uses structure and process to manage the appropriations process. For most of the postwar era, however, the dominant theme is anything but "party government." As Brady

1. The conceptual link between increasingly weak electoral parties and declining partisanship in Congress has been clearly and repeatedly made. Brady and Bullock (1983, 623), for example, write: "When party becomes a less important determinant of voting in elections, then candidates, issues, organization, money, and the professionalization of campaign staffs become more important. Representatives elected to Congress under these conditions are less likely to follow party cues."

and Bullock (1983, 623) put it, "Anyone reviewing the literature on elections, congressional reforms, and congressional policy making cannot fail to be impressed by the extent to which they show party declining in the United States."

1.1   THE LIMITED ROLE OF PARTIES

Although many believe that congressional parties have declined in importance, this is not to say that they are ignored. But their role is often seen as quite limited. A survey of works on Congress yields three basic ways in which the role of parties is limited.

First, there is the idea that parties are primarily *floor voting coalitions* that have relatively little systematic influence on prefloor (i.e., committee) behavior. In this view, party leaders' sphere of action is confined mostly to the floor stages of legislation.[2] The crucial prefloor stages of legislation are the domain of the committees, and party influences attenuate the deeper one gets into the committee system (Fenno 1962, 318; Jones 1977, 184). One consequence of this view is that the literature's central measure of party strength is cohesion on roll call votes rather than, say, success in structuring the committee system to their benefit or their cohesion on committee votes.[3]

A second idea is that parties are primarily *procedural coalitions* that have relatively little influence over the substance of legislation. Jones (1964, 5), for example, argues that "the political party functions to organize a conflict resolution process. The party willingly assumes the responsibility for organizing the process—providing personnel (including leadership), making rules, establishing committees—without assuming either responsibility for results or the power to control them." An oft-noted bit of evidence for this view is the pattern of party behavior on roll call votes: the parties are monoliths when it comes to electing a Speaker, adopting sessional rules, and a few other procedural votes, but they break up quickly and in myriad ways on matters of substance.

A third idea is that party leaders' actions in Congress are *conditional* on the support of the party membership on a case-by-case basis, rather

2. As Sinclair (1988, 3) puts it: "In our traditional understanding of Congress . . . , party leaders are associated primarily with coalition building, especially at the floor stage." Ripley (1967, 114) notes that "numerous case studies . . . emphasize that the parties are much more important on the floor than in committees."

3. One reason for the focus on floor rather than committee votes is that, until passage of the Legislative Reorganization Act of 1970, committee votes were not subject to public scrutiny.

than part of a more general and *unconditional* delegation of power, as
in Great Britain. Rohde (1991, 31) describes the "conditional party
government" that Democratic reformers were striving for in the 1970s:

> Unlike in parliamentary systems, party would not be the dominant influence
> across all issues, and the leadership would not make policy decisions which
> would receive automatic support from the rank and file. Rather, the direc-
> tion of influence would be reversed and there would be party responsibility
> *only if* there were widespread policy agreement among House Democrats.
> When agreement was present on a matter that was important to party mem-
> bers, the leadership would be expected to use the tools at their disposal . . .
> to advance the cause.

Each of these limitations on party activity—to the floor rather than
prefloor stages of the legislative process, to procedural rather than substantive issues, to issues on which the party is united rather than to all
issues—contrasts with the familiar notion of the responsible party. In
this view, properly reformed congressional parties would combine and
strengthen the powers attributed to them in the first two views. They
would be powerful floor coalitions capable of disciplining their members and passing their programs, and they would be powerful procedural coalitions effectively dominating the legislative agenda and taking
responsibility for the final legislative product. Moreover, the default
assumption would be that party leaders would act on every issue; an
explicit decision not to act would be necessary to make an exception.

1.2   RATIONAL CHOICE VIEWS OF PARTIES

From the perspective of those who seek responsible parties in the West-
minster mold, the postwar congressional party has been a kind of New
World Cheshire Cat: rather disreputable to begin with and slowly fad-
ing away. Moreover, the most sophisticated theoretical accounts of
Congress, those of the neo-institutional or rational choice school, are
firmly in the "committee government" camp and strongly downplay the
importance of parties. Indeed, from the perspective of currently influential rational choice theories, the very existence of parties—even in the
limited forms of floor coalitions, procedural coalitions, or "conditionally active" coalitions—seems difficult to explain.

Any attempt to view parties as floor coalitions must confront the
spatial model of voting and the influential "instability" and "chaos"
theorems that stem from it (Plott 1967; McKelvey 1976; Schofield 1980).
These theorems have been interpreted to mean that holding together

any governing coalition in a majority-rule institution is nigh on impossible (cf. Riker 1980). This conclusion, moreover, jibes with the stylized facts of Congress, according to which floor votes are controlled by continually shifting coalitions of narrowly self-interested legislators who act essentially free of any partisan constraints.[4]

As regards the procedural structure of Congress, the most influential recent work has focused squarely on the committees and the House, ignoring the parties. Shepsle's (1979) seminal work has a committee system and a House, but no parties. Weingast and Marshall (1988) explicitly assume away any partisan influence on the behavior of members of Congress. Gilligan and Krehbiel (1987; see also Krehbiel 1987a) construct a series of models in which the House and the committees play a role, but in which parties do not appear. Nowhere in recent theoretical work, in other words, does one see embodied the traditional notion of parties as procedural coalitions.[5] The reason for this exclusion seems, again, to be the spatial model and its chaos theorems. If coalitional stability is largely illusory, then to take parties as unitary actors in models of congressional structure is unjustified. As Mayhew (1974, 27) contends, "No theoretical treatment of the United States Congress that posits parties as analytic units will go very far."

1.3   THE THEORETICAL STATUS OF PARTIES

What, then, is the theoretical status of parties? Theorists in an older tradition (e.g., Truman 1959; Jones 1964; Ripley 1967; Ripley 1969b) were little troubled by issues of spatial instability and had no problem in taking political parties as analytic units for many purposes. They studied these units as they attempted to control floor outcomes and to organize the legislature for business. A central idea in many of these studies (see, for example, Cooper, Brady, and Hurley 1977; Ripley 1967; Ripley 1969b; Rohde 1991) is that party leaders are strong and active

---

4. This characterization of congressional voting can be found in many places. Thurow (1980, 212), for example, argues that "our problems arise because, in a very real sense, we do not have political parties. A political party is a group that can force its elected members to vote for that party's solutions to society's problems . . . we have a system where each elected official is his own party and free to establish his own party platform." Yoder (1990) complains that "by now parties consist, pretty much, of offices in Washington. In Congress, it is everyone for himself."

5. For other, committee-based models of Congress that ignore parties see, for example, Fiorina 1977; Mayhew 1974.

only when the rank and file is reasonably homogeneous in its policy preferences.

By contrast, many theorists in the rational choice school see so much difficulty in getting parties off the ground as anything like unitary actors that they banish them entirely from their theories, focusing instead on individual legislators and their goals. Neither parties as floor coalitions nor parties as procedural coalitions seem theoretically justified without a theory of how individual legislators can be welded together into a meaningful and stable collectivity. Moreover, this theoretical problem is qualitatively the same whether one is talking about a "homogeneous" party, like the Democrats in the Hundredth Congress, or a "heterogeneous" party, like the Democrats in the Ninetieth Congress.[6]

This book is our attempt to articulate a view of congressional parties in the postwar House of Representatives that takes the concerns of both traditional and rational choice theorists seriously. Like traditional theorists, we think that parties act as both floor and procedural coalitions and that more homogeneous parties are more likely to be active in both regards. Like rational choice theorists, we are impressed by the theoretical difficulty of taking American parties as unitary actors.

These concerns, it should be noted, are at odds with one another. The first impatiently says, "Of course parties exist. Of course they engage in various activities. Let us get on with the task of studying them." The second says, "But a dominant theme in the literature is that parties are so internally divided that they can rarely act with any vigor and purpose. Any *theory* of parties, therefore, must start at a lower, more fundamental, level—that of the individual, reelection-seeking legislator—and build up from there."

As we have struggled to reconcile these competing demands—for empirical relevance and theoretical rigor—we have come to a view of parties that differs in important respects from both the various traditional and the rational choice views. Our differences from the rational choice view will be obvious, since much of that view is a negative one—that parties are too internally divided to be either practically effective or theoretically interesting—and we would not have written this book had we agreed with it.

As regards our differences with traditional views of party, two in

6. That is, it takes extreme homogeneity of preferences, coupled with few dimensions of potential conflict, before the spatial theorems admit of anything like transitive majority preferences. See Aldrich 1988.

particular merit emphasis. First, we see a much greater tension between the traditional view of parties as procedural coalitions and the notion (discussed at length in part 1) that committees in the House are powerful, autonomous actors in the policy-making process. Traditional theorists saw little need to defend themselves against this "committee government" model. Indeed, for the most part they accepted the idea of committee government and evidently saw no reason that their limited notions of party could not peacefully coexist with the dominant emphasis on committees. But from a rational choice perspective there is considerable tension between the idea of a party as a procedural coalition that establishes the rules of the legislative game and the idea of committees as autonomous agents virtually beyond party influence. Jones's (1964, 5) acceptance of a party that organizes the process—"making rules, establishing committees"—yet does not assume that the "power to control" legislative events is out of equilibrium, from a rational choice perspective, since it seems to imply that some agent ("the party") is not taking much advantage of its position.

Second, and related, we see the procedural power that the majority party possesses in a different light than does the traditional literature. We do not differ as to how these procedural powers might be described; rather, we see the translation of procedural into substantive advantages as occurring on both "active" and "latent" tracks. Many scholars recognize the active translation of procedural into substantive advantage, as when the Speaker uses his scheduling power to expedite the progress of a bill he favors to the floor or a committee chairman uses his scheduling power to delay the progress of a bill he opposes. Much less attention has been paid to the substantive advantage that the majority party can attain simply by structuring the committee system—setting up jurisdictions, allocating resources, assigning members, and so forth—and then letting things proceed on "automatic pilot." From this perspective, the committee system is not simply an impediment to responsible party government;[7] it is also a tool through which a rather different species of party government can be implemented.[8]

7. Ralph K. Huitt, for example, argues that "the ultimate check on party government in the United States is the system of standing committees in Congress"; quoted in Uslaner 1974, 16.

8. A final way in which we differ from the traditional literature is that we spend more time worrying about how parties might be "built up" from a congeries of quarrelsome and fractious legislators. How can one part of the literature talk about the rampant individualism of Congress, the lack of party discipline, and the internal divisions within parties—all of which argues that they are not unitary actors—even as another part takes them with little discussion as if they were unitary actors?

1.4   *PLUS ÇA CHANGE...*

The debate in which we engage is hardly new. The reigning methodological canons of the discipline have changed, certainly. But questions about the relative power and importance of parties are perennial.

This point can be brought home quite neatly by quoting from the introduction to David B. Truman's 1959 monograph, *The Congressional Party*. Truman wrote in the aftermath of the famous committee report of the American Political Science Association (1950) that called for a strengthening of American political parties along broadly British lines. In light of the contemporary literature, he found it "entirely possible that many Americans hold a view of Congress . . . as a chaotic, incoherent aggregation of small-minded and shortsighted individualists" (Truman 1959, 9). He then proceeded to pose a series of leading questions:

> How close to reality is this impression of the national legislature? How much of pattern and regularity can be found beneath an appearance of unpredictability or even of chaos? Is there any evidence [that] the congressional party is a valuable or significant instrument of governing? . . . If the legislative party shows any coherent pattern as a stable organizational element in the political system, what of the structure, or structures, through which it is led? Specifically, what are the roles of its designated leaders?

Truman's questions are still of considerable interest today. They pose an implicit challenge to the standard "committee government" model of postwar congressional research. In the next section, we discuss some of the conventional wisdom associated with that model.

2.   COMMITTEE GOVERNMENT

Scholarly descriptions of the decline and weakness of parties have gone hand in hand with studies of the power of committees. Stylized characterizations of this power have been part of academic discourse and training since the nineteenth century. Just before the dramatic changes in the 1970s that ushered in "subcommittee government," the stock of generalizations could be described as follows:

> The oldest and most familiar is Woodrow Wilson's book-length assertion that committees dominate congressional decision making. A corollary states that committees are autonomous units, which operate quite independently of such external influences as legislative party leaders, chamber majorities, and the President of the United States. Other staples of committee commen-

tary hold . . . that each committee is the repository of legislative expertise within its jurisdiction; that committee decisions are usually accepted and ratified by the other members of the chamber; that committee chairmen can (and usually do) wield a great deal of influence over their committees. (Fenno 1973, xiii)

The specific items in this catalogue—asserting committee autonomy, committee expertise, the sanctity of committee decisions, and the power of committee chairs—are not all equally important for our present purposes. We focus on committee autonomy and decision-making power, discussing the latter first. Our discussion here pertains chiefly to the period of "committee government" from about 1940 to 1970, what Cooper and Brady (1981) call the "Rayburn House." But much of the discussion is relevant to the succeeding period of House history—in part because many researchers have described this period as one in which subcommittees simply take over the previous role of committees, and in part because committee autonomy from the floor is a necessary condition for subcommittee autonomy from the floor.

2.1   THE DECISION-MAKING POWER OF COMMITTEES

Scholars who refer to the "sanctity of committee decisions" in the Rayburn House usually have in mind both a fact—that committee decisions were rarely overturned by the parent chamber—and an explanation, which attributes the relative infrequency of overturned decisions to two related factors: a system of decentralized reciprocity between committees ("Don't mess with my jurisdiction and I won't mess with yours"); and mutual respect for expertise. That the Rayburn House rarely overruled its committees is usually discussed under two headings, corresponding to committee decisions to do nothing, on the one hand, and committee decisions to do something, on the other.

The negative (or veto) power of committees was (and still is) based on the long-established rules regulating the ordinary course of legislative business, according to which all bills must pass through one of the standing committees before they can be considered on the floor. Woodrow Wilson wrote sorrowfully about this necessity, noting that when a bill "goes from the clerk's desk to a committee room it crosses a bridge of sighs to dim dungeons of silence whence it will never return" (Wilson 1885, 69). Textbooks commonly make the point less dramatically by citing the high percentage of bills that die in committee and the infrequency with which committee decisions to kill a bill are overturned on the floor.[9]

The positive power of committees in the Rayburn House lay in their ability to make proposals to the floor. The sanctity of these proposals is suggested by the high percentage of all committee bills that passed entirely unamended. Ripley (1983, 200), for example, reports an average figure of 70 percent for the period 1963–71.

The explanation of why committees were so infrequently reversed on the floor during the era of "committee government" has usually hinged on notions of reciprocity, specialization, and expertise. *Reciprocity* refers to a norm of mutually beneficial forbearance on the floor: for example, even if a particular committee occasionally refused to report a bill that a majority on the floor wished to see reported, the members of that majority might not have insisted on their majoritarian rights in the expectation that their own committees would be given similar deference in the future. Everyone benefited from such reciprocal deference as long as the members of each committee valued influence over their own committee's jurisdiction more highly than they did influence over the average of the other committees' jurisdictions.

Another factor often cited as contributing to the sanctity of committee decisions was a generalized respect for expertise—for the members who "had specialized in the area, had worked hard, and had the facts" (Fenno 1962, 316). If everyone specialized in their own committee's affairs, then necessarily they would be less well informed about bills pending before other committees, hence more dependent for pertinent information on the "experts" in other committees.[10]

2.2 THE DISTINCTIVENESS OF COMMITTEES

The sanctity of committee decisions in the Rayburn House might not have mattered much had committees been faithful mirrors of the floor.

9. In the Eighty-ninth Congress, for example, 84 percent of the 26,566 bills introduced were stopped at the committee stage. Ripley's (1983, 145–46) discussion is typical: "There are ways around the committee system, but they are cumbersome and rarely successful. For example, a discharge petition to remove a bill from a committee and bring it to the floor requires the signatures of an absolute majority of the House (218 individuals). Between 1923 and 1975 only twenty-five petitions of 396 filed received the necessary signatures."

10. There are other theories of why committees are powerful, notably Shepsle and Weingast's (1987a; 1987b) model of the "*ex post* veto." But the standard view is based either on reciprocity or the informational advantages of committee experts over their floor colleagues, or both.

But the dominant view of the committee assignment process in the Rayburn House is that it accommodated member requests (Gertzog 1976; Shepsle 1978). Indeed, this is the dominant view of the assignment process in the contemporary House as well. Because members throughout the postwar period have sought assignments relevant to their constituencies, the story goes, accommodation of their requests has had predictable results:

> Committees and subcommittees are not collections of legislators representing diverse views from across the nation or collections of disinterested members who develop objective policy expertise. Rather, committees and subcommittees are populated by legislators who have the highest stake in a given policy jurisdiction, what we have termed "preference outliers." Hence, farm-state members of Congress dominate the agriculture committees; urban legislators predominate on the banking, housing and social welfare committees; members with military bases and defense industries in their districts are found on the armed services committees; and westerners are disproportionately represented on the public works, natural resources, and environmental committees. (Shepsle and Weingast 1984, 351)

From this perspective, the unrepresentativeness of committee membership, together with the sanctity of committee decisions, provided (and still provides) an ideal environment for special interests. By concentrating on a few relevant committees, special interests could (and still can) influence selected policies without needing to influence either policy in general or Congress in general—both considerably more daunting tasks. One of the key concepts in the literature on Congress—the notion of a "subgovernment"—was developed to describe the resulting policy process, in which a committee, an executive agency, and a client industry cooperate first in drafting policy in a given area and then in pushing it past a deferential Congress. The literature on subgovernments is vast, and the dominant view is of policy made by largely unrepresentative and mostly unsupervised members, in cooperation with interested external actors.

2.3   THE AUTONOMY OF COMMITTEES

The notion of a subgovernment presumes a considerable degree of committee autonomy from the floor. If committees were clearly the creatures of the floor, as they were in the early years of the republic, then much of the force of the subgovernment literature would vanish. The foundation stones of committee autonomy are usually taken to be the seniority system and the fixity of committee jurisdictions. The seniority system ensures a substantial degree of continuity in committee personnel, and well-defined jurisdictions ensure similar continuity in the legislative areas over which committees exercise influence.

Sinclair (1989, 310) outlines the importance of the seniority system in this way: "By the 1920s seniority had become the sole criterion for appointment to chairmanships, and as a result, chairmanships became independent positions of power over which the majority party had little control." Dodd and Oppenheimer (1977, 40) voice an even stronger view, questioning not just the parties' power of removal but also the amount of discretion that they could exert at the initial appointment stage:

> Throughout most of the postwar years . . . power in Congress has rested in the committees or, increasingly, in the subcommittees. Although the party caucuses nominally have had the power to organize [i.e., appoint] committees and select committee chairpeople, the norm of congressional or state delegation seniority has dominated the former (though not exclusively), while the norm of committee seniority has dominated the latter (exclusively).

Committees, insulated from partisan tinkering with their membership by the seniority norm and other norms regulating the appointment process, and enjoying statutorily fixed jurisdictions, were often "singularly unaffected by ties to . . . party" (Cater 1964, 153).

2.4 SUMMARY

To sum up the standard view, power in the Rayburn House was clearly decentralized. On one side stood the House committees, characterized by their power, distinctiveness, and autonomy. Their power was protected by far-reaching norms of reciprocity on the floor and by mutual respect for expertise. Their distinctiveness stemmed both from the process of committee assignment, which produced members on each panel who were largely self-selected, and from the process of pluralistic politics, which produced external influences on each panel that were entirely self-selected. Their autonomy was buttressed both by the seniority system, which protected members from removal, and by the fixity of their jurisdictions.

On the other side stood the parties. They seemed no longer able—perhaps no longer willing—to use the committee assignment process in a systematically partisan fashion; consequently, their influence was confined to the floor. Even their ability to hold together on the floor, moreover, was poor and getting worse.

Such a short summary of decades of research cannot do justice to the diversity of views and nuances of argument present in the literature. But our summary is faithful, we think, to the main features of "committee government" as it is portrayed in the literature. Moreover, many scholars would accept large portions of the account as accurate for the 1970s and 1980s, with subcommittees taking the place of committees.

3. OUTLINE OF THE BOOK

Any account of the postwar House that, like ours, emphasizes the role of parties must inevitably take account of the previous literature's overwhelming emphasis on committees. Accordingly, we begin in part 1 by reviewing the committee government model, probing two of its key premises—that committees are autonomous and that they are distinctive in terms of the preferences of their members.

In the rest of the book we turn from the negative task of criticizing the committee government model to the positive task of articulating an alternative model, one of limited party government. In part 2 we offer a theory of what parties are and how they might, in certain circumstances, act in a unitary fashion. We first provide a general survey of neo-institutional theories of organization, including under that rubric some recent interpretations of Hobbes's theory of the state, various models of business firms from the industrial organization literature, and studies of political entrepreneurship. We then adapt the general neo-institutional approach, in which organizations are viewed as solutions to collective dilemmas, to the specific case of legislative parties.

In part 3 we consider parties as floor coalitions. We review one of the main bodies of data—roll call votes on the floor of the House—underpinning the party decline thesis, from the perspective of the theory developed in part 2. We are led to measure party strength in a different fashion than did previous researchers, an approach that leads to different empirical findings (the decline of majority party strength has been neither steady nor statistically significant in the post–New Deal period) and to different interpretations of the role of party on the floor.

In the last two parts of the book we consider parties as procedural coalitions. In part 4 we focus on their influence over appointments to committees, furnishing statistical evidence that loyalty to party leaders influences not just the probability of receiving a desirable transfer but also the probability of getting an attractive appointment as a freshman. In part 5 we look at a different aspect of procedural power—the power to set the legislative agenda. We consider one model that emphasizes how committees compete for scarce time on the floor, in the process anticipating the desires of the majority party leadership, and another that highlights the veto power held collectively by members of the majority party.

PART ONE

The Autonomy and Distinctiveness of Committees

We reevaluate the role of parties and committees in the postwar House of Representatives, arguing that parties are a kind of legislative cartel that usurps the structural power of the House and that committees are definitely not autonomous. Such a reevaluation will not even get off the ground if the reader is committed to the dominant "committee government" model of Congress. Accordingly, in this part of the book we critique some key aspects of this model.

Virtually all researchers on the postwar House of Representatives speak of the standing committees as being "autonomous." What *autonomy* means varies from context to context. In reference to committee jurisdictions, *autonomy* refers to their statutory status and fixity. In reference to committee personnel, *autonomy* generally refers to some fairly specific "rights" conferred by the seniority system on committee members and to the lack of any real party control over who gets on most committees. In reference to committee involvement in subgovernments, *autonomy* refers to the ability of small groups of committee members, executive bureaucrats, and business lobbyists to make policy independently of the larger political arena.

In this part we deal with the latter two notions of autonomy, regarding personnel and decision making, leaving aside the issue of jurisdictional fixity. The notion of subgovernments also touches on the degree to which committees are distinctive or unrepresentative.

Our first task is to examine the autonomy of committee personnel. In colloquial usage—appropriate since the literature never offers a technical one—to say that the personnel process of committees was "auton-omous" would mean, at least, that the members of committees were neither "hired by" nor "fired by" any external agency. And there are those in the literature who argue both these points, especially the latter.

The first point, that committee members are not hired by any exter-nal principal, usually appears in one of two forms. Some scholars point to various norms that constrain the parties' freedom in making appoint-ments. Others stress the degree to which the whole committee assign-ment process is an exercise in "self-selection," with members' prefer-ences being the primary, even decisive, determinant of assignments. Either route can lead to the conclusion that parties—which formally make all committee assignments—exercise little real control.

The second point, that committee members are not fired by any ex-ternal principal, is generally discussed under the heading of the seniority system. Much is made of the customary right of reappointment that members enjoy and of the seniority rule governing succession to the chairmanship of each committee. Again, the conclusion is that parties, at least prior to the 1970s, were essentially incapable of intervening to alter committee makeups or internal seniority rankings.

We argue that it is only in an essentially rhetorical sense that one can speak of each committee's personnel process as being autonomous.[1] In chapter 1 we look at how representatives get onto committees, arguing that a pure self-selection model does not tally with the facts and that there is substantial room for partisan influence. In chapter 2 we look at how members advance within and get off committees, arguing that the seniority system's potency in the early postwar period has been misin-terpreted. Finally, in chapter 3 we investigate an implication of the view that committees are both self-selected and immune to external disci-pline—namely, that many of them should be distinctive or unrepresen-tative in terms of their public policy preferences, especially as regards policy in their own jurisdiction. We find that the number of committees that are unrepresentative—in terms of the geographical location of their members' constituencies or the ideological predispositions of their members—is far more limited than much of the literature would sug-gest.

1. That is, it stretches the meaning of *autonomy* well beyond its usual usage to say that committees are autonomous with respect to their personnel.

ONE

Self-Selection and the Subgovernment Thesis

Many students of American national politics have noticed the cozy arrangements between congressional committee members, executive agents, and interest group lobbyists that seem to dominate decision making in a wide range of policy arenas. These "iron triangles" or "unholy trinities," also known by the less pejorative tag of "subgovernments," are thought to be largely independent of presidents, party leaders, and other "outside" influences.[1]

In the standard analysis, subgovernments stem from a set of congressional reforms in the early twentieth century that redistributed power from party leaders to committee chairs. The most important of these reforms came with the revolt against "czar rule" in 1910 and 1911, when Progressive Republicans united with Democrats to strip the Speakership of much of its power. After a brief period during which the majority party caucus was active in determining policy, the House entered the era of "committee government," during which "each committee was left to fashion public policy in its own jurisdiction" (Dodd and Oppenheimer 1977, 22) and party leaders acted "as agents for, rather than superiors to, committee leaders and members of the inner club" (Shepsle 1989, 246). Policy in the decentralized, postrevolt House was

---

1. See, for example, Freeman 1955. See also Lowi 1972; Lowi 1979, 62–63; Cater 1964; Ripley and Franklin 1984; McConnell 1966; Jones 1961, 359; Davidson and Oleszek 1977; Davidson 1977, 31–33; Davidson 1981, 101–11; Griffith 1961; Schattschneider 1935; Shepsle and Weingast 1987a; Shepsle and Weingast 1987b; and Weingast 1979.

"incubated and crafted by interested members who monopolized the berths on committees important to their constituents' concerns." The result was a "gigantic institutional logroll" that "sanctified the division of labor that permitted policy making by subgovernments" (Shepsle 1989, 246–47).[2]

In this chapter we investigate one important part of the subgovernment model of congressional politics: the committee assignment process. As Shepsle (1978, 248) notes, "committee assignments are, on the legislative side, at the root of the 'cozy little triangle' problem. A system that permits 'interesteds' to gravitate to decision arenas in which their interests are promoted provides the fertile environment in which clientelism flourishes." The term generally used in the literature to characterize this process of gravitation is *self-selection*. The implication is that the most important factors in the committee assignment process are the wishes of the individual members: what members ask for, they mostly get, and—because what they ask for is generally determined by the kind of constituency they serve—each committee ends up populated by "interesteds." Some believe that self-selection dominates the committee assignment process to such an extent that essentially no room is left for the use of assignments as instruments of partisan control—with the possible exception of assignments to the exclusive committees (Ways and Means, Appropriations, and Rules).[3]

In this chapter we argue that the statistical evidence in support of a pure self-selection model is relatively limited—certainly insufficient to conclude that there is no room for partisan criteria in the process. We take a more positive tack in chapter 7, providing statistical evidence that committee assignments are influenced significantly by the desires of party leaders.

2. Dodd and Oppenheimer and Shepsle were writing about how Congress has changed. Both conclude that committee autonomy has been replaced with subcommittee autonomy, along with some coordination by the parties.

3. The Legislative Reorganization Act of 1946 defines exclusive, semiexclusive, and nonexclusive committees. Members of exclusive committees may not serve on any other committee; members of semiexclusive committees may also serve on one nonexclusive committee; and members of nonexclusive committees may serve on two nonexclusive committees or one nonexclusive and one semiexclusive committee (Masters 1961, 351).

Three of the four "control" committees—Appropriations, Rules, and Ways and Means— are also exclusive committees. The fourth control committee, Budget, is a semiexclusive committee and is excluded from our analysis. Agriculture, Armed Services, Interstate and Foreign Commerce, Banking and Currency, Education and Labor, Public Works, Post Office, Science, and Foreign Affairs are categorized as semiexclusive; and Interior, House Administration, Government Operations, District of Columbia, and House Un-American Activities are categorized as nonexclusive (Small Business and Official Conduct are excluded).

The task of this chapter, from the perspective of the book's overall purpose, is primarily critical. In this chapter and the two that follow, we hope to show that the committee "personnel process"—by which members get on committees, advance within them, and, in some cases, leave them—cannot accurately be characterized as "autonomous" at any point in the postwar era.

1. SELF-SELECTION

The committee assignment process took on most of its contemporary features in the aftermath of the revolt against Speaker Cannon, when both parties established committees to handle the task of deciding which of their members should go where. The Democrats gave formal authority for appointments to their contingent on Ways and Means (whose members were thenceforth to be elected by the caucus), whereas the Republicans settled on a separate party committee, with one member from each state having Republican representation in the House. These arrangements remained essentially intact until the 1970s, when the Democrats made some important changes. The Democratic Caucus decided in 1973 to add the Speaker, majority leader, and caucus chair to the formal membership of their committee on committees (CC) "in response to the desire for more direct leadership control of committee assignments" (Shepsle 1978, 137). This practice continued until 1975, when the power of appointment was transferred to the leadership-dominated Steering and Policy Committee.[4] The Republicans have left their assignment procedures largely untouched.

One of the foundational assumptions of the subgovernment model is that self-selection dominates the committee assignment process of both parties. Self-selection is taken to occur when two conditions are met: first, members request particular committee assignments based chiefly on the degree to which each committee affects their constituents' interests; second, each party's CC accommodates member requests.

In the pure form of self-selection, once members identify themselves as interested in particular positions, the rest of the process is relatively neutral and nondiscretionary. Gertzog (1976, 705), for example, writes that "in the 1970s it would appear that a newcomer need only state a

4. This committee, as specified in the 1975 reforms, consisted of the Speaker (as chair), the majority leader, the caucus chair, twelve members elected by the caucus from regional zones, and eight appointees of the Speaker. For more detail on the history of the appointment process in the House, see Shepsle 1978; Ornstein and Rohde 1977a.

preference for any but an exclusive committee and it is his or hers almost for the asking." Cook (1983, 1028) notes that, in the literature in general, "the leadership's decision making [regarding committee assignments] is seen largely to ratify the members' preferences."

Less pure forms of the self-selection model, however, allow other criteria—such as loyalty to the party leadership—to creep into the decisions of each party's committee on committees. Indeed, both Westefield's (1974) and Shepsle's (1978) models *assume* that the party leadership has substantial influence over appointments and is interested in securing the loyalty of members. The leadership accommodates member requests because it perceives this as an appropriate strategy to "reward past loyalty or encourage such behavior in the future" (Westefield 1974, 1594). This view seemingly implies a positive correlation between a member's loyalty to the leadership and his or her chances of receiving preferred committee assignments.

It is difficult, however, to see any consensus in the literature on the susceptibility of the assignment process to the influence of party leaders. On the one hand, several scholars emphasize the routinization of assignments: Gertzog's widely cited 1976 article emphasizes the high proportion of members who got their first-choice assignments within a few terms of their arrival in Congress. Gertzog interprets this situation as evidence that the 1970s assignment process was largely routine and nondiscretionary—leaving little room for partisan manipulation of assignments. Goodwin (1970, 77), describing the literature, approvingly quotes Masters's description of each party as "a mutual benefit and improvement society" when it comes to distributing assignments—from which he concludes that the assignment process usually accommodates members' preferences. Smith and Deering (1984, 240) indicate that "the assignment process increasingly has become a routine process of accommodating requests for House Democrats," and Smith and Ray (1983, 238) note that the reforms of the early 1970s made the process "even more a routine effort" that is "less manipulable by party leaders." The reforms, they assert, "have made it easier for a potential requester to be nominated and compete for any committee assignment, and declining levels of competition for seats have lessened the number of opportunities for CC member support to be decisive."

On the other hand, some of these same scholars emphasize the party leadership's important role in the assignment process. Goodwin (1970, 69) states that the Speaker and majority leader, in cooperation with the committee on committees, can "usually control initial appointments of committee members of the majority party." Smith and Ray (1983, 238) argue that the 1970s reforms gave the Democratic leadership "a more regularized and personal role in the assignment process," thus giving loyal Democrats an advantage. Smith and Deering (1984, 239) point out that "party leaders do occasionally make a special effort to place a member on a committee, and they usually succeed," and their interviews with Steering and Policy Committee members revealed that party loyalty was one of the criteria in making assignments in the Ninety-seventh Congress.

On the whole, however, most researchers seem definitely to lean much more toward Gertzog's view of assignments than to a view centered on the role of party leaders. Smith and his coauthors argued in the early 1980s that "although there are opportunities to do so, current party leaders do not attempt to exercise special influence over the *vast majority* of assignment decisions" (Smith and Deering 1984, 239; our emphasis) and that "there are few detectable differences between the pre- and post-reform periods in the factors that shape assignment outcomes, even when we narrow the focus to [the committee on committees'] support in contested decisions" (Smith and Ray 1983, 238). Davidson and Oleszek (1990, 204) have recently summarized the evidence as showing that "with exceptions for some committees, members generally receive the assignments they request. In most cases [as Gertzog argues], 'the assignment process has become an essentially routine, nondiscretionary procedure.' Both parties try and accommodate the assignment preferences of their partisans." Cook (1983, 1028) characterizes the literature as suggesting that "assignments are determined not by personal or policy considerations but instead by the interaction of the supply of available seats with the demand of the members for them." [5]

In the rest of this chapter we discuss evidence pertinent to the various facets of the self-selection model. We begin by examining the degree to which members' requests can be explained by their constituents' interests. We then look at the success of member requests, both for freshmen and nonfreshmen. Finally, we investigate whether the assignment process is routine and nondiscretionary.

5. For similar characterizations, see also Gilligan and Krehbiel 1990; Grier n.d.; Krehbiel 1991; Shepsle and Weingast 1987a; Shepsle and Weingast 1987b; and Weingast and Moran 1983, 771.

2.   CONSTITUENCY INTERESTS AND
ASSIGNMENT REQUESTS

There is substantial anecdotal evidence that members of Congress (MCs) seek committee assignments pertinent to their constitutents' interests (see Masters 1961; Fenno 1973; Shepsle 1978; Smith and Deering 1984). Moreover, there are good theoretical reasons to expect that they might: being in a position to do favors for one's constitutents is, after all, good electoral politics. Nonetheless, the statistical evidence in support of what might be called the *interest-seeking hypothesis* is relatively weak. For only a handful of committees is there strong and consistent statistical evidence that constituency interests drive assignment requests.

The weakness of the statistical evidence may be due in part to the relative paucity of systematic data on member requests: the largest data sets—those of Shepsle (1978) and Smith and Deering (1984)—together cover only the Democrats in only ten Congresses. Another contributing factor, which is probably more important, is the difficulty of adequately measuring the degree of pertinence of each committee to each constit-uency. As in the literature on constituency influence (cf. Fiorina 1974), scholars looking at the determinants of committee assignment requests have been forced to use relatively crude measures of constituency char-acteristics. As a result, the statistical evidence of interest seeking has been, except for a few committees, modest. This can be illustrated by reviewing the three main studies of member request behavior: Rohde and Shepsle 1973; Shepsle 1978; and Ray 1980a.

Rohde and Shepsle (1973) studied requests for assignment to five committees—Banking and Currency, Education and Labor, Interior, Armed Services, and Agriculture—chosen because they seemed likely to provide evidence supportive of the interest-seeking hypothesis. For each committee Rohde and Shepsle partitioned all Democratic freshmen in each of several Congresses into two groups: those whose constituencies might induce them to take a particular interest in the committee (the "interesteds") and those whose constituencies plausibly had no such effect (the "indifferents"). They then calculated the proportion of inter-esteds and indifferents who actually sought an assignment to each com-mittee. Their results consistently showed a difference in the expected direction, with higher proportions of interesteds than indifferents seek-ing assignment to each committee. In the case of the Committee on Banking and Currency, for example, 47 percent of those they identified as "interesteds" requested assignment to the committee while only 20 percent of the "indifferents" made such a request; the same comparison for the Committee on Education and Labor was 30 percent to 7 percent; for Interior, 65 percent to 8 percent; for Armed Services, 30 percent to 18 percent; and for Agriculture, 33 percent to 2 percent (895, table 3). They concluded that "although the relationship between ascribed interest and request behavior varies from committee to committee, it is always in the predicted direction and quite strong" (896). Nonetheless, it should be noted that the difference in proportions for the Armed Services Committee is not statistically significant (in either one- or two-tailed tests).[6]

Shepsle (1978) investigated both the initial requests of freshmen and the transfer requests of nonfreshmen for the Eighty-seventh to Ninetieth, Ninety-second, and Ninety-third Congresses (Democrats only). In studying requests made by freshmen, he focused on those seeking assignment to eight semiexclusive committees—the committees on Agriculture, Armed Services, Banking and Currency, Education and Labor, Foreign Affairs, Interstate Commerce, Judiciary, and Public Works—and one nonexclusive committee—the Interior Committee. He imposed this limitation for two reasons: first, most freshman requests involved these committees; and second, it was easier to link constituency interests to committee jurisdictions for these committees than it would have been for the exclusive committees or for many of the nonexclusive committees.

Shepsle's principal hypothesis was that district characteristics would drive freshman assignment requests. To test this hypothesis, he estimated nine separate probit regressions, one for each of the nine committees in his sample. The dependent variable in each case was whether or not a member had requested the committee in question, and coefficients were estimated for a set of "attractiveness" variables, meant to capture those district characteristics relevant to the committee's jurisdiction.

In three of the nine probit equations—for the committees on Education and Labor, Interstate Commerce, and the Judiciary—the only significant "attractiveness" variables uncovered were dummy variables identifying the freshman's occupational background. None of the actual district characteristics measured was shown to be important in requesting assignment to these three committees. Moreover, lacking either

6. Rohde and Shepsle (1973) do not report tests of the significance of the differences in proportions that they uncover. All but the Armed Services difference are significant at the .05 level.

a district measure or a prior occupation that would predict the "attractiveness" of an assignment on Public Works, Shepsle employed a dummy
variable tapping whether or not the freshman's predecessor had served
on that committee. It is problematic how much constituency interest is
actually picked up by this measure. Only for the Agriculture, Armed
Services, Banking, Foreign Affairs, and Interior committees were variables that actually measured some constituency characteristic significant in Shepsle's equations—and the coefficient for the Armed Services
Committee had the wrong sign! Thus, although Shepsle purposely limited his analysis to nine committees for which the interest-seeking hypothesis seemed likely to pan out, he found direct and positive support
for only four of the nine.

Ray (1980a) raised the question of "whether the preexisting geographic distribution of federal spending dictates representatives' committee assignments" (495). Ray's dependent variable measures the assignment requests made by House Democratic freshmen in the Ninety-
second to Ninety-fourth Congresses. The independent variable is federal outlays in congressional districts, paired with the relevant committee—Agriculture, Armed Services, Education and Labor, Banking and
Currency, Interior, and Veterans' Affairs—for the preceding election
year. He tests the hypothesis that "the geographic distribution of federal spending within each of these domains should predict which freshmen will, and which will not, request assignment to the associated committees" (497). Ray finds that "there is a tendency for members from
districts with greater-than-average involvements in a committee's jurisdiction to be over-represented among those seeking assignments" (498).
However, in the six probit equations that he estimates, one for each
committee, his "Constituency Stake" variable is significant at conventional levels for only the Agricultural Committee.

All told, the statistical evidence for the idea that members seek appointment to committees pertinent to the interests of their constituents
is relatively spotty. Investigations have been carried out for only ten of
the twenty-odd House committees, and the evidence is reasonably solid
and consistent for only half of these committees: Agriculture, Banking,
Foreign Affairs, Public Works, and Interior.[7] This does not mean, of

7. The evidence pertaining to the other five committees is mixed. For the Armed Services Committee, Shepsle (1978) finds a significant coefficient of the wrong sign, whereas
Rohde and Shepsle (1973) and Ray (1980a) find insignificant effects of the right sign. For
the Education and Labor Committee, Shepsle does not have a variable that actually taps
constituency characteristics, while Ray does not find a significant effect; only Rohde and
Shepsle find a significant effect for constituency variables. Only Shepsle studies the Com-

course, that there is no reason to believe that interest seeking is important for other committees. Interviews with members reported by Fenno (1973), Bullock (1976), and Smith and Deering (1984), for example, show that "reelection" and "constituency" interests predominate in the reasons given for the committee selection of members. Interview evidence, however, does not systematically reveal *how much* constituency drives committee selection. This argument depends on statistical data, and, as we have seen, the case has yet to be proved.[8]

3. ACCOMMODATION OF ASSIGNMENT REQUESTS

Do members of the House of Representatives receive the committee assignments that they request? In this section we consider the initial assignment requests of new members, leaving to the next section the transfer requests of returning members.

As a backdrop to the question of how many freshmen get what they ask for, tables 1 and 2 provide a summary of the assignments actually given to Democratic and Republican freshmen from the Eightieth to Hundredth Congresses. The committee assignment data used in these tables and throughout the rest of the book were derived from the *House Journal* rather than from any unofficial source and so are relatively error free.[9]

Table 1 shows that the largest percentages of entering Democrats were assigned to Public Works (8.2 percent of all Democratic freshmen between the Eightieth and Hundredth Congresses), Agriculture (7.9 percent), Veterans' Affairs (7.5 percent), Banking and Currency (8.0 percent), and Science (7.1 percent), accounting altogether for nearly 40 percent of Democratic freshman assignments. The most frequently

merce and Industry committees and, as noted in the text, he does not include actual constituency variables for either committee. Finally, only Ray studies the Veterans' Affairs Committee, and he does not find a significant effect.

8. A plausible reason for the lack of statistical relationship between constituency characteristics and committee jurisidictions is that many committees have broad enough jurisdictions so that just about any constituency might find something of interest in them. This suggests that it might be fruitful to look for evidence supporting the interest-seeking hypothesis at the subcommittee level.

9. The data were made available to us by Garrison Nelson and Polimet. We checked a large random sample of these data against the *House Journal* and found very few errors. Comparing the *House Journal* to other sources—often used in the literature—we found fairly high error rates: *Congressional Quarterly* was best with an error rate of about 4 to 6 percent. The *Congressional Directory* was worst, with an error rate as high as 10 percent in some years.

Committee	Percent of All Assignments of Democratic Freshmen					Percent of All Requests by Democratic Freshmen in Selected Congresses			
	80th to 93rd	N	94th to 100th	N	80th to 100th	1st Choice	N	Any Choice	N
Appropriations	1.4	8	1.8	9	1.6	10.4	43	4.8	58
Rules	0.0	0	0.4	2	0.2	0.7	3	0.5	6
Ways and Means	0.0	0	1.6	8	0.8	6.8	28	3.2	38
Agriculture	7.7	43	8.1	41	7.9	10.7	44	6.6	79
Armed Services	4.3	24	5.5	28	4.9	9.7	40	6.2	74
Banking	7.9	44	8.1	41	8.0	10.0	41	8.2	99
Commerce	4.3	24	4.7	24	4.5	14.8	61	12.0	144
Education and Labor	8.1	45	5.1	26	6.7	6.3	26	5.9	71
Foreign Affairs	3.6	20	4.7	24	4.1	6.6	27	4.7	57
Judiciary	5.9	33	4.0	20	5.0	5.1	21	5.1	61
Post Office	9.3	52	3.0	15	6.3	0.7	3	2.2	26
Public Works	6.5	36	10.1	51	8.2	8.0	33	8.5	102
Science	5.9	33	8.5	43	7.1	2.9	12	5.7	68
Dist. of Columbia	2.7	15	1.4	7	2.1	0.2	1	0.7	8
Gov. Operations	5.4	30	5.7	29	5.6	0.7	3	7.7	93
House Admin.	3.8	21	1.2	6	2.5	0.0	0	1.6	19
HUAAC	0.9	5	[disbanded]		0.5	0.0	0	0.4	5
Interior	8.4	47	4.9	25	6.8	4.4	18	8.7	104
Merchant Marine	5.7	32	6.1	31	5.9	0.2	1	1.9	23
Veterans	8.1	45	6.9	35	7.5	0.5	2	2.0	24

NOTES: Columns 1 and 2 report the percentage and number of Democratic freshman assignments, respectively, to House committees for the prereform period; columns 3 and 4 report the percentage and number of Democratic freshman assignments, respectively, to House committees for the postreform period; column 5 reports the total percentage for the Eightieth to Hundredth Congresses; columns 6 and 7 report the percentage and number of Democratic freshmen requesting each committee as their first choice; and columns 8 and 9 report the percentage and number of Democratic freshmen who request each committee as any one of their choices.

Numbers and percentages in columns 1 through 5 refer to initial assignments, not members. For example, of all Democratic freshman assignments to standing committees in the Eightieth to Ninety-third Congresses, only 1.4 percent (a total of eight) were to Appropriations. The denominator used in calculating the percentage just given includes assignments to all standing committees, but we do not report percentages for the committees on Budget, Standards of Official Conduct, or Small Business. Hence, the percentages do not sum to 100.

The figures in columns 6 through 9 are read similarly. For example, 4.8 percent of all freshman requests of which we have record in the Eighty-sixth through Ninetieth and Ninety-second through Ninety-seventh Congresses were for the Appropriations Committee, while 10.4 percent of first-ranked requests were for Appropriations.

TABLE 2.   ASSIGNMENTS OF REPUBLICAN FRESHMEN,
EIGHTIETH TO HUNDREDTH CONGRESSES

Committee	Percent of All Assignments of Republican Freshmen				
	80th 93rd	N	94th to 100th	N	80th to 100th
Appropriations	1.9	10	0.0	0	1.1
Rules	0.0	0	0.0	0	0.0
Ways and Means	0.6	3	0.0	0	0.3
Agriculture	6.5	35	6.3	23	6.6
Armed Services	3.1	17	4.1	14	3.5
Banking	7.0	38	3.8	30	7.7
Commerce	3.5	19	3.2	11	3.4
Education and Labor	7.2	39	6.8	23	7.0
Foreign Affairs	1.3	7	0.6	2	1.0
Judiciary	6.7	36	3.2	11	5.3
Post Office	6.5	35	2.6	9	5.0
Public Works	8.7	47	7.1	24	8.1
Science	3.3	18	10.9	37	6.2
Dist. of Columbia	4.6	25	1.2	4	3.3
Gov. Operations	9.1	49	10.3	35	9.5
House Admin.	3.5	19	2.6	9	3.2
HUAAC	1.9	10	[disbanded]		1.1
Interior	8.1	44	6.8	23	7.6
Merchant Marine	8.1	44	5.9	20	7.2
Veterans	8.1	44	4.4	15	6.7

NOTE: Columns 1–5 are the same as columns 1–5 of table 1 but refer to Republicans instead of Democrats (see table 1, notes).

received assignments were very similar for the Republicans. More than one-third of all Republican freshmen during the postwar period were assigned to five committees: Agriculture (6.6 percent), Banking and Currency (7.7 percent), Public Works (8.1 percent), Science (6.2 percent), and Interior (7.6 percent). Very few freshmen of either party were assigned to Appropriations, Rules, Way and Means, Foreign Affairs, or Interstate Commerce. The actual assignments of freshmen, of course, tell us only indirectly about the success of their requests, but they do remind us of where freshmen generally rank in the House pecking order.

Table 1 also provides a summary of which committees Democratic freshmen were most likely to *request,* and these figures, in tandem with those on actual assignments, begin to get directly at the question of how many requests were granted. This table is based on requests data from Shepsle (1978) and Smith and Deering (1984), covering the Eighty-sixth through Ninety-seventh Congresses (but excluding the Ninety-first). Both data sets consist of written requests formally submitted by Democratic freshmen to their CC in the various Congresses covered. These requests took the form of rank orderings of a few committees: a first choice, a second choice, and so on.[10]

The aggregate relationship between the percentage of Democratic freshmen requesting a committee as their first choice and the percentage actually receiving assignment to that committee—a crude measure of how many first-choice requests were granted—is relatively modest: an insignificant correlation of .14. Moreover, the relationship between how many request and how many receive assignment to a committee is highly variable. For example, although fifty-seven Democratic freshmen requested Appropriations between the Eighty-sixth and Ninety-seventh Congresses, only about a dozen were assigned to that committee. At the other extreme, there were only twenty-four requests for appointment to Veterans' Affairs, yet almost three times that many Democratic freshmen were assigned to the committee. Assignments to the committees on Education and Labor, Post Office, Science, District of Columbia, House Administration, and Merchant Marine and Fisheries also exceeded requests.[11]

Table 3 gives a more direct microlevel look at how frequently Democratic freshmen got the assignments they requested in the period from the Eighty-sixth to Ninety-seventh Congresses. The first column of the table gives the first-choice success rate reported by Shepsle for the Eighty-seventh to Ninety-third Congresses. The proportions he reported were equal to the number of freshmen who succeeded in getting their first-choice assignment at the beginning of their first term, divided by the total number of freshmen. We have tabulated a more generous measure of assignment success in the next column. Our measure equals the num-

10. See Shepsle 1978 and Smith and Deering 1984 for details.
11. The aggregate evidence of accommodation of freshmen requests is generally strongest for the semiexclusive committees (with the notable exception of Interstate Commerce, with 141 requests and only about a third that many appointments).

TABLE 3.   ASSIGNMENT SUCCESS OF DEMOCRATIC
FRESHMEN, EIGHTY-SIXTH TO NINETIETH AND
NINETY-SECOND TO NINETY-SEVENTH CONGRESSES

Congress	% Receiving First Choice at Start of First Term	% Receiving First Choice in First Term[a]	% Receiving No Requested Assignment in First Term	Number of Requesters	Requesters as % of Freshmen
Eighty-sixth	—	41.0	35.9	39	60.0
Eighty-seventh	47.4	57.9	5.3	19	65.5
Eighty-eighth	50.0	50.0	13.9	36	90.0
Eighty-ninth	59.1	63.4	12.7	71	93.4
Ninetieth	30.3	50.0	35.7	14	82.4
Ninety-second	75.0	75.0	7.1	28	77.8
Ninety-third	69.1	69.2	19.2	26	78.8
Ninety-fourth	—	57.3	8.0	75	94.9
Ninety-fifth	—	58.5	14.6	41	85.4
Ninety-sixth	—	64.3	11.9	42	95.5
Ninety-seventh	—	57.1	9.5	21	80.8

NOTE: All standing committees are included in the analysis reported here. It will be noted that the total number of requesters—i.e., the sum of the numbers in column 5—is 412, 5 more than the number of first choices given in table 1, column 8. The difference is due to table 1's exclusion of the committees on Budget, Standard of Official Conduct, and Small Business; five Democratic freshmen requested Budget over these Congresses; none requested Official Conduct or Small Business.

[a] From Shepsle 1978, table 9.1, 193.

ber of freshmen who succeeded in getting their first-choice assignment at any time in their first term, divided by the total number of freshmen. Thus, the request success rates we report are quite a bit larger for some Congresses than are the ones reported by Shepsle. In the third column we report a statistic measuring total failure rather than clear success: the proportion of Democratic freshmen who were assigned to none of the committees they requested in their first terms.

Both Shepsle's and our measures of success indicate that, on average, roughly 60 percent of Democratic freshmen received their first-choice committee assignment in their first term. Interestingly, if one simply *asks* members whether they have received their "first-choice" assignments—as did Gertzog (1976) in interviews with freshmen of both parties in the Eighty-ninth to Ninety-first Congresses—one finds a somewhat higher number: roughly 70 percent of those interviewed reported receiving their "first-choice" committee assignment.[12] On the down side, however, our figures show that an average of nearly 14 percent of incoming Democrats received none of the assignments they requested in their first term.[13] Moreover, in some Congresses—the Eighty-sixth and the Ninetieth—the proportion of freshmen not receiving any requested assignment exceeded 30 percent.

Can we conclude with Shepsle that the Democratic CC was "responsive" to freshmen Democrats' requests? It is true that the observed success rates for freshmen are fairly high. But, as Shepsle notes, there is a distinction to be made between the "true" preferences of members and the preferences that they reveal in their request lists. About as many freshmen requested Education and Labor as requested Ways and Means, for example, but this parity probably did not reflect a judgment that Education and Labor and Ways and Means were equally attractive appointments: anticipations of which request was likely to be granted came into play as well.[14] But if freshmen sometimes did not request positions that they believed they would not be granted, then the observed success rate in some sense overstates the true success rate. Shepsle also notes that there was often some communication between the members of the CC and freshmen before requests were submitted and that freshmen were frequently guided in such communications to temper their "real" preference by the "political realities" of the assignment process. These two forces—anticipation by freshmen of the likelihood of success and communication between freshmen and the CC—might have led freshmen to make requests that reflected their true preferences less accurately but had a higher likelihood of being granted. It is therefore problematic to conclude that a high observed success rate is good evidence that the true preferences of freshmen were being accommodated.[15]

Even if there were no discrepancy between "true" and "revealed"

12. For the Eighty-ninth and Ninetieth Congresses, Shepsle found a much lower "first-choice" success rate for freshman Democrats than that reported by Gertzog for freshmen of both parties.

13. Shepsle's higher figure, 19 percent, is due to the difference in definitions explained in the text.

14. Shepsle (1978, 65) writes: "Judgments about the value of serving on particular committees are not, as we noted earlier, the sole basis for requests. Committee attractiveness . . . is discounted by the likelihood of actually receiving an appointment. . . . Thus, highly valued assignments with low success likelihoods are often avoided. On the other hand, somewhat less attractive committees accompanied by high success probabilities may show up on request lists with surprising frequency."

15. Another point to note is that a high correlation between what is requested and what is received is not necessarily evidence of a causal relationship. Perhaps, for example, the prior occupation of new members influences both what they ask for and what the CC is disposed to give them.

preferences, however, the observed success rates seem to leave ample room for some discretion on the part of the CCs. For example, if the Democratic CC were disposed to deal less favorably with incoming members who seemed less likely to support core party programs, it seems to have had the leeway to do so: recall that nearly 14 percent of the freshmen got none of their requested assignments and that 40 percent did not get their first-choice assignment.

It has been suggested to us that even though we observe that many freshman requests are not fulfilled, nonetheless a system of complete accommodation of assignment requests might still be in operation. For example, assume that the size of each committee is determined independent of the assignment process and that every member must receive at least one committee assignment. Under these assumptions, the number of committee slots to be filled at the start of a new Congress depends solely on the number of slots vacated by exiting members from the previous Congress. Incumbents and freshmen submit requests for available slots; under the assumption of perfect accommodation, no member has an incentive to act strategically in making assignment (or transfer) requests. Hence, an excess of requests may be made for highly desired slots on some committees, while, simultaneously, other committees may have more slots available than there are requests made. In other words, some committees may have queues of prospective members, while the CCs may have to draft members to fill slots on other committees.

Under perfect accommodation the CC might choose randomly from the queued members to fulfill desired openings and then fill out undersubscribed slots with members who failed to "win" such lotteries. Committee slots will be filled first by members who request the committee. Only after all requests for the committee have been exhausted would members be drafted to fill remaining slots. However, we do in fact observe nonqueuing behavior: the committees on Veterans' Affairs, Education and Labor, Post Office, Science and Aeronautics, District of Columbia, House Administration, and Merchant Marine and Fisheries all had members who requested assignment but were denied even though the number of committee vacancies exceeded the total number of formal committee requests. Thus, we can reject this Lotto version of accommodation.

4. ACCOMMODATION OF TRANSFER REQUESTS

Evidence on how frequently members' committee assignment requests were accommodated in the postwar House can also be found in analyses of the transfer requests of nonfreshmen.[16] Here again we rely on data compiled by Shepsle (1978) and Smith and Deering (1984), covering the Eighty-sixth through Ninety-seventh Congresses.

Table 4 gives the proportion of Democrats in each Congress who received their first-ranked transfer request, the proportion granted at least one of their transfer requests, and the total number of request lists submitted. Not quite 55 percent of those Democrats who requested a transfer got their first-ranked assignment, whereas roughly 60 percent got some requested assignment.

Table 5 breaks the figures given in table 4 down by committee, showing that the proportion of transfer requests granted is below 70 percent for most committees—even for those committees for which vacancies exceed requests (such as Merchant Marine and Fisheries or Post Office). Success rates were particularly low on the exclusive committees. Less than half of all requests for transfer to Appropriations, Rules, and Ways and Means were granted.

The data in tables 4 and 5 tell us only the percentage of formal, written requests that were granted. But such requests do not exhaust the possibilities. Some members might have requested a transfer through informal channels. If so, then the overall success rate is uncertain, since it is practically impossible to measure the informal success rate. We have no way of determining the number of informal requests made, much less the number granted.

We can, however, put an upper bound on the overall success rate simply by assuming that the informal success rate was 100 percent—and that all transfers not formally requested were informally requested. Thus, only those members who formally requested a transfer and received no transfer would be considered as having failed. These assumptions are of course unrealistic, but they do define the situation in which the overall success rate would be the highest that it could possibly be, given the observed formal success rate. With these assumptions, the highest possible overall success rate is 74 percent. Thus, *at most* three in four continuing members received the transfers they desired. By contrast, at least one in four was refused.

These results suggest that the majority party's CC did exercise substantial discretion: nontrivial percentages of those requesting a transfer were turned down. Possible reasons are that there were more requests

16. On committee transfers generally, see Goodwin 1959; Bullock and Sprague 1969; Cook 1983; Bullock 1973; Jewell and Chi-Hung 1974; and Munger 1988.

TABLE 4.   SUCCESS OF DEMOCRATS REQUESTING
TRANSFER, EIGHTY-SIXTH TO NINETIETH AND
NINETY-SECOND TO NINETY-SEVENTH CONGRESSES

Congress	First-ranked Transfer Request Granted	Some Transfer Request Granted	Number Who Formally Requested Transfers	Successful Transfer Requests as % of All Transfers
Eighty-sixth	57.9	57.9	19	13.1
Eighty-seventh	37.0	59.3	27	19.5
Eighty-eighth	39.1	52.2	23	12.6
Eighty-ninth	80.0	80.0	25	22.5
Ninetieth	42.1	47.4	19	16.4
Ninety-second	64.7	64.7	17	11.8
Ninety-third	44.0	44.0	25	14.5
Ninety-fourth	80.0	80.0	20	13.6
Ninety-fifth	45.0	45.0	20	13.4
Ninety-sixth	50.0	51.3	39	29.9
Ninety-seventh	66.7	66.7	30	20.2

NOTE: All standing committees except Standards of Official Conduct and Budget are included in the analysis. Thus, the "number who formally requested transfers" (column 4) is the total number of members for whom there exists record of a written request for transfer submitted to the Democratic CC, except that those members who requested transfer only to Official Conduct (Charles E. Bennett in the Ninety-second and Ninety-third Congresses and Morris K. Udall in the Ninety-second Congress) are not counted and, similarly, those members who requested transfer only to Budget (13 members in the Ninety-fifth Congress, 23 in the Ninety-sixth Congress, and 15 in the Ninety-seventh Congress) are not counted. Four members in the Ninety-sixth Congress submitted request lists that included Budget and other committees; these members were counted as having submitted requests (but they were counted as having received a requested transfer only if they were transferred to one of the other committees, not Budget). The total number of members who transferred in a given Congress (used as the denominator in column 5) also excludes Official Conduct and Budget; that is, those who transfer to one of these two committees are not counted. A freshman or superfreshman who transfers sometime after receiving an initial assignment is counted as among those who have transferred; if only upperclassmen are counted, the percentages in column 5 are slightly higher.

than vacancies, so that the CC had to choose among a pool of applicants, or that the committee went outside the pool of applicants, "co-opting" or "drafting" some members into service. In the next set of tables we look at some numbers pertinent to deciding which kind of discretion was exercised.

TABLE 5. SUCCESS OF DEMOCRATS REQUESTING TRANSFER, BY COMMITTEE REQUESTED

Committee	Percent of Transfer Requests Granted (Number of Requests)		
	86th to 93rd Congresses	*94th to 97th Congresses*	*86th to 97th Congresses*
Appropriations	48.5 (33)	46.7 (3)	47.6 (63)
Rules	0.0 (3)	41.7 (12)	33.3 (15)
Ways and Means	100.0 (1)	51.7 (29)	53.3 (30)
Agriculture	75.0 (4)	100.0 (3)	85.7 (7)
Armed Services	66.7 (15)	100.0 (5)	75 (20)
Banking	100.0 (1)	—	100.0 (1)
Commerce	40.0 (10)	40.0 (5)	40.0 (15)
Education and Labor	50.0 (4)	—	50.0 (4)
Foreign Affairs	55.6 (9)	66.7 (3)	58.3 (12)
Judiciary	—	100.0 (1)	100.0 (1)
Post Office	50.0 (4)	—	50.0 (4)
Public Works	75.0 (4)	—	75.0 (4)
Science	57.1 (7)	100.0 (2)	66.7 (9)
Dist. of Columbia	63.6 (11)	—	63.6 (11)
Gov. Operations	33.3 (15)	50.0 (6)	38.1 (21)
House Admin.	50.0 (4)	0.0 (0)	50.0 (4)
HUAAC	0.0 (1)	0.0 (0)	0.0 (1)
Interior	52.6 (19)	33.3 (6)	60.0 (25)
Merchant Marine	44.4 (9)	100.0 (2)	54.5 (11)
Veterans	100.0 (1)	—	100.0 (1)

NOTE: The total number of requests—the sum of the numbers in parentheses in the last column of the table—is 259. This differs from the figure of 264 one gets by summing the numbers in column 4 of table 4. The difference is due to two factors. First, this table does not report the requests for the Committee on Small Business, whereas table 4 includes these requests. Three members listed Small Business as their first choice; if these three are added to the total derived from this table, the figure is 262, still short of the total in table 4. The remaining discrepancy has to do with the difference between the number of first requests (tallied here) and the number of request lists (tallied in table 4). Two members in the Ninety-sixth Congress (Norman Y. Mineta and Harold L. Volkmer) requested transfer to the Budget Committee as their first choice but then went on to list other choices. These two are counted in table 4, which tallies all request lists that are not confined solely to the committees on Official Conduct and Budget, but are not counted in the current table, which tallies only first requests.

TABLE 6. RECRUITMENT PATTERNS IN DEMOCRATIC COMMITTEE TRANSFERS, EIGHTY-SIXTH TO NINETIETH AND NINETY-SECOND TO NINETY-SEVENTH CONGRESSES

Number of Members Transferring

Congress	To an Exclusive Committee	% Requested	To a Semiexclusive Committee	% Requested	To a Nonexclusive Committee	% Requested
Eighty-sixth	20	10.0	48	16.7	24	4.2
Eighty-seventh	19	10.5	41	19.5	26	26.9
Eighty-eighth	19	15.3	39	10.3	36	11.1
Eighty-ninth	19	31.6	44	20.5	30	20.0
Ninetieth	11	0.0	26	7.7	21	33.3
Ninety-second	12	16.7	49	10.2	41	9.8
Ninety-third	16	18.8	30	6.7	34	17.6
Ninety-fourth	27	40.7	32	12.5	67	0.0
Ninety-fifth	13	23.1	35	2.9	27	18.5
Ninety-sixth	17	58.8	34	14.7	20	10.0
Ninety-seventh	20	45.0	51	11.8	35	22.9
Totals and Averages	193	26.4	429	12.6	361	13.9

NOTE: The sum of the number of members transferring to a control, semiexclusive, or nonexclusive committee in the Eighty-sixth Congress is $20 + 48 + 24 = 92$. With a bit of calculation, the corresponding number in table 4 is 84. The discrepancy arises because table 4 counts a member only once, no matter how many times he or she transfers. This table counts 8 members twice because each of them transferred to at least two different committees in different categories. For example, Victor L. Anfuso transferred both to Science and to Merchant Marine and Fisheries and was counted once in the column for semiexclusive committees and once in the column for nonexclusive committees. Similar differences occur in other years. The averages given in the bottom row of the table are weighted, not simple.

Table 6 gives the proportion of all transfers that were formally requested and, by implication, the proportion that were not (the latter group includes unrequested transfers, informally requested transfers, and perhaps some formally requested transfers of which we have no record). We calculate these proportions, for each Congress, for three subclasses of committee: exclusive, semiexclusive, and nonexclusive.

The data in table 6 show something quite significant: the proportion of formally requested transfers is relatively low, less than 35 percent for the eleven Congresses in the Shepsle-Smith data set. The proportion of transfers to control committees that were formally requested is the highest—57 percent—while the comparable proportion for all other committees is only 32 percent.

It is possible, of course, that a significant fraction of the transfers for which no formal request exists were informally requested. But for purposes of arriving at a reasonable estimate of how many transfers were requested, it cannot simply be assumed that all transfers not formally requested were informally requested: it is known that some members were co-opted by the leadership to serve on committees, and there is also evidence that some members were pressed into service on certain committees (Fenno 1973).

With regard to co-optation, Fenno (1973, 20) writes that "approximately one-quarter of Ways and Means members and one-tenth of Appropriations members were taken off the committee on which they sat, without their request, and were given the more prestigious assignment—not because there were no applicants for the position, but because none of the applicants was deemed acceptable." Giving a somewhat broader figure, Fenno (20, table 4) reports that 35 percent of the members of the Appropriations Committee and 29 percent of the members of Ways and Means were either "inner circle" choices or were co-opted to serve on these committees. The corresponding figures for the other four committees he studied ranged from a high of 21 percent to a low of 7 percent.

Fenno also mentions that some members are pressed into service on certain low-prestige committees, and some evidence in the Shepsle-Smith data supports this notion. Table 7 tallies the Democratic vacancies on each committee in the Eighty-sixth to Ninety-seventh Congresses, and the number of written Democratic requests—by both freshmen and nonfreshmen—for each committee. For six committees—Post Office, Science, District of Columbia, House Administration, Merchant Marine, and Veterans' Affairs—vacancies actually exceeded written re-

TABLE 7.   DEMOCRATIC REQUESTS AND VACANCIES,
EIGHTY-SIXTH TO NINETY-SEVENTH CONGRESSES

Committee	Total Written Requests		Total Vacancies
	By Freshmen	By Nonfreshmen	
Agriculture	79	7	75
Appropriations	57	65	51
Armed Services	73	24	58
Banking	99	2	61
Commerce	141	18	53
Dist. of Columbia	8	12	49
Education and Labor	70	8	53
Foreign Affairs	57	15	52
Gov. Operations	92	24	48
House Admin.	19	6	31
Interior	103	31	74
Judiciary	61	2	50
Merchant Marine	23	19	56
Post Office	26	8	55
Public Works	101	11	58
Rules	6	18	18
Science	68	15	92
Veterans	24	2	50
Ways and Means	38	31	37

NOTE: In this table we count all requests, not just first-ranked requests. So, for example, 79 freshman Democrats listed Agriculture somewhere on their request lists in the period covering the Eighty-sixth through the Ninety-seventh Congresses. The Ninety-first Congress is excluded because of missing data. Total vacancies are estimated by the number of newly appointed members at the beginning of the term.

quests. If one assumes that the number of informal transfer requests for each committee equals the number of formal transfer requests, then one can estimate the total number of requests (whether formal or informal).[17] As it turns out, the number of vacancies exceeds the total esti-

17. The total number of requests is simply the sum of three terms: (1) the number of written requests from freshmen; (2) the number of written requests for transfer by nonfreshmen; (3) the estimated number of informal requests for transfer by nonfreshmen, equal to (2). The figures for the total number of requests for the six committees just noted in the text are Post Office, 42; Science, 98; District of Columbia, 32; House Administration, 31; Merchant Marine, 61; and Veterans' Affairs, 28.

mated number of requests for three of the six committees listed above. For these committees, then, one must either assume that the number of members informally requesting a transfer to them exceeded the number formally requesting a transfer, or conclude that some members were "pressed into service."

Given the possibility of co-optation of members to serve on the more prestigious committees, and of impressment of members to serve on the less prestigious committees, the finding in table 6—specifically, that most transfers to noncontrol committees were, as far as anyone can document, unrequested—is inconsistent with the self-selection model.

5. THE ROUTINIZATION OF THE ASSIGNMENT PROCESS

Gertzog (1976, 698) interviewed a sample of freshmen from both parties in the Eighty-ninth through Ninety-first Congresses and reinterviewed them again in subsequent Congresses. He reports that "by their third term, less than one in ten of the surviving members . . . had not yet been appointed to the committee they most preferred."[18] He interprets his findings to mean that the contemporary assignment process "has become an essentially routine, nondiscretionary procedure" (705).

Gertzog's findings have been widely cited, yet his data pertain only to the freshman cohorts from three Congresses. It is therefore worthwhile to ask whether there is some other way of corroborating his results with data from other Congresses.

One possibility is to see what proportion of Democratic freshmen in the Shepsle and Smith-Deering data sets had been appointed to their first-choice committees by their third terms (table 8). Typically, fewer than 70 percent of those who lasted at least three terms in the House had by their third term been appointed to the committee they ranked first as freshmen. This figure compares with an average of 60 percent receiving their first choice in their freshman term. These two figures together indicate that the vast majority of members either get their first choice in their first term or not at all. This view is not altered if one measures the success of initial cohorts instead of surviving members. Table 8 also gives the percentage of each entering cohort that had received appointment to their first-choice committees by the cohort's third

18. By the third term Gertzog's sample consisted of less than half of the original freshman-year sample.

TABLE 8.   ACCOMMODATION OF COMMITTEE
REQUESTS OF DEMOCRATIC FRESHMEN ENTERING
THE EIGHTY-SIXTH TO NINETIETH AND
NINETY-SECOND TO NINETY-SEVENTH
CONGRESSES

Congress	1[a]	2[b]	3[c]	4[d]	5[e]	6[f]
Eighty-sixth	41.0	51.3	28.2	44.4	27.8	39
Eighty-seventh	57.9	63.2	5.3	60.0	6.7	19
Eighty-eighth	50.0	55.6	11.1	52.4	14.3	36
Eighty-ninth	63.4	69.0	9.9	71.4	14.3	71
Ninetieth	50.0	85.7	7.1	85.7	7.1	14
Ninety-second	75.0	75.0	7.1	80.0	10.0	28
Ninety-third	69.2	69.2	15.4	65.0	20.0	26
Ninety-fourth	57.3	60.0	6.7	60.7	8.2	75
Ninety-fifth	58.5	63.4	14.6	59.4	18.8	41
Ninety-sixth	64.3	71.4	9.5	76.5	8.8	42
Ninety-seventh	57.1	—	—	72.7	5.6	21

[a] Percent of Democratic freshmen receiving their first choice in their first term.
[b] Percent of Democratic freshmen receiving their first choice by their fifth term.
[c] Percent of Democratic freshmen receiving no requested assignment by their fifth term.
[d] Percent of surviving Democratic members receiving their first choice by their third term.
[e] Percent of surviving Democratic members receiving no requested assignment by their third term.
[f] Number of Democratic freshman requests.

Congress; "cohort" success is comparable to "surviving member" success.

All in all, the Shepsle-Smith data on formally submitted committee requests paint a somewhat different picture than Gertzog's interviews do. There is a noticeable discrepancy between the "observed" success rate of freshmen (60 percent) and their success rate as reported in interviews (70 percent). And there is an even larger discrepancy between the observed (70 percent) and reported (90 percent) success rates of third-termers. We do not know the source of these discrepancies, but it is clear that Gertzog's empirical findings are not as straightforward as they may have seemed.

The interpretation that Gertzog offers based on his interview data must also be questioned. Even if a substantial majority of all members have attained their first-choice assignment by their third term, this does not necessarily mean that the process is nondiscretionary. There are other possibilities. For example, those members granted their first choice in their first term may have been more loyal, whereas those denied their first choice in their first term may have known that their chances of getting it in succeeding terms would be improved by supporting the leadership—and they then acted on that knowledge. It should be noted in this regard that there is evidence (presented in chapter 7) that "first-choice" assignments do tend to go to those freshmen who are more loyal and that transfers do tend to go to those nonfreshmen who are more loyal.

6. NORMS IN THE ASSIGNMENT PROCESS

Even if members are not quite as successful as Gertzog's interview evidence indicates, the process of assigning members to committees can still be considered "routine" and "nondiscretionary" if it is substantially hedged about by informal rules, customs, and norms that limit the discretion of the members of the CCs (Smith and Deering 1984). For example, Bullock (1976) has suggested that the CCs operate under an "apprenticeship" norm that guarantees mediocre assignments to incoming members. In somewhat the same vein, Dodd and Oppenheimer (1977, 41) suggest that a "congressional seniority" norm has reserved the choicest assignments to those who have accumulated many years of House experience.

Another commonly noted constraint on each party's CC is the "same-state" norm, whereby certain committee seats are "reserved" for particular state delegations. Fenno provides an early description of this norm in his study of the House Committee on Appropriations, observing that the larger state party delegations felt "entitled" to one or more seats on the more important committees (Fenno 1966, 238)—and that vacancies on these committees were often filled by members from the same states as the departing members.[19]

Statistical documentation of the same-state norm has been provided by Bullock (1971) and Kiewiet and McCubbins (1991). Bullock (1971,

---

19. Substantial testimony from members of Congress bolsters the notion that state party delegations are important in the appointment process. Masters's (1961, 346) interviews indicated that state party deans played "a crucially important role in securing assignments" for their rank-and-file members. Clapp (1964) also mentions the state party delegations as a decisive factor in assignments. Shepsle (1978) notes that both parties' CCs have long been organized along geographic lines, with zone representatives competing vigorously to get the most preferred committee positions for their region's members.

527) measured "protracted seat control" for thirty-one Democratic and twenty Republican state party delegations. He found that of the 536 House committee seats, 205 met his criteria of state party delegation control. Excluding those cases where the state party delegation was represented on a committee by the same member for at least ten of the eleven Congresses he studied, Bullock (532) found "28 percent of House committee seats to be delegation held." Kiewiet and McCubbins (1991, 94) reexamined Fenno's "same-state norm" for the House Appropriations Committee. They found that "the Democrats were especially likely to follow this rule of thumb—49.5 percent of the 105 members they assigned to Appropriations were from the same state as their predecessor, compared to 29.1 percent for the G.O.P."

A final set of norms that appear to constrain decision making, at least on the Democratic CC, concern the representation of minorities and women. Friedman (n.d.) has found that the Democrats often replace African Americans with African Americans and women with women on many of the more important committees. Thus, it is not just state delegations that have "retentive" capacities when it comes to committee seats.

The various norms outlined above may all limit the discretion of members of each party's CC. But they are far from removing all leeway for the use of party loyalty as a criterion in the allocation of committee posts. First, the level of seat retention by the larger state delegations and by the Black and Women's caucuses is higher than it would be if assignments were made at random, but it is hardly a universal rule. Second, even when retention rules apply, the CC may still have a choice from within the relevant group, since all the "retentive" groups are fairly large.

7. CONCLUSION

We have uncovered little evidence that the assignment process in the House is one of pure self-selection. The interest-seeking hypothesis—that constituency concerns drive committee requests—seems reasonable, but the statistical evidence for it pertains only to a few committees. The accommodation hypothesis—that members' assignment requests are routinely granted—seems hard to maintain with the evidence at hand. More than 40 percent of freshman assignment requests and nonfreshman transfer requests are denied by the Democratic CC. More than 30 percent of entering Democratic freshmen fail to get their most-preferred committee assignment even by the end of their third Congress. Almost 10 percent of freshmen fail to get *any* of their initially requested committee assignments even by the end of their fifth Congress.

Even if one were to accept the interest-seeking and accommodation hypotheses, however, it is not inevitable that each party's contingent on a committee would end up unrepresentative of the party as a whole. This conclusion logically requires a third, usually unstated, assumption about committee jurisdictions. Interest seeking and accommodation together produce a committee composed solely of members with direct constituency interests in the committee's jurisdiction. But some committees, such as Ways and Means, have such broad jurisdictions that limiting their membership in this way is not much of a constraint; if their actual members were chosen randomly from all those who sought appointment (an approximation of the nondiscretionary selection from among interesteds envisioned in the pure self-selection model), the resulting committee contingent would, on average, be representative of the party as a whole. It is only for committees with narrow or special jurisdictions that interest seeking and accommodation lead necessarily to unrepresentative contingents. We pursue this notion further in chapter 8.

TWO

The Seniority System
in Congress

One of the primary building blocks of the committee government model is the idea that members, once appointed to a standing committee, are automatically ensured security of tenure and promotion by seniority. The role of seniority has, of course, changed considerably in the last generation. In the early postwar House, seniority was the "single automatic criterion for selecting chairmen" of the standing committees (Hinckley 1971, 6). Beginning in the 1970s, however, other criteria—in particular, the preferences of the majority party's caucus—became more salient. Three long-time chairmen of the House were deposed by the Democratic Caucus in 1975, and by our count uncompensated violations of committee seniority have occurred in six of the seven succeeding Congresses.[1]

In this chapter we first review the evidence from the early postwar era of the Rayburn House (Cooper and Brady 1981) and then turn to more recent developments. We argue that, although violations of seniority were indeed few in the early postwar years, to infer committee autonomy from this is invalid.

1. SENIORITY IN THE RAYBURN HOUSE: THE STANDARD VIEW

Seniority in the early postwar House was important chiefly because it determined who would chair the standing committees. Each party ranked

1. See table 9.

45

its members on each committee in order of the length of their continuous service on that committee, and the member of the majority party with the longest committee service (the greatest "committee seniority") was appointed chair.

The exceptions to this rule of succession to the committee chair were few and far between after the war. Polsby, Gallaher, and Rundquist (1969; henceforth, PGR) surveyed all violations in the Forty-seventh through Eighty-eighth Congresses. They found only five violations in the postwar Congresses (Eightieth through Eighty-eighth), and all five were "compensated": that is, the member received another appointment of (arguably) equal or superior value (PGR 1969, 794). Abram and Cooper (1968) looked at seniority violations involving not just chairs but ranking minority members as well and arrived at a similar conclusion: they found no seniority violations on the six committees they investigated in the Eightieth through Eighty-sixth Congresses. Moreover, as Abram and Cooper pointed out (76), there were several cases of unpunished partisan transgressions during the postwar Congresses: "In every Presidential election from 1948 through 1960 there were Democratic Congressmen who supported a third party candidate, a slate of independent electors, or the Republican candidate. Yet in no case was action taken to deprive these men of their place or position on the committees on which they served."[2]

Neither PGR nor Abram and Cooper concentrated on seniority violations below the level of the chairmanship or the ranking minority membership in the committee lists. Nonetheless, PGR reported in a footnote (1969, 804) that "seniority has been pretty much inviolate since 1946 for committee rank and file as well as chairmen. There are only two exceptions."[3]

The paucity of seniority violations in the Rayburn House has been interpreted as showing that early postwar party leaders had lost the power to remove committee personnel—a power that their predecessors had clearly exercised in the period of "Czar Rule" half a century earlier. PGR (1969, 789) refer to a "custom" that "guarantees members reappointment to committees at the opening of each new Congress, in rank

2. This is actually a bit of an overstatement. As we explain more fully in the text below, two of the members who supported Strom Thurmond in 1948 were removed from the House Un-American Activities Committee—although other factors were involved in addition to their presidential apostasy.

3. The two exceptions that PGR had in mind involved Albert Watson and John Bell Williams, both stripped of their seniority in the Eighty-ninth Congress (see appendix 1). Joseph Cooper tells us that he and Michael Abram looked at the full committee lists for their sample of committees and found no violations at any level. Neither did we, for those committees.

order of committee service." This customary right of reappointment—
similar to tenure in academic departments, except that MCs did not
have to do anything to get it—undercut the power of removal. At the
same time, it seemingly blocked the last avenue that party leaders might
have taken to influence the appointment of committee chairs.

The seniority system—comprising the rule of succession to chairmanships, the customary right of reappointment, and the sanctity of
each committee's seniority rankings—was interpreted by PGR as a rec-
ipe for decentralized control. As they put it in an important and influential passage (1969, 790):

> The extent of a seniority rule's application may be said to constitute a mea-
> sure of the allocation of discretion and hence of power as between party
> leaders and committee chairmen. . . . Committee chairmen subject to the se-
> lection of party leaders stand in a different relation to the leadership than
> chairmen selected by an impersonal process in which the leadership is pow-
> erless to interfere. Thus, like pregnancy, seniority is for most purposes a
> dichotomous variable. When seniority operates as a partial influence [only],
> political influence flows to those empowered to vary the application of the
> diverse criteria of choice—normally party leaders. When seniority is sover-
> eign and inviolate, power is decentralized to those accordingly protected.

Researchers have clearly taken this passage to heart. Most descriptions of seniority in the early postwar House see it as "sovereign and
inviolate"—and infer that committee chairs must, therefore, have been
largely autonomous. Indeed, the customary right of reappointment (with
seniority rank preserved) has generally been construed as insulating *all*
committee members, not just chairs, from the wishes of party leaders.
Thus, the seniority system has been widely interpreted as one of the
foundation stones of committee autonomy in the Rayburn House.

2. RECONSIDERING THE STANDARD VIEW

The core of PGR's argument that a strong seniority system leads to
legislative decentralization is contained in a simple counterfactual claim:
"When seniority is sovereign and inviolate, power is decentralized to
those accordingly protected." We interpret this statement to mean that
*when seniority guarantees committee chairs against dismissal by party
leaders,* power will be decentralized to the former at the expense of the
latter.[4] We do not have a substantial quarrel with this claim, although

4. It might seem that we have strengthened the requirement beyond what PGR meant
by substituting the italicized phrase for PGR's. But if one reads the full passage, quoted
in the text above, it seems clear that PGR mean something quite close to what we have

of course there is some uncertainty about exactly how much power is decentralized.[5]

In order for PGR's counterfactual claim to become interesting, however, they need to link it to the facts of the postwar Congress, and therein lies the problem. PGR investigate all postwar accessions to committee chairs and find none in which seniority is violated without compensation. This is the primary evidence from which they—and many others in the literature—infer that seniority was "sovereign and inviolate." But such an inference is a fallacy: it affirms the consequent.

To see why, recall that affirming the consequent entails reasoning of the following form: "If p, then q; and q, therefore p." PGR's inference takes exactly this form. They begin with the implicit (and true) premise that if seniority were sovereign and inviolate, then one would never see an uncompensated violation of seniority. They next observe that in fact one never does see an uncompensated violation of seniority in the early postwar period. They infer (invalidly) that seniority must have been sovereign and inviolate in that period.

The difficulty with PGR's inference is that a sovereign and inviolate seniority system is only a sufficient and not a necessary condition for the lack of any seniority violations. A variety of factors might have depressed the incidence of violations, so the evidence they present does not inescapably support the conclusion that any one particular factor was responsible.

PGR no doubt had in mind other evidence in addition to the quantitative data they marshaled. There is, for example, the testimony of members of Congress themselves, including the well-known reports of the Democratic Study Group.[6] Moreover, the criticism we have leveled is less than fair in that almost any effort at measurement in the social

---

said: the thrust of the pregnancy analogy, in particular, is that there are really only two states, one in which party leaders have some discretion, and one in which they do not. In the latter state, chairs have protection against dismissal, like that possessed by ordinary members—which PGR themselves describe as a "guarantee."

5. If PGR mean only to claim a small amount of decentralization, then their claim is less interesting. It seems clear that they and others in the literature mean to claim a quite sizable decentralization. But there is no quantitative statement of the degree of decentralization, and it probably would be impossible to give one. This leaves some ambiguity.

6. For example, as a 1970 DSG report (cited in Rohde 1991, 19) noted, "The seniority system has fragmented and diffused power in the House, thereby crippling effective leadership and making it impossible to present and pursue a coherent legislative program. In 60 years' time, the pendulum has swung from one extreme where virtually all power was lodged in one man, the Speaker, to the other extreme where power is scattered among dozens of powerful committee and subcommittee chairmen."

sciences runs afoul to some degree of the same criticism—including, for example, our own effort in chapter 6 to measure party loyalty. We have singled out PGR's inference for particular scrutiny only because it has been so influential.

Our criticism does not mean that PGR were incorrect in their beliefs. It may be true that seniority was sovereign and inviolate in the early postwar period. But one should not believe this claim simply because there were no uncompensated violations; there are other possible explanations of this finding, and, in fact, we prefer one of these other explanations. In our view the number of seniority violations observed in any period reflects an underlying factional equilibrium in each party's CC and caucus. There are plausible views of the nature of this equilibrium that do not imply that committee chairs or members were autonomous in the sense that that term is generally used in the literature. Before elaborating this view, we digress to reconsider the evidence in greater detail.

3. THE EMPIRICAL EVIDENCE

As noted in the previous section, PGR concentrated on violations of the seniority of chairmen or potential chairmen on all committees, whereas Abram and Cooper concentrated on violations involving chairmanships or ranking minority positions on six selected committees. This approach leaves open the possibility of undiscovered violations of two types: (1) those involving ranking minority members on committees other than the six looked at by Abram and Cooper; and (2) those involving members lower in the seniority lists. Were there any such violations of seniority?

As it turns out, there is one uncompensated violation of each kind in that part of the postwar period covered by PGR (the Eightieth through Eighty-eighth Congresses). At the ranking minority level, there is the case of James C. Auchincloss (R.-N.J.). Auchincloss had been ranking minority member on both the Public Works and District of Columbia committees in the Eighty-sixth and Eighty-seventh Congresses. In the next Congress, however, he was ranked second on District of Columbia and had acquired no new assignments. The *Washington Post* noted that Auchincloss, who served his last term in the Eighty-eighth Congress, had resigned his position because of "the press of other duties." It seems plausible that Auchincloss was feeling his years: he was seventy-eight at the beginning of the Eighty-eighth Congress. But his identification with the liberal northeastern wing of the party—and the rather steep decline in his leadership support scores over the Eighty-sixth, Eighty-seventh, and Eighty-eighth Congresses—may also have had something to do with his relinquishing power.[7] In any event, he received no compensation for stepping down, so his case must be counted as an uncompensated violation.

Lower in the seniority lists, there is the case of Christian A. Herter (R.-Mass.), another liberal northeasterner. Herter served on the Rules Committee in the Eightieth and Eighty-first Congresses. During the second session of the Eighty-first Congress, he was one of twenty-one House Republicans to dissent publicly from minority leader Joseph Martin's "GOP '50 Plan," a campaign platform for Republicans in the off-year elections.[8] He also voted with the liberal Democrats on Rules on the issue of reporting out a bill creating a Fair Employment Practice Commission and actively promoted liberal labor and tax legislation.[9] Herter was not reappointed to Rules at the beginning of the Eighty-second Congress, taking instead the eleventh-ranking position on Foreign Affairs. We count this as an uncompensated violation of seniority because ranking third out of four on Rules was, at this time, clearly a more powerful position than eleventh out of twelve on Foreign Affairs, a panel that traditionally has labored in the shadows of its more powerful Senate counterpart.

In addition to these two cases, there are others that fail to constitute seniority violations only through a narrow interpretation of what such violations entail. Consider the fates of John E. Rankin (D.-Miss.), F. Edward Hebert (D.-La.), and J. Hardin Peterson (D.-Fla.): Rankin and Hebert had supported Strom Thurmond's "Dixiecrat" candidacy for president in 1948. At the beginning of the Eighty-first Congress (January 1949), Speaker Sam Rayburn arranged their removal from the House Un-American Activities Committee (HUAAC)—in part to punish them for their presidential defection and in part to remake a committee that had launched investigations embarrassing to the party.

The technique used to remove them, however, was not a straightforward purge. Instead, the Democratic CC adopted resolutions to regulate its own decisions. The CC first considered a rule barring any chair

7. Whereas Auchincloss ranked in the top fourth of all Republicans in terms of loyalty in the Eighty-sixth Congress, he was near the median in the Eighty-seventh and in the bottom fourth by the Eighty-eighth.

8. See *New York Times,* 12 Jan. 1950 and 4 July 1950.

9. See *Congressional Quarterly Almanac 1950,* 375–79, 593; and *New York Times,* 13 Mar. 1950.

of a standing committee from service on any other committee. This rule would have affected both Rankin (who became chairman of the Committee on Veterans' Affairs in the Eighty-first Congress) and John S.Wood (who was slated to become chairman of HUAAC in the Eighty-first Congress and would have had to give up his position on Education and Labor under the proposed rule). The *New York Times* actually reported the adoption of this rule on 9 January 1949 (25), but this was not the final solution arrived at by the leadership. Instead, two much narrower and more obviously targeted resolutions were passed. The first forbade any chair of a House standing committee from serving on HUAAC. This rule affected only Rankin and effectively removed him from the committee. The second resolution committed the CC to appointing only "experienced members of the bar" to serve on HUAAC. This rule, aimed at Hebert, also removed Peterson—who, Ripley suggests, "apparently did not mind leaving."[10]

All told, three of the five Democratic members of HUAAC were removed—and a fourth, the new chair, had been threatened with removal. Yet none of these purges count as an impairment of seniority's "guarantee of reappointment" because they were all effected under the guise of general rules regulating the conduct of the CC. There are at least a score of other cases in which members simply dropped a committee assignment to which they were entitled under seniority. All of the ones that we have looked at are clearly not individual punishments of the kind visited on Rankin and Hebert, but their case does remind one that formally general rules may not always be politically neutral. A more thorough examination of all the various postwar changes in the rules governing committee appointments may turn up one or two other instances where seniority effectively was abridged.

A final set of cases pertinent to assessing the sanctity of the seniority rule concerns members bumped off committees because of changes in the partisan control of Congress. For example, several Republicans appointed to Appropriations, Ways and Means, or Rules in the Eightieth and Eighty-third Congresses found that there was no longer room for them when the Democrats regained their majority in the succeeding Congress. The custom in such cases (in both parties) was to reappoint the bumped members, in order of seniority, as soon as space became available. But this custom was not always observed:

10. See Ripley 1967, 22 n. 20; *New York Times,* 2 Jan. 1949, 31; 9 Jan. 1949, 25; 16 Jan. 1949, 1, 17; 18 Jan. 1949, 15.

A man who had once served on the Rules Committee and who had expected to return found himself shunted aside in favor of a junior who had never seen service on the committee; the explanation, in the words of one party leader, was that "our leadership didn't trust him because, in the past, he had made deals on legislation which were detrimental to our over-all program. The man who got the spot was safe from that point of view. There is nothing to hide about that situation. It is just a cold political fact." (Clapp 1964, 228)

The member described in this passage is J. Edgar Chenoweth (R.-Colo.), who served on Rules in the Eighty-third Congress but was not reappointed when space opened up in the Eighty-sixth. Chenoweth was in the bottom 15 percent of Republicans in terms of loyalty to the leadership in both the Eighty-fifth and Eighty-sixth Congresses.

Another possibly similar case is that of Otto Krueger (R.-N.D.). Krueger was appointed to the Appropriations Committee as a freshman in the Eighty-third Congress. Bumped off by the large influx of Democrats in the Eighty-fourth, Krueger was given a position on Government Operations. In the Eighty-fifth, custom would have entitled him to return to Appropriations, but instead he took—or was given—a position on Agriculture. It is possible that Krueger preferred Agriculture to Appropriations; North Dakota does, after all, have substantial farming interests. But it is probably relevant to note Krueger's steeply declining leadership support scores over his three terms in Congress: 90.9, 70.3, 53.7. Krueger was in the bottom 10 percent of all Republicans in terms of loyalty to the leadership in both the Eighty-fourth and Eighty-fifth Congresses.

If one counts only "pure" violations of seniority, in which someone's ranking is lowered or his customary right to remain on a committee is infringed, our survey adds only two cases in the early postwar era—those of Auchincloss and Herter.[11] These cases show that seniority was

11. Two more cases might be counted as uncompensated violations, though we have not done so. Polsby and his associates count one, the case of Dean P. Taylor, as a compensated violation. They report as follows: "In the Republican-controlled 83rd Congress (1953–55), A. L. Miller of Nebraska became chairman of the committee on Interior and Insular Affairs. The ranking Republican member in the previous Congress . . . failed to be renominated to Congress. The second ranking Republican, Dean P. Taylor of New York, whose seniority was violated, transferred to the Judiciary committee" (PGR 1969, 804). Taylor was given the highest seniority among all first-term members of Judiciary, and Judiciary was a more important committee then than now; but Taylor still ranked only eleventh out of sixteen, and it is possible to question the adequacy of his compensation. The second case is that of Alvin Ray Bush (R. -Pa.). Bush served on the Public Works and Commerce committees in the Eighty-third Congress. In the Eighty-fourth Congress he was appointed on 20 January to Commerce and Merchant Marine; seven days later he left Merchant Marine and was appointed to Public Works—but he was ranked lower

violated without compensation during the Eightieth through Eighty-eighth Congresses—but the frequency of violation remains low, and neither case involves the Democratic party. If one expands the notion of a seniority violation slightly to include transparent rules changes, then it is clear that the Democrats, too, violated seniority without compensation in a couple of cases (those of Rankin and Hebert). Finally, expanding the notion of a seniority violation yet further, to include members seeking reappointment to a committee from which they were bumped by changes in partisan control of the House, nets two more cases (Chenoweth and Krueger). Even using the most expansive definition of a seniority violation, the number of uncompensated violations is not large. Moreover, as PGR documented long ago, seniority is never violated when the succession to the chairmanship is at stake. But the number of seniority violations is large enough, we think, so that seniority in general cannot be described as "inviolate" in this period. If one accepts the logic of PGR's original analysis—that, whereby "like pregnancy, seniority is for most purposes a dichotomous variable"—then one must conclude that some political influence must have accrued to the account of the party leaders who exercised discretion over appointments—even in the early postwar period. In place of the pregnancy analogy we prefer an emphasis on "anticipated reactions": members knew that there were limits to acceptable behavior and that they ran a risk—even if a small one—of having their customary seniority rights removed if they pushed those limits too far. We are ready to accept that the limits on acceptable behavior were less constraining in the Eightieth through Eighty-eighth Congresses than they had been before or would be after, but not that there were no limits that party leaders could enforce.

The two "pure" cases of uncompensated seniority violations discussed above and every other such violation occurring in the Eightieth through Hundredth Congresses are briefly recounted in appendix 1 and tabulated along with compensated violations in table 9. As is already well known (PGR 1969; Hinckley 1971; Hinckley 1976; Dodd and Oppenheimer 1977), the frequency of uncompensated violations picks up in the Eighty-ninth and later Congresses. Fresh violations occur in

---

than seven others whom he would have outranked had his service been counted as continuous. This may just be a case of indecisiveness costing a member his seniority. But other members have been appointed "late" to a committee on which they had previously served and not suffered any loss in seniority. So there seems to be some element of discretion involved.

TABLE 9.   SENIORITY VIOLATIONS IN THE
EIGHTIETH TO HUNDREDTH CONGRESSES

Congress	Compensated Violations	Uncompensated Violations	Total Violations
Eightieth	4	0	4
Eighty-first	0	0	0
Eighty-second	0	1	1
Eighty-third	1	0	1
Eighty-fourth	0	0	0
Eighty-fifth	0	0	0
Eighty-sixth	0	0	0
Eighty-seventh	0	0	0
Eighty-eighth	0	1	1
Eighty-ninth	0	3	3
Ninetieth	0	2	2
Ninety-first	3	1	4
Ninety-second	2	1	3
Ninety-third	3	1	4
Ninety-fourth	5	13	18
Ninety-fifth	6	1	7
Ninety-sixth	2	1	3
Ninety-seventh	6	1	7
Ninety-eighth	6	0	7
Ninety-ninth	7	6	13
Hundredth	9	6	16

NOTE: A violation is counted for each member whose seniority is violated in a Congress. We continue to count the violation as long as the member's seniority is not respected.

seven of the twelve Congresses after the Eighty-eighth, and some members had their seniority violated in all but one of the Congresses after the end of PGR's time series.[12]

There are substantial differences in the pattern of evidence for the two parties. There have been only three uncompensated violations of the seniority of Republican members in the entire postwar era. This lack of seniority violations on the Republican side reflects fewer sex and

12. Also, the view of committee chairs as agents of the majority party makes a clear reappearance. In a letter to Daniel Rostenkowski (D. -Ill.), for example, Speaker James C. Wright was quite explicit: "As Chairman of the House Committee on Ways and Means, Danny, you are the designated agent of the Democratic Caucus" (Barry 1989, 179).

bribery scandals, fewer members supporting the other party's presidential nominees, and fewer members willing to fight over their party's top committee slots. Because there are so few Republican seniority violations, in the remainder of this chapter we concentrate on the Democrats.

4. INTERPRETING THE EVIDENCE

What should one make of the Democratic evidence on seniority violations? The first point to make is that even finding *no* uncompensated violations of seniority in a given period of time does not mean that such violations were impossible or unthinkable. It just means that in all cases where someone might have lost seniority, there were enough votes in the CC or in the party caucus to prevent it or even to prevent the issue from being formally raised. This lack of votes might be due to a variety of factors, but we focus on two possible causes in particular.[13]

A first possible cause, often suggested in the literature, is the self-interest of senior members: these members—in sight of a chairmanship of their own—wish to prevent the establishment of any precedent that might some day be used against them; therefore, they usually oppose any violation of seniority, and because they are collectively powerful, their opposition is sufficient to make uncompensated seniority violations rare, even nonexistent. This idea has been linked to the dramatic events of 1975, when three full committee chairs were deposed by the Democratic Caucus: Hinckley (1976) points out the unusually large Democratic freshman class in the Ninety-fourth Congress and argues that they played a key role.

13. One possible explanation that we do not examine views the seniority norm as an informal consensus on the abstract virtues of experience and age, especially in determining succession to positions of authority. We doubt that such a norm has ever been markedly more important in Congress than elsewhere. Why do we say this, in light of the extensive research into the socialization of new members, showing how they were instructed in the niceties of the seniority-apprenticeship system and their (quite limited) role in it? Because we do not believe that this propaganda effort on the part of the senior members was particularly convincing. It surely was convincing in communicating to new members what was expected of them by those with power over their advancement. But as a philosophy of government it was merely a convenient, not entirely bankrupt but nonetheless transparent, rationalization of the status quo. Every organization with long career paths within it is prone to discover the virtues of seniority at some point. The question is why the senior members of the House were more successful than senior managers elsewhere in imposing the reality of seniority-based promotion. In explaining this difference their understandable efforts at promoting the abstract virtues of seniority, as against energy or competence, seem relatively unimportant. More important was the factional balance of power in the majority party.

A second possible explanation for the paucity of seniority violations in the early postwar years is stalemate between the regional wings of the Democratic party. According to this view, variations over time in seniority violations do not follow the twists of "class warfare" between juniors and seniors so much as the turns of factional warfare between southerners and northerners. In this view the story of seniority violations might go something as follows: In the early postwar years, the southern wing of the party was either a majority or close to it. Both wings of the party effectively possessed a "veto" on the CC and in the caucus. The South used this veto to protect a series of their own members who strayed from the straight and narrow path in presidential politics. When William Colmer (D.-Miss.) supported an unpledged slate of electors in 1960, for example, liberal members of the party sought to purge him from the Rules Committee as retribution.[14] The reason they failed seems to be primarily that Colmer, albeit out of tune with northern liberals, was very much in tune with southern conservatives, who were sufficiently numerous to make his removal costly. As Clark (1964, 132) puts it, "To remove Colmer could have meant tampering with seniority . . . risking a rupture with the Southern wing of the party." Most of the other instances of members failing to support the Democratic nominee for president also involved southerners, and in each case it seems plausible that southerners, rather than senior members, provided the main insurance against reprimand.

Some credence is lent to this view of seniority violations by the punitive demotions of Albert Watson (D.-S.C.) and John Bell Williams (D.-Miss.) for their support of Goldwater in 1964. In the Eighty-seventh Congress, which declined to punish Colmer, southerners constituted 38 percent of the Democratic Caucus.[15] In the Eighty-ninth Congress, which did punish Watson and Williams, southerners constituted only 30 percent of the party—their lowest percentage in the postwar era to that point.

The southern percentage *after* the Eighty-ninth Congress has fluctuated between 28 and 33 percent of the party, whereas *before* the range had been from 35 to 55 percent. This decline in the southern wing of the party has also been linked to the events of 1975. Hinckley (1976) notes that southerners were substantially overrepresented among committee chairs by the Ninety-fourth Congress: their earlier numerical

14. See *New York Times*, 3 Jan. 1961, A-1; 4 Jan. 1961, A-1, A-25.
15. By *southerner* we mean members from the eleven states of the former Confederacy.

preponderance at all levels of seniority had survived disproportionately as a preponderance at the most senior levels. All three deposed chairmen, of course, were southerners.

Were the 1975 dethronings caused primarily by regional warfare or by "class" warfare? Was the previous era of surface tranquility caused primarily by regional stalemate or by successful oppression of juniors by seniors? We incline strongly to the regional stalemate hypothesis. But even if regional conflict were not the most important factor, it seems clear that it played a major role in the pattern of seniority violations over time. If one accepts this argument, however, then one's interpretation of the seniority evidence—and in particular its relationship to committee autonomy—must differ from the standard view.

To make the point clear, suppose that regional conflict among Democrats was the primary explanation for the lack of seniority violations in the early postwar era. The "independence" of committee chairs in this case would be due to the fact that both wings of the party could veto any major sanction, so that the range of acceptable behavior for committee chairs (and other members) was quite broad: members needed to please only one wing to retain their positions.

It is important to note that this view does not imply that committees or their chairs were "autonomous" in any normal sense of that word. If some committee chair had sufficiently antagonized *both* wings of the party in the 1950s, there seems little reason to doubt that he would have been removed. Most of the anecdotal evidence regarding "independent" committee chairs concerns southerners who were independent of liberal northern Democrats but were clearly dependent on the support of the southern wing of the party, which they served well. Certainly this seems a reasonable reading of Howard W. Smith's stewardship of the Rules Committee. Smith delayed much legislation that the northern wing wanted passed. But, as he said, "it was a helpful slowing down or else Congress would not have tolerated it all these years" (*Congressional Quarterly Weekly Report*, 2 Jan. 1959, 24). To whom was it helpful? To the southern wing, which was sufficiently numerous to maintain Smith in his position.

Another way to drive home the point that we are trying to make is to take a comparative perspective. Imagine a two-party coalition government in some parliamentary democracy and ask the following question: as the disagreements between the two coalition partners increase, should we expect the separate ministries to be more autonomous, in the sense that the two partners will delegate more decision-making authority to them and give their decisions less scrutiny in cabinet? We think not. As disagreements mount between two coalition partners, each will wish to ensure that the other does not dominate important ministries. For each ministry, this situation will mean either that (1) both partners have sufficient representation in the ministry to protect their interests, in which case the ministry can be as "autonomous" as it ever was but will not obviously be any more so; or (2) one partner will feel underrepresented on the ministry, in which case it will use whatever resources it has to interfere with the "autonomous" functioning of the ministry (see McCubbins 1985 for a similar argument regarding delegation to executive agencies). Every time Judge Smith and the Rules Committee delayed or derailed the legislation of other committees, scholars see evidence of the "autonomy" of the Rules Committee; one might just as well see evidence that other committees were not "autonomous" and that the decentralization of power was incomplete.

5. CONCLUSION

There was clearly a big change in the relationship between party leaders and committee chairs after the revolt against Joseph Cannon. Prior to the revolt, Speakers made all committee appointments and considered committee seniority as only one among several criteria. The Speaker, in other words, could both "hire" and "fire" committee personnel. After the revolt, in contrast, committee assignments have been made by committee. The top leaders have retained, even in the postwar era, influence over initial appointments and transfers, but they can no longer independently remove committee personnel or violate their seniority.

Nonetheless, this erosion of the top leadership's control over committees has never meant committee autonomy. Early postwar committees were certainly not autonomous in the sense of being unaccountable to their party. Removal or demotion of committee personnel has always been possible, either on the recommendation of the CC or by direct caucus action. That removals and demotions were rarely observed in the Rayburn House did not reflect some change in the organizational chart of the parties or the House. Committees were never like independent executive agencies are supposed to be vis-à-vis the president. Seniority violations were rare because (1) the party was divided into two regional factions, both of which could veto the punishment of any of their own; and (2) the seniority system produced a mix of committee chairs that, until the 1970s, accurately reflected the regional balance in the party (Hinckley 1971; 1976). The stalemate began to dissolve when the relative size of the southern contingent in the Democratic Caucus shrank after the 1964 elections, so that the North was able to punish MCs who transgressed in their support of presidential candidates. A decade later, when a regional imbalance appeared at the level of committee chairs, the caucus took action to remove chairs merely because they were unrepresentative.[16] The extent of seniority violations does not measure committee autonomy or decentralization of power so much as it measures the degree of factional stalemate in the majority party.

16. One might ask what the pattern of uncompensated seniority violations looked like before the North-South split in the Democratic party emerged in the late 1930s. PGR do not break violations down by party, so we cannot say for sure at this point whether *Democratic* violations were higher before the Seventy-fifth Congress (1937–38) or not. But overall violations certainly were. This may not be good evidence, however, if most seniority violations are accounted for by the majority party—as has been the case in the postwar period.

THREE

Subgovernments and the Representativeness of Committees

One of the key notions entailed in the committee government model, especially in its more extreme "subgovernment" version, is that many congressional committees are unrepresentative of their parent chambers. It is easy to see why this notion is important: if most committees mirrored the range of interests found on the floor, then the autonomy that they are assumed to possess would have much less far-reaching consequences.

The belief that many committees are unrepresentative is partly based on a deduction from the assumptions that members seek assignment to committees pertinent to the interests of their constituents (the interest-seeking hypothesis) and that most assignment requests are routinely accommodated by each party's CC (the accommodation hypothesis).[1] We believe the premises of this deduction to be shaky (see chapter 1); however, unrepresentative committees may arise even if members do not self-select committees. Self-selection focuses on the unrepresentative character of those who enter a committee, but it can also be that those who exit are unrepresentative, and either process is sufficient to produce unrepresentative panels. If we accept the possibility that subgovernments may arise whenever there are unrepresentative committees (unrepresentativeness + autonomy = subgovernment), then committee unrepresentativeness itself is of interest to those who would assess the

---

1. An ancillary assumption, that districts are small enough so that many of them are dominated by one or another interest that looks special from a national viewpoint, is usually unstated.

plausibility of the view that Congress is something like a giant logroll among subgovernments.[2]

The view that a system of reciprocity exists among autonomous committees, which trade support on the floor (or "defer" to one another's policy-area expertise), seems to require a certain number of unrepresentative committees. After all, if a committee is representative of floor preferences, then legislation that passes muster in committee will also be likely to pass muster on the floor—without need for any intercommittee deals or deference. Thus, if reciprocal noninterference among autonomous and distinctive committees is to be the dominant story line in Congress, then many members must be assigned to unrepresentative committees. Indeed, a majority of members must be so assigned; otherwise, intercommittee logrolls would be ineffective because too few members need them.

A little bean counting is sufficient to show that this condition puts a fairly strong requirement on the number of unrepresentative committees. It has long been recognized that the control committees in the House—Appropriations, Ways and Means, and Rules—are broadly representative of the House's regional and ideological groupings.[3] Thus, if the subgovernment thesis is true, then more than half of the remaining committees must be unrepresentative of the regional and ideological groupings in the House. Otherwise, the pervasive necessity and centrality of intercommittee logrolls is brought into question.

The first section of this chapter reviews the previous scholarly literature dealing with the representativeness of House committees. The next two sections update previous results while trying to improve the data and methods used. Our findings are in general agreement with those reported in earlier studies: a few committees are frequently unrepresentative, but most do not differ in a statistically significant manner from the full House membership. Section 4 considers how these results square with the subgovernment thesis and with the committee government model more generally.

1.   THE PREVIOUS LITERATURE

Committee representativeness has been examined in numerous case studies of individual committees.[4] Here we focus on those scholars who

2. See, for example, Shepsle 1990; C. Miller 1962, 110.
3. See below and also Shepsle 1978; Kiewiet and McCubbins 1991.
4. These include Appropriations (Kiewiet and McCubbins 1991); the House Budget

have looked at more than one committee over a span of Congresses.

The dimensions along which a committee might be unrepresentative of its parent chamber are many. Researchers have typically concentrated on just two: a regional dimension (is the South overrepresented on committee X?) and an ideological dimension (are liberals overrepresented on committee Y?). The natural suspicion is that committees will represent not the broad spectrum of societal interests but rather the narrow regional or ideological interests of the constituencies affected by the policies over which they have some influence.

Of the two criteria of representativeness, regional balance is the easier to measure. It is mostly just a matter of seeing whether the pattern of regional representation in the House as a whole is reflected in each of its panels. There is substantial agreement that several committees have been persistently unbalanced in terms of the geographical location of their members' constituencies: for example, the South often has been overrepresented on Agriculture, the East on Education and Labor, the West on Interior, and the coasts on Merchant Marine and Fisheries. In addition, various other committees have been identified as regionally unbalanced in one or more Congresses. Table 10 summarizes those identified by Goodwin (1970), Fenno (1973), and Smith and Deering (1990).[5]

Measuring ideological representativeness is a bit more complicated, since it is easier to find out the region from which members hail than to classify them unambiguously as liberal, moderate, or conservative. Most of the literature relies for such classifications on the roll call ratings produced by interest groups such as the Americans for Democratic Action (ADA), the United Auto Workers (UAW), and the League of Conservation Voters (LCV).

These scores are thought to tap into two different types of ideology. First, they might measure the *general* ideological predispositions of members—how liberal or conservative they are. Second, they might measure more *specific* ideological predispositions—whether a member is a social liberal, a defense hawk, and so forth.[6] In either case, however, substantial problems loom.

Committee (Kiewiet and McCubbins 1991; Palazzolo 1989; Schick 1980); Agriculture (Jones 1961; Ornstein and Rohde 1977b; Hall 1989); Armed Services (Ray 1980b; Goss 1972; Arnold 1979); Ways and Means (Manley 1970); Post Office and Judiciary (Ogul 1976); and Rules (Robinson 1963).

5. We do not analyze these findings here. The interested reader can refer to Fenno 1973; Goodwin 1970; and Smith and Deering 1990.

6. Of course, as we get more and more specific about ideological predispositions, they begin to look increasingly like issue preferences of one kind or another.

Consider first the difficulty of taking interest group scores as measures of general ideology. As Fowler (1982) indicates, interest groups do not intend their ratings to measure ideology. They are designed instead to identify interest groups' friends and expose their enemies. Unfortunately, a group may have both conservative and liberal friends and both conservative and liberal enemies (especially if it has a fairly narrow issue focus). To the extent that it does, the effort to separate friends from enemies will interfere with the separation of conservatives from liberals.

Another problem is that many interest groups, especially the more broadly focused ones, such as the Americans for Constitutional Action (ACA) and the ADA, choose controversial but nonpartisan issues to calculate their ratings. These groups want to rate their friends and enemies in Congress regardless of party. Partisan issues clearly separate Democrats from Republicans, of course, but they provide little intraparty variance—thus the incentive to include important votes that produce intraparty divisions. The question then arises as to whether the ACA and ADA scores are based on too many nonpartisan issues—proportionally more than occur in Congress. If they are so based, then they will provide a picture of Congress that is misleadingly nonpartisan. If we believe that salient ideological divisions lie along party lines, then using these ratings as general measures of ideology will be problematic.

Another consequence of interest groups' choosing controversial but nonpartisan votes to include in their scores is that many scores are better at discriminating among Democrats than among Republicans. (The reason is that most controversial but nonpartisan votes are squabbles among the members of the majority party; many are on amendments that the minority designs specifically to split off some segment of the majority, if it can.) The ratings of the American Security Council (ASC) for the Ninety-seventh Congress (figure 1) and of the ADA for the Ninety-seventh Congress (figure 2) are typical. More than 90 percent of all Republicans received a rating of 85 percent or higher on ASC's National Security Index; Democrats, by contrast, are dispersed more or less uniformly over the entire range, from 0 to 100 (figure 1). The distribution of ADA ratings for the Ninety-fifth Congress shows the Democrats more or less uniformly distributed over the full range of scores but over 90 percent of the Republicans concentrated below 45 (figure 2).

This problem is still worse for ratings by the more specialized interest groups, such as the National Education Association (NEA); the American Federation of State, County, and Municipal Employees (AFSCME);

TABLE 10. GEOGRAPHICAL UNREPRESENTATIVENESS ON COMMITTEES IN THE HOUSE

Committee	Fenno[a]	Goodwin[b]	Smith and Deering[c]
Agriculture		South overrepresented	South and Midwest over-represented
Banking		East overrepresented	
Dist. of Columbia		South overrepresented	
Education and Labor	East and West overrepresented; South underrepresented	East and West overrepresented	
Foreign Affairs	Midwest overrepresented	East and Midwest overrepresented	
Gov. Operations		East and Midwest overrepresented	
HUAAC		Midwest overrepresented	
Interior	West overrepresented	West overrepresented	West overrepresented, South underrepresented

Committee			
Judiciary			East overrepresented
Merchant Marine	South and East overrepresented	East and West overrepresented	East overrepresented, Midwest underrepresented
Post Office		Balanced	
Rules		South overrepresented	
Ways and Means	Balanced overall; South slightly favored, West and Midwest underrepresented		Balanced overall; South slightly favored, East slightly underrepresented

[a] Fenno considers the regional representativeness of six committees in the Eighty-fourth through Eighty-ninth Congresses, using a five-way regional breakdown (East, Midwest, Border, South, West). He offers no significance tests. See Fenno 1973, table 3.3, 47–79.

[b] Goodwin computes an index of regional overrepresentation for all committees for the Eightieth through Ninetieth Congresses, using a four-way regional breakdown (East, Midwest, South, West). He offers no significance tests. See Goodwin 1970, table 6.3.

[c] Smith and Deering compare regional representation on selected committees to regional representation in the House as a whole in the Eighty-ninth to Ninetieth, Ninety-sixth to Ninety-seventh, and Ninety-ninth to Hundredth Congresses, using the same five-way regional breakdown as Fenno. They offer no significance tests. See Smith and Deering 1990, 98, table 3-7.

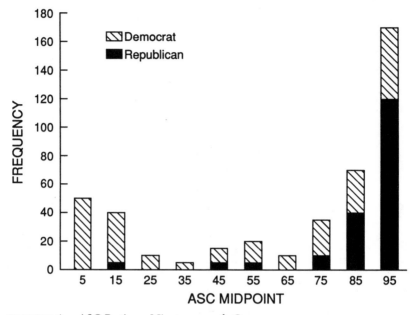

FIGURE 1. ASC Ratings, Ninety-seventh Congress

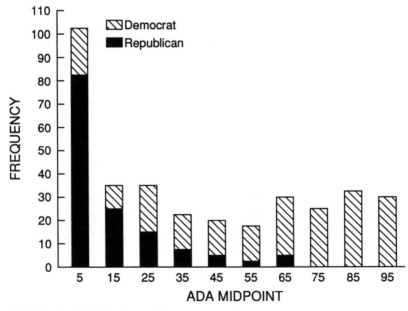

FIGURE 2. ADA Ratings, Ninety-seventh Congress

the UAW; and the AFL-CIO's Committee on Political Education (COPE). These groups have been closely affiliated with the Democratic party and thus identify Republicans as implacable enemies. They consistently place Republicans in the lowest part of the ratings order, with little or no variance among Republican members.

One might argue that there is little variance among the Republicans because they are ideologically homogeneous. But an alternative possibility is that interest groups' use of controversial but nonpartisan votes in their scores, in combination with the tendency of most such votes to split the majority rather than the minority party, overstates the divisions among Democrats and understates the divisions among Republicans.[7]

Consider next the use of interest group scores as measures of specific ideology. There is an important potential benefit from using interest group ratings, especially those produced by the more narrowly focused groups, in this way. If every group that calculates and publicizes a rating is part of some subgovernment, then each may pick roll call votes that highlight the divergence of interest between the members of "its" committee and other members of the House. Thus, the interest groups may solve the analyst's problem of identifying the relevant issue cleavage(s) between committee and noncommittee members.[8]

It should be noted, however, that none of the interest groups include enough roll call votes in their ratings to cover the whole range of issues that come before any House committee. Moreover, in producing their ratings most interest groups choose votes on bills from several committees. Thus, because the typical view of "iron triangles" holds that there is only one committee per subgovernment, the potential advantage of using ratings produced by special interest groups—that the issues they include in their ratings correspond to the policies most important to a particular subgovernment—may be illusory. (We say more on this score in chapter 8.)

Whether one seeks to use interest group scores as measures of general or specific ideology, another deficiency is that they typically are based

7. In spatial modeling terms, if the status quo is already somewhere near the center of Democratic opinion and an attempt is being made to move it in some direction, then the Democrats are likely to be split, the Republicans to be unified.

8. The very existence of such roll calls, however, undercuts the assumption of reciprocity in the subgovernment thesis. Logically, if one of the reasons that subgovernments are considered undesirable is that the members of each subgovernment deferentially vote in favor of legislation produced by the other subgovernments—in a gigantic logroll—then all participants in the logroll would have very similar voting records.

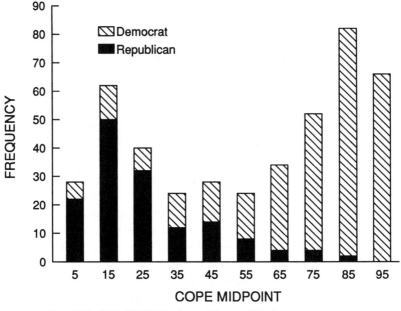

FIGURE 3.   AFL-CIO COPE Ratings, Ninety-fifth Congress

on only a few roll call votes. One consequence of this approach (together with the desire to identify friends and enemies) is that the distribution of scores is skewed toward the extremes and away from the
middle. This result further reduces the discriminatory power of data
that are lumpy enough to begin with.

The U-shaped distribution of ratings is clear in figure 3, which presents a histogram of the ratings produced by COPE for the House in
the Ninetieth Congress. More than half of the members in the Ninetieth
Congress were placed at the very extremes of the distribution of COPE
ratings. Similar examples could be adduced for the ACA's ratings or for
the *National Journal*'s conservative coalition score.

Another consequence of the low number of votes included in interest
group ratings is that the scores for individual members of Congress over
time are not very stable. For example, ratings by groups such as the
National Taxpayers' Union (NTU), the National Farmers' Union (NFU),
and the UAW often fluctuate wildly. This fluctuation is particularly dis-
turbing in a measure of ideology (whether general or specific), as we do
not generally expect a member's ideology to change greatly from one
Congress to the next.

Putting aside these caveats about the use of interest group scores, we can turn to some of the results obtained in the previous literature (table 11). There is general agreement that conservatives have been consistently overrepresented on some committees (e.g., Agriculture and Armed Services), liberals on others (e.g., Education and Labor and Foreign Affairs). There is not agreement on the overall tenor of the data, however. Davidson (1981b, 111), articulating the conventional wisdom, concludes that "many congressional workgroups are not microcosms of the parent houses, but are biased in one way or another." Krehbiel (1990, 159), lodging a dissent, argues that "few contemporary committees are composed predominantly of high-demand preference outliers."

2. DATA AND METHODOLOGY

Our own research into the geographical and ideological representativeness of committees differs slightly from the previous literature in terms of both data and methodology. In addition to spanning a longer period than have previous studies (the Eightieth to Hundredth Congresses), our data on committee membership are derived directly from the *House Journal* rather than from unofficial sources such as the *House Directory*.[9]

We use essentially the same methodology as employed by previous researchers in investigating the geographical balance of committees. The primary difference is that we adopt a three-way regional classification (North, South, and West) rather than a four- or five-way classification.[10] If a committee is representative of the House, then the proportion of members from each geographic region on the committee should not differ significantly from the analogous proportion for the House as a whole. This hypothesis can be tested using a simple t statistic. It is possible, however, for the distribution of regional affiliations on a committee to be skewed relative to the regional breakdown in the House as a whole while none of the individual regional discrepancies is alone significant (i.e., none of the t statistics is significant). We can capture

9. These data were compiled by Garrison Nelson. As noted in chapter 1, note 9, we found that alternative sources of committee assignment data have fairly high error rates. We checked Nelson's data by comparing them to the committee lists published at the beginning of committee hearings and to assignments data given to us by Keith Poole.

10. The motivation for including only three regions was simply to vary the analysis slightly from that conducted by previous researchers to see if it made any difference. As will be seen, it made little. The regions were defined as follows: South (former Confederacy plus border states), North (New England, Middle Atlantic, Midwest), and West (Mountain plus Pacific).

TABLE 11. IDEOLOGICAL REPRESENTATIVENESS ON COMMITTEES IN THE HOUSE

Committee	Fenno[a]	Goodwin[b]	Hinckley[c]	Krehbiel[d]
Agriculture		Conservative	Conservative	Balanced (slightly conservative)
Appropriations	Conservative	Balanced	Balanced (slightly conservative)	Balanced
Armed Services		Conservative	Conservative	Conservative*
Banking		Liberal	Liberal	Conservative
Dist. of Columbia		Conservative	Fluctuates	Liberal*
Education and Labor	Liberal	Liberal	Liberal	Liberal*
Foreign Affairs	Liberal	Liberal	Slightly liberal	Liberal*
Gov. Operations		Liberal	Liberal	Conservative
HUAAC		Conservative	Slightly conservative	
Merchant Marine		Liberal	Balanced	Conservative

Post Office	Balanced (slightly conservative)	Balanced	Balanced	Liberal*
Science			Balanced	Conservative
Official Conduct			Conservative	Conservative
Veterans	Balanced	Balanced	Balanced (slightly conservative)	Conservative

[a] Fenno considers the ideological range and representativeness of six committees in the Eighty-fourth through Eighty-ninth Congresses. He offers no significance tests. See Fenno 1973, table 3.1, 47–79.

[b] Goodwin uses conservative votes identified by the *New Republic* to compute an index of ideological overrepresentation for the Eightieth through Ninetieth Congresses. He offers no significance tests. See Goodwin 1970, table 6.4, 105, 110.

[c] Hinckley looks at the Eighty-sixth, Ninety-first, and Ninety-fifth Congresses, using a measure of conservative coalition support. She neither offers significance tests nor discusses the import of the ideological spread that she finds. We classify one of Hinckley's committees as liberal, for example, if she showed it to be liberal in at least one of the three Congresses she looked at and not significantly conservative in either of the other two. See Hinckley 1983, figure 6.1.

[d] Krehbiel (1990), using interest group ratings for the Ninety-sixth to Ninety-ninth Congresses, concludes that most committees accurately reflect the House as a whole most of the time. He tests his results (difference of medians) at the .05 level and finds that only five committees differ significantly from the entire House.

* Significant at the .05 level.

such distributional unrepresentativeness by using a chi-square statistic computed across the three regional categories.[11]

Our methodological differences are larger when it comes to measuring ideological representativeness. We use two different approaches. One, pursued for the sake of comparability with previous research, measures ideology in terms of interest group scores. Though we originally included twelve interest group ratings in our analysis,[12] we ultimately restricted our analysis to scores produced by the ADA, the ACA, and the *National Journal* (conservative coalition). The conclusions to be drawn from the omitted ratings do not differ substantially from those we draw from these three.

Our second approach to measuring the general ideological predispositions of members relies on the one-dimensional spatial coordinate estimated by Poole and Rosenthal's (1985) Nominal Three-step Estimation (NOMINATE) procedure. This score registers a member's location in an underlying spatial dimension derived from the scaling of all non-unanimous roll call votes taken during a session of Congress.[13] Although the NOMINATE procedure consistently identifies two or more dimensions in roll call votes, the first accounts for most of the variance (more than 70 percent) in the votes. Moreover, because they are derived

11. The chi-square distribution is used in goodness-of-fit tests of contingency table data. The test statistic is calculated by dividing the expected frequency in each cell under the null hypothesis into the squared difference of the expected frequency from the actual observed frequency in the cell, repeating the calculation for all cells in the table, and then summing the values calculated for each. This statistic is then compared to "critical" values of chi-square, the rule of thumb being to reject the null hypothesis of no relationship between the two categorical variables if the test statistic is larger than the critical value of chi-square. For more on chi-square tests, consult any introductory text in statistics.

12. The twelve ratings were produced by Americans for Democratic Action (ADA); the AFL-CIO's Committee on Political Education (COPE); the National Farmers' Union (NFU); Americans for Constitutional Action (ACA); Conservative Coalition; the American Security Council (ASC); United Auto Workers (UAW); the National Education Association (NEA); the National Taxpayers' Union (NTU); the League of Conservation Voters (LCV); the Consumer Federation of America (CFA); and the American Federation of State, County, and Municipal Employees (AFSCME).

13. The NOMINATE measure has its detractors. For example, Koford (1989) argues that though NOMINATE represents a significant improvement over previous techniques, it overstates the statistical fit of the first dimension extracted relative to subsequent dimensions. In his view the issue space in which congressional voting takes place is not as unidimensional as Poole and Rosenthal's results suggest. In any case, our use of this measure does not require us to assume that all issues facing Congress can be projected neatly onto a single dimension. The advantage to using Poole and Rosenthal's measure is that no other simple measure accounts for more of the variance in roll call votes. Moreover, NOMINATE scores are unbiased; as long as the other dimensions are orthogonal to the one liberal-conservative dimension we use, there can be no bias resulting from our reliance on the one-dimensional NOMINATE scores.

from hundreds of roll call votes, the NOMINATE scores constitute a very fine-grained measure.

It should be kept in mind, however, that like the interest group ratings just discussed, the NOMINATE rankings are based solely on roll call votes and do not reflect behavior in committee. Variance between actions taken in these two different legislative arenas may compromise the value of these ratings as measures of ideology.

Another problem the NOMINATE scores share with interest group ratings is the arbitrary nature of the underlying scale.[14] This problem can be partly remedied by utilizing only the ordinal properties of these scores. We have accordingly converted the NOMINATE scores into percentile rankings. Thus, if Representative X's score is 30 percent in a given Congress, this means that 30 percent of the House in that Congress was to X's left, 70 percent to the right. By construction, the distribution of the NOMINATE percentage scores in each Congress is uniform over the range from 0 to 100, with the median (and mean) at 50.

Our solution to the problem of defining the null hypothesis—of how to tell when a committee is representative—is simple but arbitrary. We compare the distribution of rating scores (ADA, ACA, conservative coalition, or NOMINATE) on each committee to the distribution in the House, using a difference-of-means test for the interest group scores and a Wilcoxon difference-of-medians test for the NOMINATE scores.[15]

3. RESULTS

In examining ADA, ACA, conservative coalition, and NOMINATE scores, along with our measure of regional diversity, for the twenty-one Congresses from 1947 to 1988, we found even less support for the subgovernment thesis than our review of the literature would lead us to expect. For most committees in every Congress, we could not reject the hypothesis that the committee was representative of the rest of the House.

14. The scale is arbitrary because there are no fixed or external (to Congress) referents that we can use to rate members. Moreover, we have no way of measuring the *size* of ideological differences between MCs: all we can do is state that member A is to the left of member B (perhaps with some other members between them). We cannot say how great the ideological difference between A and B actually is.

15. This latter statistic is calculated by ranking each observation in the sample and multiplying this rank by 1 if the observation is greater than the predicted median and −1 if the observation is less than the predicted median. The Wilcoxon statistic is then the sum of these weighted ranks. See Hogg and Craig 1978, 314–20.

Only five committees (discussed below) showed any persistent tendency to be unrepresentative of the House as a whole.

Table 12 displays the differences between mean ADA scores for each committee and mean ADA scores for the rest of the House in the Eighty-seventh through Ninety-seventh Congresses.[16] The mean ADA score for the Agriculture Committee was significantly lower than the chamber mean in the Eighty-seventh and Ninetieth to Ninety-second Congresses. Further, the membership of the Armed Services Committee was less supportive of the ADA's position than was the rest of the House in the Ninety-second to Ninety-seventh Congresses. Education and Labor and Government Operations were significantly more likely than the rest of the chamber to support the ADA-endorsed position for all but a few Congresses. The Judiciary and Banking committees were occasionally more supportive of the ADA than was the rest of the House.

Only the Agriculture, Armed Services, Education and Labor, and Government Operations committees were unrepresentative of the House membership more than a few times. Only Armed Services (after the Ninety-second Congress) and Education and Labor were consistently unrepresentative. Perhaps the only surprise here is Government Operations, which is not considered a major policy committee and therefore was not expected to be unrepresentative. By contrast, the committees on Foreign Affairs, Interior, Commerce, Merchant Marine, Post Office, Public Works, Science, and Veterans' Affairs tend to be representative on this measure, contrary to the expectations of the subgovernment thesis.

We performed the same kind of difference-of-means analysis using ACA ratings from the Eighty-seventh to Ninety-seventh Congresses. The results (table 13) show a consistent pattern of unrepresentativeness in only two committees—Armed Services and Education and Labor.

The difference-of-means tests based on the *National Journal*'s conservative coalition support scores are in close agreement with those based on ADA ratings. The results (table 14) again show the committees on Agriculture and Armed Services to be frequently unrepresentative (Agriculture for all but the Ninety-fourth to Ninety-sixth and Armed Services for the Ninety-second to Ninety-seventh Congresses). The members of both committees on average were more supportive of the conservative coalition than were the rest of the members of the House.

---

16. In this chapter we ignore the comments of Hall and Grofman 1990; we deal with them in chapter 8.

TABLE 12.   SUMMARY OF DIFFERENCE-OF-MEANS
TESTS ON ADA SCORES FOR HOUSE COMMITTEES,
EIGHTY-SIXTH TO NINETY-SEVENTH CONGRESSES

Committee						Congress						
	86	87	88	89	90	91	92	93	94	95	96	97
Agriculture		−			−	−	−					
Appropriations												
Armed Services							−	−	−	−	−	−
Banking		+	+				+					
Education and Labor				+	+	+	+	+	+	+	+	+
Foreign Affairs						+		+		+		
Gov. Operations			+	+	+	+	+		+	+		
Interior												
Commerce												
Judiciary						+	+	+				
Merchant Marine												
Post Office												
Public Works										−		
Rules												
Science												
Veterans											−	−
Ways and Means												

NOTES: + = Mean committee ADA score significantly greater than House mean: that
is, significantly less conservative.
− = Mean committee ADA score significantly lower than House mean: that
is, significantly more conservative.

TABLE 13. SUMMARY OF DIFFERENCE-OF-MEANS TESTS ON ACA SCORES FOR HOUSE COMMITTEES, EIGHTY-SIXTH TO NINETY-SEVENTH CONGRESSES

Committee	Congress											
	86	87	88	89	90	91	92	93	94	95	96	97
Agriculture					+	+						
Appropriations												
Armed Services						+	+	+	+	+	+	+
Banking												
Education and Labor						−	−	−		−		−
Foreign Affairs										−		
Gov. Operations						−						
Interior												
Interstate Commerce												
Judiciary												
Merchant Marine												
Post Office												
Public Works												
Rules												
Science												
Veterans											+	+
Ways and Means												

NOTES: + = Mean committee ACA score significantly greater than House mean.
− = Mean committee ACA score significantly lower than House mean.

Committee	86	87	88	89	90	91	92	93	94	95	96	97
Agriculture	+	+	+	+	+	+	+	+				+
Appropriations												
Armed Services							+	+	+	+	+	+
Banking	−	−	−					−				
Education and Labor	−		−	−	−	−	−	−	−	−	−	−
Foreign Affairs						−		−		−	−	−
Gov. Operations			−		−	−						
Interior												
Interstate Commerce												
Judiciary						−	−	−				
Merchant Marine												
Post Office												
Public Works											+	
Rules												
Science												
Veterans											+	+
Ways and Means												

NOTES: + = Mean committee conservative coalition score significantly greater than
House mean.
− = Mean committee conservative coalition score significantly lower than
House mean.

By contrast, the membership of the Committee on Education and Labor was consistently less supportive of the conservative coalition than was the rest of the House. This generalization holds true as well for the Banking Committee for the Eighty-sixth, Eighty-seventh, Eighty-eighth, and Ninety-third Congresses; the Foreign Affairs Committee for all but two Congresses after the Ninetieth; the Government Operations Committee for the Eighty-eighth, Ninetieth, and Ninety-first Congresses; and the Judiciary Committee for the Ninety-first to Ninety-third Congresses.

The difference-of-medians tests we derived from the one-dimensional NOMINATE scores reveal much the same pattern among committees as did the difference-of-means tests for ADA and conservative coalition scores (table 15). The members of the Agriculture Committee in the Eighty-sixth and the Eighty-ninth to Ninety-second Congresses, and of the Armed Services Committee in the Ninety-second to Hundredth Congresses, were significantly more conservative than was the House as a whole. In the Eighty-ninth, Ninety-second, Ninety-fourth, and Ninety-eighth Congresses the membership of the Committee on Education and Labor was significantly more liberal than was the House as a whole. The members of the committees on Foreign Affairs, Government Operations, and Judiciary occasionally were significantly more liberal than the membership of the House. The remaining committees, including the control committees, are representative of the House over the full period from the Eightieth to Hundredth Congresses (i.e., we cannot reject the null hypothesis for any of those Congresses).[17]

Similarly, we find very little evidence to support the notion that committees are geographically imbalanced. In fact, we can reject the null hypothesis that a committee is representative of regional groupings in the House only for the Agriculture and Interior committees. While Agriculture overrepresented southern and western members in twelve of twenty-one Congresses, Interior overrepresented westerners in twenty of twenty-one Congresses. We could find no significant regional imbalances, based on a three-way regional breakdown, in any other committees in any of the Congresses we examined.

We thus have very little evidence in support of the subgovernment thesis. Only a handful of committees—Agriculture, Armed Services, Education and Labor, Government Operations, and Interior—are fre-

17. The results of the difference-of-means test for ADA, ACA, and conservative coalition scores and the difference-of-medians test for NOMINATE agree about 90 percent of the time.

quently unrepresentative of the ideological or regional groupings in the House. This list falls far short of containing all of the major policy committees in the House.

4. CONCLUSION

The evidence presented here on committee representativeness does not support the subgovernment thesis. By our measures, a majority of members of Congress do not serve on committees that are dominated by preference outliers. A handful of semiexclusive and nonexclusive committees tend to be persistently unrepresentative of regional or ideological groupings in the House. For most committees, however, we were unable to reject the null hypothesis that the committees were representative of the interests and preferences in the House.

The tests conducted in this chapter were, of course, limited to only two of the many dimensions along which one might look for unrepresentativeness in committee personnel. In particular, we did not use measures of preference specific to each committee's jurisdiction. However, we doubt that such measures would yield additional support for the subgovernment thesis. In examining eight additional policy-specific interest group ratings, from the National Security Index compiled by the ASC to the ratings of the League of Conservation Voters, we found less support for the subgovernment thesis for each relevant committee than we found using the more general interest group ratings or the one-dimensional NOMINATE scores.

Given these results, is it necessary for committees in the House to maintain a norm of reciprocal deference to each other's handiwork? Most committees are representative of the broader interests of the House. These committees can presumably draft legislation reflecting the diversity of interests in the chamber. Although such legislation no doubt will reflect extensive intracommittee logrolling, it can pass without the need for any intercommittee logrolling.[18] Only a handful of committees are dominated by preference outliers and can be expected to draft legislation that, not being reflective of broader House interests, requires reciprocity among House committees to be passed. But reciprocity would not be forthcoming from the vast majority of House committees since

18. By *intercommittee logroll* we mean either an explicit logroll—votes for bill X in exchange for votes for bill Y—or an implicit logroll of the kind envisioned in the concept of deference.

TABLE 15. SUMMARY OF DIFFERENCE-OF-MEDIANS TESTS ON NOMINATE RANKINGS FOR HOUSE COMMITTEES, EIGHTIETH TO HUNDREDTH CONGRESSES

Committee	Congress								
	80	81	82	83	84	85	86	87	88
Agriculture							+		
Appropriations				+					
Armed Services									
Banking									
Education and Labor									
Foreign Affairs									
Gov. Operations									
Interior									
Interstate Commerce									
Judiciary									
Merchant Marine									
Post Office									
Public Works									
Rules									
Science									
Veterans									
Ways and Means									

NOTES: + = Median committee NOMINATE score significantly more conservative than House median.

− = Median committee NOMINATE score significantly more liberal than House median.

	Congress										
89	90	91	92	93	94	95	96	97	98	99	100
+	+	+	+								
			+								
			+	+	+	+	+	+	+	+	+
−			−		−				−		
		−									
	−	−									
		−									
	−	−				+	+				

they have no need for intercommittee logrolls and would therefore only bear the cost of passing legislation that did not reflect their interests.

This line of argument is far from showing that intercommittee logrolls do not or cannot occur. But it is sufficient to raise some doubts about the simplest version of the committee government model, in which distinctive panels reciprocally defer to one another's proposals on the floor. Only about a quarter of House committees have been persistently unrepresentative of chamber preferences in the postwar era. Is this number enough to sustain a system of committee-based reciprocity as the dominant feature of legislation?

PART TWO

A Theory of
Party Organization

In the previous part we scrutinized several of the key building blocks of the committee government model, concentrating on the notions that committees are autonomous and distinctive. Autonomy can mean many things; we focused on the extent to which the committee personnel process can reasonably be described as autonomous, concluding that it cannot. Distinctiveness also can mean many things; we focused on the geographical and ideological representativeness of House committees, concluding that most committees are representative most of the time.

In this part we shift gears from an examination of empirical details to a broad theoretical question: Why and how might a group of legally equal and often contentious legislators nonetheless create and maintain parties? The answer that we give to this fundamental question is similar in essential respects to the "theory of the firm" developed in the industrial organization literature over the past two decades. But one need not be familiar with this literature to follow the argument. The basic ideas—which are also available in the Hobbesian theory of the state, the theory of political entrepreneurship, and elsewhere—boil down to this: parties are invented, structured, and restructured in order to solve a variety of collective dilemmas that legislators face.[1] These "collective dilem-

---

1. This statement may suggest that we emphasize the degree to which organizational design and reform are intentional. We certainly do emphasize this intentionality more than, say, Hayek (1960) does. But we do not mean to imply that those who attempt to design institutions are infallible or to preclude the kind of evolutionary perspective articulated in Alchian (1950).

mas"—situations in which the rational but unorganized action of group members may lead to an outcome that all consider worse than outcomes attainable by organized action—are inherent in the drive to be reelected in a mass electorate and in the process of passing legislation by majority rule.

The primary method of "solving" the collective dilemmas that legislators face, we argue, is the creation of leadership posts that are both attractive and elective. In chapter 4 we survey theories of organizational leadership, explaining how it is that the institution of leadership positions can ameliorate the dilemmas facing groups of workers, citizens, legislators, and so forth. In chapter 5 we adapt the ideas sketched out in chapter 4 to the specific case of elected legislators.

FOUR

Institutions as Solutions to Collective Dilemmas

Starting with this and the next chapter, we begin to articulate a view of parties as legislative cartels. This metaphor seems apt to us in part because both cartels and parties—indeed, organizations in general—face a variety of collective dilemmas that must be solved if the organization is to operate effectively. This chapter accordingly deals with the general topic of organizational design and structure. The next chapter then focuses more specifically on legislative parties.

Social scientists from a variety of disciplines study institutions such as legislatures, business firms, public and private bureaucracies, armies, and trade associations. This chapter reviews what we consider to be the most satisfying and comprehensive theory of institutional origins and design: what we shall refer to as the neo-institutional or neo-contractarian theory. This theory, exposited fully in no single source, appears in remarkably similar form in a variety of fields. It will be familiar to normative political theorists as a generalized version of the Hobbesian theory of the state, to positive political theorists as a variant on the idea of a "political entrepreneur," and to industrial organization economists as an elaboration on the Alchian-Demsetz theory of the firm. Our purpose here is to underscore the similarity of these various theories—all of which seek to explain institutional features in terms of the choices made by rational individuals facing collective dilemmas—and to examine the answers given to two key questions: How do institutions "solve" collective dilemmas? What are the costs entailed by institutional solutions?[1]

In the first section of this chapter we define the notion of a collective dilemma more precisely by looking at two examples. In the rest of the chapter we concentrate specifically on the prisoner's dilemma, by far the most studied of collective dilemmas, and on a particular "institutional" solution to it: central authority.[2] In sections 2 and 3 we describe the basics of central authority and why it is resorted to in theory and practice. In sections 4 and 5 we consider some of the costs of central authority and the possibility of doing without it.

1. COLLECTIVE DILEMMAS

A collective dilemma is a situation in which rational behavior on the part of individuals can lead to unanimously dispreferred outcomes.[3] More formally, collective dilemmas are situations that can be modeled by games possessing Pareto-inefficient Nash equilibria.[4] Two well-known game situations can illustrate what we mean.

1.1   STANDARDIZATION

Consider first some problems of standardization. Two railroads would both benefit if they used the same gauge of track, but each prefers the gauge that fits its own trains. Two grain merchants would both benefit if they used the same unit of weight to measure the grain, but each prefers the unit with which he has experience. Two politicians would both benefit if they joined forces to promote the same bill, but each

1. We do not ignore criticisms of the neo-institutional view, but it is not our primary task to deal with them here.
2. Other, more decentralized, institutional solutions, such as a system of property rights, are not dealt with here.
3. We thus agree with the usage in Taylor 1987, 19; and Bates 1987.
4. The usual games included under the rubric of "collective dilemmas" are the prisoner's dilemma, chicken, battle of the sexes, assurance games, and pure coordination games. The formal definition given in the text yields—in light of the folk theorem, discussed in the text below—a great many collective dilemmas when iterated games are considered. In light of the multiplicity of (inefficient) Nash equilibria in the theoretical world, it would seem sensible to adopt some stronger equilibrium concept. Unfortunately, the standard refinement of Nash equilibrium—subgame perfection—also falls prey to a folk theorem. At present there is no well-worked-out refinement of the Nash concept that avoids the multiple equilibrium problem in iterated games. Consequently, we do not pursue any refinements here.

prefers her own version of the bill.[5] In each of these situations, the two
agents—call them A and B—have two basic strategies: they can either
stick with their current standard or switch to the other player's standard. In the case of the politicians, it may also be reasonable to offer a
compromise of some sort, but we will not consider that possibility here.

In some situations of standard setting, the benefits of coordinating
are high enough so that both players would prefer to switch to the
other's standard rather than fail to coordinate on a standard at all.
These situations pose the following problem of interaction: if the other
player is going to insist on his or her standard, then it is wise to switch
to that standard; but if the other player will soon give in, then one
should insist on one's own standard.

The standard-setting problem poses a collective dilemma because both
players may rationally insist on their own standard, resulting in an outcome (no shared standard) that both consider inferior to some other
that could have been attained (both adopting A's standard or both
adopting B's standard). Plausible real-world examples of this inefficient
outcome include the multiplicity of different railroad gauges in the nineteenth century and the difference between the U.S. and metric measuring systems.

If we turn to the more formal definition of a collective dilemma—a
situation that can be modeled by a game possessing Pareto-inefficient
Nash equilibria—then some care must be taken in the present example
to choose the right game. A *game* is a formal representation of a strategic choice or a class of strategic choices. It consists of a set of players
(in this case, A and B); a specification of the options or strategies of the
players (A can either stick with his standard or switch to B's, and similarly for B); a specification of what outcome results from each possible
set of options chosen by the players (e.g., if A sticks and B switches,
then coordination is achieved on A's standard and B pays some costs in
switching); and a specification of how players rank the various possible
outcomes (A most prefers that they coordinate on his standard, next
that they coordinate on B's standard, next that neither switch, and last
that both switch). A matrix representation of the standardization game—
in which the value of agreeing on a standard is (arbitrarily) taken to be
5 and the cost of switching to be 2—is given in figure 4.[6]

5. Obviously, the example of the politicians begins to stretch the usual meaning of
standardization into something one would more usually describe as *coalition*. The point
of including it is to emphasize the abstract similarity of these problems, which, in game
theory, are both discussed under the general heading of coordination games.
6. If one assumes that "both switching" means that both actually switch to the other's

Player B

		Stick	Switch
	Stick	0, 0	5, 3
Player A			
	Switch	3, 5	-2, -2

FIGURE 4.   A Standardization Game

Given a game, a *Nash equilibrium* for that game is a set of strategies, one for each player, such that each player does best playing his equilibrium strategy (all other players continuing to play their equilibrium strategies). In the example above, the pair of strategies (Switch, Stick)— where A's strategy is listed first—is a Nash equilibrium because A prefers the equilibrium outcome (coordination on B's standard, with some costs of switching) to the outcome she could get by changing her strategy to Stick (failure to coordinate on either strategy, with no costs of switching). This equilibrium outcome is also *Pareto efficient,* meaning that no other outcome exists that both players prefer to it. A little thought will reveal that the only other equilibrium is (Stick, Switch) and that this, too, is efficient.

It might appear that as the game we have described has no inefficient equilibria, there is by our definition no collective dilemma. However, another game that models the same situation a bit more accurately *does* possess inefficient equilibria. This game consists simply of repeated plays of the game sketched above. Intuitively, such a game introduces the element of time into the situation facing A and B; if they fail to coordinate in the first period, they have another chance. This situation opens up the possibility that each will try to outlast or outbluff the other. Farrell (1987) has shown that this game does have inefficient equilibria, the reason being simply that each player tries to get the other to switch before giving in himself. Thus, in equilibrium, a few rounds of bluffing are ex-

---

standard—and pay the associated costs—then it seems reasonable that this option would be ranked last, as in figure 4. If one takes switching to be "giving in at the negotiating table," then simultaneous switching would presumably give rise to further negotiation. One particularly simple form of further negotiation would be to flip a coin. In this case the entries in the Switch, Switch cell in figure 4 should be 4, 4 rather than $-2, -2$. This change would make the game one of chicken. As it stands, it is a variant on the battle of the sexes.

Player B

		Bribe	Do Not
Player A	Bribe	-1, -1	1, -2
	Do Not	-2, 1	-0, 0

FIGURE 5.   A Prisoner's Dilemma

pected in which neither party gives in and both forgo the benefits of coordination. This problem might be exacerbated if each player invested more and more heavily in his or her particular standard as time went by, for there might come a time when standardization would no longer be worth it to either (the costs of switching having become too high).

1.2   THE PRISONER'S DILEMMA

In standardization or coordination games the problem is one of strategic uncertainty: will the players settle on one of the multiple Nash equilibria in the game (and if so, which one), or will they fail to coordinate entirely? Another collective dilemma is the famed prisoner's dilemma, in which the problem is one of a "nasty" incentive structure. A two-person version of this game (figure 5) models the situation facing candidates for elective office before effective bribery laws were enacted (e.g., in England before 1883). Each candidate can either bribe some voters or not. Bribery, of course, is costly but—depending on what the other candidate does—it can secure an electoral advantage. Specifically, if both (or neither) bribe, then neither gains an advantage; but if one bribes and the other does not, then the briber is advantaged. If one assumes that the advantage gained by bribing exceeds the cost, then the situation facing the candidates is a prisoner's dilemma. In figure 5 we assume that the utility of the electoral advantage is 2 for both candidates, with a symmetric utility loss of 2 for the disadvantaged candidate; and that the cost of bribery in utiles is 1 (this cost includes the monetary expenditure on bribery; the fines to be paid if caught, discounted by the probability of being caught; and any moral repugnance the candidate may feel). Both candidates have a dominant strategy to bribe; that is, their best strategy is to bribe regardless of what they think their opponent will do. Thus, the strategy pair (Bribe, Bribe) is a Nash equilibrium. The collective dilemma comes in that this equilibrium is inefficient: both candidates could be made better off if neither bribed. Unfortunately, neither can trust the other not to bribe, and so both incur the costs of bribery without realizing any benefits.[7]

Another prisoner's dilemma (actually a close cousin) can be illustrated by the difficulties facing teams of laborers. In prerevolutionary China large gangs of men would tug fair-sized boats up the Yangtze. The problem was that each man was tempted to slack off a bit. After all, if enough others were pulling, the boat would still progress; if too few others were pulling, it did not matter how hard one pulled anyway.[8] This situation is a collective dilemma because it is a Nash equilibrium for no one to pull at all (if no one else pulls, then the efforts of just one person are futile); yet this equilibrium is inefficient because everyone prefers the outcome in which everyone both pulls and gets paid.

In the remainder of this chapter we discuss some solutions to the prisoner's dilemma, focusing in particular on central authority. In many cases, of course, action can be taken to *create* prisoner's dilemmas. Examples include the district attorney's separation of the suspects in the original prisoner's dilemma, antitrust laws, and open shop laws. We are not concerned with institutions or rules that create dilemmas, however, only with those that solve them.

2. CENTRAL AUTHORITY: THE BASICS

This section concerns what we call "central authority." The gist of this notion can be suggested by recalling the case of the Chinese riverboat pullers discussed above. Cheung (1983, 8) has noted that the problem of loafing was so severe that workers "actually agreed to the hiring of [someone] to whip them," thereby ensuring that everyone both pulled and got paid. This simple idea underpins a wide array of institutional

7. One plausible explanation of the timing of the Corrupt Practices Act of 1883 in the United Kingdom is that the aristocratic politics of the prereform era, in which the prisoner's dilemma could fairly often be kept in bounds by negotiation between candidates who knew one another personally, gave way to an increasingly competitive and open system in which the prisoner's dilemma became less tractable to solution by repeat play.

8. If just the right number of others are pulling, then whether or not you pull can make the difference between the boat progressing and stalling. For this reason, shirking is not a dominant strategy. Analysts generally reserve the term *prisoner's dilemma* for situations in which noncooperation is a dominant strategy—e.g., Schelling 1978; Taylor 1987. Kavka 1987 calls this type of case a "quasi-prisoner's dilemma."

theories, including Frohlich and Oppenheimer's (1978) theory of political entrepreneurship (see also Olson 1965; Salisbury 1969; Frohlich, Oppenheimer, and Young 1971), the Alchian and Demsetz (1972) theory of the firm, and Hobbes's theory of the state (see Gauthier 1969; Kavka 1987).

2.1 POLITICAL ENTREPRENEURS

The theory of political entrepreneurship suggests that n-prisoner's dilemmas can be solved by "political entrepreneurs." Political entrepreneurs have three essential features: (1) they bear the direct costs of *monitoring* the community faced with the collective dilemma; (2) they possess *selective incentives* (individually targetable punishments and rewards) with which to reward those whom they find cooperating or punish those whom they find "defecting"; (3) they are *paid,* in various ways, for the valuable service they provide.

A recent example of political entrepreneurship is Dan Rostenkowski's handling of what became the 1986 Tax Reform Act. The Democratic leadership was anxious to avoid the impression that the Democratically controlled House of Representatives had killed tax reform. Rostenkowski, as chair of the tax-writing Ways and Means Committee, was faced with the formidable task of ensuring that the members of his committee did not cave in to special and constituency interests clamoring for the preservation of tax loopholes (the collective dilemma arose because each committee member wished to preserve loopholes benefiting his constituency, but if enough loopholes were preserved, the Democrats could be accused of gutting reform). The selective incentives Rostenkowski had available to reward cooperative members included a variety of legislative favors at his disposal as chair, the most obvious of which were the so-called transition rules—special dispensations publicly justified on the grounds that they allowed a smooth transition from the old to the new tax rules, and politically justified on the grounds that they enabled key supporters to deliver benefits to important constituents. Rostenkowski made liberal use of the transition rules and ultimately was successful in reporting out a bill that made substantial reforms in the tax system (at the same time clearly benefiting traditional Democratic constituencies more than Republican constituencies). The chair was paid for his troubles with a share of the transition-rule largesse, continuance in office, and (perhaps) an increased chance that he would someday become Speaker.

The moral of this story is that a long-standing feature of the institutional structure of the House—to wit, the office of chairman of the Ways and Means Committee—facilitated the successful handling of a potential dilemma for the Democratic party. The basic reason (on which we expand greatly in the next chapter) is that the position is both powerful and essentially elective so that its occupant has both the wherewithal and the incentive to ameliorate collective dilemmas.

2.2 ECONOMIC ENTREPRENEURS

The above view of political institutions has a direct analog in the theory of the firm advanced by Alchian and Demsetz (1972). Business entrepreneurs, in their view, have three distinguishing features. First, they are specialists in monitoring, whose function it is to prevent shirking by workers engaged in team production. Second, they alone have the right to hire and fire individual workers and to negotiate pay. Third, they have a residual claim to all profits produced by the enterprise. Each of these features is directly analogous to the features of political entrepreneurship identified above. First, Alchian and Demsetz define team production in such a way as to make the problem of shirking essentially an n-prisoner's dilemma, very similar to the problem facing the Chinese riverboat pullers. Thus, monitoring serves the same purpose in the Alchian-Demsetz firm as in the Frohlich-Oppenheimer political organization. Second, the right to hire, fire, and negotiate pay gives the business entrepreneur some particularly potent selective incentives with which to reward cooperative and punish noncooperative behavior. Third, the business entrepeneur's residual claim is compensation for services rendered. Alchian and Demsetz emphasize the inadequacy of paying a flat salary to the monitor, who then has no economic incentive other than the fear of dismissal to perform his or her duties. Having a claim to all profits in excess of the sum needed to pay workers' wages, however, motivates the entrepreneur to promote efficient collective action in order to maximize output and thus profits.[9]

9. There are several other major versions of the theory of the firm. A good recent review can be found in Tirole 1988. Here it suffices to note that collective dilemmas lurk at the heart of the other major theories as well. Consider, for example, Williamson's (1975) notion of specific investment—an investment of time or money that will have a high range of payoffs if the investor can trade with a specific party and a low range of payoffs if the investor is forced to trade with others. If the specificity of the investment is known to the prospective trading partner, then once the investment is made, the partner may be able to "hold up" the investor for essentially its full value. This possibility, if anticipated, removes the investor's incentive to invest. Williamson argues, among other

2.3 THE HOBBESIAN STATE

A final example of central authority as a solution to a prisoner's dilemma is the Hobbesian state. The "war of all against all" can be viewed as the collectively irrational outcome of an n-prisoner's dilemma (Gauthier 1969; Kavka 1987; Taylor 1987). Hobbes's suggested solution is the institution of an absolute sovereign—an individual or assembly with unlimited authority to act for all members of the polity and with accompanying unlimited lawmaking and enforcement. The monarch monitors and punishes unlawful and aggressive behavior (Kavka 1987, secs. 4.4, 6.1). He is *able* to do so because of the vast power of his office, and he is *motivated* to do so by the fees collected in his courts, by the taxes collected by his officials, and by other devices that provide monarchs with a personal interest in promoting the peace and prosperity of their kingdoms (Hirschman 1977). *Olson 1993*

2.4 CENTRAL AGENTS

All of the institutional theories surveyed here involve a central agent—whether political entrepreneur, businessperson, or monarch—with three common features: (1) the agent bears the direct costs of *monitoring* the population faced with the collective dilemma; (2) the agent possesses, by virtue of his or her institutional position, *selective incentives* with which to punish noncooperative and reward cooperative behavior; and (3) the agent is motivated to bear the costs of monitoring and to expend scarce resources on selective incentives in punishing and rewarding those whom he or she monitors, either by receiving a substantial share of the collective output, or by receiving a claim to the residual of collective output above some preassigned level, or by some other compensation scheme designed to align the personal interests of the agent with the level of collective output. The essential purpose of establishing a central authority is to create an institutional position whose occupant has a personal incentive to ensure that the collective dilemma is overcome. In Olson's terms, one can think of central authority as an institutional means of transforming latent groups into privileged ones (Olsen 1965).[10]

---

things, that problems of investment and asset specificity—which are wrinkles on the prisoner's dilemma—are easier to solve within firms than between them. This is one reason why firms exist.

10. One criticism of theories that point to central authority as a solution to collective

It might be noted that central agents are not always confined in the literature to the role of supervisors, as they have been in the discussion above. In some recent versions of the theory of the firm, for example, corporate management is viewed as an arbiter of intrafirm disputes. The gist of this view is that (1) many important transactions carried out within corporations are difficult to fully specify in advance; (2) this vagueness may lead to costly disputes when unforeseen contingencies arise; and (3) the CEO of the corporation thus has an interest in providing cheap, knowledgeable, and rapid "justice" when disputes arise. Part of the reason the corporation exists, then, is that the "legal system" provided within the firm by management is more flexible, cheap, and fair than the state-provided legal system to which the divisions of the corporation would have to appeal were all their transactions conducted in the open market.

This notion of central agent as provider of justice is, of course, a familiar one in the history of the state. The economic value of establishing a reliable system of property and justice, even in a local area, is evident throughout history. From a contractarian perspective, it is one of the clearest reasons to have a state.

The central agent as provider of justice is also visible within parties. Mayhew's *Party Loyalty among Congressmen* (1966) provides a number of examples of the leadership helping to hold together Democratic logrolls on the floor. We pursue this idea at greater length below.

3. WHY CENTRAL AUTHORITY IS SOMETIMES NECESSARY

This section discusses why purely voluntary agreements cannot always be relied on to solve organizational dilemmas. We focus on economic organization, contrasting the fortunes of workers who organize into an Alchian-Demsetz firm with those of workers who remain unorganized

---

dilemmas is that they presuppose the solution of a prior collective action problem—that is, the creation and support of the central authority (Taylor 1987, 22). This is a valid point, but the collective action problem entailed in creating a position of authority is often more tractable than the original problem. In the case of the riverboat pullers, for example, the workers need only agree that someone be given a whip and a share of the pay. Those who refuse to contribute toward the purchase of a whip—should this be necessary—are simply excluded from the group. The whipper's share is just as secure as that of any ordinary puller. More generally, Hardin (1991) points out that the problem of creating a state when none exists is a coordination problem (of the battle of the sexes kind) rather than a prisoner's dilemma.

(leaving all their transactions to "the market").[11] The focus on economic rather than political organization is chosen for a variety of reasons: political scientists generally are less familiar with this literature and may profit from exposure to it; the theory of economic organization is more fully and formally developed than is the corresponding political theory; the principles of economic and political organization are fundamentally similar despite the fairly obvious initial differences (e.g., economic organizations produce private goods almost exclusively, whereas political organizations usually produce a mixture of both private and public goods). Political organization will, of course, come in for the bulk of our attention in the remaining sections and chapters.

But for now we shall concentrate on the organization of production. Consider a group of n workers producing for sale in the marketplace. Each worker i chooses an action, a_i, from a set of available actions, $A_i = [0,\infty)$. We shall interpret the action $a_i = 0$ as "exert no effort" or "do nothing" and adopt the convention that action a_i requires more effort than action b_i if and only if $a_i > b_i$. Effort is assumed to be costly, so that the ith worker bears a cost—$v_i(a_i)$—for taking action a_i, where v_i is strictly increasing and such that $v_i(0) = 0$. Given a vector of actions, $a = (a_1, \ldots, a_n)$, one for each of the n workers, a total output, $y(a)$, is determined. For simplicity, we shall assume that the price of the output y is \$1, so that the total revenue produced is simply $y(a)$. Can a group of n unorganized workers agree on a method of sharing this revenue such that all workers are properly motivated to work?

This question has been posed, in a precise fashion, by Holmström (1982), who makes three assumptions. (1) *Unobservability:* The particular action taken by each worker is unobservable, so that the share each receives can depend only on total revenue. Holmström denotes i's share as $s_i(y)$. (2) *Budget balancing:* Regardless of the level of total revenue, the shares of the n workers add up to one ($Rs_i(y) = 1$ for all y). (3) *Concavity of production:* The function y is strictly increasing, concave and differentiable with $y(0, \ldots, 0) = 0$ (no effort, no output). Under these conditions Holmström shows that no n-tuple of actions exists that is both a Nash equilibrium and Pareto efficient. Put another way, he shows that any Nash equilibrium must be Pareto inefficient, so that any group facing the three conditions of unobservability, budget balancing,

---

11. The reader will notice similarities between the theory of the firm summarized in the following paragraphs and the Hobbesian theory of the state, which contrasts the fortunes of individuals who organize into a state with those of individuals who remain unorganized (leaving all their transactions to "anarchy").

and concavity of production must be mired in what we have called a collective dilemma.

The reason for this can be seen in the context of a simple example. Suppose that $s_i(y) = y/n$ for all i (that is, each worker gets one nth of the total revenue). Each will choose an action a_i in order to maximize the difference between his share of total revenue $(y(a)/n)$ and the cost of his action $(v_i(a_i))$. Denoting the partial derivative of y with respect to a_i by y_i', this implies that $y_i'/n = v_i'$. That is, the worker continues increasing his level of effort until the marginal cost of this effort equals one nth of his marginal contribution to total output. But Pareto efficiency requires that each worker equate marginal cost to his full marginal contribution to total output.

It is important to note some limitations on Holmström's result. Gary Miller (1987, 28) interprets it as showing that "with any budget-balancing incentive scheme . . . there will be a tension between individual self-interest and group efficiency—exactly the tension described by the prisoner's dilemma." But schemes satisfying the budget-balancing and unobservability assumptions do exist that support efficient Nash equilibria.

As an example, suppose that $n = 3$, $s_i(y) = y/3$ for all i, $v_i(a_i) = a_i$ for all i, and $y(a) = 0$ unless a_1, a_2, and a_3 are all at least 1, in which case $y(a) = 99$. Note that the specification of y violates the concavity assumption. It says that all three workers must exert a particular minimum level of effort or no salable output is produced at all. All the other major conditions of Holmström's model are satisfied. In this example, however, there exists a Nash equilibrium that is Pareto efficient. Pareto efficiency requires that all three workers choose action $a_i = 1$, yielding a payoff to each of $99/3 - 1 = 32$. But no worker has an incentive unilaterally to depart from this triple of actions. On the one hand, if i lowers her level of effort below 1, her share of output drops 33 (to zero) while she saves at most \$1 in costs. On the other hand, if i raises her level of effort, no more output is produced but additional costs are incurred.

The message of this example is that unorganized workers with unusually complementary skills may achieve efficient equilibria via simple share-of-output agreements. What is required is that the value of total output be quite low until all workers perform their tasks at an acceptable level. In other and more evocative terms, each worker's contribution must be like a link in a chain, not like a drop in the bucket.[12] An

---

12. This terminology was suggested to us by our colleague Samuel Popkin.

economic example approximating such a production function might be coauthorship when neither coauthor has the other's expertise. A political example sometimes occurs in voting: against a solid minority of 49, a majority of 50 can produce "victory" (and, with it, spoils) only if all members of the majority do their part and vote.

Despite this caveat regarding extreme complementarities in production, however, Holmström's result does show that for a wide class of situations, when actions are unobservable and budgets are balanced, inefficient equilibria are unavoidable. This suggests that a group of workers in an industry where workers cannot monitor one another are inevitably faced with a collective dilemma.

Holmström suggests that the way around this problem is to relax the balanced-budget assumption. In other words, let the workers share the output in some budget-balancing way if output attains the efficient level; otherwise, give all the output away to some third party or destroy it. This scheme does, in principle, allow for efficient equilibria: supposing that everyone is currently working at efficient levels, each is faced with a choice between shirking (which saves some effort but costs the entire output) and not shirking (which requires effort but is remunerated with some share of the total output). As long as each worker's share of the total output exceeds the total cost of his effort, a condition that is satisfied *ex hypothesi*, each worker will work.[13] Holmström's technique works for basically the same reason that efficient equilibria can be attained with extreme production complementarities. Indeed, Holmström can be interpreted as using sharing rules, together with detailed knowledge of the production function *y*, to *create* the same interdependencies among workers that were posited as a feature of production technology alone in the above example. However, just as such production technologies are the exception rather than the rule, so, too, does it appear that Holmströmian employment contracts are exceptional.

The *rule* in employment contracts is based on a violation of the unobservability assumption. Business entrepreneurs expend resources to monitor the actions of employees and base their pay chiefly on their observed actions rather than on total output. This corresponds to the Alchian-Demsetz model of the firm, or what we have referred to generally as central authority. Central authority can ameliorate the collec-

13. When all workers work at the efficient level, the value of total output must exceed the total social cost of effort for there to be a collective dilemma in the first place. Thus, there always will exist sharing rules that give each worker sufficient remuneration to cover his or her effort costs.

tive dilemma facing workers (in the sense of effecting a Pareto improvement) because workers can be effectively motivated to work by the system of monitoring and sanctions that the central agent implements. Monitoring of employee actions need not be perfect in order to achieve a Pareto improvement. Holmström has shown that partial information about the actions of workers is always valuable in the sense that were such information available at no cost, and workers' pay based in part on it, then all workers could in principle be made better off. The reason for this is simply that the workers' incentives actually to work are greatly improved when their pay is based to some extent directly on their level of work. Output thus can go up rather dramatically when pay is based on direct information about effort (how much it increases depending on the quality of the information), and in principle everyone can share in the profits from increased production. In practice, of course, information is costly. Because of its value in stimulating effort, however, it may be worth a substantial price. It may even be worth the cost of hiring an $(n + 1)$st worker whose only job is to monitor and sanction the original workers, as in the example of the Chinese riverboat pullers.

The possibility that monitoring can so improve incentives to work that Pareto improvements result, even after the cost of monitoring is taken into account, is one of the central insights of the Alchian-Demsetz model of the firm. Nonetheless, it should be noted that full or "first-best" efficiency is never attained in Alchian-Demsetz firms. The first-best solution is for every worker to perform the efficient action, a_i^*, and for no resources to be expended on monitoring. The Alchian-Demsetz firm mitigates the incentive problem but does so at the cost of expending real resources in monitoring—an otherwise useless endeavor. A lower bound on the amount by which such firms fall short of first-best efficiency is simply the amount of resources devoted to monitoring (it is a lower bound because workers may shirk even with monitoring—albeit less than without it).

If infinitely high penalties can be imposed on workers caught shirking, then the amount of actual monitoring can be reduced to near zero while still providing workers with sufficient incentives to work at the efficient level. Such a scheme could approximate first-best efficiency as closely as desired (Mirrlees 1976). But, although a "Pascal's wager" solution might work if managers could rent fire and brimstone, bankruptcy laws and other legal devices seem to prevent the infliction of some punishments utilized in hell.

To summarize the discussion so far, it it difficult to achieve first-best efficiency in group production of private goods. If there are extreme complementarities in production, or if these complementarities are mimicked by the employment contract as suggested by Holmström, then full efficiency can be attained in equilibrium by a simple share-of-output contract with no need for the organization brought by a central agent. But the typical real-world case involves neither extreme complementarities nor extreme contracts, and in this case workers are insufficiently motivated to work if they merely receive a share of total output. This insufficiency of motivation prompts the development of firms in which certain agents monitor and sanction the actions of others. This monitoring cum sanctions gives workers an incentive to work, and output can increase enough to cover the costs of monitoring. Nonetheless, monitoring is costly and would be avoided in a first-best world.[14]

4. MULTIPERIOD CONSIDERATIONS

The model of collective production considered in the last section was for the short term, focusing on the more or less immediate rewards and punishments available to motivate behavior. But the possibility of voluntary or anarchistic cooperation in long-term interactions recently has been prominently argued in the literature. Taylor (1976; 1987) and Axelrod (1981; 1984) have shown that a simple tit-for-tat strategy in two-person iterated prisoner's dilemmas can support cooperation in equilibrium without any apparent institutional structure.[15] The gist of this result is that current noncooperation can be deterred by the threat of future retaliation in kind. If one takes this "shadow of the future" argument seriously enough, the question arises as to why central authority is ever necessary.

14. The results regarding group production of *public* goods are even less encouraging as regards Pareto efficiency. Because by definition everyone consumes the entire quantity of a public good available, whether or not he or she has contributed to its production, the incentive to contribute cannot be manipulated by adjusting the share of output that an agent receives. If extreme complementarities in production exist (everyone must contribute or nothing is produced), the efficient level of output may be achieved. Otherwise, production of the public good would have to rely on the type of selective incentives that Olson (1965) identifies and that Frohlich and Oppenheimer (1978) expand on; that is, some central agent would have to monitor the contributions of individuals and mete out rewards and punishments accordingly. The analog to Holmström's technique would require that the public good be destroyed if not produced in the efficient amount. This is hard to imagine in concrete instances. Would a group failing to clean up a local pond to the extent agreed on then set about the costly task of restoring all the pollutants they had extracted?

15. The equilibrium they identify is not perfect. See, for example, Sugden 1986 for a robust perfection.

Part of the answer has to do with two of the assumptions that make the "shadow of the future" formidable—that both parties can observe whether or not the other has cooperated and that both expect the interaction to last a long time. Both of these assumptions rely for their approximate fulfillment in the real world on the existence of appropriate institutions.

Consider first the problem of unobservability. If the players in an iterated prisoner's dilemma can neither observe whether others have cooperated in each stage of the game nor infer this from what they can observe, then policing noncooperation by in-kind retaliation is obviously problematic. This is essentially the difficulty facing many arms control agreements. An agreement not to develop certain kinds of weapons may be concluded, but typically neither side can easily observe compliance. Moreover, neither side can observe a payoff in increased security from which compliance might be inferred. Hence, elaborate verification procedures are resorted to in an attempt to provide sufficient observability so that both sides feel they have a credible deterrent threat. The role of U.N. monitors in verifying the winding down of the Iran-Iraq war provides a recent and more explicitly institutional example of the same point.[16]

A second prerequisite for decentralized, purely voluntary cooperation is that both players believe their interaction will last long enough so that the possibility of *future* gains can deter *present* noncooperation. On the one hand, this belief can be endangered in a number of ways, giving rise to a collapse of cooperation. On the other hand, it can be shored up institutionally. For example, Kreps (1990) illustrates how business firms—artificial persons with indefinitely long lives—can replace natural persons for the purposes of many transactions. If an individual has a reputation for dealing honestly with customers whom he might cheat, there is a possibility that his customers will become nervous when they believe he is near retirement or death. If a firm has a reputation for dealing honestly with customers whom it might cheat, there is less reason to become nervous when the current owner nears retirement or death, for a firm's reputation for honest dealing is a valuable asset that contributes to the sale price of the firm. Thus, the owner nearing retirement recognizes that any cheating of customers in the twi-

---

16. On the U.N. monitors, see *Maclean's,* 29 Aug. 1988, 10–17. Another important function of the U.N. troops was to raise the cost of violating the agreement, since violation might entail casualties among noncombatant nations.

light of his career may cost more (in the form of a lowered sale price) than it is worth.

In addition to the problems of unobservability and shortness of interaction, which hinder voluntary cooperation even between two persons, several other difficulties appear or are exacerbated when the number of players grows beyond two. The most straightforward of these difficulties is illustrated by the steady erosion of incentives to contribute to public goods that often occurs as a group's size increases. Theoretically, this erosion follows in models in which the importance of individual contributions declines with group size (cf. Hardin 1982).

An institutional response to the problem of maintaining voluntary cooperation in large groups is illustrated in the Hutterite communes. The Hutterites have developed an elaborate procedure for regularly splitting their communities whenever a certain optimal size (sixty to one hundred individuals, or about six to ten families) is exceeded (Bullock and Baden 1977). A similar emphasis on smallness (plus a bit of isolation) characterizes other successful communal life-styles (e.g., that of the Israeli kibbutzim).

A second difficulty, which appears in two-person prisoners' dilemmas but is more troublesome in n-prisoners' dilemmas, is the problem of multiple equilibria. This can be explained by adverting to one of the more remarkable results in the theory of repeated games: the "folk theorem." The folk theorem, so called because it is widely known to game theorists but of obscure authorship, deals with repeated noncooperative games (games in which the players cannot make binding agreements). Let G be a noncooperative game in normal form (two examples of such games are given in figures 4 and 5). Denote by G^* the "supergame" of G—that is, the game that consists of an infinite sequence of plays of the "stage game" G. Roughly put, the folk theorem states that, if the players of G^* have enough information (in particular, at the end of each stage they are informed of the strategy chosen by all other players in that stage), then *any* outcome that is individually rational can be supported by some Nash equilibrium.[17] An outcome is individually rational if the payoff each player gets is not less than his *security level,* defined as the worst payoff that can be forced on him by the remaining players. Thus, very little restriction is placed on the outcomes that one

17. The only other restriction to note is that the outcome be feasible—that is, that it be possible to attain such an outcome via some strategy n-tuple in G (or via some *correlated* strategy n-tuple in G). See Aumann 1981.

might predict in a repeated noncooperative game by the notion of Nash equilibrium alone.

An industry has arisen in game theory in response to the problem of multiple equilibria, devoted to finding such refinements of Nash equilibria as perfect or sequential equilibria (see, for example, Selten 1975; Kreps and Wilson 1982; Kalai and Samet 1982; Banks and Sobel 1987). It is safe to say, however, that none of the refinements of Nash equilibria proposed so far produces unique and widely accepted equilibrium predictions for all games; indeed, the only refinement concept offered that produces unique predictions is that of Harsanyi and Selten (1988). The multiplicity of equilibria, however, means that a coordination problem similar to the standardization game discussed in section 1 can arise over which of the many equilibrium outcomes will be selected. One view of leadership (or central agency, in our terms) is as a mechanism for preventing any efficiency losses through lack of coordination (see Calvert 1985; Kavka 1987, 247).

A third impediment to decentralized cooperation in large groups is what we refer to as the "group punishment" feature. In a repeated prisoner's dilemma, if one player defects at time t, the only way to punish her (if side payments are not allowed) is for some other player to defect at some future date. But any such future defection unavoidably hurts not just the original defector but all other players as well. It is therefore questionable whether collective action can hold together on a purely voluntary basis, just on the threat of in-kind retaliation. Should Ms. A really resume polluting in order to punish Mr. B's act of pollution, given that she thereby also punishes C, D, and E? Can a group of laborers gain a reputation for reliability if shirking by any one of them is punished by retaliatory shirking? When the strategy of in-kind retaliation is carried to its logical extreme—in the so-called grim trigger strategy—cooperation is enforced by the threat of universal and perpetual defection. But if this threat ever gets carried out (in a model in which mistakes are possible, presumably), the result is tantamount to the utter dissolution of the organization. We do not believe that many important organizations are held together by a well-understood threat of dissolution should any member defect. It is possible to bypass the group punishment feature if side payments—transfers of private goods—are feasible. In this case, a defector can be punished directly: whipped, fined, ostracized, frowned on, whatever. But the other problems—unobservability of actions, shortness of time horizons, insignificance of individual contributions, and multiplicity of equilibria—remain and may be severe.

5. PROBLEMS WITH CENTRAL AUTHORITY

Although institutionalizing central authority can in principle be effective in overcoming collective dilemmas, there is no guarantee that it will do so in practice.[18] Central authority can be either too weak or too strong. It is _too weak_ when the selective incentives at its command are insufficient to deter noncooperative behavior, so that the potentially capturable benefits of cooperation are not in fact captured. This is the case of the king who cannot maintain internal order or of the businessman who cannot prevent shirking by his employees. Central authority is _too strong_ when the selective incentives at its command allow the incumbent central agent to appropriate all of the rents produced by collective effort, to deter any attempt to remove him, and even to extract resources produced by individual (noncollective) action. This is the case of the strong queen who maintains order but extracts taxes so high that each citizen is nearly indifferent between that order and war of all against all.

These twin problems besetting the institution of central authority recall Madison's comment in _Federalist_ 51: "In framing a government to be administered by men over men, the great difficulty lies in this: you must first enable the government to control the governed; and in the next place oblige it to control itself." When Madison wrote this passage, the American people had recently experienced both government too strong (under George III) and government too weak (under the Articles of Confederation); his dictum simply recalled this experience to his readers' minds. From a contractarian perspective, Madison's statement haunts any institution that relies on central authority to solve collective dilemmas: what is the point of central authority if it fails, through weakness or through strength, to effect a Pareto improvement?

The rest of this section is devoted to a discussion of one horn of this dilemma: the problem of authority that is too strong. This problem has, of course, received considerable attention from political theorists through the years. In particular, the motivation of the central agent has received extensive attention. Alchian and Demsetz (1972) argue that the central agent will have the incentive to monitor at the efficient level only if he has a claim to all revenues above a certain fixed level (i.e., only if he is the residual claimant). Frohlich and Oppenheimer (1978) are less precise but emphasize the importance of the central agent having a substantial stake in the collective action being organized. Some versions of

18. See Kiewiet and McCubbins 1991.

the theory of absolute monarchy emphasize the monarch's ultimate ownership of all land (cf. Hirschman 1977).

It is not clear that any of these techniques of motivating the central agent—giving him the residual claim, a substantial stake, or reversionary ownership rights—adequately deals with the problem at hand. A residual claimant may profitably devote her time to driving her employees' wages down rather than helping to increase their productivity.[19] A political entrepreneur may sell his followers out. A king may prosecute ruinous foreign wars or pursue a luxurious life-style rather than sticking to his Hobbesian functions. These defects of motivation have given rise to a variety of institutional supplements. We discuss them here under three headings: establishing mechanisms for the central agent's removal, lengthening the agent's time horizon, and putting central authority into commission.

The first of these techniques is the most straightforward. If the central agent can be removed by the group whose agent he is, then actions detrimental to all or most of the group should presumably be discouraged. From this perspective, it is an important part of the total compensation package that CEOs can be removed by the stockholders (but not, usually, by the workers); that legislative party leaders are elected (usually by members of their party serving in parliament); that pirate captains (Ritchie 1986) and the kings of the ancient Germanic tribes were elected by their followers; and that the right of the people to overthrow "unjust" monarchs, even those reigning by divine right, was clearly understood. Of course, the practical importance of the possibility of removal depends on how real the possibility is. At one extreme, if removal requires revolution and revolutionaries can be hung, then a substantial prisoner's dilemma arises over who is to bear the cost of providing the collective good of removing the tyrant. At the other extreme, competitive and regular elections with low costs to losing challengers may impose a substantial constraint on the incumbent central agent.

Another technique of shoring up the incentives of the central agent, which complements the possibility of removal, is to lengthen his time horizon. This strategy makes the threat of removal more potent because there is more to be lost in the future. Time horizons of monarchs can be extended by making monarchy hereditary.[20] Time horizons of cor-

19. There is a substantial literature in economics on managerial incentives in large corporations, much of it concerned with managers who maximize their own utility rather than firm profits. Major examples include Baumol's (1962) sales maximization hypothesis and Williamson's (1967) managerial discretion model.

20. English law considered kings and bishops to be corporations sole, with infinite lifetimes.

porate managers can be extended by the development of marketable reputations and "good will" (Kreps 1990) or by the posting of bonds (Jensen and Meckling 1976). Time horizons of politicians can be extended by attractive (but forfeitable) pension schemes, such as peerages and knighthoods in England or retirement benefits in the U.S. Congress, and by putting no limit on the number of terms that may be served.

A third and quite common technique of getting around the problem of too-strong central authority is to make it collective. The institutionally simplest way to do so is to put central authority into commission. Examples include plural executives, such as the Roman triumvirates or the Swiss Federal Council, and corporations, whether civil, eleemosynary, business, or municipal. Institutionally more elaborate schemes fall under the rubric of "checks and balances": the independent judiciary, the separation of executive and legislative powers, bicameralism, the independent comptroller in business firms, and so forth (Lijphart 1984; Baylis 1989; Watts and Zimmermann 1983).

The simpler examples of collective authority, where central power is shared but not institutionally divided and balanced, raise an obvious trade-off. On the one hand, the more central agents there are, the less likely that all will collude in schemes of corruption or oppression. Ideally, each will watch the others. On the other hand, the more members there are, the smaller the stake and say of each in collective affairs; hence, it is less likely that the collective action problem among the central agents will be overcome. The trick is to replace a single central agent, who ideally can convert a latent into a privileged group but who cannot quite be trusted, with a group of central agents that is (1) small enough, and in frequent enough interaction, so that voluntary cooperation in sharing the costs of monitoring can emerge; (2) composed in such a way that it can be trusted; and (3) large enough or given a large enough stake in the success of collective action so that it is viable in Schelling's sense (that is, each member of the group will benefit if the group cooperates in policing collective action, even if they bear all the costs themselves; see Schelling 1978).[21]

21. Other factors promote "good behavior" by central agents but are not endogenous to a single group. An example is the market for top corporate managers. Fama (1980) notes that a manager's future remuneration depends substantially on the past performance of the firms managed. Thus, each individual firm does not need to solve the problem of managerial motivation solely by internal means; it is helpful by the existence of a properly functioning market for managerial talent. A political analogue is implicit in Schlesinger's (1966) idea of "progressive ambition."

6. CONCLUSION

This chapter has surveyed theories of organizational design from several fields: the theory of political entrepreneurship from the political economy literature; the theory of the firm in the industrial organization literature; and the Hobbesian theory of the state. From this survey we have pieced together a common view of the origin and functioning of organizations.

In rough outline, this view goes as follows: Collective action in any field of endeavor can produce a surplus, in the sense that collective output exceeds the sum of individual outputs. This surplus appears in firms, for example, whenever the production process is such that what worker A does increases the marginal productivity for worker B, and it appears in armies whenever what soldier A does increases the marginal effectiveness of soldier B. Such a surplus from collective action is an incentive to collective action. Unfortunately, even if the product is private (widgets or plunder) instead of public (national defense), a substantial free-rider problem stands in the way of voluntary cooperation. Absent unusual conditions, any single-period contract based solely on sharing the collective output leaves substantial incentives to shirk and free ride (Holmström 1982); and any multiperiod contract based solely on in-kind retaliation for shirking is implausible in large organizations. Thus, simple sharing rules and in-kind retaliation rules cannot sustain large organizations. Some attention to the actual actions taken by the various workers, soldiers, political activists, and so on is needed.

This necessity for keeping track of the actual effort and actions taken leads to the creation of specialists in monitoring—and gives rise to the profusion of auditors, managers, and supervisors observable in all real-world organizations of any size. But *quis custodiet ipsos custodes?* The answer has always been to arrange the incentives of auditors so that they will in fact ameliorate problems of collective action. The two basic forms this tinkering with incentives has taken are checks and balances (getting the auditors somehow to watch one another as well as those they audit) and hierarchy (placing auditors above the auditors). The latter solution, of course, leaves the top auditor unwatched, and here the solution has been twofold: to give the top auditor—whether general, CEO, or prime minister—a substantial personal stake in the success of the collective enterprise; and to provide a mechanism—coup, proxy fight, election, or whatever—for his or her removal.

FIVE

A Theory of
Legislative Parties

Definitions of political parties have been offered from two main perspectives, one emphasizing structure, the other purpose. The structural perspective defines parties according to various observable features of their organization. Studies of the historical development of parties, for example, take pains to distinguish "premodern" parties from "modern" ones, typically by pointing to the increasing elaboration of extraparliamentary structures in the latter (Duverger 1954; LaPalombara and Weiner 1966). The purposive approach, by contrast, defines and categorizes political parties by the goals that they pursue. Typical examples include Edmund Burke's definition of a party as a group of men who seek to further "some particular principle in which they are all agreed" (Burke 1975, 113); Schattschneider's definition of a political party as "an organized attempt to get . . . control of the government" (Schattschneider 1942, 35); and Downs's definition of a political party as "a team of men seeking to control the governing apparatus by gaining office in a duly constituted election" (Downs 1957, 25).[1]

Neither the structural nor the purposive definitions of parties are suited to the needs of this chapter. The structural definitions take as defining features the kinds of things that we hope to explain. Moreover, these definitions generally turn on extraparliamentary organization rather than on the intraparliamentary organization that is our main concern.

---

1. Another approach, which defines parties in terms of the actions that they take, is pursued in Panebianco 1988.

The purposive definitions of party, by contrast, assume too much about the internal unity of parties. Indeed, the more formal definitions make parties into unitary actors who single-mindedly seek to maximize votes, probability of victory, policy-derived utility, or some such maximand.[2]

The unitary actor assumption has proven valuable for many purposes—spatial models of elections and models of coalition formation come readily to mind—but it is not a useful starting point from which to build a theory of the *internal organization* of parties. Such a theory must begin with individual politicians and their typically diverse preferences, explaining why it is in each one's interests to support a particular pattern of organization and activity for the party. Accordingly, we begin not with parties and postulated collective goals but rather with legislators and postulated individual goals. The task of this chapter is to explain how a party with substantial if not perfect coherence of collective purpose might emerge from the voluntary interaction of individual politicians. Put another way, we seek to answer the following question: How can a group of formally equal and self-interested legislators, with demonstrably diverse preferences on many issues, agree on the creation or maintenance of a party, on the organizational design of a party, and on the setting of collective goals? In answering this question, we borrow from the general perspective on organizational design developed in chapter 4.

The (admittedly partial) answer that we give to this question can be described as either neo-institutional or neo-contractarian, in the sense that these terms were used in the previous chapter. Those familiar with the economics literature will find it similar in intellectual content to the theory of the firm. We begin in section 1 by discussing the goals of individual legislators, accepting the usual emphasis on reelection but highlighting factors that improve the reelection probabilities of all members of a given party. Section 2 notes that not enough attention will be paid to these common factors—which are public goods to members of the same party—absent organized effort of some kind. In section 3 we argue that an important reason for the existence of legislative parties is to attend to the collective component in the reelection chances of its members. The arguments we employ are abstract enough that they might apply to a number of national and historical contexts. Our pri-

---

2. Downs (1957, 25) is explicit in stating that his party teams are "coalition[s] whose members agree on all their goals." A vast array of spatial models and studies of coalition formation also explicitly consider parties as unitary actors.

mary concern here, however, is suitability to the specific context of interest—the post–World War II American Congress.

1.   THE REELECTION GOAL

The possible goals of rational legislators are many, including reelection, internal advancement, "good" policy, social prestige, advancement in the hierarchy of political offices, and so forth. Many studies, however, concentrate on the reelection goal, noting that reelection is typically necessary to satisfy other plausible goals. Although we do not assume that legislators are "single-minded" in their pursuit of reelection (Mayhew 1974), we do believe that it is an important component of their motivation and that, to begin with, it is reasonable to consider this goal in isolation.

The primary task of this section is to defend the notion that the probability of reelection of the typical member of Congress depends not just on such individual characteristics as race, sex, voting record, and so forth, but also on the collective characteristics of the member's party (cf. Arnold 1990). For some, this point might be entirely unobjectionable. After all, how many empirical studies of American voting behavior ignore the partisan attachments of the electorate as unimportant? Even some who have prominently argued that the electorate is "dealigning" judge contemporary levels of partisanship to be far from the point of "zero partisanship" (see Burnham's introduction to Wattenberg 1984, xi). And partisan attachments in the electorate imply a collective component in the reelection fates of candidates of the same party—as indicated in such venerable political science concepts as partisan "electoral tides" and presidential "coattails."

Nonetheless, many have noted that in the twentieth century the president's coattails have been getting shorter and shorter as the congressional and presidential party systems have become more and more separate (Calvert and Ferejohn 1983; Schlesinger 1985). It may also be that the steady stream of articles proclaiming party decline has planted seeds of doubt about the meaning of partisan electoral tides for today's well-entrenched House incumbents.

It is to those who entertain such doubts that we address this section. We start with a simple model in which the reelection probability of a typical House member may depend both on that member's characteristics and on the characteristics of the member's party. Notationally, we shall write $R_i = R_i(c_i; p_i)$, where R_i represents the ith legislator's probability of reelection, c_i represents the ith legislator's individual characteristics, and p_i represents the ith legislator's party's characteristics.[3] This notation reflects the "holy trinity" of voting research—party, personal characteristics, and issues—but collapses the latter two factors into c_i.

In order to say anything substantive about reelection, of course, we need more than this formal notation, which allows the possibility that R_i is a constant function of c_i, p_i, or both. We take it as uncontroversial that R_i depends substantially on c_i. Any reader who finds it uncontroversial that R_i also depends substantially on p_i may skip the rest of this section. Given the recent literature on the decline of party, however, we feel it necessary to defend this assumption explicitly.

1.1   THE PARTY RECORD

The degree to which p_i affects the probability of reelection depends, of course, on what exactly p_i stands for. Our interpretation is that p_i represents the *public record* of the ith legislator's party. Very briefly defined, this record consists of actions, beliefs, and outcomes commonly attributed to the party as a whole. For example, issue positions adhered to by substantial majorities of the party—especially if opposed by majorities of the other party—become part of its public record. Somewhat more carefully defined, a party's record is the *central tendency* in citizens' *beliefs* about the actions, beliefs, and outcomes attributable to the *national* party. Each of the italicized terms in this definition deserves some comment.

Taking the second term first, note that *party record* refers to *beliefs* about parties, not evaluations of them. This definition differs from notions of party identification—certainly from older versions that hinge on early socialization (Campbell et al. 1976), but also from revisionist versions that hinge on how voters evaluate the outcomes that they attribute to a party (Fiorina 1977). We follow Fiorina's account of party identification in our use of the term *party record* to refer to the things that might go into a voter's evaluative process; however, we construe these things more broadly, to include actions—and even beliefs—in addition to outcomes. A party's record, thus, is a commonly accepted summary of the past actions, beliefs, and outcomes with which it is

---

3. For each legislator i in the same party, p_i will be equal—but this does not mean that each legislator's reelection fate depends in the same way on the party's record, as we explain below.

associated. Of course, it is quite possible under this definition that some aspect of a party's record (some particular action, belief, or outcome) will help some of that party's incumbents, have no effect on some, and hurt still others. This does not mean that the party's record varies from district to district, but just that evaluations of it vary.

A party's record is best understood as the *central tendency* in mass beliefs rather than as a single primordial belief with which everyone is somehow endowed. Different individuals may identify the party with different actions, beliefs, and outcomes. Some may have no view at all. Others may have "erroneous" views (e.g., identifying the Republicans with more liberal policies). Nonetheless, there is generally a systematic and more or less "correct" component in mass opinions about the parties. Moreover, because *district* perceptions of what actions, beliefs, and outcomes should be associated with the parties are averages of *individual* perceptions, the systematic component in district perceptions is larger, and the idiosyncratic component smaller. Thus, incumbents—who, electorally speaking, face district rather than individual perceptions (or other group perceptions, such as that of the reelection constituency) of their party's record—tend to be faced with a similar perception of their party's record, regardless of where they run. The central tendency of district perceptions is symbolized formally by p_i.

Of course, the difference between the Democratic party's record in Alabama and in Massachusetts is rather large, which is why our definition refers to *national* parties. There is no doubt that the Democratic party's record in Alabama was influenced by George Wallace and other state party figures. The actions, beliefs, and outcomes attributed to the national party, however, can vary independently of state and local factors. The national factors that have the best-documented impact on electoral results are the state of the economy and the performance of the president. But major pieces of legislation passed on a party basis presumably have some impact as well.

National events can have an impact both because of the evaluative response of voters—no doubt mediated by press reactions—and because potential candidates and contributors anticipate voters' responses (Jacobson and Kernell 1983). As Jacobson (1990, 4) puts it:

> When national conditions favor a party, more of its ambitious careerists decide that this is the year to go after a House seat. Promising candidates of the other party are more inclined to wait for a more propitious time. People who control campaign resources provide more to challengers when conditions are expected to help their preferred party, more to incumbents when

conditions put it on the defensive. . . . The collective result of individual strategic decisions is that the party expected to have a good year fields a superior
crop of well-financed challengers, while the other party fields more than the
usual number of underfinanced amateurs.

The ultimate result is that general anticipations of a bad year help to
bring about a generally bad year.

The logical extreme of Jacobson's argument could take the form of
a self-fulfilling prophecy, with candidates' and contributors' responses
to electoral chimeras working to transform rumor into reality. But as
Jacobson (1990, 4) notes, "Decisions based on illusion are hardly strategic; national conditions must have some independent effect on the
outcome for the argument to make sense."

As we noted above, a party's record may affect the reelection probabilities of its members in different ways: witness the civil rights issue
in the 1960s. Nonetheless, substantial components of a party's record
affect all its members similarly: for example, all are hurt by scandal or
helped by perceptions of competence, honesty, and integrity; all or nearly
all are helped by the party's platform, when taken as a package. Thus,
party records often can be changed in ways that affect the vast majority
of party members' reelection probabilities in the same way (either helping all or hurting all).[4]

If this claim is true, the election statistics for the House should reveal
that the electoral fates of members of the same party are tied together,
as suggested in the old metaphor of *electoral tides*. We shall now discuss
three slightly different methods of testing whether this is the case in the
postwar period.

1.2   THE EXISTENCE OF PARTISAN ELECTORAL TIDES

The first method of testing for the existence of electoral tides is that
employed in the literature on the nationalization of electoral forces (Stokes
1965; Stokes 1967; Claggett, Flanigan, and Zingale 1984; Kawato 1987).
The national partisan forces found in this literature are essentially what
we are looking for: their statistical definition entails that they affect all
candidates of the same party similarly. Much of the literature does not

---

4. This is not to deny that what is good for the legislative party may be bad for the
presidential party. Individual Democratic legislators can run for reelection by picking and
choosing the aspects of the overall party record that they wish to emphasize, avow, or
disavow. Walter Mondale, by contrast, found it hard to repel the image of a party be-
holden to special interests that candidate Reagan conjured up during the 1984 presidential campaign.

bother to report tests of whether the national forces discovered are statistically significant, however. Thus, we briefly conduct our own analysis of variance, focusing on interelection vote swings to the incumbent party.

The vote swing to the incumbent party can be computed for every pair of consecutive elections held in a given district simply by taking the percentage of the two-party vote received by that party's candidate at the later election and subtracting from it the percentage of the two-party vote received by that party's candidate in the earlier election. If there are national factors that affect all candidates of a given party in similar fashion, then an analysis of the variance in these interelection swings should reveal a partisan effect: all Democratic candidates should tend to move together, and similarly for the Republicans.

We have examined this possibility. We shall not present the details of the analysis here, but the bottom line is that if party and year are included as main effects, along with their product as an interaction effect, all three factors are statistically significant in explaining interelection vote swings. This finding provides evidence that candidates of the same party do tend to be pushed in the same direction from year to year.[5]

Another way of demonstrating this sharing of electoral experience is to look at a subset of the data used in the analysis of variance—namely, those districts in which an incumbent was running against a major-party opponent. There were 292 such districts in the 1948 election, for example. If we regress the swing to each of these incumbents on a dummy variable equal to 1 if the incumbent was a Democrat and 0 otherwise, the resulting coefficient gives the difference between the average swings to Republican and Democratic incumbents; the associated t statistic tests whether the difference in average swings to the two parties' incumbents is statistically discernible from zero. The difference in average swings to the two parties' contingents of incumbents in 1948 was 14.6 percent, statistically significant at the .0001 level. Table 16 gives the corresponding significance levels (with the coefficient and its standard error) for all years from 1948 to 1988. The difference in swings to the two parties is significant at the .05 level (or better) in all years except 1968. This result is consistent with the hypothesis that there is some common element in

_____

5. This analysis is essentially the same as that conducted by Kawato (1987), except that he deals with a longer time period and uses the components of variance technique. Kawato also found a statistically significant national or common element in interelection swings (personal communication).

TABLE 16. PARTISAN DIFFERENCES IN INTERELECTION VOTE SWINGS, 1948–88

Dependent Variable: Interelection vote swing to incumbent candidate[a]

Year	Absolute Value of Estimated Coefficient of Party Dummy[b]	Standard Error	Significance Level
1948	14.6	.76	.0001
1950	5.1	.60	.0001
1952	4.8	.74	.0001
1954	8.1	.56	.0001
1956	4.6	.59	.0001
1958	13.6	.64	.0001
1960	5.9	.62	.0001
1962	2.0	.68	.004
1964	10.2	.68	.0001
1966	14.6	.73	.0001
1968	1.2	.74	.112
1970	7.3	.75	.0001
1972	3.6	1.00	.0004
1974	13.3	1.05	.0001
1976	4.8	.87	.0001
1978	5.5	.98	.0001
1980	7.2	1.02	.0001
1982	7.0	.94	.0001
1984	8.6	.83	.0001
1986	6.5	.76	.0001
1988	2.0	.81	.014

[a] Defined as the percentage of the two-party vote received by the incumbent candidate at election t, minus the percentage of the two-party vote received by the incumbent candidate at election $t-1$. Only contests with incumbent candidates are analyzed.

[b] The party dummy variable equals 1 if the incumbent was a Democrat, 0 otherwise. Third-party incumbents are excluded.

the electoral fates of incumbents of the same party that distinguishes them from the other party.[6]

A third method of illustrating the existence of such a common element looks directly at the probability of winning, which we have posited to be of central concern to all incumbents. Pooling all contests with opposed incumbents in the period 1948–88, we have estimated each incumbent's probability of victory (using probit) as a function of two variables: the percentage of the vote garnered in the previous election, and the average swing to all *other* incumbents of the same party in that year (the value of the swing variable for Tony Coelho in 1984, for example, is the average of the 1982–84 swings to all Democratic incumbents other than Coelho). The coefficient of the party swing variable is of the expected (positive) sign and statistically significant at the .0001 level (table 17).

What this coefficient means in terms of the typical incumbent's probability of victory is explored in the lower panel of table 17. It should first be noted that one would expect the impact of national electoral tides to vary from district to district. After all, even a very large positive swing cannot improve the chances of an incumbent already certain to win, but the same swing may substantially improve the chances of an incumbent who is in a close race. Thus, the answer to the question, How much would a one-percentage-point change in the swing to an incumbent's party change her chances of victory? depends on the initial probability from which the change is to be made. The "Initial Probability" column in the lower panel gives a series of such hypothetical initial probabilities. The impact of a one-percentage-point decrease and of a five-percentage-point decrease in the swing to the incumbent's party is

---

6. We performed a similar analysis for open seats. In 1948 (again) there were thirty-five contests in which no incumbent candidate ran. The swing to the incumbent party in these districts was regressed on a dummy variable equal to 1 if the Democrats were the incumbent party, 0 otherwise. The coefficient on the dummy variable tests the hypothesis that there is no difference in the average swing to two groups of candidates: (1) Democratic candidates defending a seat from which a Democratic incumbent has retired; and (2) Republican candidates defending a seat from which a Republican incumbent has retired. If we did not include the dummy variable and simply regressed swing on a constant term, the results would give the average swing to a party losing an incumbent candidate— that is, an estimate of what is usually called the "retirement slump." By including the party variable, we test whether the slump a party suffers on retirement of one of its incumbents is worsened—or offset—by national partisan swings. The results can be summarized as follows: prior to 1966 all but two of the party coefficients are significant at the .05 level; afterward, as one would expect from the literature on the "incumbency effect," all but two of the party coefficients are insignificant. The last year in which open seats were identifiably affected by national partisan trends was 1974.

TABLE 17.   PARTISAN SWINGS AND INCUMBENT
CANDIDATES' PROBABILITIES OF VICTORY

Dependent Variable: Equal to 1 if incumbent
candidate won election, 0 otherwise

Independent Variables	1948–88	1966–88
Constant term	−3.996	−2.950
	(.350)	(.374)
Incumbent candi-date's vote in last election[a]	.095	.076
	(.006)	(.006)
Average swing to incumbent's party[b]	.156	.140
	(.009)	(.012)
N	6,249	3,639

Interpretation of Results

	Decrease in Probability Due to a Decrease in the Swing to Incumbent's Party of	
Initial Probability	1%	5%
.99	.005	.051
.95	.018	.144
.90	.030	.208
.75	.052	.292

[a] The percentage of the two-party vote received by the incumbent in the previous election.
[b] The average of the swings to all other incumbents in the incumbent's party.

given in the columns headed "1%" and "5%." Thus, for example, an incumbent with an initial probability of victory of .90 would suffer a decline of .03 (to .87) were unexpected events to generate a one-percentage-point decrease in the swing to her party. A five-percentage-point decrease would produce a decline of .208 (to .692). The interpretation, of course, is not that the swing itself produces such effects but that the unobserved forces that harm other members of the party also hurt the member in question. In other words, the common factors in the reelection chances of incumbents of the same party are large enough that the chances of each can be predicted by the average experience of the rest.

1.3   SECULAR TRENDS AND REGIONAL DIFFERENCES

The three sets of results just presented are sufficient to show both that there really is a common element in the reelection fates of incumbents of the same party and that it is large enough to be worth doing something about. Nonetheless, two questions about these results might occur to those who view House elections as essentially local phenomena in which the impact of any national or common element is negligible. First, it might be thought that the size of the common element will have declined substantially in and after the 1960s, with the growing importance of the "incumbency effect." Second, it might be thought that the degree of commonality has been overstated for the Democratic party because of an underrepresentation of southern Democrats in the data. We turn next to these two concerns.

A slight decline in the strength of partisan electoral tides can be seen in three different analyses. First, the average difference in the swings to Democratic and Republican incumbents has declined a bit: from 7.2 percent in the 1950s to 6.8, 6.9, and 6.3 percent in the succeeding three decades (table 16, column 1). Second, table 17 provides a probit estimation of incumbents' probabilities of victory for the period from 1966 to 1988 (chosen because 1966 is often found in the literature on incumbency to be an important turning point); the coefficient on the party swing variable declines from .156 to .140, remaining significant at a high level. Third, Jacobson (1990) has estimated similar probit equations for the 1972–86 period and found quite comparable results. His equations have the additional merit of controlling for several variables not included here: whether the challenger had held previous elective office, how much the challenger's campaign spent, and how much the incumbent's campaign spent.[7] All told, the evidence points to only a slight decline in the magnitude of national partisan tides over the postwar period.

As for the southern Democrats, it is best to start with an account of

7. Jacobson (1989) recently performed a probit analysis over the entire 1946–86 period in which time trend interaction terms were included for all his variables. He found a statistically significant decline in the party swing coefficient, but the decline was not particularly large in a substantive sense.

why they are underrepresented in the data. Any analysis of House election results must make a decision regarding uncontested races. We have followed conventional procedure and excluded these races.[8] Because most uncontested races are in the South, and because the vast majority of southern representatives are Democratic (especially in the early postwar years), the result is that a smaller proportion of southern than of northern Democrats who sought reelection make it into the analysis: 29 percent as opposed to 86 percent. This in turn means that the southern Democrats constitute 34 percent of all Democrats seeking reelection but only 15 percent of all Democrats in the analysis.

Because of this underrepresentation of southern Democrats, it is possible that our results overstate the magnitude of the common or national element in Democratic electoral chances. One way to test this hypothesis is to look at the average interelection vote swings to three groups of incumbents—Republicans, southern Democrats, and northern Democrats—for the twenty-one election years from 1948 to 1988. The correlation between the yearly swings to the northern and southern contingents of the Democratic party is .79 (significant at the .0001 level). By comparison, the correlations between the yearly swings to Republican incumbents and to the two groups of Democratic incumbents (northerners and southerners) are −.92 and −.68, respectively. These figures suggest that the difference in electoral experience *between* the parties has been far larger than any internal Democratic difference.

Another way to assess the differences in electoral experience of northern and southern Democrats is to look at how well the average swing to the northerners predicts success in the South, and vice versa. If the South were sui generis, then presumably electoral tides there would not be a good clue to northern success, nor would northern tides predict southern success. Table 18 presents the results of a test of this null hypothesis. Equation 1 in that table is the same as the first equation in table 17, except that only Democratic incumbents are included; the estimated coefficients for Democratic incumbents by themselves are quite similar to those for Democrats and Republicans together. The second equation in table 18 uses the average swing to incumbents in the "other" region of the party in place of the average swing to the full Democratic party; that is, the value for southerners is the swing to northerners, and the value of northerners is the swing to southerners. The coefficient on

---

8. An *uncontested race* is defined as one in which only one major party candidate seeks election to the seat in question.

TABLE 18.   NORTHERN DEMOCRATIC SWINGS, SOUTHERN DEMOCRATIC VICTORIES, AND VICE VERSA[a]

Dependent Variable: Equal to 1 if incumbent candidate won election, 0 otherwise

Independent Variables	*Equation 1*	*Equation 2*
Constant term	−3.672	−3.516
	(.502)	(.484)
Incumbent candidate's vote in last election[b]	.089	.086
	(.009)	(.009)
Average swing to incumbent's party[b]	.164	—
	(.016)	
Average swing to regional Democrats[c]	—	.078
		(.008)
N	3,176	3,176

Interpretation of Results

	Decrease in Probability Due to a Decrease in the Swing to Regional Democrats of	
Initial Probability	*1%*	*5%*
.99	.002	.016
.95	.009	.055
.90	.014	.086
.75	.025	.138

[a] Only Democratic incumbents were included in the analysis.
[b] See table 17.
[c] For northern (southern) Democrats, this is the average of the swings to southern (northern) incumbents.

"regional party swing" is significantly different from zero at the .0001 level but about half the size of that on "full party swing": .078 versus .164. As shown in the lower panel of the table, this translates into impacts on probability of victory that are about half the size of those reported in table 17. The conclusion to draw from this evidence is that there is some regional variation in interelection vote swings, with southern and northern Democrats facing somewhat different electoral tides.

But there nonetheless remains a detectable common element, so that tides in one region are a good clue to success in the other.

1.4   THE PERCEPTION OF PARTISAN ELECTORAL TIDES

The last subsection provided evidence of a common element in the electoral chances of House incumbents of the same party. We now ask whether members of the House recognize this commonality.

One way to answer the question is by asking members directly. Responses in interviews are not always frank or well thought out, however, and in any event we do not know of any interviews that have asked the appropriate question. Another method is to note those instances in which members seem clearly to act on the hypothesis that there is a common element in electoral politics. As Thomas B. Edsall noted (*Washington Post Weekly,* 27 Mar. 1989, 29), for example, Newt Gingrich's attack on Jim Wright's ethics seems to have been motivated by such a belief. Unfortunately, we do not know quite how to assess this kind of evidence—how many such episodes would be convincing?—and so have not pursued it.

The method that we have pursued is to allow members of Congress to speak for themselves through their retirement decisions. If partisan electoral tides are perceived by members of Congress in roughly the same fashion (so that there is rough agreement on which way the tides will be flowing), then there ought to be a negative correlation between the rates at which incumbents of the two parties retire. Examining data from 1912–70, Jacobson and Kernell (1981, 54) report that "removing the secular growth of careerism by examining change scores and omitting [the 1942 war election], we find that Republican and Democratic retirements do move in opposite directions. The $-.43$ correlation (significant at .01) of the partisan retirement ratio indicates a pronounced systematic component in behavior which heretofore has been viewed as idiosyncratic." Jacobson and Kernell note that the post-1970 period has seen substantial changes in retirement benefits, which have altered the pattern in retirement rates.

1.5   SOME CRUCIAL PREMISES

The argument in the rest of this chapter depends crucially on the premise that party records have at least a "noticeable" impact on the reelection probabilities of their members. We cannot quantify the degree of impact, but we can say that the stronger the reader believes the electoral impact of party records to be, the more convincing will be the arguments to come.

The evidence presented above should at least convince the reader that there is a common element in the electoral chances of members of the same party. This does not prove that party records must be important, of course, because there may be other mechanisms that produce a correlation between the electoral fates of members of the same party, mechanisms that are not related to or mediated through the party record and reactions to it. Nonetheless, we believe that any plausible explanation for electoral tides must to some degree involve party records and voter responses to parties as collectivities.[9]

It is not enough that what parties do—as encapsulated in their party records—affects the (re)election chances of their members. Some researchers view national partisan swings as largely outside the control of members of Congress. For example, Mayhew (1974, 28) writes that "national swings in the congressional vote are normally judgments on what the president is doing . . . rather than on what Congress is doing." He cites Kramer (1971) as showing that "the national electorate rewards the congressional party of a president who reigns during economic prosperity and punishes the party of one who reigns during adversity." A bit later (30–31) he notes the difficulty of finding "an instance in recent decades in which any group of congressmen . . . has done something that has clearly changed the national congressional electoral percentage in a direction in which the group intended to change it." If one accepts this view, then the prospects for the remainder of our argument—or for any argument that views congressional parties as instruments to improve the collective electoral fate of their members—are bleak.

We need, therefore, to reconsider the evidence. Two points bear

9. What form would be taken by an explanation for electoral tides that made no reference to party records? One might suppose that Republicans do worse on average than Democrats in some given year because most of them have supported some specific policies that their constituents have judged harshly. But then one must ask why more Republicans than Democrats were unable to predict what the reactions of their constituents would be to their legislative actions. If all politicians are equally good at catering to their constituencies, then tides of this type should rarely occur. Another possibility is that most of the Republicans bought into a particular policy stand that events then undermined. Voters do not think of the policy as a Republican policy; they just think of it as a failed policy, and most of the candidates who supported it happen to be Republicans. Of course, this scenario provides what are seemingly ideal conditions for collective responsibility to be assigned, and one must ask why it is that voters blame individual Republicans for the failure of a policy to which they as individuals contributed only one vote.

stressing. First, although the extant literature (e.g., Kramer 1971; Tufte 1975; Bloom and Price 1975) does find that macroeconomic conditions and presidential popularity account for a substantial portion of the variation in the aggregate House vote, these variables are far from accounting for all the variation.[10] Second, even that portion of the variation that is accounted for *statistically* by presidential popularity and macroeconomic conditions is not beyond congressional influence. If one believes that legislation can have a substantial impact on presidential popularity (or macroeconomic health) and that members of Congress are aware of this, then one must conclude that presidential popularity (or macroeconomic health) is the outcome of a game in which both Congress and the president have a role (see Kernell 1991). Members of Congress, in other words, collectively can influence the variables that influence partisan electoral tides.[11]

2. REELECTION MAXIMIZERS AND ELECTORAL INEFFICIENCIES

The argument of the rest of the chapter is simply that the element of commonality in the electoral chances of incumbents of the same party is strong enough to merit attention; parties that organize sufficiently to

10. Kramer (1971), for example, explains about 64 percent of the variation. Tufte (1975) explains 91 percent but has only eight data points. Respecifications of Tufte's model on longer time series show significantly lower R^2s. Are congressional actions important in explaining that part of the variance not accounted for by the economy (and presidential popularity)? To show this positively, one would need some way of measuring what Congress does. But such measurement is unavoidably difficult because of the nature of legislative action. Social Security legislation, for example, has not waxed and waned over the years as has the economy. It is therefore difficult to find its effect in aggregate time-series analysis—and the same problem besets virtually any issue. One might resort to some sort of analysis focusing on the point in time that the legislation was first passed. But suppose one were to find an issue that seemed to spark a noticeable gain for one party. That would beg the question of why this issue, if so profitable, was not pushed earlier. Finding an issue big enough to be clearly identifiable in the way that Mayhew (1974) demands is equivalent to finding a big mistake—a protracted failure to recognize the growing salience of the issue—by one of the parties. If the parties are actively sniffing out electoral advantage, then big issues with a clear national impact should be rare. This is not to say that congressional parties do not contribute to the record on which their collective interests ride, but only that the contribution comes in many small payments, each difficult to be sure of by itself.

11. Another route to showing that not all the action is extracongressional is to run the probits in table 17 again, including economic variables and presidential approval ratings. We have done so and found no change in the size and significance of the party swing variable. The common element in the electoral fates of incumbents of the same party cannot be explained simply by economic and presidential variables.

capture these potential collective benefits will be more successful electorally, hence more likely to prosper, than parties that do not.[12]

Before showing how the organized may prosper, however, we shall consider how the unorganized may not. We assume, to begin with, that each legislator seeks to maximize her probability of reelection and can take a variety of actions in the legislature (e.g., speaking and voting) that affect either her individual reputation, her party's collective reputation, or both. Because individual reputations (c_i) are essentially private goods, it is not difficult to explain why legislators undertake activities—such as pork barreling and casework—that enhance their own reputations. In contrast, the party's reputation, based on its record (p), is a public good for all legislators in the party. This means that party reputations may receive less attention than they deserve, for the usual kinds of reasons (Olson 1965).

Consider, for example, the transition rules employed by House Ways and Means Committee chairman Dan Rostenkowski to facilitate passage of the 1986 Tax Reform Act. Certainly the Democratic members of Congress who benefited from these transition rules were in favor of them. Yet, had Rostenkowski been too liberal in his distribution of this largesse, presumably there would have come a point at which the damage done to the reputation of the party as a whole would have outweighed the sum of individual benefits. Republicans nationwide would have champed at the bit to run against the party that had sold out so completely to the special interests, and everyone in the Democratic party could be made electorally better off by some package of retrenchments on transition rules and alternative, less-sensitive side payments to those bearing the brunt of the retrenchment. Yet no individual Democrat would have an incentive unilaterally to give up her transition rule(s), and so—absent collective action of some sort—the party's reputation on matters financial would be tarnished.

Another scenario in which both party and individual reputations might be tarnished, absent collective action, arises when legislation confers collective benefits and costs on many voters in many districts. Such legislation by definition poses at least two collective action problems that

---

12. A somewhat different starting point for a theory of parties would see them as organizations designed to facilitate passage of those policies that members of the party hold in common. We do not intend to deny the validity of this approach by pursuing the one that we do in the text. Rather, just as in the literature on party behavior, it seems fruitful to pursue an analytical policy of "divide and conquer"—considering the main motivations behind party development one at a time. (We intend to address the concept of parties as vehicles for producing policy in future work.)

interfere with its being translated into electoral profit. First, benefits and costs are not excludable: they accrue to all citizens regardless of whether they individually have supported or opposed any legislators deemed responsible. Second, because bills are enacted by majority vote in a large assembly, no individual legislator can credibly claim personal responsibility for providing the benefit (Fiorina and Noll 1979). Both these problems make it less likely that any single legislator can turn her support of legislation conferring collective benefits into electoral profit. This difficulty in turn makes it theoretically less likely that legislation conferring collective benefits would ever get passed—or, more to the point, that it would ever get pushed far enough along in the legislative process so that it might actually come up for a vote.

The difficulty facing collective-benefits legislation of this kind can be exposed in the simple question, Who is to bear the costs of drafting and negotiating logrolls in support of such legislation? This problem does not arise in complete information models, as can be seen in the following example.

Suppose that the majority party is divided into two factions, N and S. They face a unified opposition, R, and any two voting blocs constitute a majority. Only two bills are under consideration, N (proposed by N) and S (proposed by S). It is common knowledge that all legislators seek to maximize their own probability of reelection and that preferences over the bills are as follow (where Ns stands for the outcome in which bill N passes and bill S does not, ns means that neither bill passes, and so forth):

> everyone in N: Ns > NS > ns > nS
>
> everyone in S: nS > NS > ns > Ns
>
> everyone in R: ns > Ns > nS > NS

Given these preferences, both bills will fail if everyone votes sincerely and the bills are voted on separately. But N and S can do better if they agree to package their bills and vote directly on the question "both (NS) or neither (ns)?" Moreover, there is no informational impediment in this model to N and S concluding this deal. Any individual in N or S would happily bear the apparently trivial costs of proposing such a package during floor consideration—and so the logroll might well occur. (The only "problem" in this model—and it does not obviously impede the logroll—is majority-rule instability: once NS is passed or about to be passed, N and R could both do better by supporting Ns, and so forth.)

Now consider a more complex model in which (1) everyone in N wants a bill, N, whose characteristics are common knowledge; (2) everyone in N (and S) thinks that there probably exists some sweetener S that will induce S to go along with them; but (3) no one knows exactly what this sweetener is; and (4) it would be costly to "invent" an appropriate sweetener and sell it to S (and N). In this model, a free-rider problem arises for the members of N (and S): no single one of them wishes to bear or contribute to the costs of searching for the sweetener, because this action is invisible to voters and they cannot credibly claim credit for it. Hence, collective-benefits legislation will be underproduced, entailing an *electoral inefficiency:* even though everyone in N and S could be made better off if a sweetener were produced, no one wants to contribute to the costs of its production, and so none (or too little) is produced.[13]

3. PARTY LEADERSHIP

In the last section we sketched two theoretical accounts of how unorganized groups of reelection-seeking legislators might overproduce particularistic-benefits legislation and underproduce collective-benefits legislation in an electorally inefficient fashion. We now argue that political parties can help to prevent electoral inefficiencies of this kind.

The way in which parties do this can be seen by considering the incentives of party leaders. So far, we have assumed that every legislator seeks simply to maximize her probability of reelection. This assumption led directly to the inefficiency result of the last section. Yet not all reelections are created equal. The payoff to being reelected is higher if one's party wins a majority, as evinced by the obvious payoffs in terms of the Speakership and committee chairmanships, by the chronic and sometimes loud complaining of the Republicans in the House of Rep-

---

13. It is interesting, although tangential to our present purposes, to note that the free-rider problem in the production of collective-benefits legislation is prior to, and partially alleviates, the problem of instability. To get instability one needs complete and costless information about the electoral effects of all potential legislation, coupled with costless drafting of legislation. If drafting bills, communicating their characteristics (e.g., their likely effects), and negotiating logrolls are costly, then a free-rider problem may considerably reduce the supply of collective-benefits legislation—and hence the potential instruments by which instability could be revealed.

resentatives, and by the pattern of voluntary retirements from the House.[14] Moreover, there may well be a purely electoral payoff to majority status: how much less money would Democrats get from business political action committees if they were in the minority? It seems likely that they would lose more than could be accounted for simply by the loss in members. The payoff to being reelected is also higher if one is elected or appointed to a leadership position in one's party, rather than remaining in the rank and file. Both of these features are endogenous: majority status and leadership posts can be made more or less attractive by changes in House and caucus rules.

These simple facts—that majority status can be made preferable to minority status, that leading can be made preferable to following—suggest a rather different view of the motivation of rational legislators than that adopted in the last section. Reelection remains important, even dominant, but its importance can be modified significantly by the desire for *internal advancement*—defined both in terms of a party's advancement to majority status and in terms of the individual MC's advancement in the hierarchy of (committee and leadership) posts within her party. If internal advancement is to some extent contingent on the servicing of collective legislative needs, then the desire for internal advancement can play the leading role in solving the problems of electoral inefficiency mentioned in the last section. We show how this follows in the case of the Speaker of the House (other cases being similar in general outline).

We must first select a point in time at which to analyze the Speaker's preferences. There are two possibilities: the (short) period just after a

14. The Republicans have controlled the House only twice in the postwar period, in the Eightieth and Eighty-third Congresses. Thus, there is little variance in the majority status of the parties. Nonetheless, majority status, not party, predicts retirement rates. This can be shown as follows. Let the dependent variable be the retirement rate (computed, for a given party and Congress, as the percentage of all that party's sitting members who do not seek reelection, for some reason other than death). We have two observations per Congress, for a total of forty-two. Regress this dependent variable on the following independent variables: Party ($=1$ for the Democrats, 0 for the Republicans); Majority Status ($=1$ if the party controlled the House, 0 otherwise); and Presidential Status ($=1$ if the party controlled the presidency in November of the election year ending the Congress, 0 otherwise). The result can be expressed as follows: Retirement $= 8.99 - .04 *$ Party $- 2.67 *$ Majority Status $+ 1.87 *$ Presidential Status. The t statistics for Party and Majority Status were 0.03 and 1.95, respectively. Given that there was considerable collinearity between the Party and Majority Status variables (the Democrats were almost always in the majority), the results are surprisingly strong. They indicate almost no partisan effect and a substantial majority status effect: holding constant other variables, majority status is worth a decrease of 2.67 percentage points in the retirement rate of a party. The Presidential Status variable, which reflects the federal appointments available to a representative whose party controls the presidency, has a t of 2.30.

potential Speaker is elected to Congress but before he is elected as Speaker, and the (long) period after the Speakership election but before the next congressional election. In the first period, the goal of reelection to Congress has already been attained, as has the goal of majority party status. All that remains as an *immediate* goal is winning the nomination of the majority party as Speaker (which leads automatically to election by the House). In the second period, all three goals have been resolved for the present Congress but remain to be attained in the next Congress. Of course, all three goals must be achieved anew in the *next* Congress. The primary difference in preferences, then, is simply one of which goal is most immediate (i.e., least discounted). We have chosen to focus on the second and longer period because it yields a technically simpler maximand. (We do not make the assumptions necessary to drive a real wedge between *ex ante* and *ex post* preferences, as does Kramer (1983); nonetheless, some similar problems arise and are discussed below.)

Given a focus on the period after the Speakership election but before the next congressional elections, we can write out the implied maximand for the Speaker of the House. We normalize the utility of failing to be reelected to the next Congress to be zero and use the following notation:

u_{11} = the utility of being reelected, having one's party secure a majority, and being reelected as Speaker

u_{10} = the utility of being reelected, having one's party secure a majority, and *not* being reelected as Speaker

u_{01} = the utility of being reelected, having one's party secure a minority, and being reelected as leader of one's (now minority) party

u_{00} = the utility of being reelected, having one's party secure a minority, and *not* being reelected as leader of one's party

x = a vector of actions taken by the Speaker

$R(x)$ = the Speaker's probability of reelection, given x

$M(x)$ = the probability that the Speaker's party will secure a majority, given x and that he wins reelection

$S(x)$ = the probability that the Speaker will be reelected as Speaker, given x, that he wins reelection, and that his party secures a majority

$L(x)$ = the probability that the Speaker will be reelected as leader of his party, given x, that he wins reelection, and that his party secures a minority

In terms of this notation, the Speaker's maximand can be written as follows (we suppress the functional dependence of R, M, S, and L on x for convenience):

$$R[MSu_{11} + M(1-S)u_{10} + (1-M)Lu_{01} + (1-M)(1-L)u_{00}]$$

The practical meaning of this expression is that Speakers are faced with a mixture of three motivations: increasing their personal probability of reelection (R); increasing the probability that their party secures a majority (M); and increasing the probability that they are reelected as leader of their party (S and L). It is important to note that these three goals can in principle conflict but that the degree to which they do so in practice is endogenous to the majority party.

Consider first the possibility of conflict. The three goals of maximizing R, M, and S/L differ most clearly in terms of the set of districts to which the Speaker needs to pay attention in order to satisfy those goals. To win reelection to Congress, he can focus primarily on his own district; to win reelection as leader of his party, he will probably focus on those districts that returned or are expected to return members of his party (representatives from these districts constitute the "electorate" for the leadership contest); to secure a majority for his party, he may consider all districts. (If the action x that the Speaker takes is construed to be simply the selection of a policy from a unidimensional policy space— and if some rather heroic assumptions are made, which need not detain us here—then the potential conflict between a Democratic Speaker's goals can be expressed as follows: to maximize R he should choose x equal to the median of *his own* district; to maximize S/L he should choose x equal to the median of the *median Democrat's* district; to maximize M he should choose x equal to the median of *the median legislator's* district. The model that generates this result should not be taken too seriously, but it conveys the flavor of the possible conflict among the Speaker's goals.[15])

15. The heroic assumptions are as follows: Assume that the policy space is unidimensional and interpret the action (x) that the Speaker takes as simply the selection of a policy that he will support using the power and resources of his office. This choice is made after the election of the Speaker in a given year; he anticipates the impact that his choice will have on R, M, and S/L two years hence. In this model, what is required to maximize R is

Despite the *potential* for conflict among the Speaker's goals, they may not conflict much in equilibrium. As we show below, this is primarily because the Speaker is elected and faces competition for the post *within his party.*

1. *R versus S/L:* If maximizing the probability of being elected as party leader requires, let us say, being in the middle of the party's ideological range, then presumably those who *are* in this range and have contituencies that allow or support this position are more likely to win the leadership election. Other things equal, party leaders are more likely to come from districts that are typical of the mainstream of their party than from atypical districts. But this should mean that those who actually win leadership elections are unlikely to face strong conflicts between the goal of reelection to Congress and reelection to the leadership.

This argument implicitly assumes that there is some equilibrium position that is best for winning one's party's nomination. But various instability results in the literature (McKelvey 1979; Schofield 1980; Schwartz 1986) imply that there will always exist some alternative set of actions and policies, regardless of what the Speaker's current set of actions and policies, such that some majority in the party would prefer the alternative to what the Speaker does. So why is a Speaker not always vulnerable to a "redistributive" attack from within his party? And why does this not make what is required to maximize S/L rather unpredictable, so that it is hard to say whether R and S/L conflict or not?

Our answer to the second of these questions hinges on some results in the spatial theory of electoral competition (N. Miller 1980; McKelvey 1986; Cox 1987). These results pertain to a model in which two aspirants for an elective office compete by announcing the policies that

---

clearly choosing x equal to the expected median of the Speaker's district. What is required to maximize M and S/L is more complicated. If we think of the individual reputation of each legislator (c) as being determined by his or her own choice of what policy to support, the party reputation (p) as being determined by the Speaker's choice of policy, and make the heroic assumption that the impact of c and p on R is additively separable, then each legislator will simply choose the median of his or her own district. In this case, maximizing S or L requires setting x equal to the expected median of the *median Democrat's* district, whereas maximizing M requires setting x equal to the expected median of the *median legislator's* district. This reveals a fairly clear potential tension between maximizing M and maximizing S/L. In the much more likely case that the impact of c and p on R is not additively separable, things are less clear. For example, if voters care a lot about any divergence between c and p, maximizing M may require something like minimizing the average divergence between c and p. In this case, the tension between maximizing S or L on the one hand, and M on the other, would be lessened.

they would pursue if elected. The model is multidimensional (there are many policy issues), and so in general there will be instability; that is, any given set of policies will be vulnerable to defeat by some other set of policies. McKelvey (1986), following N. Miller (1980), shows that the competitors in such an election would nonetheless confine themselves to a subset of the possible policy platforms, the so-called uncovered set. The important properties of the uncovered set are two. First, the uncovered set can be small, located near the "center" of the electorate's distribution of ideal points. Indeed, when the special conditions necessary for the existence of a multidimensional median are met, the uncovered set collapses to this single point; and when the conditions are "almost" met, the uncovered set is tiny. Second, in order to conclude that a competitor will choose a platform from within the uncovered set, one needs only to make the relatively mild assumption about motivation that no competitor will announce a platform X if there is another platform Y which is at least as successful against any platform the opponent might announce and is better against some. That is, one need only assume that no competitor will play game-theoretically *dominated strategies*.[16]

The uncovered set is relevant to the problem at hand because it shows that there are definite limits to the policy platforms that those seeking leadership positions will adopt—limits much more restrictive than the full range of opinion in the party. These restrictions in turn imply that a member whose constituency interests dictate something rather far from the competitively optimal platforms in the uncovered set is less likely to *seek* leadership positions—because implementing the optimal policies would be electorally hazardous—and also less likely to *win* those positions—because other members of the party will recognize the constituency conflict and therefore doubt the member's reliability in office. Thus, we are led again to predict that leaders will be chosen in such a fashion that their personal reelection is not too incompatible with the duties of office.

The primary weakness in the foregoing argument is that it relies on results that presume a two-way contest. What if there are more than two competitors for the Speakership nomination of the majority party? Cox (1989) has shown that certain types of voting procedures (what he

16. Of course, there are other assumptions—for example, regarding voters and the nature of competition—that must also be accepted. These assumptions, too, seem relatively mild. McKelvey (1986) used a somewhat restrictive assumption about voter utility functions to derive the result, but this restriction has been relaxed by Cox (1987).

calls "majority Condorcet procedures") induce candidates to adopt positions in the uncovered set regardless of the number of candidates. Although we have no formal results, we believe that the method used by the Democratic Caucus—which requires a majority for nomination—also places significant constraints on the range of policies that look good for winning the nomination.

There remains the question of why Speakers are not forever being turned out of office, as might be expected on the basis of the spatial instability theorems. The answer has to do with violations of the assumptions underlying these theorems. Instability theorems can be interpreted in two ways: either as statements about preferences or as statements about behavior. If they are interpreted as statements about preferences, then their assumptions are quite general and their conclusion compelling: there will always be some majority, all of those members could be made better off if policies were changed. If they are taken to refer to behavior, however, they entail the assumption that any coalition, all of whose members would individually benefit were another set of policies adopted, will in fact form and take action to ensure that appropriate change is forthcoming. This assumption ignores the costs of identifying coalitions and organizing them sufficiently so that their members' collective interests can be served. It ignores, in other words, the existence of the prisoner's dilemma that faces any hypothetical coalition seeking to overturn the status quo.

In our view, the legislative process in the House of Representatives is in important respects more like research and development than it is like the costless and instantaneous voting that occurs in the spatial model. We view each Speakership as embodying a certain set of policy deals within the majority party, but the alternatives to these deals are not as clear as they are in the spatial model. More to the point, *attainment* of one of these alternatives is not a matter of a single motion on the floor changing everything that needs to be changed all at once. It is instead a matter of many votes taken over an extended period, with many details too costly to specify in advance, and ultimate success uncertain. For this reason, we view Speakerships as Hobbes viewed governments (Hardin 1991): as (noncooperative) equilibria to coordination games rather than as (cooperative) equilibria to spatial voting games.

Once a Speakership has been launched, the Speaker serves to police and enforce a particular set of deals. It is true that some other set of deals might be preferred by some majority in the party. But ousting the incumbent Speaker and his deals and installing a new regime cannot be accomplished by a single costless vote: it requires a series of political battles, each with uncertain outcome. While the revolutionary battle rages, the value of the deals struck by the old Speaker may be lost to all members of the party. Moreover, when the dust settles and a new regime is in place, the original revolutionaries may or may not have gotten what they wanted.

2. R versus M: Potential conflict between R and M can be lessened by choosing a Speaker from a "safe" district, defined as one in which a wide range of values of x can be chosen, all of which maximize or nearly maximize R. A Speaker who is electorally safe in this sense is less likely to sacrifice collective goals (M or, for that matter, those implicit in maximization of S/L) for personal goals (R) simply because there is little need to do so. Hence, other things equal, party leaders are more likely to come from safe seats than from marginal seats. In view of the large number of safe seats in the postwar period, this hardly constrains the choice of leaders.

3. M versus S/L: The potential tensions between winning a majority and retaining support within the party were no doubt quite evident to Neil Kinnock, leader of the Labour party in Britain throughout the 1980s. But Kinnock's problems, it should be remembered, were not internal to the parliamentary party; those who seemed to be least interested in the electoral consequences of Labour party positions were the constituency activists, who were not running for office (Jenkins 1988). In general, it would seem that the goals of winning a majority and retaining support within the *legislative* party are not much at odds, if at all. Peabody (1967, 687), in a study of party leadership in the U.S. House of Representatives, notes: "Strong victories promote good will and generally reflect to the benefit of party leaders. Conversely, defeat results in pessimism, hostility and a search for scapegoats. If the net losses are particularly severe . . . then the possibilities of minority leadership change through revolt are greatly enhanced."

From a theoretical perspective, the best way to maximize the probability that one's party will win a majority next time may very well be to concentrate on getting the current majority reelected. After all, they have shown that they can win and have all the advantages of incumbency; challengers, by contrast, are much more risky. To the extent that this is true, of course, there should be very little conflict between the goals of maximizing M and maximizing S/L.

The bottom line of this discussion is that, by creating a leadership post that is both attractive and elective, a party can induce its leader to internalize the collective electoral fate of the party. In Olsonian terms, creation of a position whose occupant is *personally* motivated to pursue *collective* interests serves to make the party a privileged group.[17]

The parameters of the model make clear what promotes and hinders this internalization of collective electoral interests. The more attractive is the leadership relative to rank-and-file status (the more intraparty inequality), the more attractive majority party status is relative to minority status (the more interparty inequality), and the less the leader has to worry about personal reelection, the more completely will the leader's induced preferences be a combination of a purely collective goal (maximizing the probability that his party wins a majority at the next election) and a goal (maximizing the probability that he is reelected as party leader) that is unattainable for those who neglect to service collective interests.

Party leadership in the United Kingdom seems to have been designed particularly well to achieve internalization. First, the inequality in power between the back benches and the front benches is quite large, so retaining the leadership is important relative to retaining a seat in Parliament. Second, the inequality in power between the majority and minority is large, so that retaining majority status is important relative to retaining a seat in Parliament. Third, important party leaders are always run in safe districts and, if they happen to lose nonetheless, are immediately returned at a by-election (some obliging backbencher having resigned his seat for the purpose). Party leaders thus have very little in the way of *parochial* electoral concerns.

U.S. parties cannot compete with their U.K. counterparts in purity of organizational design, but the same principles are evident nonetheless. Intraparty power in Congress may be decentralized, but there are still lumps of it piled up in the leadership positions that are worth striving for. The minority party may be more capable of influencing legislation in the House of Representatives than in the House of Commons, but it is still decidedly preferable to be in the majority. This can be seen

---

17. An example of how this logic might play out in practice can be given by continuing the example of the Tax Reform Act of 1986. Dan Rostenkowski, as chair of the committee on Ways and Means, is clearly in a position of great authority and power. This position has been to some degree elective for quite some time. Rostenkowski can be said to be from a typical Democratic district and to be reasonably safe. From our perspective, the reason he did not distribute "too much" in the way of transition rules is because he had partially internalized the collective costs of such a course of action. He did make sure that Chicago got its share of transition rule benefits, but he did not hand out such large amounts to his own or other districts as to lessen the Democratic party's chances of securing a majority or his own chances at retaining his seniority on Ways and Means.

in the significantly higher retirement rates among minority party members. The average postwar retirement rate for the Democrats, when in the minority, was 8.91 percent; when in the majority, 7.03 percent. The comparable figures for the Republicans were 9.96 percent and 6.37 percent. A multivariate explanation of retirement rates finds most of the action not in party, but in majority status.[18] Finally, party leaders in the United States may not have a guaranteed return comparable to Margaret Thatcher's, but who was the last Speaker to be denied reelection by his constituents?[19]

If party leaders do internalize collective electoral interests along the lines suggested, then the rest of the argument is fairly close. Electoral inefficiencies that can potentially accumulate because of the free-rider problems inherent in legislation (of both the particularistic-benefits and collective-benefits kind) are prevented because party leaders have a *personal* incentive to prevent them. Thus, for example, leaders will be on the lookout for profitable logrolls within their party, for institutional arrangements that will encourage the discovery of information about potential logrolls and prevent their unraveling by bipartisan coalitions, and so forth.[20]

4. CONCLUSION

In this chapter we have articulated a view of parties as solutions to collective dilemmas that their members face. Several points about this view merit notice here.

First, we have focused solely on collective dilemmas that entail *electoral* inefficiencies. Another perspective on parties might focus instead on collective dilemmas entailing *policy* inefficiencies (see Rohde 1991; Aldrich 1988; Cox, McCubbins, and Schwartz n.d.). For the purposes of our discussion here, however, the differences between these two views are inconsequential.

Second, the collective dilemmas facing a party are "solved" chiefly through the establishment of party leadership positions that are both

18. See note 15.

19. The answer is William Pennington, Whig Speaker in the Thirty-sixth Congress (1859–61).

20. Note that in the logrolling example given above, the Speaker's preferences would plausibly be NS first, regardless of whether he was in the N or S faction. He would prefer this outcome because he internalizes the reelection probabilities of all parts of the party. If true, then the logroll has an element of stability: the party leadership is interested in preserving it and will presumably seek to scuttle any legislation that would unravel it.

attractive and elective. The trick is to induce those who occupy or seek to occupy leadership positions to internalize the collective interests of the party, thereby converting the party into a privileged group (Olson 1965) for some purposes.

Third, solutions to collective dilemmas—that is, the institutions of leadership and particular elected leadership teams—are stable because they are, in essence, equilibria in n-person coordination games. Nearly everyone in the party prefers that there be *some* agreed-upon leadership team rather than that there be *no* agreed-upon leadership team, even if they disagree on which team would be best. Because each leadership team carries with it particular policy predispositions and deals, leadership stability leads to a certain amount of policy stability as well.

PART THREE

Parties as Floor Voting Coalitions

In the previous part we focused on the leadership of parties as the key to understanding their collective action. This suggests that investigations of parties as floor voting coalitions ought to be conducted in terms of loyalty to party leaders and not, as has usually been done in the previous literature, in terms of general party cohesion. In other words, voting together (or failing to so vote) when the leadership is inactive or divided is one thing, and voting together (or not) when the leadership is active and united is quite another. Chapter 6 uses this basic point to reinvestigate and reinterpret the data on party voting in the House since the New Deal era.

Our reinterpretation relates to the notion of "conditional party government" (Rohde 1991). Conditional party government refers to a system in which the majority party leadership is active on an issue only when the party rank and file is substantially in agreement on what should be done. In such a system, decreases in party homogeneity will lead, not to decreases in the support that leaders receive when they take a clear stand, but rather to leaders taking fewer stands. This suggests a different view of how to measure the weakness (or strength) of parties as floor coalitions. In pursuing this view, we find little indication of a secular trend in the strength of the majority party on the floor of the House in the postwar era.

SIX

On the Decline of Party
Voting in Congress

The literature on recorded votes in Congress is vast (for recent surveys, see Collie 1984; Thompson and Silbey 1984). Most of it, including that portion that deals with the postwar House of Representatives, concludes that party is the single best predictor of congressional voting behavior (Turner 1951; Truman 1959; Matthews 1960; Marwell 1967; Turner and Schneier 1970). At the same time, however, those who take a historical view emphasize the declining importance of party voting in Congress during the twentieth century (Cooper, Brady, and Hurley 1977; Brady, Cooper, and Hurley 1979; Collie 1988a; Clubb and Traugott 1977; Collie and Brady 1985). Collie (1984, 8) summarizes recent research in this vein showing "an erratic but overall decline in the levels of both intraparty cohesion and interparty conflict since the turn of the century."

Our purpose in this chapter is threefold: first, to discuss some recent work dealing with trends in party voting in the 1980s, a period not included in the literature cited above; second, to review the methods used and results found in the literature on the pre-1980 period; and third, to provide a new perspective on historical trends in party voting since the New Deal. The new perspective for which we argue centers on the activity of party leaders rather than party majorities. Thus, for example, instead of focusing on such standard measures as the number of *party votes*—roll calls in which a majority of Republicans oppose a majority of Democrats—we look at *party leadership votes*, defined as roll calls in which the Republican and Democratic leaderships oppose one another. If one seeks to assess the importance of parties as organizations, we argue, the appropriate measures are (1) the cohesion of each party in support of its leadership on those roll calls on which the leadership takes a clear stand and (2) the number and importance of such roll calls. When we reexamine the data from this perspective, we find little indication of a long-term secular decline in the importance of party voting cues in the period after the New Deal—at least for the majority party.

1. PARTY VOTING: TRENDS IN THE 1980s

Systematic study of historical trends in party voting in Congress first became feasible in the mid-1970s, with the compilation of machine-readable roll call votes by the Inter-University Consortium on Political and Social Research. Soon thereafter, the first entries into the field appeared in print, providing and analyzing long time series of data on party voting (Cooper, Brady, and Hurley 1977; Clubb and Traugott 1977). These works obviously could not cover the later 1970s and 1980s, and most of the subsequent literature does not look beyond the 1970s.

The chief exception to this characterization is a series of important papers by David Rohde (1988; 1989; 1990b).[1] Using essentially the same methodology as previous researchers, Rohde has extended the time series to the late 1980s. He finds, first, an increase in the frequency of party votes (as a percentage of all roll calls) from the mid-1970s to present and, second, a strong increase in cohesion on these party votes. "Democratic party unity, which had stabilized at a low point between 70 and 72 percent during the first Nixon term (1969–72), began increasing sharply in the 1980s. . . . The average for the 100th Congress (1987–88) was 88 percent, and to find a Congress in which that level was exceeded one has to go back to the 61st (1909–11)" (Rohde 1990b, 6).

The importance of Rohde's findings, for present purposes, is not just in what they show—a significant increase in party voting in the 1980s— but also in what they suggest about the previous trends. Rohde notes that previous researchers found a long-term decline in party voting prior to the 1980s, and most gave no indication that they expected it to end, much less reverse itself. Party decline in the legislative arena was seen as linked to party decline in the electoral arena, and both seemed to

1. See also Schlesinger 1985.

have considerable inertia behind them. As Rhode (1990b, 32) points out, however, "the apparent immutability of partisan decline that was explicit or implicit in earlier research has to be taken as disproved."

2. PARTY VOTING: TRENDS FROM 1910 TO THE 1970s

Even if reversible, the decline in party voting down to 1980 may still have been substantial and steady. Was it? To answer this question, we consider the evidence in greater detail, concentrating in particular on the two variables that have received the most attention in the literature: the relative frequency of party votes and average levels of party cohesion.

2.1 PARTY VOTES

Consider first the relative frequency of party votes.[2] Cooper, Brady, and Hurley (1977) provide the appropriate figures for the Fiftieth (1886–87) through Ninetieth (1966–67) Congresses. Regressing these figures on time, they find a slope of −.52, indicating that party votes as a percentage of all roll calls fell, on average, by about half a percentage point per Congress.[3] Extending the time series forward ten Congresses and performing the same regression for the Sixtieth through Hundreth Congresses produces a slightly smaller (but still statistically significant) slope of −.45.

What these results mean depends on what constitutes evidence that parties are important in structuring floor voting. Cooper, Brady, and Hurley argue that intraparty cohesion *and* interparty conflict must both exist before one can say that parties are important. Indeed, they measure the importance of party in structuring floor votes by *multiplying* intraparty unity (measured by Rice's coefficient of cohesion) and interparty conflict (measured by party vote percentages). They clearly state that high internal cohesion alone is not evidence of party strength: "in a context of low divisiveness [internal cohesion] does not testify to the strength of party as a determinant of voting" (Cooper, Brady, and Hurley 1977, 35–36).

2. Party votes are defined as recorded votes in which a majority of nonabstaining Republicans oppose a majority of nonabstaining Democrats (with pairs counted as nonabstaining). Their frequency is, in the present context, measured relative to the total number of recorded votes.

3. They measure "time" by Congress number, as do we in the regression reported next in the text.

Given this view of party strength, it follows that the decline in the relative frequency of party votes is straightforward evidence that "party strength" is declining. We do not share this multiplicative view of party strength, however. Consider the hypothetical case of a cohesive majority party that succeeds in passing its program against an opposition so divided (or co-opted) that the relative frequency of party votes is very low. Is party really not very important in this situation? It is *ex hypothesi* important to what gets passed. And it is important, too, in structuring the votes of the majority. It is only for the minority that party seems unimportant.

What, then, should one make of the trend in party votes? Recent work by Collie (1988a) fills in some more pieces of the puzzle by tracking not just party votes but also two other categories: roll calls on which at least 90 percent of the voting members vote in the same direction, which can be called *universal votes,* and a *residual category* of roll calls that are neither party votes nor universal votes. At least for the period that Collie studies (1933–80), the decline in party votes as a percentage of all roll calls is not mirrored by an accompanying incline in the residual category of votes. Collie finds that there is essentially no trend in the residual category. The bulk of the action is in party votes and universal votes, with the latter increasing as the former declines. Thus, the relative decrease in party votes does not reflect the increasing activity of shifting cross-party coalitions so much as the increasing activity of universal coalitions. The chief puzzle is not why moderately sized bipartisan coalitions have become more prevalent but why nearly unanimous coalitions have become more prevalent.

It seems quite possible to answer this question in a way that does not do much damage to one's image of how important parties are in determining floor votes. What seems to need explaining is why "motherhood and apple pie" votes are recorded more and more frequently or, perhaps, why small minorities find it more and more worthwhile to push things to a vote—not why parties are less powerful or important.[4]

Suppose one excluded the nearly unanimous votes from analysis, as is often done in computing internal cohesion. Would there still be any substantial trend? The answer is less clear than when dealing with all

---

4. In the early 1880s in Great Britain, Irish obstructionists forced a huge number of divisions on the issue of home rule. Both major English parties opposed these initiatives overwhelmingly, and consequently the party vote percentages for these years are much lower than for either preceding or succeeding years. Yet no one argues that any significant decline in the strength or opposition of the parties occurred.

roll calls. If one regresses party votes (as a percentage of nonuniversal votes) on time for the period examined by Collie, there is still a significant negative declivity. The slope is no longer significant, however, if one deletes the Seventy-third Congress (1933–34).[5] Moreover, the decline is far from steady. The average party vote percentages by decade for the 1930s though 1970s are 73.1, 60.3, 65.5, 62.1, and 57.0. The decline from the 1930s to the 1940s seems relatively large; but not much happens from the 1940s to the 1960s.

How much should one make of the 8 to 13 percentage points that separate the House in the 1930s from that in the succeeding three decades? This difference is not always clearly interpretable as party decline. Suppose, for example, that the Republicans stopped opposing core New Deal programs in the later decades after their popularity became obvious. Then votes on such programs should have been passed by bipartisan majorities, where previously they had been passed by the Democrats alone. Such a change says that the minority party is throwing in the towel, not that party—the majority party in particular—is less important in understanding what policy is passed and what is not. It would be hard to argue, on the basis of the party vote evidence alone, that the congressional parties were markedly less important in the 1940s, 1950s, and 1960s than they were in the 1930s.

2.2   INTRAPARTY COHESION

Let us consider also the evidence on intraparty cohesion. This category can be divided into two subcategories depending on whether cohesion is averaged over all roll calls or just over party votes. The first type of evidence (cohesion on all roll calls) is presented by Cooper, Brady, and Hurley (1977) and Clubb and Traugott (1977). Both find little trend over the periods that they examine (1887–1969 and 1861–1974, respectively). As Clubb and Traugott (1977, 394–95) report, based on an investigation of the longer period, "the average index of cohesion for the Republicans is effectively uncorrelated" with time, and the correlation for the Democrats is "at best only moderately higher." They conclude, "Taken in total, it appears that declining trends in party voting

5. The Seventy-third Congress is the first in the series and has the second highest party vote percentage in the entire data set. That the regression slope is no longer significant when this Congress is excluded reflects the well-known sensitivity of bivariate OLS regressions to the value of the dependent variable corresponding to extreme values of the independent variable.

in the House can best be characterized as involving diminution of differences between the parties [as reflected in the decline in the relative frequency of party votes] rather than generalized and increasing partisan disunity" (397). Nonetheless, the cohesion figures in certain subperiods do show a decline. In particular, Clubb and Traugott report regressions on time for the period from 1897 to 1933 and find large and significantly negative slopes for both parties.

Clubb and Traugott also examine party cohesion on party votes alone rather than on all roll calls. These data corroborate the negative slope for both parties in the 1897–1933 period—and show a continuing decline in the 1933–74 period. Similarly, Collie (1988a) finds that the average percentage of party members voting with a majority of their party in the 1933–80 period falls from nearly 90 percent in the Seventy-third Congress (1933–34) down almost to 70 percent in the Ninety-first and Ninety-second Congresses, recovering thereafter.

Although the trends in cohesion on party votes are fairly clear, what they tell us about parties is less so. Some roll calls concern minor issues on which the parties do not oppose one another; those who discard universal votes before computing average cohesion are usually attempting to correct for such minor issues. Others employ a similar rationale in looking at cohesion only on party votes, since roll calls on which party majorities oppose one another are more likely to involve important partisan issues.

Even roll calls on which party majorities oppose one another, however, may not be "party votes" in the sense that some party leader wished to bring them on, was active in organizing support behind one side or the other, or held out the possibility of punishment or reward for members of the party. Yet if one is interested in the strength of parties as organizations, then the attitude of party leaders is crucial.

The point can be made clearer by reference to a distinction made in British politics between "whip" votes and "open" votes. Whip votes are those on which a party's whip organization is active—and this activity demonstrates that the party leadership is united in favor of the position that the whips are urging. Open votes, in contrast, are those on which the party leadership—hence, the whip organization—is silent. No one would think to measure the strength of the leadership of British parties by the levels of party cohesion on open votes. We think a similar restriction should apply to studies of party cohesion in the United States.

It is true, of course, that party leaders in the United States are much less powerful than are their counterparts in the United Kingdom. But that is beside the point. The leadership of a U.S. party varies in the degree to which it is united and in the degree to which it communicates its intent to its followers. The importance of party leaders as voting cues should be measured by the frequency with which they give fairly clear cues and the cohesion of their followers when they do.

Following this line of thought, we adopt the following definitions: for a given party, the *party agenda* is the set of all roll calls on which its top leadership is active and unified, and a *party agenda vote* is a roll call in the party agenda. A *party leadership vote* is a roll call on which the top leadership of one party is unified in opposition to the top leadership of the other. (We give operational definitions of both these terms in the next section.)

Cohesion on party leadership votes and on party agenda votes seems more readily interpretable than is cohesion on party votes conventionally defined. On party leadership votes, for example, the parties clearly confront one another in a meaningful sense. On party votes as usually defined, however, issues devoid of organized partisan conflict may very well find majorities of the parties opposed simply because of the like-mindedness of members of the same party. If like-mindedness is of interest, then perhaps such roll calls should be included. But if the strength of the parties as organizations is at issue, then one presumably wants to isolate those roll calls on which the organizations are indeed active. The appropriate measures of a party's strength then are (1) the *size* of the party's agenda and (2) the party's cohesion in support of its leadership on the party agenda. In the next section we take this approach.

3.   PARTY AGENDAS AND PARTY LEADERSHIP VOTES

One might identify roll calls on which the leadership of a given party was active in any of a number of ways. One method would be to include only those roll calls prior to which the party's whip organization had polled the membership and made clear the leadership's position. Another method would be to include roll calls only on issues that the party leaders had identified publicly as of concern to them as leaders of the party.

The problem with these methods is that getting information on the relevant actions is difficult. Except for a few Congresses, we simply do not know the issues on which the parties' whip organizations have been active. And there is no single forum in which party leaders have announced their agendas so that one could be assured of comparability across time.

The method that we have employed to identify party agendas relies on the voting behavior of the majority and minority leaders and whips. On each roll call we have ascertained how the floor leader and whip for each party voted. If a party's leader and whip both voted on the same side, then that side was taken to be the party leadership's position (which, henceforth, we also refer to as the party's position). The party agenda can then be defined in either of two ways. One way is to include all roll calls on which the party has a position, though this definition yields party agendas that are probably too large: roll calls on which both leader and whip vote on the same side constitute about 70–75 percent of all roll calls in the typical Congress (at least in the 1933–89 period). Moreover, on many votes both parties' leaders are on the same side of the issue, indicating that it is not a matter of partisan division. A second definition of the party agenda—the one that we shall use in what follows—excludes these votes. Thus, the *party agenda* is the set of all roll calls on which the party has a position and on which the other party takes either no position or an opposed position. If both parties have a position and these positions are opposed, then the roll call is considered to be a *party leadership vote*.

These operational definitions obviously do not perfectly capture the original conceptions of party agendas and party leadership votes. On the one hand, the operational definitions are likely to be too inclusive. The floor leader and whip of a party may both vote on the same side of a roll call without taking any stand or exerting any effort *as party leaders*. Their votes may both be cast in a purely private capacity. On the other hand, the operational definitions may also, on occasion, be too exclusive. Illness or unavoidable commitments may prevent a leader from voting, even on an issue to which he and the other top leaders have devoted considerable attention.

Nonetheless, our definitions have the considerable advantage of being systematically implementable for a large number of Congresses. Party floor leaders and whips are both identifiable by the opening decade of the twentieth century. There are several gaps in the lists of Democratic whips in the first three decades of the century, but by the 1930s the lists are complete and the office well established.

We have chosen to begin our analysis with the New Deal, conforming to one of the conventional cutting points in the literature (cf. Clubb and Traugott 1977; Collie 1998a). We end our analyses with the Ninety-sixth Congress, thus omitting the 1980s, in order to make our results comparable with those of earlier studies.

3.1 PARTY AGENDAS

We look first at the size of party agendas, the levels of support for leaders on these agendas, and the trends in these two variables. The measure of size is simply the number of roll calls in the party agenda as a percentage of all roll calls. The relevant figures for both parties are presented in table 19. For the Democrats, the size of the party agenda ranges from a low of 23.6 percent of all roll calls to a high of 67.7 percent, with a median of 45.4 percent. The Republican figures are similar but generally lower. Over the period stretching from the Seventy-third to the Ninety-sixth Congress, regressions on time reveal a decline in the size of the agenda for both parties. However, the decline is statistically discernible from zero only for the Republicans.

Support for the party agenda is measured by a leadership support score, calculated as the percentage of times a legislator voted with party leaders or paired in their favor on party agenda votes (the denominator for the percentage being the total number of party agenda votes on which the legislator participated, either voting or pairing).[6] The average of these leadership support scores, for each party and each Congress, is reported graphically in figure 6 (the Democrats) and figure 7 (the Republicans). Regressions on time of these averages show a large ($-.66$) and significant ($t = 7.1$) decline for the Republicans, a small ($-.09$) and insignificant ($t = .4$) decline for the Democrats.

These results merit some consideration. Previous investigators have found that cohesion declines significantly for both parties when averaged over all party votes. Our results show a significant decline only for the Republicans. What explains the difference in conclusions regarding the Democrats?

The difference is not due to the use of average *support scores* rather than average *cohesion coefficients*. These measures correlate at a very high level, when averaged over the same roll call base. Indeed, if every legislator votes in every roll call, then the average across legislators of

---

6. This measure of party loyalty or leadership support is essentially the same as that used by Mayhew (1966).

TABLE 19.   THE SIZE OF PARTY AGENDAS,
SEVENTY-THIRD TO HUNDREDTH CONGRESSES

Congress	Total Roll Call Votes	Democratic Party Agenda as % of All Roll Calls [b]	Republican Party Agenda as % of All Roll Calls [b]	Party Leadership Votes as % of All Roll Calls [c]
Seventy-third	143	65.7	56.6	40.6
Seventy-fourth	212	23.6	55.2	10.4
Seventy-fifth	158	67.7	48.7	35.4
Seventy-sixth	227	52.0	53.3	33.0
Seventy-seventh	152	65.1	32.9	30.2
Seventy-eighth	156	44.2	54.5	32.1
Seventy-ninth	231	57.1	45.9	35.1
Eightieth	163	42.3	59.5	33.7
Eighty-first	275	46.5	39.3	23.6
Eighty-second	181	62.4	47.0	35.9
Eighty-third	147	27.9	50.3	23.8
Eighty-fourth	149	41.6	34.9	26.2
Eighty-fifth	193	39.9	44.0	21.8
Eighty-sixth	180	52.2	43.9	35.6
Eighty-seventh	240	52.9	38.8	24.2
Eighty-eighth	232	52.2	41.8	32.2
Eighty-ninth	394	41.9	43.9	26.4
Ninetieth	478	40.2	34.9	19.7
Ninety-first	443	26.2	25.1	13.1
Ninety-second	649	33.1	37.6	17.1
Ninety-third	1,078	42.1	32.8	18.7
Ninety-fourth	1,273	49.4	36.2	22.5
Ninety-fifth	1,540	41.4	32.9	16.3
Ninety-sixth	1,276	45.4	34.4	18.9
Ninety-seventh	812	40.3	38.2	21.8
Ninety-eighth	896	45.3	45.6	27.3
Ninety-ninth	890	52.9	49.6	33.9
Hundredth [a]	488	63.5	53.7	42.4

[a] First session only.

[b] The Democratic party agenda is defined as the set of all recorded votes on which (1) both the Democratic floor leader and the Democratic chief whip voted on the same side; and (2) it was not the case that both the Republican leader and whip agreed with the Democratic leaders. The Republican party agenda is defined similarly.

[c] The set of party leadership votes consists of all recorded votes such that the Democratic floor leader and whip oppose the Republican floor leader and whip. It is the intersection of the two party agendas, as defined in note b.

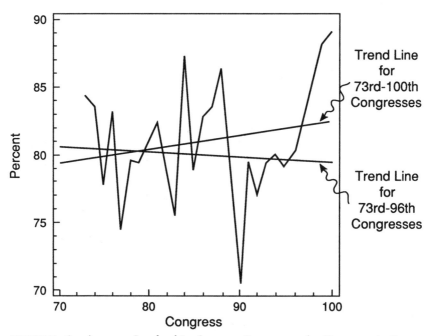

FIGURE 6. Average Leadership Support Scores on the Democratic Party Agenda, Seventy-third to Hundredth Congresses

party support scores must equal the average across roll calls of cohesion coefficients.[7]

So the difference in results must be traced to the difference in roll calls used: the set of votes on which a party's leadership takes a united stand (and is not joined by the other party's leaders) is not coextensive with the set of party votes as conventionally defined. Consider some figures for the Eighty-fourth through Eighty-sixth Congresses. There were 255 party votes in these three Congresses, only 177 of which were in the Democratic party agenda. The other 78 (or 31 percent) divide into three classes: (1) 10 votes on which the Democratic leader and whip voted against one another; (2) 36 votes on which either the leader or the whip abstained; and (3) 32 votes on which the Democratic leadership and the Republican leadership agreed. Clearly, there were enough

7. This point holds, simply as a mathematical identity, if the party support scores used tally the percentage of times a legislator agrees with the majority of his or her party. It holds for the leadership support scores used here only if unified party leaderships are always supported by a majority of their followers. Even if this condition does not always hold, however, if it holds in the vast majority of cases, then the claim is approximately true; and, more important, the broader point made in the text is largely valid.

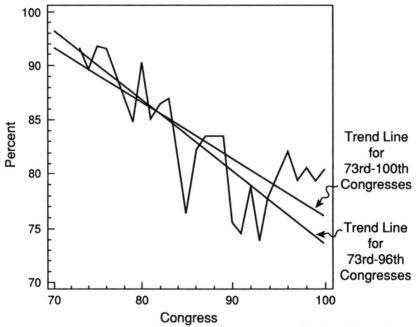

FIGURE 7. Average Leadership Support Scores on the Republican Party Agenda, Seventy-third to Hundredth Congresses

party votes not in the Democratic agenda—and, for that matter, enough party agenda votes that were not party votes[8]—so that cohesion figures calculated over party votes and cohesion figures calculated over party agenda votes need not be the same in any given Congress. Thus, trends in the two measures may differ, and indeed we found that they do: Democratic cohesion declined over time on party votes, but not on party agenda votes.

This difference should probably have been expected. The regional split in the Democratic party between North and South is well known and well represented among party votes (Rohde 1988; 1989; 1990b). Thus, as the North-South split in the Democratic party worsened (with the onset of civil rights issues), it automatically produced a decline in the cohesion figures for party votes. But there are two reasons why this split is probably underrepresented on the Democratic party agenda. First, what goes into the agenda is a matter of choice. If the top leaders of the majority party seek to avoid being drubbed on the floor, they may choose

8. There were fifty-six such votes in the Eighty-fourth through Eighty-sixth Congresses.

to abstain on certain issues. But abstention by either leader or whip removes the roll call from the party agenda. Second, on issues that split the Democratic party, the floor leader and whip may themselves be split. This circumstance also would remove the roll call from the party agenda.

The primary effect of the North-South split, therefore, should not have been to reduce cohesion on the party agenda, but rather to make the party agenda smaller. Assuming that the leadership got neither better nor worse over time at anticipating defeats and avoiding them, one would expect no particular trend in cohesion, but a decline in the size of the agenda. Similarly, if the floor leader and whip became neither better nor worse as barometers of splits in the party, then one would again expect a decline in the size of the agenda but no decline in cohesion.

This is basically the pattern of evidence that we find: no significant trend in Democratic cohesion and a decline in the size of the agenda. The decline is not significant, however, and one might wonder why. If the North-South split was large enough to produce a significant declivity in cohesion on party votes, but cohesion on the party agenda shows little trend, does this not suggest that increasingly many party votes must have been excluded from the agenda, so that it should have shrunk significantly?

There are two points to consider in this regard. First, if one looks at the size of the *majority party's* agenda, rather than at the size of the Democrats' agenda (using the Republican figures for the Eightieth and Eighty-third Congresses), one finds a significant decline. Two of the smallest Democratic agendas occur in these Congresses, when the Democrats were in the minority. As both Congresses are in the first half of the period investigated, they tend to flatten the slope of decline. By contrast, two of the largest Republican agendas occur in these Congresses, so substituting the Republican figures strengthens the downward trend in the size of the majority party's agenda.

Second, the Seventy-fourth Congress was an unusual one for the Democrats. Their floor leader, William B. Bankhead, was seriously ill throughout the first session and did not vote at all.[9] This poor attendance record translates into the smallest party agenda for the Democrats in the entire period: 23.6 percent. If the Seventy-fourth Congress is omitted as an outlier, then the decline becomes significant.

---

9. See *New York Times*, 22 Dec. 1935.

If one adopts one or both of the latter two explanations, then one finds an average decline of 0.73 to 1.09 percentage points per Congress in the size of the majority party's agenda, this decline being statistically discernible from zero. Over the span of about twenty Congresses, these figures translate into an estimated decline from about 65 percent in the early 1930s to about 45 percent in the late 1970s.

3.2   PARTY LEADERSHIP VOTES

A set of questions similar to those just asked about party agendas can be asked also about party leadership votes (i.e., those roll calls in the intersection of the two parties' agendas). How many party leadership votes have there been, relative to all roll calls? How much support from their followers have the top leaders received? How have these two variables changed over time?

The answers can be given briefly. First, party leadership votes as a percentage of all roll calls have declined significantly (table 6). This decline was to be expected given that (1) the size of both parties' agendas declined and (2) the set of all party leadership votes is the intersection of the two party agendas.

Second, average levels of support for the leadership decline for both parties (see figures 8 and 9). The decline for the Republicans, however, is much larger and much steadier. The decline for the Democrats, although statistically discernible from zero, needs to be hedged by caveats similar to those we noted above when discussing the size of the party agenda. First, if one excludes the Seventy-fourth Congress (in which the Democrat's floor leader was absent unusually often), then the decline in average leadership support scores is no longer statistically significant for the Democrats. Second, if one looks at the figures for the majority party—which entails substituting the Republican averages for the Democratic averages in the Eightieth and Eighty-third Congresses—then, again, there is no statistically significant decline.

Moreover, the plot of average leadership support scores for the Democrats over time (figure 8) shows virtually no trend over the period from the Seventy-third to the Eighty-eighth Congresses (confirmed by a regression slope of 0.003 for this period). This period of practically no change was followed by a sharp decline in the Eighty-ninth and Ninetieth Congresses, fluctuations in the Ninety-first through Ninety-fifth Congresses, and a large, monotonic increase thereafter. It would be hard to explain this pattern with a story of secular party decline.

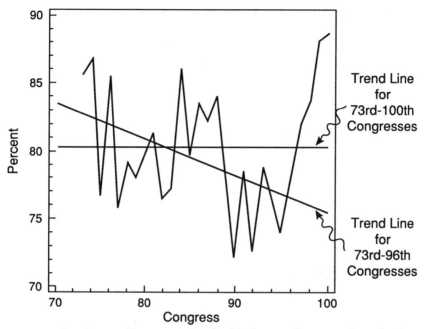

FIGURE 8.   Average Democratic Leadership Support Scores on Party Leadership Votes, Seventy-third to Hundredth Congresses

Another way to underscore this point is to look directly at the majority party leadership's "batting average": the percentage of all leadership opposition votes that it wins. In the Seventy-third through the Seventy-ninth Congresses, the majority party leadership won, on average, 75 percent of the time; in the Eightieth through Eighty-eighth, it won 77 percent of the time; in the Eighty-ninth through Ninety-fifth, 74 percent of the time; and in the Ninety-sixth through Hundredth, 81 percent of the time. [10] These figures, too, provide little support for any notion of secular decline.

It would seem that when civil rights, the Great Society, and the Vietnam War came to dominate the Democratic agenda, southern Democrats abruptly became more disloyal to the leadership. This conjecture

10.   These figures are calculated as follows: First, within each period, the total number of leadership opposition votes was counted, excluding votes that pertained to suspension of the rules or to attempts to override a presidential veto; these votes were excluded because they involved a two-thirds rather than a simple majority vote. Second, within each period the number of leadership opposition votes, not involving suspensions or veto overrides, won by the majority party was counted. Third, this latter number was divided by the former to yield the majority party leadership's batting average on "ordinary" votes (those not requiring a two-thirds vote to pass).

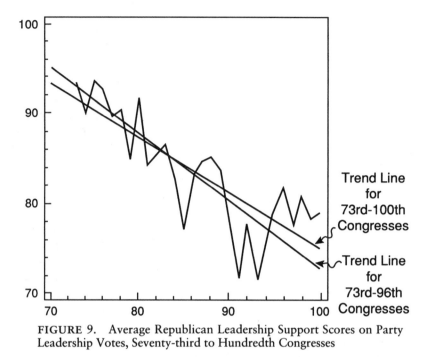

FIGURE 9.   Average Republican Leadership Support Scores on Party
Leadership Votes, Seventy-third to Hundredth Congresses

is confirmed by figure 10, which plots separately the average leadership
support scores for northern and southern Democrats; there is essentially no trend in the loyalty of northern Democrats. The drop-off in
the overall figures in the Eighty-ninth through Ninety-fifth Congresses
is produced primarily by the large decline in southern loyalty. Similarly,
the marked recovery in overall Democratic party loyalty in the late 1970s
and 1980s is primarily due to the return of southern loyalty to pre–
civil-rights levels.

4.   CONCLUSION

All told, the roll call evidence does not suggest a secular decline for both
parties in the post–New Deal era. The decline for the Republicans can
accurately be characterized in this way: both the size of their party agenda
and their cohesion on this agenda diminished considerably, and fairly
steadily, from FDR to Reagan. But the story is different for the Democrats. Their party agenda does shrink (growing again in the 1980s), but
there is no evidence of a long-term erosion of party cohesion on the
party agenda. Rather, there is a sharp dip in the Eighty-ninth through

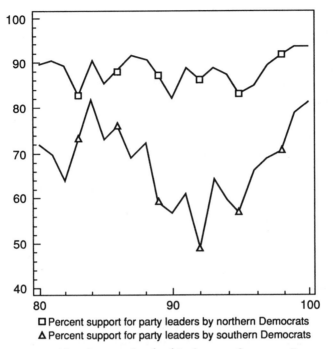

☐ Percent support for party leaders by northern Democrats
△ Percent support for party leaders by southern Democrats

FIGURE 10.   Average Leadership Support Scores on Party Leadership Votes, Northern and Southern Democrats, Seventy-third to Hundredth Congresses

Ninety-fifth Congresses, produced mainly by the reaction of southern Democrats to civil rights and the Vietnam War, with a substantial recovery thereafter.

These results seem to us precisely those that would be expected were a system of "conditional party government" (Rohde 1991) in operation throughout the postwar era. The gist of conditional party government is that the party leadership is active only when there is substantial agreement among the rank and file on policy goals. If this hypothesis is true, one would expect that decreases in party homogeneity should lead, not to decreases in the level of support given to leaders when they take a stand, but rather to leaders taking fewer stands. This is essentially what we find.

Our results also cast an interesting light on an old debate about the interpretation of roll call evidence. It is well known that a legislator's party affiliation is the single best predictor of his roll call voting behavior (Truman 1959; Turner and Schneier 1970). But many (e.g., Shannon 1968; Fiorina 1974, 2–3) have pointed out that this statistical result does not necessarily testify to the strength of the congressional party. After all, members of the same party tend to have similar reelection constituencies, distinct from those of the other party.[11] Thus, Democrats may vote differently from Republicans simply because they are responding to a different set of constituency pressures. Credence is lent to this view by the finding that a major determinant of the level of party cohesion in a Congress is the homogeneity of the party's constituency base (Cooper, Brady, and Hurley 1977; Brady, Cooper, and Hurley 1979).

Because party and constituency are so obviously collinear, some question whether the party organization has exerted any independent influence at all on voting behavior. In the skeptics' eyes, the only real evidence that the party organization has influenced voting behavior consists of scattered anecdotes about Speakers lining up "pocket" votes on key issues (see, e.g., Ripley 1969b)—and these anecdotes are counterbalanced by many others that show postwar leaders (especially John McCormack and Carl Albert) to be inactive and weak.

We think that the debate over the strength of party as an influence on voting behavior has focused too narrowly on the meting out of tangible rewards and punishments by party leaders. Another reason that members of the same party might vote together, above and beyond the similarity of their constituents' interests, is that they have entangled themselves in various logrolls or policy alliances. Thus, for example, urban Democrats support agricultural subsidies in return for rural Democrats' support of food stamps (Ripley 1969a; Ferejohn 1986). This deal may have been facilitated by the party leadership, but the reason that urban and rural Democrats voted together more often than they might otherwise have done is not that the leadership raced around threatening dire consequences to all and sundry; dire consequences needed to be visited only on those who took a "free ride" on the deal without a good excuse.

From this perspective, the abrupt decline in the loyalty of southern Democrats in the Eighty-ninth Congress is intriguing. Our interpretation of this decline is that the southern conservatives, seeing that the

---

11. *Reelection constituency* refers to those voters in a member's geographical constituency who have voted for him in the past and will continue to do so, with a little nursing, in the future; see Fenno 1978.

single most important part of their deal with the dominant liberal wing—keeping civil rights off the agenda—had been broken in spectacular fashion, no longer felt disposed to enter into new deals or to carry through their end of old deals. Thus, the size of the decline in average loyalty among southerners is a crude indicator of the component of party cohesion created by intraparty logrolls.

PART FOUR

Parties as Procedural Coalitions: Committee Appointments

In articulating our view of parties, we have thus far discussed the incentives of party leaders (part 2) and the behavior of parties as floor coalitions (part 3). In this and the next part of the book we focus on the extent to which parties—the majority party in particular—can control the standing committees of the House. To put the question in another way, we are interested in whether committees function to some degree as agents of the majority party.

The literature presents at least three different views on the question of agency: committees have been considered as agents of no one but themselves, as agents of the House, and as agents of the majority party. The first of these views, in which committees are agents of neither the House nor the majority party, is associated with the purer versions of the "committee government" model. From this perspective, committees are autonomous agents, acting to further the interests of their own self-selected and "tenured" members. The second view, in which committees are agents of the House, finds clearest expression in historical surveys of the early development of the committee system (e.g., Cooper 1970), but it is also apparent in, for example, Robinson's description of the Rules Committee (Robinson 1963) and Fenno's description of the Appropriations Committee (see, for example, Fenno 1966; Oppenheimer 1977). The last view of committee agency appears mostly in descriptions of Congress at the turn of the century, during the era of strong Speakers. Implicitly, this view sees the ties between the majority party and its various committee contingents as strong enough so that committees are reliable vehicles for party government; any competing ties between the committee as a whole and the House as a whole, or tendencies toward autonomous action, are of secondary importance.

Much of the postwar literature is an uneasy compromise between the first two views. Committees are seen as autonomous actors in their own right, exerting important and independent influence on policy; but they are also viewed as anticipating what will fly on the floor.[1] Depending on how this anticipation of floor preferences affects internal committee deliberations, the model ends up veering toward one or the other of the polar possibilities: complete autonomy or complete agency.

If committees are modeled as having substantial (and exogenous) institutional powers—*ex post* vetoes and the right to bring bills to the floor under closed rules, for example—then they end up exerting considerable influence over policy (Shepsle and Weingast 1987a; 1987b). They look rather autonomous and their anticipation of floor preferences is simply a necessary preliminary to circumventing them. By contrast, if committees are modeled as creatures of the House (so that none of their institutional powers is exogenous), then their independent impact on policy begins to fade away and their anticipation of what will fly on the floor begins to look like the mechanism whereby the floor gets what it wants (Gilligan and Krehbiel 1990).

In the empirical literature this progression of models can be seen as one goes from the subgovernment literature, with its strong emphasis on the autonomy of the "iron triangles" that dominate different fragments of policy, to the literature on, say, Wilbur Mills's Ways and Means Committee, with its strong emphasis both on Mills's concern with anticipating what would win on the floor and on his ability to craft bipartisan coalitions that would stand up there. Even the literature on Ways and Means, however, has a considerable admixture of the first or "committee autonomy" model: in particular, Ways and Means' privileged access to the floor and its tradition of going to the floor under a closed rule have commonly been viewed as giving it substantial influence.

In this part we emphasize the third of the models listed above, wherein committees are vehicles of party government. We are certainly not arguing that some pure version of this model provides a complete explanation of congressional politics. But we do think that the ways in which

---

1. Although Cooper clearly sees committees as agents of the House, he also finds a large amount of slack in the agency relationship. For example, he finds evidence of committee autonomy, based on intercommittee deference and vote trading, even in very early Congresses. See Cooper 1970, 16.

the majority party influences the committee system are not adequately appreciated.

Many scholars recognize that the majority party might in principle exert control over committees—by creating and destroying them, assigning them tasks and giving them the resources to accomplish those tasks, regulating their personnel, and providing for the review and revision of their decisions. But the dominant view is that most of these potential levers of control are not often or effectively pulled by the majority party.[2]

We think that several key techniques of control, especially those pertinent to setting the legislative agenda, have been regularly used throughout the postwar era: party and staff ratios have been consistently set in the majority party's favor; the appointment power has, we argue in chapter 7, been consistently used to advance those more loyal to the party leadership; and the scheduling power has been used consistently for partisan purposes. It is on these more constant elements that we will focus in this part of the book. Specifically, we focus on the appointment power in this part of the book and on the scheduling power in the next part of the book. This approach leaves plenty of other avenues of influence uninvestigated: we see a whole range of structure and process employed, but these are two of the most important.[3]

2. For example, it is often noted that discharge petitions are very rarely successful (e.g., Ripley 1983, 145–46). What is less often noted is that they may be unsuccessful for many reasons other than committee power and autonomy. For example, the committee may have correctly calculated that there is not a floor majority in favor of the bill at issue, whereas the filer of the petition incorrectly believes otherwise. Alternatively, perhaps there is a majority in favor of the bill being reported. In this case the committee chair may agree to schedule hearings after the petition is filed but before it has the required number of signatures; or the committee may report some other, related bill that satisfies enough of the majority for discharge so that actual discharge is averted; or the Senate may send a related bill to the House so that the issue becomes moot before the petition acquires enough signatures; and so on.

3. For example, in studies of the appropriations committees and the congressional spending process, Fenno (1966) and Kiewiet and McCubbins (1991) examine how House and Senate rules serve to constrain and direct the activities of the appropriations committees. Fenno details how the rules requiring prior authorization before appropriations can be made put checks on the committees' actions. Kiewiet and McCubbins examine the procedures specified in the Congressional Budget and Impoundment Control Act and how they serve to channel the choices of the appropriations committees and to impart greater leadership influence into their decisions.

SEVEN

Party Loyalty and Committee Assignments

The evidence presented in chapter 1 led us to question whether the committee assignment process in the postwar House has been mostly an exercise in self-selection, as often asserted. There seems ample room in the process for discretion and, in particular, for partisan discretion. In this chapter we investigate whether partisan criteria enter the assignment process in a statistically discernible fashion. This issue is important because it relates to one of the key structural powers that party leaders might exercise. If they do not in fact use this power, then our view of how parties operate will need revision.

We are interested in particular in whether *party leaders* are able to affect committee assignment decisions. Certainly, the power of party leaders is not what it once was. Until the revolt against Boss Cannon in 1910 the Speaker made all majority party assignments (and, before the turn of the century, all minority party assignments as well).[1] Since the revolt both parties have resorted to a system in which a party CC recommends all assignments, with the caucus ratifying (or rejecting) the committee's recommendations. No one, however, has argued that party leaders have had no influence over the appointments made by the parties' CCs. Indeed, many anecdotes illustrate the ability of party leaders to secure committee assignments for those they favor (thereby denying them to others less favored).[2] Moreover, there is widespread agreement

---

1. See Shepsle 1978 for a historical survey.
2. Some of the best are reviewed by Shepsle 1978; Smith and Deering 1990; Hinckley 1983; Gertzog 1976; and Rohde 1991.

that the "interest-advocacy-accommodation syndrome" does not fully apply to what Goodwin (1970) termed the *control committees:* Appropriations, Rules, and Ways and Means.

In this chapter we reassess the role of party leaders in determining committee assignments. We first review the literature on assignments to the control committees of the House. We then examine committee transfers, testing the null hypothesis that loyalty to the party leadership has no effect on the success of a member's transfer requests. Finally, we test a similar null hypothesis for the assignments received by freshman members.

1.   ASSIGNMENTS TO CONTROL COMMITTEES

The special nature of appointments to the control committees has long been appreciated. Masters (1961, 352), for example, writing of the early postwar House, noted that "the three exclusive committees . . . are regarded by all in both parties as being of special importance." As a consequence, appointments to these committees were made differently than were appointments to other committees:

> [Members are] selected by the party leadership in consultation with the members of the committee on committees, rather than the other way around. A nominee's name may be first brought up by the party leaders, a committee member, or even by someone not involved with the mechanics, but whatever the technical circumstances surrounding the introduction of his name, if the nominee is assigned, he bears the party leaders' stamp of approval. This is true in both parties.

In his study of the Committee on Ways and Means, Manley (1970, 24) stresses that its membership was of special importance to the Democratic leadership:

> Year in and year out the Committee handles legislation that is vital to the administration's foreign and domestic policy, and it is the party leader's job to get this legislation through the House. . . . The jurisdiction of Ways and Means, then, is enough to generate leadership concern about who is recruited to the committee. But there is another reason too. . . . The Speaker, if he is to exert any influence over the vital committee assignment process, has to work through and with the Ways and Means Democrats.

Manley's interviews seem to indicate active and purposive intervention by the Democratic leadership in assignments to Ways and Means in the 1950s and 1960s. All of the Ways and Means Committee members Manley interviewed affirmed this special interest by the Democratic leadership, and "thirteen of the eighteen [Ways and Means] Democrats interviewed mentioned the leadership as playing an important part in their successful candidacies. In at least six known cases . . . the leadership took the initiative by asking the members to go on Ways and Means, and in the others the members made a call on the leadership first or second priority in their campaign for the Committee" (Manley 1970, 25).

Similarly, in his analysis of the Ways and Means Committee in the 1960s and 1970s, Shepsle (1978, 145) finds that "leadership endorsement . . . is an important, though not always decisive, element in recruitment to the Ways and Means Committee. . . . As one current member of the committee remarked, 'We are elected by the *party* as you know. You have to be acceptable to get on Ways and Means.' " Shepsle also notes that special attention was given to the other control committees and, indeed, that the assignment process accorded them a certain pride of place. In the meetings of the Democratic CC, Shepsle reports, "the usual practice is to take up Appropriations and Rules first, along with one or two semiexclusive committees, e.g. Interstate, for which there is considerable competition. After disposing of these, the remaining semiexclusive committees are taken in alphabetical order, followed by the nonexclusive committees in alphabetical order" (179).

In summarizing the evidence on Democratic assignments to control committees in the 1960s and 1970s, Shepsle notes that

> assignments to the exclusive committees (Appropriations, Rules, Ways and Means) constitute a unique subprocess of the committee assignment process in which the interest-request-assignment pattern that dominates assignments to the substantive legislative committees does not have as much force. Only for Appropriations may it be said that the request/assignment linkage is a strong one, and even here a substantial number of assignments are prearranged, bypassing normal request channels. Ways and Means assignments, of course, are determined by Caucus election, and Rules assignments are dominated by the preferences of the Speaker. (228)

In the 1980s, Hinckley (1983, 149) reports, party loyalty has been an overt criterion for assignment to a variety of "important" committees:

> On the committees the leadership considers most critical, party loyalty is an important assignment criterion. During the sessions of the Steering and Policy Committee in the Ninety-sixth Congress, members reportedly brought in various measures of party loyalty and wrote these on a blackboard next to

the nominee's name. As one of the leaders commented: "we tried to put reasonable people on the [important] committees. Some members who wanted new assignments didn't get what they wanted. Members who never go with the leadership—never help out. It's not only [the other leaders] and I who did this. The other Steering and Policy members—the elected ones—feel the same way."

2. PARTY LOYALTY AND TRANSFERS TO HOUSE COMMITTEES

There is substantial evidence from interviews, reviewed in the previous section, that party leaders have influenced appointments to the control committees—and that they have done so with an eye to putting those loyal to the party in key positions. There is also consistent evidence from interviews (Masters 1961; Smith and Ray 1983) that members of the Democratic CC use party loyalty as one of many criteria in allocating assignments. In this section we consider what *statistical* evidence there is that party loyalty correlates with success in securing desirable transfers. We first review some previous findings regarding transfer success in the Eighty-sixth through Ninety-seventh Congresses and then provide new results, some of which are pertinent to the entire postwar period.

2.1 PREVIOUS RESEARCH

Rohde and Shepsle (1973) investigated the success of nonfreshman Democrats in securing requested transfers in the Eighty-sixth, Eighty-seventh, Eighty-eighth, and Ninetieth Congresses. Comparing those whose party support scores surpassed "the mean for the party in the previous Congress with those who gave the party less than the mean support,"[3] they found that "in each of the four Congresses, high party supporters were more successful in securing assignments . . . than low party supporters" (904). The number of requests in their sample was not sufficiently large, however, for the differences they found to attain conventional levels of statistical significance (even when all four Congresses were polled).[4]

Smith and Ray (1983) also examined the committee assignment pro-

3. The support scores used were those given in the *Congressional Quarterly Almanac*.
4. The appropriate test is a chi-square test of independence in the two-by-two tables they present. For their table E, this test gives a figure of about 3.55, not significant at the .05 level.

cess, estimating six probit equations in which the dependent variable was whether or not a nonfreshman Democrat received an assignment for which he or she was nominated.[5] They included a measure of party loyalty—the member's *Congressional Quarterly* party unity score in the previous Congress—as one of the regressors in two of these specifications. In the first specification including party loyalty, where the only other regressors measured characteristics of the member requesting transfer, loyalty had a positive but statistically insignificant effect.[6] In their fully specified probit, with no fewer than twenty-four regressors, party loyalty's impact was both positive and significant.

Rohde and Shepsle's and Smith and Ray's results support the notion that members who are more loyal to their parties are more likely to be granted transfers that they request.[7] However, these studies have substantial limitations from the point of view of assessing the impact of party leaders on assignments in the postwar period.

First, neither of them is designed specifically to address the issue of leadership impact: both use party loyalty as a control variable in analyses constructed primarily to assess self-selection; and they both measure loyalty not to party *leaders* but to party *majorities*. Smith and Ray (1983, 224) do note that the Democratic CC has in recent years used party loyalty scores provided by the leadership in its deliberations, but they opine that the impact of these scores on assignment decisions "cannot be determined."

Second, even if Rohde and Shepsle's and Smith and Ray's studies were directly focused on the issue of leadership influence, their data are limited in several ways. Both cover only Democratic assignments. Both cover only transfers made at the beginning of Congresses, thereby excluding about a fourth of all transfers. Both investigate the importance of party loyalty only as it pertains to improving a member's chances of

5. The Democratic CC requires that members be nominated for a position on a committee before voting on the issue. See Smith and Ray 1983 for details.

6. The other regressors were vote percentage garnered in last election to Congress, region, and number of committees to which a transfer was requested.

7. Also supportive is a study by Ripley (1967) in which he investigates the success of twenty-one Democrats who requested transfer in the Eighty-eighth Congress. Of these twenty-one, eleven succeeded and ten failed in getting the transfer that they requested. Averaging "party loyalty scores for the two groups in the previous Congress," he finds that "the eleven 'successes' had a score of 67 and the ten 'failures' had a score of 34" (Ripley 1967, 60). The party loyalty score used was computed by subtracting the *Congressional Quarterly*'s party opposition score from its party unity score. No significance tests were reported. Robinson (1963, 104–5) also has some supportive data regarding the Rules Committee. Bullock (1985, 804) reports a contrary result for U.S. Senate committee assignments.

being granted a *written request* for transfer. And the two studies together cover fewer than half of the postwar Congresses.

Finally, the results they present are statistically mixed, with only one analysis in which the party loyalty coefficient attains conventional levels of significance. Moreover, Shepsle's later work (1978) is sometimes cited as showing that party loyalty has little impact on committee assignments. Waldman (1980, 377–78), for example, writes (citing Shepsle) that "work on the committee assignment process has shown that general party loyalty has . . . failed to affect assignments to most House committees." Although we cannot see that Shepsle's research supports such an inference in any straightforward way,[8] it does contribute to a perception that party loyalty matters little in the allocation of committee assignments.

2.2   WHO TRANSFERS?

In this section we consider the extent to which past loyalty to the party leadership determines who transfers and who does not. In so doing, we attempt to overcome some of the limitations just alluded to in the previous literature. Thus, the study is designed specifically with an eye to assessing the impact of party leaders and, accordingly, measures party loyalty in terms of loyalty to leaders rather than majorities. Previous studies of committee assignments, as noted above, have measured party loyalty using published *Congressional Quarterly* party unity scores. These scores give the proportion of times a member votes with a majority of his or her party on "party votes," defined as those in which majorities of the two parties are in opposition. However, not all "party votes" are ones on which we should expect the leadership to be active. We therefore use a score (explained below) defined directly in terms of support for the party leadership.

The present study also includes a larger array of data than have previous studies. In some of the analyses we include Republican assignments. We also include transfers made *during* a Congress as well as at

8. Shepsle (1978) estimated a probit equation predicting the success of nonfreshman transfer requests during the Eighty-seventh through Ninety-third Congresses. He included, as one of several regressors, a "party support differential" variable. This variable, however, was defined as the *absolute* value of the difference between the requesting member's *Congressional Quarterly* party support score and that of his or her zone representative on the Democratic CC. Thus, high scores on this variable could reflect either *low* party support scores (relative to the zone representative's) or *high* party support scores (again, relative to the zone representative's). This variable does not, therefore, test the importance of loyalty to the leadership in any straightforward way.

its beginning; transfers made pursuant to informal requests or no requests at all, as well as those made pursuant to formal written requests; and, in some of the analyses, transfers from all of the postwar Congresses (up to and including the Hundredth).

The previous literature has not marshaled any systematic statistical evidence on whether loyalty has varied in importance over the postwar era. To the extent that this issue is addressed at all, the consensus seems to be that in the 1970s there was less and less room for loyalty to play a role. For example, Smith and Ray (1983, 238) speculate that "the process has become even more a routine effort to accommodate the requests of as many members as possible." Waldman (1980, 375), writing of the late 1970s, argues that "'members do not need or depend on party leadership . . . to get desirable committee assignments as they did in the 1960s and early 1970s." Shepsle (1978, 160) sees Speakers McCormack and Albert as being "decidedly less activist" in the committee assignment process than was Speaker Rayburn. We explicitly take into account the important reforms of the 1970s, addressing for the first time in a systematic fashion whether these reforms changed the relationship between loyalty and assignment success.

2.3   DATA AND METHODS

Our analysis begins with a test of the hypothesis that the likelihood of transferring between committees increases with a member's loyalty to the party leadership, all else constant. To test this expectation, we tracked the assignment history of each member in every Congress from the Eightieth to the Hundredth. The unit of observation is thus a member-Congress.[9] For each member-Congress the dependent variable is whether or not the member transferred onto a new committee in that Congress.

Of course, not all committees are created equal. Therefore, we looked separately at transfers to four different categories of committee—all committees, control or exclusive committees, semiexclusive committees, and nonexclusive committees.[10] In other words, we defined not just one but four dependent variables:

9. Each member from each Congress appears in the analysis once. Party leaders, however, were excluded, as they typically are not eligible for committee assignments. Also excluded were freshmen and superfreshmen (those returning to Congress after an absence of one or more Congresses), since we have no data on loyalty in the previous term for such members.

10. See chapter 1, note 3, for a discussion of control, exclusive, semiexclusive, and nonexclusive committees.

1. ANYTRANS, equal to 1 if the member transferred to *any* committee in the Congress, 0 otherwise;

2. CONTRANS, equal to 1 if the member transferred to a *control* committee in the Congress, 0 otherwise;

3. SEMTRANS, equal to 1 if the member transferred to a *semiexclusive* committee in the Congress, 0 otherwise; and

4. NONTRANS, equal to 1 if the member transferred to a *nonexclusive* committee in the Congress, 0 otherwise.

By defining our dependent variables in this way, we are pooling transfers within categories of committee rather than investigating transfers committee by committee. Some such pooling is useful both from a statistical standpoint (as it increases the number of cases to examine) and from an interpretational standpoint (as it obviates the necessity of looking at twenty different equations). The pooling categories we use reflect the distinctions made by House Democrats in assigning members and are well known in the literature (Masters 1961, 351).

For each dependent variable, we estimated a probit equation with the following independent variables:[11]

1. LOYALTY: *Party loyalty,* as we use the term here, is loyalty to the leadership, defined as the percentage of times in the previous Congress that a member voted with his party leader and party whip in opposition to the party leader and whip of the opposing party.[12] Each Democratic member has a raw loyalty score computed as follows: First, all roll calls from the previous Congress in which the Democratic leader and whip voted together against the Republican leader and whip are identified. These roll calls are called *party leadership votes.* Second, the number of times that a given member votes *with* his party leaders on party leadership votes is divided by the total number of times that that member votes at all on party leadership votes (counting pairs as votes). This formula yields the member's raw loyalty score. The next step is to standardize these raw scores. First we computed the average loyalty score

11. The literature on seniority argues that members have enjoyed security of tenure on standing committees since shortly after the revolt against Cannon, which would imply that any changes in a member's assignments must reflect the member's preferences. Although we registered some qualms with this view in chapter 2, here we take this meaning of seniority at face value. Thus, in interpreting the probits to follow, we assume that all transfers are voluntary, hence desirable.

12. For simplicity, we use only a member's loyalty in the previous Congress rather than his or her entire record of loyalty over several Congresses. To use the record over several Congresses would of course reduce the number of cases available for analysis.

for both Democrats and Republicans in each Congress, along with the standard deviations for both groups. The raw loyalty scores were then standardized for both parties in the usual fashion, yielding the variable we call LOYALTY in tables 20–24.[13] Thus, we measure the loyalty of members by how many standard deviations above or below the mean loyalty for their party they were in the previous Congress. The purpose of this standardization by Congress and party is to allow us to focus on the relative loyalty of MCs, controlling for trends and cross-party differences in the overall level of discipline. We expect a positive relationship between LOYALTY and the probability of transfer.

2.   SOUTHERN: For Democrats, this variable takes on a value of 1 if the member is from the South (former Confederacy and border states) and 0 otherwise. Numerous studies have examined the differences between northern and southern Democrats in Congress (see, for example, Rohde 1991). Though we have no explicit theory about how such differences should affect committee assignments, we include it for the sake of completeness and comparability with the previous literature.

3.   TERMS: Previous studies of transfers have also found that chamber seniority matters. The greater an MC's seniority, the higher the likelihood that she will receive a transfer, all else constant. But the longer a member has been on a given committee, the less likely she is to want a transfer because of accrued committee seniority. Thus, we expect a curvilinear relationship between chamber seniority and transfers. Accordingly, we include both TERMS (equal to the number of terms a member has served) and TERMSQ (equal to the square of TERMS) in our equation, with the expectation that the coefficient on TERMS will be negative, the coefficient on TERMSQ positive. (However, we expect less of an effect for transfers to control committees, since members are likely to want promotion to a control committee almost any time they can get it.)

4.   VACANCIES: This variable gives the number of party vacancies to be filled on the committees included in each category. We measure vacancies on a committee after the fact—as the size of the party contingent on the committee in the current Congress minus the number of carryovers from the previous Congress.[14] In the probits for ANYTRANS,

13. The standardized variable, LOYALTY, is simply (1) the difference between a member's party loyalty score and the mean party loyalty score for his or her party in a given Congress, quantity divided by (2) the standard deviation of the party loyalty scores of the member's party in a given Congress.
14. We measure vacancies as follows: $V_{jt} = N_{jt} - R_{jt}$, where V_{jt} = the number of party assignments to be made on committee j at time t; N_{jt} = the number of party seats on committee j at time t; and R_{jt} = the number of party members on committee j at time $t-1$ who remain on the committee at time t. V_{jt}, however, can be rewritten as $V_{jt} = O_{jt} + T_{jt} + DS_{jt}$,

all Democratic (or all Republican) vacancies for all House committees (except Budget, Small Business, and Official Conduct) for each Congress are counted; in the probits for CONTRANS, only vacancies on the control committees are counted; similarly, for SEMTRANS and NONTRANS, only vacancies for semiexclusive and nonexclusive committees, respectively, are counted. We expect the coefficient on VACANCIES to be positive for semiexclusive and exclusive committees, since there typically is excess demand for these committees. For nonexclusive committees, however, vacancies sometimes greatly exceed formal requests (and, we assume, total requests), indicating that there is excess supply of seats; for these committees, then, the coefficient on VACANCIES will probably be smaller.[15]

5. POSTREFORM: Last, many scholars have noted that the committee reforms of the 1970s expanded the formal role of the majority party leadership in assignment decisions. One might wonder whether this increased formal role translated into an increase in the importance of loyalty as a criterion in allocating transfers. To investigate this possibility, we included an interactive term, LOYALTY∗POSTREFORM, where POSTREFORM is a dummy variable that takes on a value of 1 for the Ninety-fourth through Hundredth Congresses, and 0 otherwise.[16]

---

where O_{jt} = number of party members of committee j at time $t-1$ who do not return to Congress at time t; T_{jt} = number of party members on committee j at time $t-1$ who transferred off the committee at time t; and DS_{jt} = the change in the size of the party contingent on committee j from time $t-1$ to time t (positive or negative). The number of vacancies is thus partly endogenous to the transfer decision (see footnote 16).

15. The number of vacancies on a committee depends in part on how many members decide to transfer off that committee; there is thus some simultaneous interaction between VACANCIES and our dependent variable. (This point is ignored in the literature and probably cannot be addressed within the limits of current data.) For the most part, however, committee vacancies are determined prior to transfer decisions—by the retirement or electoral defeat of previously sitting members and by the decisions of party leaders to expand or contract the size of committees—and thus we agree with the previous literature in treating that total as predetermined.

16. Those familiar with the previous literature may wonder why we do not include variables tapping the amount of competition for a given committee or class of committees. Both Shepsle (1978) and Smith and Ray (1983) find a few such variables to be important in explaining the success of those who request transfer. We expect, however, that MCs will apply a logic reminiscent of Jacobson and Kernell's (1983) *Strategy and Choice* model for electoral competition. Jacobson and Kernell argue that prospective candidates for House seats choose strategically whether or not to run for office, depending on the quality of the competition. An inexperienced candidate is unlikely to do well against a field of experienced candidates, all else equal. Similarly, we argue that the less loyal anticipate failure if they request a spot for which there is much high quality (i.e., more loyal) competition; hence, they request assignments for which there is less competition. Further, competition is clearly endogenous to both the request decision and the assignment decision.

TABLE 20.   PARTY LOYALTY AND DEMOCRATIC
COMMITTEE TRANSFERS, EIGHTIETH TO
HUNDREDTH CONGRESSES

	Dependent Variables			
Independent Variables	ANYTRANS	CONTRANS	SEMTRANS	NONTRANS
Constant	− 0.000	− 1.604*	− 0.255*	− 0.958*
LOYALTY	0.100*	0.150*	− 0.015	0.121*
LOYALTY * POSTREFORM	− 0.054	− 0.015	− 0.020	− 0.088
SOUTHERN	0.090	0.161	− 0.037	− 0.034
TERMS	− 0.366*	− 0.095	− 0.352*	− 0.254*
TERMSQ	0.012*	− 0.004	0.015*	0.009*
VACANCIES	0.005*	0.034*	0.001	0.013*
N	4,407	4,407	4,407	4,407
% correctly predicted	83.96	96.23	93.26	93.24
Log Likelihood Ratio	1.87	4.87	3.30	3.14

* Significant at the .05 level.

In the first set of probits, reported in tables 20 and 21, we do not include a variable identifying members who requested a transfer for the simple reason that member requests are unknown for the Eightieth to Eighty-fifth, Ninety-first, and Ninety-eighth to Hundredth Congresses. In section 2.5 we reestimate the probits reported in table 20 for those Congresses for which Democratic transfer requests are known. In that section we also discuss the possibility of simultaneous interaction between requests and transfers.

2.4   RESULTS

2.4.1 *Democratic Transfers*   The results of the four probit regressions described above—with dependent variables ANYTRANS, CONTRANS, SEMTRANS, and NONTRANS—are presented in table 20 (Democrats only). The coefficient on SOUTHERN is insignificant in all four probits: southern Democrats were neither more nor less likely to transfer than were their nonsouthern colleagues. The coefficient on the VACANCIES variable, not surprisingly, is positive for all categories of Democratic transfers (though it is insignificant in the equation for transfers to semi-exclusive committees). This finding indicates simply that more available committee slots mean a better chance of landing a transfer. Finally, the coefficients on TERMS and TERMSQ were as predicted (negative and positive, respectively) in all but the probit for transfers to control committees. This is largely as we expected. Whereas members are less eager to move as they accumulate seniority (and approach positions of leadership within their original committees), many members will accept a transfer to a control committee from a noncontrol committee at any time.

Turning now to the main focus of the analysis—the impact of party loyalty on probability of transfer—we see that the coefficient on LOYALTY was positive and significant in the ANYTRANS equation. That is, if one asks what distinguishes those who transfer from those who do not (regardless of where they transfer), one factor is loyalty to the party leadership.[17] The effect is such that an increase in a member's loyalty ranking from the 50th to 67th percentile would increase that member's probability of receiving a transfer by as much as 3.3 percent, while an increase in a member's loyalty ranking from the 50th to the 95th percentile would yield up to a 6.4 percent increase in likelihood of transferring.[18]

The effect of party loyalty on Democratic transfers to control and nonexclusive committees is also positive and significant. In the case of transfers to control committees, a drop in loyalty from the 95th to the 50th percentile would yield a drop of as much as 11.1 percent in the likelihood of getting these highly coveted transfers. The same drop in loyalty would yield a decline of up to 9 percent in the likelihood of a transfer to a nonexclusive committee. Party loyalty is insignificant, however, in the probit equation we report for transfers to semiexclusive committees. The problem with this last result is that we are in part comparing apples and oranges. The average loyalty of Democrats who receive transfers to semiexclusive committees is in fact slightly above

17. If we exclude returning members of control committees (on the grounds that they are not really in the pool of potential transferers), the coefficient on our loyalty variable is even larger and more significant.

18. We say "as much as" and "up to" because probit coefficients do not translate as straightforwardly as OLS coefficients into statements of the kind "A one-unit change in the independent variable will produce an x-unit change in the dependent variable." In the case at hand, how much a given change in loyalty affects the probability of transfer depends on the initial or base probability. For example, a member whose characteristics give him a .999 probability of transfer could not improve his chances much by an increase in loyalty, whereas one whose characteristics give him a .7 probability of transfer could.

the mean loyalty of Democrats as a whole (standardized to equal zero), even though this whole includes members already sitting on or just transferring to a control committee. But these members are, first, much more loyal than the average Democrat and, second, extremely unlikely to seek or receive a transfer to a semiexclusive committee. When we compare apples with apples—those who might have transferred to a semiexclusive committee to those who actually did—we get a somewhat different picture. We excluded those already on or just transferring to control committees from the analysis, leaving a pool of those who might transfer to semiexclusive committees. A probit equation on this subset of Democrats (not reported here) produced coefficients for our loyalty measure that were of the right sign, though insignificant.

We sought to test the effect of the committee reforms in the Ninety-second and Ninety-third Congresses with the interactive term LOYALTY∗POSTREFORM. A positive coefficient for this variable would show that party loyalty became more important after the committee reforms, whereas a negative coefficient would show that loyalty became less important. The interactive term was insignificant in all four probits.[19] The lack of any significant coefficient says simply that there was little or no change in the degree to which those more loyal to the leadership were advantaged in the competition for desirable transfers.

2.4.2 Republican Transfers   The results for the Republicans (table 21) are similar to those just described for the Democrats. The party loyalty term is positive and significant as a predictor of transfers to any committee and to control committees, but it is not significant for transfers to semiexclusive or nonexclusive committees. The estimated effect in the overall equation (with dependent variable ANYTRANS) was such that a decline in a Republican's loyalty from the 95th to 50th percentile would yield a decline of as much as 6.2 percent in the likelihood of transferring.[20]

We included the interactive term LOYALTY∗POSTREFORM in the equations for the Republicans as we had for the Democrats. The formal role of the Republican leadership in the committee assignment process changed little, but the variable is still useful as a crude test of whether there was

19. Indeed, dropping the LOYALTY ∗ POSTREFORM variable from our probits has almost no effect on the error structure of the regression. The removal of this variable from the four probits in table 20, moreover, has no effect on the level of significance of the other included variables.

20. The coefficients on the control variables—TERMS, TERMSQ, and VACANCIES—were as predicted in all four probits, almost all of them significant.

TABLE 21.   PARTY LOYALTY AND REPUBLICAN
COMMITTEE TRANSFERS, EIGHTIETH TO
HUNDREDTH CONGRESSES

Independent Variables	Dependent Variables			
	ANYTRANS	CONTRANS	SEMTRANS	NONTRANS
Constant	− 0.087	− 1.120*	− 0.426*	− 0.866*
LOYALTY	0.086*	0.311*	− 0.023	0.060
LOYALTY * POSTREFORM	− 0.149*	− 0.100	− 0.083	− 0.192
TERMS	− 0.435*	− 0.263*	− 0.415*	− 0.223*
TERMSQ	0.019*	− 0.010*	0.019*	0.008*
VACANCIES	0.007*	0.043*	0.011*	0.004
N	3,036	3,036	3,036	3,036
% correctly predicted	81.42	95.03	90.61	94.05
Log Likelihood Ratio	1.63	3.98	2.53	3.34

* Significant at the .05 level.

any change over time in the importance of loyalty as a criterion in the allocation of Republican transfers. In both the ANYTRANS and NONTRANS probits, the estimated coefficient on LOYALTY*POSTREFORM turned out to be negative, significant, and larger in magnitude than the coefficient on LOYALTY. For some reason, the statistical association between loyalty to the Republican leadership and transfer among committees was significantly weaker (even negative) in the later Congresses. This finding merits further investigation, but we do not pursue the matter here.

2.5   DEMOCRATIC ASSIGNMENT REQUESTS AND TRANSFERS

In this section we respecify the probits in table 20 to include a variable identifying those Democratic members who requested a transfer. Since information on members' requests for transfer are available only for the Eighty-sixth to Ninetieth and Ninety-second to Ninety-seventh Congresses, the analysis is confined to these Congresses.

Naturally, the precise definition of the variable identifying whether or not a member submitted a formal request for transfer differs depending on the dependent variable. In the probit for ANYTRANS, the variable

TABLE 22. DEMOCRATIC TRANSFERS AND
REQUESTS, EIGHTY-SIXTH TO NINETIETH AND
NINETY-SECOND TO NINETY-SEVENTH CONGRESSES

Independent Variables	Dependent Variables			
	ANYTRANS	CONTRANS	SEMTRANS	NONTRANS
Constant	−0.255*	−2.058*	−0.446*	−1.201*
LOYALTY	0.122*	0.214*	.009	0.118*
LOYALTY * POSTREFORM	−0.056	−0.014	0.003	−0.066
SOUTHERN	0.138*	0.234*	0.064	−0.009
TERMS	−0.322*	0.023	−0.307*	−0.237*
TERMSQ	0.011*	−0.011	0.010*	0.008*
VACANCIES	0.004*	0.027*	−0.000	0.016*
REQUEST	0.965*	1.634*	1.759*	1.730*
N	4,407	4,407	4,407	4,407
% correctly predicted	85.14	96.42	93.94	93.62
Log Likelihood Ratio	1.96	5.51	3.60	3.39

* Significant at the .05 level.

(labeled REQUEST) is defined to be 1 if the member filed a written request for any transfer in that Congress, and 0 otherwise; in the probit for CONTRANS, REQUEST is defined to be 1 if the member filed a written request for transfer to a control committee (Appropriations, Rules, or Ways and Means), and 0 otherwise; and so on.

Several points should be kept in mind before we turn to the results of our reestimation. First, as discussed in chapter 2, we can observe only those requests submitted in writing to the Democratic CC (and subsequently collected by Shepsle and Smith). But it seems likely that a substantial number of members for whom we have no data may have requested transfer through other, more informal, channels. If these informal requesters enjoyed a higher likelihood of success, then the estimated coefficient on REQUEST in the probits in table 22 will underestimate the true relationship between requests (defined broadly) and transfers.

Second, and more seriously, requests are probably simultaneously determined with transfers. That is, asking for a transfer may increase one's chances of getting it, but one's anticipation of success may affect

whether or not one asks to begin with. If requests and transfer decisions
are simultaneously determined, then it is difficult to say—based on the
kind of estimation procedure used here—how much influence requests
actually have on transfer decisions: if requests are made only when the
likelihood of transfer is high, then the coefficient on REQUESTS reflects
not simply the accommodation of requests but rather the joint decision
to grant a transfer and to file a request.

The two problems just identified—that we can observe only a fraction of all requests and that requests and transfers are simultaneously
determined—suggest that the interpretation of the coefficient on RE-
QUESTS in the respecified equation is far from straightforward. More
worrisome for our purposes is the possibility that these problems, especially the second, may bias the estimation of the impact of LOYALTY
(both in table 22 and in tables 20 and 21).

One might ask why we do not simply specify and estimate a full
system of simultaneous equations, one for transfers and one for requests. The answer is partly lack of data: we do not have a very prom-
ising set of exogenous variables for the REQUEST equation.[21] But it is
also true that the estimates we do provide are largely sufficient for the
points we wish to make.

If there is a simultaneity problem, then the results to be presented in
table 22 can be interpreted as those that one gets from running OLS on
one of the reduced-form equations.[22] There are some general arguments
for using OLS in this fashion, even on underidentified equations. Maddala (1988, 322–23), for example, discusses conditions under which
OLS will be consistent "for all practical purposes," and Bartels (1985)
contains some discussions in a similar vein. Moreover, if one adapts the
formulas for OLS bias to the present context (a technical exercise that
we confine to a footnote), one can at least put some bounds on what
can go wrong. Reassuringly, it seems unlikely that the true structural
relationship between loyalty and probability of transfer could be negative, if the OLS estimates in table 22 turn out to be positive: we at least
will get the sign of the relationship right, even if there is (upward or
downward) bias.[23]

21. This means both that we would get pretty lousy first-stage instruments in any
attempted 2SLS estimation and that we might have trouble identifying the system to begin
with.
22. If some exogenous variables from the REQUEST equation were not included in the
TRANSFER equation, then the specification in table 20 would not quite be the reduced
form.
23. The (quick and dirty) argument goes as follows: Suppose we model the process

As it turns out, the results in table 22 are virtually identical to those presented in table 20. As before, the coefficient on LOYALTY is positive and significant in the ANYTRANS, CONTRANS, and NONTRANS probits and positive but insignificant in the SEMTRANS equation. In each case, the coefficient on LOYALTY is greater in table 22 than in table 20. The coefficients for most of the other exogenous variables—LOYALTY∗POSTREFORM, TERMS, TERMSQ, AND VACANCIES—were also virtually identical to the results reported earlier. The one difference between the two sets of probits regards the coefficient on the dummy variable SOUTHERN. The probits for ANYTRANS and CONTRANS produced positive and significant coefficients on SOUTHERN, whereas previously these coefficients, though positive, were not significant. This finding indicates that, other things equal, southerners were more likely to transfer.

2.6   DEMOCRATIC REQUEST SUCCESS AND FAILURE

One interesting topic not yet addressed concerns request success and request failure. That is, among those who request a committee transfer, who succeeds and who fails? Presumably, loyalty to the party leadership should increase the likelihood of receiving a requested committee transfer. One obvious way to address this topic would be to examine a new dependent variable—the probability of getting a requested transfer—and assess the importance of loyalty and other independent variables in another probit equation.

This, however, is not an attractive estimation procedure. As we point out in chapter 3, only about 20 percent of all committee transfers are requested formally. Yet it seems likely that a substantial proportion of the remaining transfers, for which we have no record of a request in the

---

as a pair of OLS regressions:

$$T = \check{A}R + \check{S}L + w$$
$$R = \acute{A}T + v$$

where $T = 1$ if the member transferred, 0 else; $R = 1$ if the member formally requested transfer, 0 else; L is the member's standardized loyalty score; and w and v are stochastic disturbance terms. Since these are linear probability models, one certainly hopes that $\acute{A}$ will lie between zero and one, and it seems likely that $\bar{A}$ will not be far from this range either. The OLS estimator of $\check{S}$, d, will equal (assuming the covariance between w and v is zero; cf. Maddala 1977, 246) $\check{S}[1 + (\acute{A} - \check{A})\acute{I}_w{}^2/(\acute{I}_w{}^2 + \acute{I}_v{}^2)]$, where $\acute{I}_w$ is the standard deviation of w and $\acute{I}_v$ is the standard deviation of v. If $\check{S}$ is less than zero, than d can be greater than zero if and only if the term in square brackets is less than zero, which is equivalent to $\acute{A} > \acute{A} + (\acute{I}_w{}^2 + \acute{I}_v{}^2)/\acute{I}_w{}^2$. Thus, the only way that we can get the sign wrong, in this simplified example, is if the effect of R on T is greater than the effect of T on R plus a term greater than one. Since $\acute{A}$ is not likely to be much greater than one, it seems unlikely that d could be positive when $\check{S}$ is negative.

Shepsle-Smith data set, were nonetheless requested through informal channels. What this implies—for any study of request accommodation—is that most requests are censored from our analysis: we cannot observe the dependent variable for some unknown but probably large proportion of the cases.

Censoring would not be an insurmountable problem if the observed sample of formal requests were a random draw from the set of all requests. We suspect, however, that formal requests differ systematically from informal requests. Members' requests for transfer depend on their estimates of the probability that they will be granted. It may be that the formal requests of which we have record in the Shepsle-Smith data set are made by members who lack the clout to obtain transfer through informal channels (the analogy between academics who apply for an advertised position and those who are specifically asked to apply comes to mind). If so, then any analysis of request success and failure (such as that of Smith and Ray 1983) faces very serious problems of the kind explained at length in any of the standard sources (e.g., Achen 1982).[24] As a consequence, we do not attempt such an analysis here.

This does not mean, however, that what information we have on members' requests for transfer cannot be used. We can place Democrats into four categories:

1. DO-NOTHINGS, defined as those members in each Congress who neither formally requested nor received a committee transfer;

2. REQUEST-FAILURES, defined as those who formally requested a transfer and received either no transfer or one different from any they requested;[25]

3. REQUEST-SUCCESSES, defined as those who received a formally requested transfer;

4. DRAFTEES, defined as those for whom there was no written request but who nonetheless transferred to a new committee.

We can estimate the effect of loyalty and our other independent variables on the likelihood that members fall into one of these four categories. In estimating these likelihoods, however, once three of the likeli-

---

24. In particular, such an analysis would certainly run the risk of downward bias in estimating the impact of party loyalty on request success.
25. Members submit ranked lists of committees to which they would like to transfer. Often these lists consist of only one committee, but sometimes they have two or more. We count a member as failing only if she gets none of the committees requested.

hoods are known, we of course know the fourth. Thus, if we were to estimate parameters defining all four likelihoods, the parameters of the first three would define the fourth. The problem is similar to multicollinearity: the independent variables defining the first three likelihoods are perfectly correlated with the variables defining the fourth.

Thus, we estimate, by means of a categorical logit, the determinants of the odds of a member's placement into three of these four categories relative to an excluded fourth category. The excluded comparison group in our analysis consists of those members in each Congress who neither formally requested nor received a transfer—the DO-NOTHINGS. In a sense, then, we really have three dependent variables: the odds of a member falling into each of REQUEST-FAILURE, REQUEST-SUCCESS, or DRAFTEE categories rather than the DO-NOTHING category. The estimated coefficients from the categorical logit procedure tell us how important party loyalty is in determining the odds of being a REQUEST-SUCCESS (or REQUEST-FAILURE or DRAFTEE) rather than a DO-NOTHING.

The results (table 23) support our suspicion that there are differences between those who formally requested a committee transfer and those who transferred without a written request: the coefficients on LOYALTY, TERMSQ, and VACANCIES differed across all three categories. Interestingly, in comparison to those who neither requested nor received a transfer (DO-NOTHINGS), those members who requested but failed to get a transfer (REQUEST-FAILURE) were significantly *less* loyal. By contrast, there was no significant difference between the comparison group, the DO-NOTHINGS, and those members who received a requested transfer, REQUEST-SUCCESS, in terms of party loyalty. But the coefficient on LOYALTY in the comparison between DRAFTEES and DO-NOTHINGS is positive and significant.

These results are consistent with our expectations that written transfer requests are used largely by those who fail to gain a desired transfer informally. They also show that only those from the pool of formal requesters who are at least of average loyalty are granted their request. For transfers made through informal channels (i.e., the bulk of transfers), party loyalty is an important determinant of transfer success.[26]

Last, the number of Democratic committee vacancies is significant only for the comparison between DRAFTEES and DO-NOTHINGS. This result indicates that request success does not depend on vacancies.

26. As Fenno (1973, 19–20) points out, written transfer requests are often made at the behest of party leaders. A member will apply for a particular committee slot, especially to a control committee, when asked to do so by the party leadership. Fenno refers

TABLE 23. MULTINOMIAL ANALYSIS OF
DEMOCRATIC TRANSFERS AND REQUESTS,
EIGHTY-SIXTH TO NINETIETH AND NINETY-
SECOND TO NINETY-SEVENTH CONGRESSES

Independent Variables	Log Odds of Request Failure (REQUEST-FAILURE) Coefficients	Log Odds of Request Success (REQUEST-SUCCESS) Coefficients	Log Odds of Being Drafted (DRAFTEE) Coefficients
Constant	0.432	0.389	−0.627
LOYALTY	−0.331*	0.127	0.227*
LOYALTY * POSTREFORM	0.344*	−0.190	−0.053
SOUTHERN	−0.342	0.167	0.180
TERMS	−0.731*	−0.921*	−0.555*
TERMSQ	0.025*	0.030*	0.018*
VACANCIES	0.001	0.004	0.008*
% of sample	6.78	6.16	9.47

$N = 2,450$
% correctly predicted $= 77.592$
Log Likelihood Ratio $= 2.10$

* Significant at the .05 level.

2.7 SUMMARY

Putting together the various findings reported above, we can confidently
reject the null hypothesis that party loyalty has no effect on committee
transfers. In fact, party loyalty seems to be a criterion in making assignment decisions to most House committees. Thus, whether or not party
leaders are directly involved in assignment decisions, the process produces results whereby those whose roll call votes demonstrate loyalty
to the leadership are rewarded with committee transfers. This of course
makes committees and their members more responsive to both the party's leadership and goals.

---

to this procedure as "cooptation" and notes that it was used fairly frequently to pick
members for control committees, but that "it is a method never used" for the other committees in his study. In this case, we assume that members issue a formal, written request
because of the structural separation between the party leadership and the CC. Co-optation may be one reason that members make formal requests for committee assignments,
but it is distinct from the motivation we believe pertains here.

3. ASSIGNMENT SUCCESS OF FRESHMEN

In this section we ask whether postwar freshmen who were more loyal to their respective leaders in their first term were also more likely to do well in terms of their initial committee assignments. Because committee assignments are made at the beginning of the term, before a freshman has had an opportunity to establish a voting record, the causal relationship in the analyses to follow is less clear than in the case of transfer requests. A positive correlation between first-term loyalty and assignment success might arise because each party's CC is able to *predict* how loyal a member will be—and rewards anticipated loyalty. However, such a correlation might also arise because those given more desirable assignments respond with gratitude in the form of higher levels of support. As long as this response was anticipated, however, the story is not much different. Because both these causal paths rely on anticipations of future loyalty rather than assessments of past loyalty, one expects the evidence relating to the initial assignment requests of new members to be weaker than that relating to the transfer requests of returning members.

Nonetheless, the evidence turns out to be generally positive. This can be seen in three different analyses, one involving the probability that an entering Democrat will get his or her first-choice assignment, one involving those appointed to control committees in their first year, and one involving the seniority rank that entering members receive.

Consider first the probability that a freshman Democrat will be granted his or her first choice.[27] Table 24 presents the estimates from a probit equation predicting this probability as a function of the following variables: (1) LOYALTY—the standardized loyalty score described in section 2.3; (2) CONTROL—whether the request was for a control committee or not; (3) MAJOR—whether the request was for a "major" noncontrol committee or not;[28] (4) SOUTHERN—whether the requester was from the South or not; and (5) interaction terms involving LOYALTY and the other three regressors.

The rationale for this specification is straightforward. The probability that a request is granted ought plausibly to depend on the kind of committee requested. Our first two dummy variables, CONTROL and MAJOR, are an attempt to capture this notion by dividing committees

---

27. Note that because almost all freshmen submit requests, this analysis does not face the same kind of simultaneity problems that confront similar analyses of transfers.

28. The variable MAJOR was equal to one for the following committees: Commerce, Armed Services, Public Works, Banking, and Agriculture.

TABLE 24.   LOYALTY AND FIRST-CHOICE
ASSIGNMENTS

Dependent Variable: Equal to 1 if Democratic freshman got
first-choice assignment, 0 else

Independent Variables	Coefficients (Standard Errors)	
Constant	.312	(2.47)
LOYALTY	.485	(2.97)
CONTROL	−.769	(−3.90)
MAJOR	.089	(.59)
SOUTHERN	−.016	(−.11)
LOYALTY * CONTROL	−.228	(−1.02)
LOYALTY * MAJOR	−.472	(−2.73)
LOYALTY * SOUTHERN	−.216	(−1.51)

$N = 408$
% correctly predicted = 66.4

into three groups—control, major noncontrol, and the rest. The coefficients on CONTROL and MAJOR will indicate whether those requesting control and major noncontrol committees were more or less likely to be successful than those requesting a committee in the residual category of committees. The SOUTHERN dummy variable is included to see if southern Democrats enjoyed any advantage or suffered any disadvantage in the committee assignment process. The various interaction terms involving LOYALTY are included to allow for the possibility that loyalty to the leadership might matter less for some committee requests than for others (LOYALTY * CONTROL, LOYALTY * MAJOR) or might matter less for some members than for others (LOYALTY * SOUTHERN). If, for example, it is especially important to be loyal in order to get on a control committee, then perhaps the slope coefficient on LOYALTY will be larger for those requesting control committees than it is for those requesting run-of-the-mill committees.

The actual results show that not all of the possible effects for which we allow turn out to be significant. Nonetheless, the variable of primary interest—LOYALTY—has a positive and significant coefficient. This result indicates that, among those *northern* Democratic freshmen requesting a *residual* committee, those who were more loyal in their first term were more likely to be granted their first choice. The insignificant coefficient on LOYALTY*SOUTHERN shows that we cannot reject the hypothesis that the same basic relationship holds among southern Democratic freshmen—although it appears to be a bit less pronounced. The insignificant coefficient on LOYALTY*CONTROL similarly indicates that the story is not much different for those few freshmen who requested control committees: the more loyal ones were more likely to have their request granted. There is a difference, however, for those requesting the second tier of committees. The estimated coefficient on the LOYALTY*MAJOR interaction term is negative and only slightly smaller in magnitude than is the coefficient on LOYALTY. Thus, the relationship between first-term loyalty and request success for those requesting major noncontrol committees is, albeit positive, nearly zero. The Democratic CC apparently does not use anticipated first-term loyalty as a criterion to distinguish among those seeking appointment to such committees.

Altering the definition of what is a "major" noncontrol committee does not change the results much. Two committees, Armed Services and Commerce, stand out as different from the rest, however. In particular, these two committees do not pool with the rest for purposes of estimating the coefficient on LOYALTY: whereas the estimated coefficient on LOYALTY is positive and significant when considering all committees except these two, it is negative and significant for these two considered alone. This result makes some sense for Armed Services, which has traditionally been a conservative committee, but we do not know why the results for the Commerce Committee are similar.

In any event, the bottom line is clear. Higher first-term loyalty scores correlate positively with higher probabilities of receiving requested assignments for most categories of freshmen and committees.

A second way of assessing whether first-term loyalty is anticipated and rewarded in the appointment process is to examine those who were appointed to a control committee in their first year (regardless of whether they requested the appointment or not): Were they significantly more loyal in their first term than was the rest of their cohort? The answer is positive for both the Republicans and the Democrats, although the number of Republican freshmen appointed to control committees in the postwar era (twelve) is sufficiently small so that the effect does not attain conventional levels of statistical significance.

A final bit of evidence that first-term loyalty matters is that commit-

tee seniority rank among freshmen correlates positively and significantly, albeit modestly, with committee loyalty rank. We looked, for
each Congress from the Eightieth to the Hundredth, at each committee
to which more than one freshman Democrat was assigned. For each
such committee we coded the committee seniority rank among the
freshmen as well as how they ranked in loyalty in their first term. The
(Spearman) correlation was .32, significant at the .0001 level. The results were similar for the Republicans (a correlation of .29, also significant at the .0001 level).[29]

4. CONCLUSION

In this chapter we have asked whether those members who are more
loyal to their party's leadership have a statistically discernible edge in
the committee assignment process. Although there is considerable anecdotal evidence indicating that loyalists are rewarded, especially when
it comes to assignment to the control committees, there is a surprisingly
scanty body of corroborating statistical evidence. The impact of party
loyalty either has not been investigated at all (in the case of freshman
assignments) or has been investigated only with limited data and mixed
results (in the case of nonfreshman transfers).

Our results, based on a substantially larger data set than previously
available, indicate that loyalty to the party leadership is a statistically
and substantively important determinant of who gets what assignment.
The effect is particularly strong in determining who transfers, but it is
noticeable even in determining the initial assignment of freshmen.

The motivation for marshaling the statistical evidence that loyalists
are rewarded is to counterbalance the growing tendency in the literature
to view the committee assignment process as a neutral, nondiscretionary, or routine one in which members' preferences are the primary determinant of where they end up. We certainly do not deny that members' preferences for assignment are important and determine much of
the pattern of actual assignment, but this fact does not make the process
one of "self-selection" pure and simple, where member requests are
neutrally processed. The statistical evidence is clear: more loyal members are more likely to transfer (and more likely to get better assignments as freshmen). Because there are almost always more members
who *want* assignment to a committee (at least if it ranks relatively high

29. The results are similar if the postwar period is split into two subperiods, from the
Eightieth to the Ninetieth and from the Ninety-first to the Hundredth Congress.

in the pecking order) than there are available slots on that committee, there is a standing incentive to become more loyal. The assignment process seems to us inherently discretionary. This discretion, moreover, is consequential in that it provides a route by which the collective goals of the party, as internalized by the party leadership, are represented in the composition of committees.

EIGHT

Contingents and Parties

In the previous chapter we explored a key expectation of our model—namely, that party leaders would have a systematic influence on committee assignments. If party leaders do influence committee assignments, one might expect that the overall composition of each party's contingents on the standing committees would be affected. In this chapter we consider how they ought to be affected and then turn to data pertinent to testing our expectations.

In thinking about whether or not one should expect contingents to be representative, we appeal to two different perspectives on how the appointment process works: the self-selection model and the partisan selection model. We have already discussed the first of these perspectives in chapters 1 and 3. In a nutshell, the self-selection model posits, first, that members request appointment to committees based primarily on the interests of their constituencies and, second, that members' requests are routinely accommodated by each party's CC. As Shepsle (1978) puts it, committee assignments are made in a way that "permits 'interesteds' to gravitate to decision arenas in which their interests are promoted" (248) and allows "most members for most of their careers [to be] on the committees they 'want'" (236). Given this view of the assignment process, one would expect a committee contingent to be representative only if the committee's jurisdiction was broad enough to attract a representative cross-section of the party. Other committees with less widely appealing jurisdictions would be expected to have more or less unrepresentative contingents.

An alternative view of the appointment process is embodied in what we call the partisan selection model. In this model of the appointment process, assignments to committees are made in order to further some collective goal, such as the number of seats that the party will win at the next election. Although this would seem to be a polar opposite of the self-selection model, in many cases the predictions the two models make about which contingents will be representative are indistinguishable. After all, a CC interested in winning as many seats as possible for its party may well be one that gives its members the opportunity to participate in policy arenas of interest to their constituents. Committees that have very narrow jurisdictions—and whose decisions do not adversely affect other members of the party—can be allowed to be unrepresentative of the party as a whole. Committees with broad and important jurisdictions, by contrast, will be kept more firmly in hand by making sure that the party's contingent is broadly representative of the party as a whole.

In the next section we sketch out the partisan selection model in a bit more detail. Section 2 elaborates the predictions that this model makes about each standing committee (do we expect it to be representative or not?). Section 3 then tests these predictions against the empirical record, with section 4 concluding.

1.   A MODEL OF PARTISAN SELECTION

The simplest and starkest model of a committee assignment process in which partisan interests are represented is one in which the leaders of both parties decide which of their followers should serve on which committees. Having themselves internalized their party's collective interests along the lines discussed in chapter 5, party leaders would structure committees to further those collective interests.

What exactly this structuring would mean depends on what the collective interests of the party are. We shall assume that party leaders make appointments in order to maximize the number of seats that their party will win at the next election. Although this sounds rather precise, in fact the discussion to follow will be intuitive rather than formal.

There are two basic ways for a party to use committee appointments in order to increase its number of seats at the next election. First, it can furnish party members with opportunities to advertise themselves, claim credit for particularistic benefits delivered to their constituents, and in other ways enhance their personal standing with their voters (cf. Mayhew 1974). Second, it can foster the kinds of elaborate intraparty deals that are needed to unite the party behind broad legislation with national impact, thereby affecting the party's collective reputation with the electorate. Most issues involve trade-offs: if everyone claims credit for delivering public works projects to their districts, the party as a whole may find itself saddled with a "tax and spend" reputation; unqualified support for fundamentalist Christian values may be an attractive addition to the party reputation as far as some Republicans are concerned, but it would be deleterious to others. Seat-maximizing party leaders must be sensitive to these trade-offs.

What this means in terms of committee appointments depends on the committee's jurisdiction. Consider first a hypothetical committee whose jurisdiction is composed of very narrowly targeted issues that affect only a small, fairly well defined subset of districts. By definition, this committee's decisions have minimal impact on the individual electoral standing of members whose districts are *not* in the affected subset. Moreover, the impact of committee decisions on the party's national reputation will also likely be small. To the extent that this is so, a seat-maximizing leader need not be much concerned with negative electoral externalities from this committee. The optimal strategy is to let those members who are interested in the policy area join the committee and do what they will. If they occasionally deal with issues that potentially have major effects on other members of the party, the leader can rely on the Rules Committee, the Appropriations Committee, and his own scheduling powers to ensure that these effects are taken into account. In the case of low-externality committees with narrow jurisdictions, then, both the self-selection hypothesis and the partisan selection hypothesis would lead to the prediction that such committees will tend to be unrepresentative.

By contrast, a committee whose jurisdiction concerns "national" policy—defined as policy whose costs and benefits reach every constituency—will need to be handled differently. The seat-maximizing leader will be concerned with regulating the electoral externalities that such a committee's decisions can entail. The most straightforward way to regulate potential externalities is to ensure that the contingent on the committee is representative of the party as a whole. Contingents that are representative of the important currents of opinion in the party will be able to "decentralize" intraparty arguments so that the outcome of the arguments in the party's committee contingent are representative of the outcome of the arguments in the party as a whole; all the party's varied electoral interests will be internal to the committee's decisions.

2. WHICH COMMITTEES' CONTINGENTS WILL BE REPRESENTATIVE?

The previous section sketched the beginnings of a partisan selection model, the gist of which is that committee contingents will be structured so that they internalize all of the party's significant electoral interests.[1] We do not argue that the postwar appoint process has been purely partisan, but we do think that each party's CC has internalized collective goals enough so that the partisan selection model is a useful benchmark. Accordingly, we use it to answer the question, Which committees should we expect to be representative and which to be unrepresentative?

The key variable in determining whether a committee will be representative or not, according to the partisan selection model, is the character of the committee's jurisdiction. We characterize jurisdictions along two (closely related) dimensions: an "external effects" dimension and an "extramural effects" dimension. We first discuss the notion of external effects and offer a three-way classification of committees in terms of the kind of potential external effects of their decisions. We then return to the notion of extramural effects and further differentiate committees on this basis. That approach allows us to make specific predictions about each committee and to test those predictions against the empirical record.

2.1   THE EXTERNAL EFFECTS OF HOUSE COMMITTEE DECISIONS

By *external effects* we mean essentially what an economist would mean: effects that are external to the narrowly self-interested calculus of committee members. Because we define self-interest here in terms of electoral prospects, *external effects* refers to the effects that committee decisions have on the probabilities of victory of party members not on the committee.

The external effects for a single issue might be described both in

1. A similar notion concerning the effects of one committee's decisions on another committee's members is articulated by Collie and Cooper's (1989) work on multiple referral.

terms of size—how much the issue, on average, affects probabilities of reelection—and distribution—whether everyone is affected to about the same extent or whether there are subsets of affected and unaffected members. It is a bit harder to characterize the pattern of external effects of committee *jurisdictions* because a single jurisdiction may contain all kinds of issues. Here we ignore the full complexity of jurisdictions and attempt to classify them simply on the basis of central tendency.

In particular, we distinguish three classes of jurisdiction, based on the uniformity or skewness of their typical external effects. Jurisdictions whose external effects on average fall about equally on all noncommittee members are described as "uniform" or possessing "uniform externalities"; those whose external effects usually fall primarily on a well-defined subset of noncommittee members and leave the rest largely unaffected are described as "targeted" or possessing "targeted externalities"; and those whose external effects do not fall into either of the first two categories are put in a residual category and said to be "mixed" or to possess "mixed externalities."

Note that a jurisdiction can be uniform without being particularly important. We think of a jurisdiction as uniform if it touches most districts about equally, regardless of how much it touches them. A targeted jurisdiction, in contrast, has a very skewed distribution of external effects: a small, well-defined subset of noncommittee members care a lot, the rest relatively little.

We recognize that these definitions are loose, but they should be sufficiently precise to categorize the committees. We think it is noncontroversial to say that the committees on Appropriations, Interstate and Foreign Commerce, Rules, and Ways and Means possess among the widest-ranging jurisdictions in Congress; accordingly, as they offer "something for everyone," we put them in the uniform externalities category. The other fifteen committees (we do not deal with Small Business, Official Conduct, HUAAC, or Budget) are somewhat less clear and deserve individual discussion.

2.1.1 Committees with Uniform Externalities   The decisions of committees that authorize "projects" on a national scale can affect most districts in the nation simply because most districts can qualify for a project (grant, contract, subcontract) at some point. The construction projects authorized by the Committee on Public Works and Transportation, for example, leave few districts unaffected (Murphy 1974; Ferejohn 1974). Similarly, although the outlays may not be as great, the

Science Committee authorizes projects, contracts, and grants in virtually every congressional district (Cohen and Noll 1991). Accordingly, we put both of these committees in the uniform externalities category.[2]

The Committee on Post Office and Civil Service has jurisdiction over policies affecting federal and postal employees. Once the core patronage committee of the majority party, Post Office is now a relatively minor panel. Nonetheless, the policies recommended by the committee affect virtually every congressional district: the average congressional district in 1970 had 6,820 federal or postal employees (or roughly 3 percent of the average district employment); of the 262 below-average districts, only 37 had fewer than 3,000 employees. Not surprisingly, the distribution of federal employment is quite even across congressional districts. Because Post Office policies concern a vocal minority in essentially every district, so that its policy decisions have the potential to affect the electoral prospects of virtually every member, we put this committee in the uniform externalities category.

The Committee on Veterans' Affairs oversees the two hundred thousand employees of the Veterans' Administration and recommends policies with respect to pensions, insurance, health, and housing programs for the nation's more than twenty million veterans. The effects of these programs are important to constituents in every congressional district: the average number of veterans per district in 1970 was over fifty-one thousand, and the district with the smallest number of veterans still had more than twenty-four thousand. Thus, for reasons similar to those articulated above, we put Veterans' Affairs in the uniform externalities group.

The committees on House Administration and Government Operations perform management or "housekeeping" functions for the House of Representatives and the executive branch, respectively.[3] Most of the decisions these committees make have little electoral impact on any member. Nonetheless, each occasionally is in a position to affect a wide range of members. The House Administration Committee may not produce any direct electoral externalities, but many of its allocational decisions are of great interest to members generally. The Government Op-

2. It is true that virtually nobody other than the member in whose district the project is placed cares about single projects. But projects are usually packaged in omnibus bills, and most members care about these bills because most members have a project in them.

3. On House Administration, see Bolling 1974, 11. On Government Operations, see Ornstein and Rohde 1977b, 209, 246–52; and Bolling 1974, 1.

erations Committee can, by conducting oversight hearings, poke its nose into virtually anything that the executive bureaucracy does. We thus place both House Administration and Government Operations in the uniform externalities category.

2.1.2 *Committees with Targeted Externalities*   According to Ornstein and Rohde (1977b, 230), the Agricultural Committee serves "a very limited and specific set of interests." Moreover, agricultural policy has been of central importance in an ever-shrinking minority of districts in the postwar period. The court-ordered redistricting of the 1960s led to a rapid decline in the number of members elected from predominantly rural districts so that by 1973 only 130 remained (McCubbins and Schwartz 1988, 391). Further, the crop subsidy and loan programs administered by the committee, which once accounted for over 6 percent of federal spending, now account for little more than 1 percent (McCubbins and Schwartz 1988, 409). Most of the commodity-support programs, moreover, have little or no effect on the prices consumers pay for food (Cochrane 1958). Thus, the effects of agriculture policy are largely concentrated on a narrow set of constituents in a small and decreasing number of districts, with few significant externalities on constituents in other districts. For these reasons, we put Agriculture in our targeted externalities category.[4]

An even purer case of a narrowly targeted, regional policy committee is the Committee on Interior and Insular Affairs. The federal land-use policies overseen by the committee are important to only a few western states, with virtually no external effects outside of these areas and with correspondingly small general budget effects.[5] Indeed, the narrow clien-

4. Ornstein and Rohde (1977b, 230) note that clientelism in agricultural policy has not been altered by expansion of the Agriculture Committee's jurisdiction to include consumer interests and some social social welfare programs: "The lack of a major urban or consumer focus on agricultural policy is . . . related to the nature of subcommittee assignments on Agriculture. Through a process of self-selection, the few urban-oriented members . . . have avoided the commodity subcommittees and have chosen operational subcommittees like Domestic Marketing and Consumer Relations for their first assignment option and their major time commitment. Thus the agricultural legislation which goes through the commodity subcommittees remains dominated by legislators who represent particular commodity interests." The makeup of the committee, however, has changed as a result of this jurisdictional expansion. As Ornstein and Rohde (1977b, 195) show, the membership of the committee, especially the Democrats, became significantly more liberal, on average, relative to the House, between the Ninety-first and Ninety-fourth Congresses.

5. Land-use policies include grazing rights, park management, and so forth. The federal government owns about one-third of all land in the United States, but about two-thirds of all land in western states (*Economist,* 22 Oct. 1988, 21). Although these re-

tele interests of the committee were recognized in the report of the Bolling Committee, which proposed to broaden the Interior Committee's jurisdiction by making it an energy and environment committee, a plan that was only modestly successful (Davidson 1977, 42). Interior, too, is classified in the targeted externalities group.

The Bolling Committee also remarked on the narrow jurisdiction of the Merchant Marine and Fisheries Committee—responsible, as its name suggests, for regulating the United States' merchant fleet and fisheries (Davidson 1977, 40). Its decisions have little impact outside a hundred or so coastal and riverine districts, and so we put it in the targeted externalities group.

District of Columbia is a housekeeping committee, most of whose decisions have little electoral impact. However, the large African-American population in the District of Columbia has meant that the district's governance has been of special concern to the Black Caucus in Congress. Thus, we categorize District of Columbia as having a targeted jurisdiction.[6]

2.1.3 Committees with Mixed Externalities The Judiciary Committee is hard to categorize. Much of its work is of a housekeeping nature, with little electoral impact.[7] This fact would argue for a uniform classification, but the committee's long-standing involvement with civil rights legislation has made it of special interest to southern conservatives and northern liberals.[8] Thus, we put Judiciary in the mixed externalities category.

---

sources represent public assets, for most of our nation's history the problem facing the central government has not been a "tragedy of the commons," where too many people have tried to use public resources. Rather, from the perspective of national income, the problem has been underutilization. Thus, for the most part, particular interests have held sway over collective ones. The committee also oversees the regulation of coal, coal mines, and mine reclamation, all of which are narrowly targeted regional matters.

6. Perhaps District of Columbia should be classified as having uniform externalities for the Republican party; however, we do not bother here to differentiate between the parties.

7. Perkins (1980, 381) relates that members "expressed a lack of interest in Judiciary Committee legislation, calling it unimportant and of a 'housekeeping' nature." An examination of Judiciary Committee reports for the Ninety-second and Ninety-third Congresses shows that the bulk of the committee's work is on private bills (2,658 in the Ninety-second Congress), mostly relating to immigration and naturalization. Most of the rest of the committee's activities related to revisions and codification of the laws, holidays and commemorations, antitrust law, the courts, and prisons. The committee occasionally deals with civil rights and congressional redistricting issues. Unlike the Senate Judiciary Committee, the House committee has no formal role in the appointment of federal jurists.

8. According to Ogul (1976), the Judiciary Committee was a sought-after appoint-

The Committee on Foreign Affairs also has a mixed jurisdiction. On the one hand, it handles such issues of national importance as international relations and disarmament negotiations. (These jurisdictional items do not attract much attention because the committee's constitutional position is weak in comparison to its Senate counterpart, but their external effects are more or less uniform.) The foreign aid bill, on the other hand, attracts fairly lively interest from the narrow subset of members whose districts contain a large number of recent immigrants, Jews, or favored export industries.[9]

Throughout its history the Committee on Education and Labor has been concerned with the political agenda of organized labor. According to Munger and Fenno (1962), "When the Committee was established in 1946, its main focus was considered to be the field of labor—not education" (111), and this focus continued to the time of their study (177). Davidson (1974, 53), too, emphasizes the union labor focus of the committee, noting that "the AFL-CIO informally clears prospective Democratic committee members."[10] Constituents affected by these activities are largely concentrated in the Northeast and the Great Lakes region. From this perspective, the committee's jurisdiction is targeted. But occasionally, as with the Taft-Hartley Act, the committee is responsible for labor legislation of national significance. Moreover, the committee's educational jurisdiction also includes some policies of national importance.[11] Thus, the committee's jurisdiction falls into neither pure case, consisting as it does of much that is of only regional significance with occasional forays into nationally important issues.

The jurisdictions of the remaining two committees—Banking and Armed Services—changed dramatically in the postwar period, a shift that makes them particularly difficult to classify. The Banking Committee shapes public programs that deal with the nation's financial institutions and with a wide variety of urban policy matters. In the 1950s— when only about 130 members were elected from central city districts—

---

ment in the late 1950s and 1960s (138–39), with civil rights being the committee's most attractive (if not most important) subject matter. This view of the committee changed in the early 1970s, however, as the flood of civil rights legislation that the committee processed from 1957 to 1970 dried up (Ogul 1976, 151). See also Bolling 1974, 1.

9. Many foreign aid programs are not simply handouts; rather, they provide subsidies to foreign countries to purchase particular U.S. export goods. This connection means that foreign aid is likely to be of considerable particularistic interest.

10. The committee's report of activities in the Ninety-third Congress indicates that it spent about three-fourths of its time on labor matters.

11. However, many large educational programs were placed under the jurisdiction of other House committees.

these programs had a substantial effect on relatively few districts and imposed relatively modest externalities on the rest. As a result of court-ordered redistricting in the 1960s, however, the number of substantially urban districts grew from 221 in 1964 to more than 300 by 1974.[12] This growth, coupled with an expansion in jurisdiction in the 1960s to include the urban renewal and housing programs of the Great Society, meant that a much greater proportion of members were affected by the committee's policies in 1973 than had been affected a decade earlier. One option is to put the committee in different categories depending on the period of time under discussion. Here, however, we shall simply put it in the mixed externality group.

The Armed Services Committee has jurisdiction over matters that can simultaneously be of great national and local importance: every major weapons system is simultaneously a contribution (positive or negative) to our national defense and a cornucopia of targetable defense contracts. The other major policy in the committee's jurisdiction, the deployment of our armed forces, is of much less widespread concern now than it used to be. From 1952 to 1974, 125 major military installations were closed (Arnold 1979). By 1970, 255 districts had fewer than 1,000 military personnel stationed within their borders, and 20 percent of all districts had no defense-related employment (Goss 1972, 217); only 59 districts had more than 10,000 military personnel (roughly two standard deviations from the average of 4,500). By the early 1970s base closing had become an important matter for many of the members representing districts with major military installations threatened by closure (Arnold 1979, 126). At any one time, of course, base closing is an important issue to only a few handfuls of the roughly 150 members representing districts with major military installations (Arnold 1979). These members, largely from rural districts, have a stake in the committee's deployment policies. The remaining members of Congress have little or no stake in the issue.

The jurisdiction of the Armed Services Committee, then, was transformed in the early 1970s. During the early postwar period, the committee had a national policy jurisdiction with substantial external effects on all members of Congress. After the changes described by Arnold

12. For sources on changes in district composition, see McCubbins and Schwartz 1988. The categories *central city* and *substantially urban* are defined somewhat differently. *Substantially urban* includes all districts with more than 60 percent of the district's residents living in a Standard Metropolitan Statistical Area (SMSA). It is impossible to get consistent and meaningful measures of the degree of urbanization of particular districts.

(1979), the committee's jurisdiction was somewhat more mixed, containing national as well as more narrowly targeted policy issues. We put Armed Services, too, in the mixed externalities category.

2.1.4 Summary We have classified House committees into three groups based on the character of their jurisdictions. In the first group (uniform externalities) are Appropriations, Rules, Ways and Means, Interstate and Foreign Commerce, Public Works and Transportation, Science, Post Office and Civil Service, House Administration, Government Operations, and Veterans' Affairs. The second group (targeted externalities) consists of Agriculture, District of Columbia, Interior and Insular Affairs, and Merchant Marine and Fisheries. In the third group (mixed externalities) are Judiciary, Foreign Affairs, Education and Labor, Banking, and Armed Services.

We expect that committees in our uniform externalities group will tend to have contingents that are microcosms of their party caucuses. There is, by definition, no strong bias in the type of member willing to serve on these committees; everyone is equally interested in the important uniform jurisdictions and, perhaps, equally uninterested in the unimportant uniform jurisdictions. Moreover, neither party's CC has an incentive to prefer one type of member over another, for it wishes to create a committee that will produce legislation consistent with the maximization of seats. Appointing a committee that is not representative of the party as a whole simply runs the risk of its members' pursuing their own individual or factional interests at the expense of others' individual or factional interests. This risk, of course, is not very great if the committee's jurisdiction is unimportant (generates uniformly low externalities). Thus, the more important the committee's jurisdiction, the stronger the expectation of a representative contingent.

We expect the committees in our targeted externalities group to have party contingents that are unrepresentative of the party caucus on one or more dimensions. Indeed, if the committee's legislation produces no externalities outside of a well-defined group, we would expect only members of that group to be appointed to the committee. This pattern of appointment would serve the collective interests of the party because, by hypothesis, no "uninterested" member's probability of reelection can be affected much by committee decisions. Thus, because the interested members fully internalize everything of collective interest, there is no electoral need for uninterested members to be on the committee. In this case, of course, the contingent would be unrepresentative at least with respect to the characteristics that differentiate interested members from uninterested ones.

Finally, it is harder to say anything definitive about committees with mixed externalities jurisdictions. The closer they are to the uniform externalities end of the spectrum, the more representative they should be; the closer they are to the targeted externalities end, the more unrepresentative they may be.

2.2   EXTRAMURAL EFFECTS

The notion of external effects may be clear enough as a broad abstraction, but it is difficult to measure with any operational precision. A check on our classification can be provided by looking at extramural effects.

By *extramural effects* we mean effects that are felt by organized actors outside of Congress: pressure groups, trade associations, and the like. A clue to the breadth of a committee's jurisdiction is the number and diversity of groups that (regularly) attempt to influence the committee's deliberations by lobbying, appearing at hearings, and so forth. In principle, one might conduct a census of groups appearing at each committee's hearings in order to measure the size and character of extramural effects. All we do here is to subdivide each of our three categories—targeted, mixed, and uniform—based on an impressionistic judgment of which committees faced a more homogeneous and which a more heterogeneous group of lobbyists on a regular basis.

The result of this exercise is our final classification of committees (table 25). In addition to our expectations regarding committees with targeted, mixed, and uniform jurisdictions, we expect that *within* each of these categories the committees with the more homogeneous set of clientele groups will be less representative. The rationale behind this expectation is that a more homogeneous group of lobbyists is evidence that a narrower group of issues dominates the committee's jurisdiction.[13] Moreover, extramural actors may lobby for a particular kind of member to be appointed to "their" committee (recall the AFL-CIO's influence over Democratic appointments to Education and Labor), and

---

13. It should be noted that less-representative committees do not necessarily produce more targeted external effects, since the narrow group of issues may be important to a minority that is evenly distributed among congressional districts. But within each category of external effects, homogeneity of lobbying groups seems a reasonable clue that external effects may be more targeted.

TABLE 25.   CLASSIFICATION OF COMMITTEES BY
            TYPE OF EXTERNALITY

		Externalities		
		Targeted	*Mixed*	*Uniform*
Clientele	*Homogeneous*	Dist. of Columbia	Education and Labor Armed Services Banking	Science Post Office Veterans Public Works
Groups	*Heterogeneous*	Agriculture Interior Merchant Marine	Judiciary Foreign Affairs	Appropriations Rules Ways and Means Commerce Gov. Operations House Admin.

committee members, once appointed, may be exposed to incentives (such as campaign contributions) that induce them to vote in distinctive ways. This last point is relevant when the representativeness of a committee contingent is assessed in terms of how its members vote in comparison to the party as a whole.

2.3   A DIGRESSION

The discussion thus far has proceeded as if there were no constraints on a party CC's ability to appoint members. But in fact there are constraints, both in the form of various norms that are commonly thought to regulate CC behavior and, possibly, in the form of interactions with the other party. We discuss each of these kinds of constraint in turn.

The best-known and most obviously constraining regulatory norm is the seniority norm—which, among other things, confers security of committee tenure on members. If the CC could violate members' security of tenure with impunity, remaking committee rosters anew each session, it could ensure that the membership of each committee reflected the party's position on the issues before them. But CCs typically have been reluctant to violate members' tenure, even in the postreform era.

Barring a change in this equilibrium, both parties' ability to alter the composition of committees will depend, at least in the short run, on the number of vacancies to be filled.[14] As it turns out, the typical number of vacancies on most committees with uniform jurisdictions seems to have been enough for the parties' CCs, were they so inclined, to fashion a representative contingent. In other words, the vacancies constraint has not often been binding.

The primary exception to this observation is the Appropriations Committee. Kiewiet and McCubbins (1991) report that cumulative turnover among Democrats on the Appropriations Committee in the postwar era has been 10 percent less than among all House Democrats. This low turnover has made it difficult for appointments to Appropriations to keep pace with the steady liberalization of the Democratic party (as the southern conservative wing has disappeared).

Other norms that regulate CC behavior pose little or no constraint on the fashioning of balanced or representative contingents. For example, Democratic appointments to the larger and more important committees are influenced by three "group-retentive" norms: one that stipulates replacing a departing member from a medium-sized or large state with another member from the same state; one that stipulates replacing a departing female member with another female member; and one that stipulates replacing a departing African-American member with another African-American member (Bullock 1971; Friedman n.d.). Each of these norms can be viewed as furthering rather than hindering the achievement of balance on Democratic committee contingents.

With regard to interactions with the other party, we have two points to make. First, the majority party decides both the total number of seats that each committee will have and how many of these seats each party will get. In principle, it can use this power to "pack" committees—as was done, for example, with Rules in 1961 and Ways and Means in 1975 (Shepsle 1978). The minority party, lacking this power, faces an additional constraint in achieving balance in its contingents.

Second, one might suppose that each party's CC anticipates the appointments to be made by its opposite number. This supposition would make particular sense if, as much of the formal modeling literature explicitly supposes, parties matter little in committee and committee pol-

14. Of course, the mere existence of this constraint on each party's ability to structure its committee contingents indicates an element of party weakness. Before the revolt against Boss Cannon, members did not enjoy security of tenure on committees, and Speakers could restructure rosters as thoroughly as they wished.

icy recommendations reflect the interests of the median committee member. If everyone knows that the median committee member determines policy, should not those empowered to make appointments take this fact into account? If they do, a game results between the two parties' CCs. We shall not say much about this game except to note that, if it is analyzed under the standard spatial modeling assumption that parties do not matter, it generates predictions that are falsifiable and false.[15]

3. RESULTS

We turn now to an empirical investigation of the representativeness of party contingents. We begin, in sections 3.1 through 3.5, with a series of "static" tests that assess the degree to which contingents have been, at a given time, representative of the parties from which they were drawn. One might assess representativeness along any number of different dimensions: Is the contingent representative in terms of its general policy predispositions? Is it representative in terms of some more specific policy predispositions pertinent to the committee's jurisdiction? Is it representative in terms of the geographic location of its members' constituencies? Our strategy is to look at each of these kinds of representativeness using an array of different measures and methodologies.

Following the static tests, we look in section 3.6 at some "dynamic" tests that compare two sets of committee members: new appointees and continuing members. In any given Congress, the continuing members on a committee contingent may be unrepresentative of their party as a whole simply because of other party members who failed to secure reelection, retired, or transferred to another committee. If the continuing members on a uniform externality committee *are* unrepresentative in some fashion, we expect that the party CC will attempt to remedy the situation by appointing new members who restore the contingent's balance.

---

15. Consider the Democratic CC's appointments to a committee with thirty Democrats and twenty Republicans. The median member of the Democratic CC ("Ernie") wants to ensure that the median member of the committee being appointed ends up as close to his ideal point as possible. Suppose that all twenty of the Republican appointees are to Ernie's right. Then Ernie wants twenty Democrats to be to his left to balance the Republicans, and the other ten split evenly around him, for a total of twenty-five out of thirty Democrats to his left. This is not, of course, how appointments turn out.

3.1 CONTINGENT VERSUS PARTY MEANS: ADA SCORES

The ADA has rated the roll call voting records of members of Congress since 1947, with higher scores going to more liberal members. In tables 26 (for the Democrats) and 27 (for the Republicans) we investigate whether the mean ADA score on each committee contingent differs significantly from the mean ADA score of the party from which it was drawn. In each table a plus sign (+) indicates that the contingent had a mean ADA score significantly greater than the mean for the party (thus indicating that the contingent was more liberal than the party), whereas a minus sign (−) indicates a mean ADA score significantly lower than the party's.[16] Both tables rate all committees—except Budget, HUAAC, and Small Business—for the Eighty-seventh through Ninety-seventh Congresses.

First, the Democratic contingents on seven of our ten "uniform externalities" committees *never* had mean ADA scores that differed significantly from the mean for the remainder of the party (table 26). The only uniform committees that were ever unrepresentative in terms of their ADA scores were Public Works (in one Congress), Government Operations (in two), and Veterans' Affairs (in four).

Second, among the "mixed externalities" committees, Democratic contingents were occasionally unrepresentative on three (Foreign Affairs, Judiciary, and Banking) and often unrepresentative on two (Armed Services and Education and Labor). Democrats on Education and Labor were significantly more liberal in all Congresses, whereas those on Armed Services were significantly more conservative starting in the Ninety-second Congress.

Finally, among the "targeted externalities" committees, two (Interior and Merchant Marine and Fisheries) never had unrepresentative Democratic contingents, whereas two (Agriculture and District of Columbia) were unrepresentative in almost half the Congresses covered. In interpreting these results, it should be remembered that committees with targeted jurisdictions are predicted to be unrepresentative along some, but not necessarily all, dimensions. In the case of Interior and Merchant Marine and Fisheries the cleavage between committee and noncommittee members is easiest to discern in geographical terms, as discussed in section 3.5.[17]

16. The .05 significance level is used throughout. We thus ignore the comments of Hall and Grofman 1990 in this section. They are addressed in the following sections.
17. We also ran difference-of-means tests for two other scores: the ACA score and

TABLE 26. SUMMARY OF DIFFERENCE-OF-MEANS TESTS ON ADA RATINGS BETWEEN DEMOCRATIC COMMITTEE CONTINGENTS AND THE PARTY, EIGHTY-SEVENTH TO NINETY-SEVENTH CONGRESSES

Committee	Congress										
	87	88	89	90	91	92	93	94	95	96	97
Agriculture	−				−	−	−			−	
Appropriations											
Armed Services						−	−	−	−	−	−
Banking		+					+				
Commerce											
Dist. of Columbia	−	−					+				+
Education and Labor	+	+	+	+	+	+	+	+	+	+	+
Foreign Affairs					+				+		
Gov. Operations		+							+		
House Admin.											
Interior											
Judiciary					+	+	+				+
Merchant Marine											
Post Office											
Public Works									−		
Rules											
Science											
Veterans		−		−					−		−
Ways and Means											

NOTES: − = Mean contingent ADA score significantly lower than party mean.
+ = Mean contingent ADA score significantly higher than party mean.

TABLE 27. SUMMARY OF DIFFERENCE-OF-MEANS TESTS ON ADA RATINGS BETWEEN REPUBLICAN COMMITTEE CONTINGENTS AND THE PARTY, EIGHTY-SEVENTH TO NINETY-SEVENTH CONGRESSES

Committee	Congress										
	87	88	89	90	91	92	93	94	95	96	97
Agriculture	−	−	−	−	−						
Appropriations	−										
Armed Services							−	−	−	−	−
Banking									+		
Commerce					−	−	−				
Dist. of Columbia		+							+		
Education and Labor	−						+				
Foreign Affairs						+	+	+		+	+
Gov. Operations					+		+	+			
House Admin.								−		−	
Interior			−				−	−			−
Judiciary					+	+	+				+
Merchant Marine					+	+	+	+			
Post Office					−						
Public Works				−			−	−	−	−	
Rules	−	−									−
Science											
Veterans											
Ways and Means	−	−	−	−	−	−				−	

NOTES: − = Mean contingent ADA score significantly lower than party mean.
+ = Mean contingent ADA score significantly higher than party mean.

The results for Republican contingents are presented in table 27. Somewhat surprisingly, in seven of the eleven Congresses investigated, the average member of the Republican contingent on Ways and Means was significantly less likely to support the position advocated by ADA than was the average member of the party; in other words, Ways and Means Republicans have tended to be significantly more conservative than their party as a whole. Also contrary to expectation, the Republicans on Public Works were frequently more conservative than their party. The Republican contingents on Rules, Commerce, and Government Operations were unrepresentative of their party in three of the eleven Congresses. The remaining Republican contingents fit more clearly with our expectations.[18]

What explains the Ways and Means and Public Works Republicans? One might answer this question with a careful historical analysis of Republican factional politics or of their traditional opposition to New Deal "tax and spend" politics—the "tax" side of which went through Ways and Means and much of the "spend" side of which went through Public Works. But it should also be noted that getting committee appointments right matters less for a hopeless minority than it does for a majority party. The value of fashioning representative contingents for the majority is that the deals struck within such contingents are likely to stick within the party as a whole. If they do stick, then they are likely to pass, since the party has a majority. For the minority party, however, equally representative contingents may agree on alternative legislation, and they may even carry their colleagues on the floor, but they can rarely hope to succeed in passing it; so the payoff to careful balancing is somewhat less.

3.2 CONTINGENT VERSUS PARTY MEDIANS: NOMINATE SCORES

In chapter 3 we introduced Poole and Rosenthal's NOMINATE scores as a more informative alternative to the use of interest group ratings such

---

the conservative coalition support score compiled by *National Journal*. The results were similar to those reported in table 26, the chief difference being that the Democratic contingent on Veterans' Affairs was unrepresentative in seven of twelve Congresses on the basis of ACA scores, rather than four of eleven on the basis of ADA scores.

18. The results in table 27 for Republican ADA scores are closely replicated for Republican ACA scores, with two exceptions. The Republicans on Agriculture and Armed Services are only rarely unrepresentative of the Republican party in terms of their ACA scores. The results for Republican conservative coalition scores also closely approximate the results given in table 27.

as ADA. Here we use the Wilcoxon difference-of-medians test to assess whether each contingent in each Congress is representative of the party from which it is drawn in terms of its NOMINATE scores.[19] Thus, in contrast with the previous section we use both a different measure of general ideological predisposition (NOMINATE rather than ADA scores) and a different measure of central tendency (the median rather than the mean). The point is simply to show that the findings sketched in the previous section do not depend crucially on a particular measure or methodology. An additional benefit from using NOMINATE scores, beyond the technical advantages indicated in chapter 3, is that these scores are available for every postwar Congress in our purview (the Eightieth through the Hundredth).

The null hypothesis in the Wilcoxon tests is that each contingent is as if drawn at random from the party as a whole. If this null is rejected, we take the committee to be unrepresentative; otherwise, we take it to be representative.[20]

Our results are given in tables 28 (for the Democrats) and 29 (for the Republicans). Because NOMINATE scores are larger for more conservative members, plus signs indicate contingents that are more conservative than their party, and minus signs indicate contingents that are more liberal.

We look first at Democratic contingents and differences significant at the .05 level. There are four groups among the "uniform externalities" committees: the contingents on Interstate and Foreign Commerce, House Administration, Rules, and Ways and Means were never significantly different from the rest of the Democratic party; those on Public Works, Science, and Post Office were each significantly different in two of the twenty-one Congresses; those on Appropriations and Government Operations were significantly different in three Congresses; and that of Veterans' Affairs was significantly different in five Congresses. Among the "mixed externalities" committees, one finds two groups: Judiciary and Foreign Affairs both differ significantly in about a quarter of the Congresses investigated; by contrast, the three intermediate com-

---

19. We discuss this test more fully in chapter 3.

20. It is obvious that contingents are not chosen at random, so one may ask what the point is of testing the null hypothesis that they are. The reasoning—implicit in previous studies that use the same basic methodology—is as follows: The difference between the contingent median and party median is a rough measure of the contingent's unrepresentativeness—the larger the difference, the more unrepresentative. If one wishes to classify contingents as either "representative" or "unrepresentative," however, where should the cutoff be made? The cutoff here is the .05 critical value for rejecting the null. The interpretation is that differences that might have arisen by chance, *had assignment been random*, are not large.

TABLE 28. SUMMARY OF WILCOXON DIFFERENCE-OF-MEDIANS TESTS ON NOMINATE RATINGS BETWEEN DEMOCRATIC COMMITTEE CONTINGENTS AND THE PARTY, EIGHTIETH TO HUNDREDTH CONGRESSES

Committee	Congress								
	80	81	82	83	84	85	86	87	88
Agriculture		+	+	+		+	+	+	.15
Appropriations							.10		+
Armed Services	+			.10	.15				
Banking		−	−	−	−	−	−.10	−	−
Commerce									
Dist. of Columbia			−.15				−.15		
Education and Labor					−	−	−	−	−.10
Foreign Affairs	−	−.10	−.15		.15		−.15		−.10
Gov. Operations		−.10		−	−.10				−
House Admin.		.15							
Interior				.15					
Judiciary									
Merchant Marine									
Post Office									
Public Works									
Rules				.15					
Science	N/A	N/A	N/A	N/A	N/A	N/A			
Veterans			+					.10	
Ways and Means									

NOTES: + = Contingent median is significantly greater than the party median at the .05 level.
− = Contingent median is significantly smaller than the party median at the .05 level.
.10 (−.10) = Contingent median is significantly greater (smaller) than the party median at the .10 level.
.15 (−.15) = Contingent median is significantly greater (smaller) than the party median at the .15 level.

					Congress						
89	*90*	*91*	*92*	*93*	*94*	*95*	*96*	*97*	*98*	*99*	*100*
+	+	+	+	+		.10	+	.10	+	+	+
.10	.15	+	.10	+	.10						
.10	.15	+	+	+	+	+	+	+	+	+	+
−	−		−					−.10			
				−			−	−	−	−	−
−	−	−	−	−	−	−	−	−	−	−.10	−.10
−.10	−.10	−	−.15		−.15	−	−.15		−	−	−
−.15		−			−.10	−.10					
							−.15				
.15											
		−.10	−	−	−		−.15		−	−.10	−
									.10	.10	.10
		−.15		−.10	−.10	−		−	−.10	−.10	−.10
	.15					+	+				
						−.10					
				.10		.15	.15			+	+
					.10	+	+	+	+	+	.10

TABLE 29. SUMMARY OF WILCOXON DIFFERENCE-OF-
MEDIANS TESTS ON NOMINATE RATINGS BETWEEN
REPUBLICAN COMMITTEE CONTINGENTS AND THE
PARTY, EIGHTIETH TO HUNDREDTH CONGRESSES

| | | | | | Congress | | | | |
Committee	80	81	82	83	84	85	86	87	88
Agriculture						+		.10	+
Appropriations				+		.10	.15	+	.10
Armed Services						−		−.10	
Banking									
Commerce	−			−.10	−.10				
Dist. of Columbia				−.15	−			−	−
Education and Labor	.15		.10		+				
Foreign Affairs	−.10			−			−.10	−	
Gov. Operations									−.10
House Admin.	.15								
Interior	−.15		.10						
Judiciary									
Merchant Marine		−.10	−.10						−
Post Office		−.10		−					
Public Works									
Rules					.15		.10	.10	.10
Science	N/A	N/A	N/A	N/A	N/A	N/A	−.15		−.10
Veterans	−.15	−.15	−	−				−.15	
Ways and Means	+	+						+	.10

NOTES: + = Contingent median is significantly greater than the party median at the .05 level.
  − = Contingent median is significantly smaller than the party median at the .05 level.
  .10 (−.10) = Contingent median is significantly greater (smaller) than the party median at the .10 level.
  .15 (−.15) = Contingent median is significantly greater (smaller) than the party median at the .15 level.

					Congress						
89	90	91	92	93	94	95	96	97	98	99	100
.10	+	+	+								
									−.10	−	
		.15	+						.15		.10
−.15											
									.15		+
					−.15	−.15					
					−.10						
		−.10	−		−		−.10	−.15			−.15
	−.10	−	−.10	−	−.15						
					+	.15	.15			+	+
		.15			.10			.10		+	+
		−	−							+	
−.10	−.10		−					−.15			−.10
		+	.15								
	.15			.10		.15	+				.10
.10								.10			
								−.15			
	−.15								−.15	−.15	
.10	.15			.15	.10				.15		

mittees with the most homogeneous clientele groups—Armed Services, Banking, and Education and Labor—differ significantly about half the time. Finally, among the "targeted externalities" committees, the Democratic contingents on Interior and Merchant Marine and Fisheries never differed significantly from the rest of the Democratic party, while the contingent on DC differed eight times and that on Agriculture fifteen times.

These results jibe, for the most part, with our expectations and with the results using ADA scores reported in the last section.[21] We expected that committees with uniform jurisdictions would not differ significantly on any politically important dimension. If we arbitrarily say that a committee contingent is "generally representative" if it differs significantly from its party less than 10 percent of the time, we find that only three of the uniform committees—Appropriations, Government Operations, and Veterans' Affairs—fail to qualify as generally representative. As Kiewiet and McCubbins (1991) have argued at length, the Appropriations case seems to be one in which there were not enough vacancies on the committee to keep up with changes in the caucus. Veterans' Affairs may be a case in which the influence of a monolithic clientele group—organized veterans—outweighs the possible external effects.

Hall and Grofman (1990), in a critique of Krehbiel (1990), have noted that conventional Type I error rates—.05 in our case—may not be appropriate if one wishes to show that a committee *is* representative. The logic is simply that the probability of a Type II error (acceptance of a false null) is quite large when the probability of a Type I error (rejection of a true null) is set to .05; but the Type II error ought to be set to a lower value by a researcher who wishes to infer from acceptance of the null that committees are representative (cf. Blalock 1979, 157–65).[22] The only way of obtaining a lower probability of Type II error, of course, is by choosing a somewhat higher significance level (Type I error probability). Accordingly, table 28 also reports contingent-party differences

21. The primary differences between the ADA difference-of-means test and the NOMINATE difference-of-medians test concern two committees: Appropriations and Banking. Democratic contingents on both committees are judged more frequently unrepresentative in terms of their median NOMINATE scores than in terms of their mean ADA scores.

22. Although this point is well taken in some contexts, we are not sure that this is one of them. After all, the null hypothesis—that contingents are drawn at random from their respective parties— is obviously false, as demonstrated by the fact that any previous member who wishes to stay on a committee may do so. In the present context, the .05 level is being used simply as a benchmark, a slightly less arbitrary way of deciding which contingents are representative and which are unrepresentative.

that are significant at the .15 level; this modification substantially changes the results for only five of the uniform externalities committees—Science, Post Office, Appropriations, Government Operations, and Veterans' Affairs—all of which are found to differ significantly in three to six more Congresses. It should be noted that after Veterans' Affairs, Post Office and Science have the most homogeneous clientele groups among the committees with uniform jurisdictions.

The results in table 29 (taking the .05 significance-level results first) generally show Republican contingents on the "uniform externalities" committees to be less unrepresentative than they were in terms of ADA scores. In particular, Ways and Means and Public Works Republicans, as well as those on Interstate and Foreign Commerce, Government Operations, and Rules, were less frequently unrepresentative of their party in terms of their median NOMINATE scores than they had been in terms of their mean ADA scores.[23] Otherwise, the NOMINATE results are similar to the ADA results. Differences at lower levels of significance show the Republican contingents on both Rules and Ways and Means as unrepresentative considerably more often (in six or more Congresses).

3.3   CONTINGENT VERSUS PARTY DISTRIBUTIONS: NOMINATE SCORES

The Wilcoxon tests just reported reveal whether the median member on a contingent differed significantly from the median member of the party as a whole. It remains possible, of course, that the *distribution* of NOMINATE scores on a contingent is unrepresentative even if the median is not. For example, the members on a contingent might be more (or less) tightly clustered around the median than are their party colleagues in general. But our model suggests that the entire distribution of scores on a "uniform externalities" committee will be representative of that in the party.

Accordingly, in this section we use a quintile-based chi-square to assess the representativeness of party contingents. To compute this statistic, we first rank the members of each party from most liberal to most conservative, based on their NOMINATE scores, then divide each party into fifths. The chi-square measures under- or overrepresentation of each

23. Recall that we suggested in explanation of the ADA results that the Republicans were emphasizing their opposition to New Deal policies by putting their most committed opponents on the relevant committees. If this line of thought has merit, then the results just noted in the text presumably show that ADA scores are more focused on the traditional New Deal political agenda than are the more broadly based NOMINATE scores.

TABLE 30. SUMMARY OF QUINTILE-BASED CHI-SQUARES ON NOMINATE RATINGS FOR DEMOCRATIC COMMITTEE CONTINGENTS, EIGHTIETH TO HUNDREDTH CONGRESSES

Committee	80	81	82	83	84	85	86	87	88
Agriculture			+			+	.10	.15	
Appropriations									.10
Armed Services							.15		
Banking					.15	+		.15	.15
Commerce									
Dist. of Columbia					.15			.15	+
Education and Labor					+	.10	+	.10	
Foreign Affairs		.10	.10						
Gov. Operations				+					
House Admin.		+		.15					
Interior								.10	
Judiciary									
Merchant Marine				.15					
Post Office									
Public Works								.15	
Rules				.10					
Science	N/A	N/A	N/A	N/A	N/A	N/A			
Veterans									+
Ways and Means				.15					

NOTE: + = Chi-square values are significantly greater than zero at the .05 level; .10 and .15 denote significance at those lower levels.

				Congress							
89	90	91	92	93	94	95	96	97	98	99	100
.10	+	+	.10	.15					+		+
				.15							
	.15	.15	+	+	+	+	+	+	+	+	+
	+			.15							
+											
+	.15			+			.15	.15	.15	+	+
+	+	+	+	+	.15		.15	.15	.10		
	.10	+				.10			+		+
					+	+					
.15					+		.15				.15
					.15						
		+	+				.15	+		+	.10
		.15				+					
	.15					.15	.10				
	.10		.10	.15							
										.15	.15
.10		+	.15	.10		+	+	+	.10		

TABLE 31. SUMMARY OF QUINTILE-BASED
CHI-SQUARES ON NOMINATE RATINGS FOR
REPUBLICAN COMMITTEE CONTINGENTS, EIGHTIETH
TO HUNDREDTH CONGRESSES

					Congress				
Committee	80	81	82	83	84	85	86	87	88
Agriculture				.15					+
Appropriations				+	.10				
Armed Services						.15			
Banking									+
Commerce				.15					
Dist. of Columbia	.15			.15				.15	
Education and Labor		.15			.15				
Foreign Affairs			.15	.15				+	
Gov. Operations									.15
House Admin.									.15
Interior				.10	+				+
Judiciary	+							+	
Merchant Marine			.10		+				
Post Office	.15	.15							
Public Works									
Rules	.10					.10			
Science	N/A	N/A	N/A	N/A	N/A	N/A			
Veterans	.15			+					
Ways and Means									

NOTE: + = Chi-square values are significantly greater than zero at the .05 level; .10 and .15 denote significance at those lower levels.

					Congress						
89	90	91	92	93	94	95	96	97	98	99	100
								.15			
										+	
			+								
						+		.10	.10		
+				.15				+			
					.15	.15	.15				
										+	
			+	+			.10				
		.10								.10	+
										.15	
		+									
		+								+	
.10	.10		.10	+	.15			.15			
										.15	.10
		.10					+				
	+		+								
.10								.15			
			.15						.15		
									.10		

of these quintiles: the greater the departure from equal representation for each, the greater the value of the statistic. We present the results in tables 30 and 31. Chi-square values significantly greater than zero at the .05 level are denoted with a plus sign (+); values greater than zero at the .10 and .15 levels are explicitly labeled in the tables.

Five of the uniform externality committees had Democratic contingents that were never significantly different (at the .05 level) from the Democratic party as a whole (table 30). Of the five that did differ, two (Interstate and Foreign Commerce and Post Office) did so in only one Congress, while another two (Government Operations and House Administration) did so in three or fewer. Only Veterans' Affairs, with probably the most homogeneous clientele group of the lot, tended to have unrepresentative contingents more frequently (in five of the twenty-one Congresses).

These results show that discrepancies between the distribution of opinion on Democratic contingents and the distribution of opinion in the Democratic party as a whole are even rarer than discrepancies between contingent medians and party medians—at least as regards the uniform externality committees. This result is particularly true of the Appropriations Committee, which, although it tended to deviate in terms of central tendency fairly often, did not in terms of overall distribution. Little is changed in this assessment if one counts differences at the .15 level as significant.

The results for contingents dealing with mixed jurisdictions are also similar to those obtained previously. Once again, one finds Democratic contingents on Judiciary and Foreign Affairs differing less often (three or four times in twenty-one Congresses), the contingents on Armed Services and Education and Labor—both with relatively homogeneous clientele groups—differing more often (seven to nine times). The only change involves the contingent on Banking, which in this analysis differs significantly from the Democratic Caucus in only two Congresses.

The results for Democratic contingents on targeted externality committees were essentially the same as those obtained with the difference-of-medians test. The contingents on Agriculture and District of Columbia differ significantly fairly often, while those of Interior and Merchant Marine and Fisheries never do.

The results for Republican contingents are presented in table 31. None of the contingents on uniform externality committees was unrepresentative in terms of the distribution of their NOMINATE scores in more than two Congresses. This finding is roughly in accord with the difference-of-medians tests, although there is a general tendency for contingents to be unrepresentative in terms of distribution less often than they are in terms of medians.[24]

3.4 CONTINGENT VERSUS PARTY BEHAVIOR ON COMMITTEE-RELATED ROLL CALLS

Thus far we have investigated the representativeness of committee contingents only in terms of their general ideological stance, as measured by ADA or NOMINATE scores. But a contingent may be representative in general terms and at the same time unrepresentative in terms of the specific issues with which the committee deals. To explore this possibility, we supplement the analyses of the previous three sections with one that looks for unrepresentative behavior on just those roll calls pertinent to the committee's jurisdiction.

One way of focusing the analysis on committee-specific roll calls—that employed in the previous literature (Weingast and Marshall 1988; Krehbiel 1990)—is to rely on the evaluations of a special interest group. For example, one might use the National Security Voting Index compiled by the American Security Council to assess the behavior of members of the Armed Services Committee, the score compiled by the Committee on Political Education of the AFL-CIO to assess the behavior of members of the Education and Labor Committee, and so forth.

Although using interest group scores to measure behavior along more narrowly defined issue dimensions is convenient, there are some problems with this approach. First, one cannot find an appropriate interest group score for every committee. Second, as discussed in chapter 3, special interest groups often construct their scores in order to identify friends and expose enemies. This desire usually entails concentrating on a few litmus test votes rather than on the entire range of votes related to the issue of concern, so that the difference between friends and enemies will be put into starker relief. But the stark differences on the litmus tests may not be entirely representative of the milder differences on the whole range of votes.

Instead of relying on interest group scores to tap into each committee's jurisdiction, we have constructed our own scores. These, too, have substantial weaknesses, as we explain below, but they complement the more often used interest group scores.

---

24. The only uniform externality committee for which a distributional difference showed up more frequently than a difference in medians is Rules.

Our scores can be explained most easily by considering a specific example—say, the Agriculture Committee in the Ninety-eighth Congress. As it turns out, a total of twenty-three roll calls pertinent to bills were reported out by the Agriculture Committee in the Ninety-eighth Congress.[25] Our strategy is to gauge the representativeness of the Democratic members on Agriculture by comparing their voting behavior on these twenty-three votes to that of their noncommittee colleagues.

First, for each of the twenty-three roll calls we compute the difference between the proportion of the contingent voting yes and the proportion of the rest of the party voting yes. Second, we take the absolute value of each of these twenty-three differences and average them. This approach yields a straightforward statistic, the mean absolute difference (MAD), which is essentially Rice's "index of likeness" applied to the difference between contingents and parties instead of the difference between parties. If MAD is zero, then the contingent and the rest of the party never differed, and there is no evidence of unrepresentativeness; as MAD grows larger, the contingent appears more and more distinctive in its behavior vis-à-vis the rest of the party.

Although MAD is easy to calculate, there are two important problems of interpretation. First, the distribution of MAD under the null hypothesis of "no difference between contingent and party" is not known, so it is difficult to judge statistical significance. Part of the problem is that distributions involving absolute values are always a bit tricky. But even if we were interested in the mean difference rather than the mean absolute difference there would be a problem because one cannot assume that all the votes related to a given committee's bills are statistically independent. Often there will be several votes on a single committee bill, all of which concern procedural attempts to kill it; these votes are obviously not statistically independent. Indeed, they are essentially the same vote taken over and over again. More generally, even votes on different bills from the same committee are not independent for present purposes because the process by which votes are generated is nothing like a random draw from some big bin of possible votes. Votes on committee bills are generated in two steps, both of which may involve strategic calculation: first, the committee has to decide to report a bill; second, someone has to decide to call for a vote on some aspect of the bill. Because the membership of the committee contingent remains the same

25. This figure includes roll calls held on rules for the consideration of Agriculture's bills.

over all votes in a given Congress (ignoring midterm changes in personnel), the same selection pressures on bills will be evident throughout the term. Any procedure that counts votes as if they were independent draws from some fixed distribution will underestimate standard errors and hence be too likely to find statistically significant differences.

Second, and more serious, the size of MAD is far from being a direct and unproblematic measure of the representativeness of the committee contingent under investigation. Committee and noncommittee Democrats may vote differently on committee-related roll calls either because they have different underlying preferences on the issues at stake (i.e., the committee contingent is unrepresentative) or because committee Democrats are involved in a nexus of logrolls and side payments that boosts their support for committee handiwork above what it would otherwise be on preferential grounds alone. For example, if the proportion of Ways and Means Democrats voting yes on final passage of some tax bill exceeds the analogous proportion of noncommittee Democrats, is this because of an ideological difference or because some committee Democrats, who might have opposed the bill, were brought on board with generous transition rules or other particularistic favors incorporated in the bill? Similarly, if the proportion of Commerce Democrats voting yes on final passage of some energy bill exceeds the analogous proportion of noncommittee Democrats, is this because of some ideological difference or because some committee Democrats, who might otherwise have opposed the bill, were using their votes to purchase their committee colleagues' support on another committee bill?

A large MAD might indicate simply that a committee is highly integrated, in the sense that committee members trade with one another, using votes as the primary medium of exchange.[26] From this perspective, a high value of MAD for a particular committee might measure how much logrolling goes on within the committee. The extent of logrolling within a committee might in turn depend on both the breadth of its jurisdiction (broader jurisdictions creating the potential for more trades) and the availability of particularistic side payments (more side payments also creating the potential for more trades).

All these matters, of course, make the interpretation of MAD values

26. For some committees, members' ability to trade with one another might itself depend on underlying preference characteristics. For example, if most members of the Armed Services Committee have military bases in their districts, then member A will oppose closing B's bases in return for B's opposition to closing A's bases; the committee Democrats thus will support military spending more than noncommittee Democrats will.

difficult. For example, if MAD measures unrepresentativeness, we should expect Appropriations to have a small MAD value; but if MAD measures committee integration, we might expect Appropriations to have a high MAD value.[27]

With these caveats in mind we can turn to table 32, which gives the total number of pertinent roll calls for each committee in all even-numbered Congresses from the Eighty-fourth to the Hundredth, inclusive, together with the mean absolute difference between the proportion of the committee and noncommittee Democrats voting yes.

There are three points to note about these figures:

First, in substantive terms there does not seem to be much to distinguish the various committees. Only two stand out from the pack: Veterans' Affairs, which has the lowest MAD value (2.3 percent); and Armed Services, which has the highest MAD value (17.9 percent). Most of the rest cluster in the range from 7 to 13 percent.

Second, there is only a small correlation (.27) between a committee's MAD values in succeeding Congresses; that is, if one wanted to predict a committee's MAD value in Congress t, the same committee's value in Congress t-2 would be of little value. This suggests either that MAD does not measure unrepresentativeness very well or that committees change frequently in how they rank in terms of unrepresentativeness. If there were some stable ranking of committee representativeness—as indicated for example by the substantial stability of committee rankings based on NOMINATE scores—and MAD tapped into it well, then we should find the same ordering of committees in Congress after Congress. We do not.

Our conclusion from this analysis is that trying to measure how unrepresentative a committee contingent is with regard to (some subset of) issues within the committee's jurisdiction is problematic. Using roll calls that *do not* pertain to bills reported out by the committee in ques-

---

27. With enough data, the uncertainty over the interpretation of MAD might be reduced. Suppose, for example, that we identified all Democrats who transferred to Armed Services in the postwar period. For each of them, we could calculate how frequently they supported the majority position among Armed Services Democrats in (1) the Congress just before they joined the committee and (2) the Congress in which they joined. If MAD measures underlying preference disparity, and committees are fairly stable over time in terms of the preferences of their members (as suggested in the literature on self-selection), then we should find little difference in the voting behavior of transferees before and after transfer. They have a general predisposition similar to that of the rest of the committee Democrats, and they express this predisposition both before and after they join the committee. By contrast, if MAD measures the extent of intracommittee logrolling, then one would expect higher rates of support for committee Democrats after than before transfer. Unfortunately, we do not at present have the data to perform this analysis.

TABLE 32.   MEAN ABSOLUTE DIFFERENCE
(MAD) IN PERCENT VOTING YES BETWEEN
COMMITTEE AND NONCOMMITTEE DEMOCRATS,
SELECTED CONGRESSES

Committee	MAD (%)	Roll Calls (N)
Agriculture	11.5	203
Appropriations	10.3	866
Armed Services	17.9	254
Banking	9.7	232
Budget	15.6	13
Commerce	7.0	348
Dist. of Columbia	11.9	60
Education and Labor	11.9	304
Foreign Affairs	12.4	217
Gov. Operations	8.0	101
House Admin.	10.4	33
Interior	8.2	179
Judiciary	8.6	270
Merchant Marine	7.0	128
Post Office	12.2	89
Public Works	11.1	118
Science	8.9	107
Veterans	2.3	48
Ways and Means	10.7	352

NOTE: The first column gives the MAD between the percentage of committee Democrats voting yes and the percentage of noncommittee Democrats voting yes on committee-related votes. The second column gives the
number of these votes in the Eighty-fourth, Eighty-sixth, Eighty-eighth,
Ninetieth, Ninety-second, Ninety-fourth, Ninety-sixth, and Ninety-eighth
Congresses. The average is taken over all votes from all Congresses.

tion, one faces Scylla: Are the bills actually relevant to the committee's
jurisdiction? And if so, why are they not in it? Using roll calls that *do*
pertain to bills reported out by the committee, one faces Charybdis: To
what extent do differences between how committee contingents and
their party colleagues vote reflect logrolling within committees rather
than distinct preferences? This dilemma faces not just the method investigated here but also the traditional method of relying on the voting
scores compiled by special interest groups.

3.5 REGIONAL REPRESENTATIVENESS

In this section we consider the geographic representativeness of committee contingents. Part of the motivation for doing so is to shore up the evidence on the targeted externality committees. We have predicted that contingents on these committees will tend to be unrepresentative of their parties along some dimension. Two of these committees—Interior and Merchant Marine and Fisheries—have shown no tendency toward *ideological* unrepresentativeness, as measured either by ADA or NOMINATE scores. It is well known, however, that both are *geographically* unrepresentative, with Merchant Marine and Fisheries attracting coastal members and Interior attracting western members (see, for example, Smith and Deering 1990). We have found that this committee-wide tendency is reflected in both parties' contingents. For example, the pattern of regional representation on the Interior Committee's contingents is sufficiently unusual so that it is unlikely to have arisen by chance in any postwar Congress. It should also be noted that both parties' contingents on another targeted externality committee—Agriculture—are geographically unrepresentative in virtually every postwar Congress.

A second motivation for discussing the issue of geographic representativeness is simply to test the uniform externality committee contingents along another dimension. The investigation proceeds by first categorizing members into three regions—North, South, and West—and then testing each contingent (with a chi-square statistic) to see if the overall pattern of regional representation was different from that in the party as a whole. The results (not reported here) show that on only two uniform externality committees—Veterans' Affairs and Public Works—were contingents of either party geographically unrepresentative in more than two of the twenty-one postwar Congresses in our purview.

3.6 CONTINUING MEMBERS AND NEW MEMBERS

Thus far, all of our investigations have been "static" in the sense that they compare the characteristics of a contingent to the party from which it was drawn at a given time. In this section we ask a slightly different and more "dynamic" question: if the *continuing* members of a contingent are unrepresentative in some fashion, will the party CC attempt to use whatever new appointments it has to redress the balance?[28]

28. By *continuing members* we mean members of the committee who both won re-election and chose to retain their positions on the committee.

In the case of uniform externality committees, we expect that each party will attempt to restore balance on its contingent if electoral vagaries or unusual transfer patterns disrupt it. One crude way to test this expectation is as follows: First run the Wilcoxon difference-of-medians test on the continuing members of the contingent only, then on the full membership.[29] Classify each committee in a two-by-two table, according to whether (1) the continuing members' median was or was not significantly different from the party median and (2) the full membership's median was or was not significantly different from the party median.[30] We expect that if the median of the continuing members' NOMINATE scores does not differ significantly from the party's, then the contingent will be "left alone": the new appointments will not push the median into the "significantly different" range. By contrast, if the continuing members are unrepresentative, we expect that the new appointments will be used to pull the contingent back into greater conformity with the party as a whole.

How these expectations stack up against the data can be seen in tables 33 (for Democratic contingents) and 34 (for Republican contingents). In this analysis we consider only Appropriations, Rules, and Ways and Means.

For the Democrats, our predictions are confirmed. The returning Democratic members of both the Rules and the Ways and Means committees were unrepresentative of their party only once in the postwar era. In both cases the new appointments made to the committee counterbalanced the returning members enough so that the full contingent was no longer unrepresentative. Moreover, when the continuing Democratic members of Rules or Ways and Means were already representative of their party, the new appointees never disturbed this relationship sufficiently to produce an unrepresentative contingent.

The evidence is slightly more complicated for the Appropriations Committee. The returning Democratic members of Appropriations were unrepresentative of their party on seven occasions—and on only four of these occasions did the new appointees move the contingent back into greater conformity with the party. The explanation for the three "failures," however, is straightforward: there simply were not enough vacant seats to move the median enough to produce a representative contingent (cf. Kiewiet and McCubbins 1991, chap. 5).

---

29. *Full membership* refers to the membership at the beginning of the Congress, just after committee assignments have been announced.

30. We can construct the same tables comparing quintile-based chi-square statistics instead of Wilcoxon statistics. The results are equivalent.

TABLE 33. DEMOCRATIC REALIGNMENT OF CONTROL COMMITTEES, EIGHTIETH TO HUNDREDTH CONGRESSES

Appropriations

		Full Membership	
		NS	S
Returning Members Only	NS	12	0
	S	4	3

Rules

		Full Membership	
		NS	S
Returning Members Only	NS	18	0
	S	1	0

Ways and Means

		Full Membership	
		NS	S
Returning Members Only	NS	18	0
	S	1	0

Control

		Full Membership	
		NS	S
Returning Members Only	NS	48	0
	S	6	3

NOTES: NS = Wilcoxon test was not significant for this group.
S = Wilcoxon test was significant for this group.

TABLE 34. REPUBLICAN REALIGNMENT OF CONTROL COMMITTEES, EIGHTIETH TO HUNDREDTH CONGRESSES

Appropriations

		Full Membership	
		NS	S
Returning Members Only	NS	17	1
	S	0	1

Rules

		Full Membership	
		NS	S
Returning Members Only	NS	19	0
	S	0	0

Ways and Means

		Full Membership	
		NS	S
Returning Members Only	NS	14	1
	S	2	2

Control

		Full Membership	
		NS	S
Returning Members Only	NS	50	2
	S	2	3

NOTES: NS = Wilcoxon test was not significant for this group.
S = Wilcoxon test was significant for this group.

The Republicans do not seem to have balanced their contingents on the control committees as consistently as the Democrats have. The continuing Republican members on the Rules Committee were never unrepresentative, and the new appointees never made the contingent as a whole unrepresentative.[31] The returning Republican members of Ways and Means were unrepresentative on four occasions, yet the imbalance was corrected only twice. Moreover, in one instance the Republicans' new appointees to Ways and Means created an imbalance where none had existed before. Finally, the Republicans failed to redress one imbalance and actually created another on Appropriations.

4. CONCLUSION

This chapter has sketched out a partisan selection model of the committee appointment process in which each party's CC seeks to maximize the number of seats that the party will win at the next election. We suggested that pursuit of this goal would entail allowing a considerable amount of self-selection while at the same time keeping an eye out for electoral externalities. We characterized the pattern of the external effects that each committee's decisions were likely to entail on nonmembers as either uniform, mixed, or targeted and argued that committees whose decisions imposed uniform externalities on everyone in the party would need the most careful regulation, whereas those that affected only a small subset of the party could be left more or less to the vagaries of self-selection.

Our empirical analysis shows that Democratic contingents on uniform externality committees were generally representative of the party both in ideological and geographical terms. The primary exception, the contingent on Veterans' Affairs, is influenced by a particularly homogeneous and powerful clientele group.

Democratic contingents on mixed externality committees were as a class more likely to be unrepresentative than were the uniform externality committees. Among mixed externality committees, however, there was a clear distinction between the "housekeeping" committees (Judiciary and Foreign Affairs), which were rarely unrepresentative, and the substantive committees (Armed Services, Banking, and Education and Labor), which were more often unrepresentative.

Democratic contingents on targeted externality committees were the

31. In any event, there are so few Republican members of Rules that statistical significance is hard to attain.

most likely to exhibit unrepresentativeness of some kind. The Agriculture Committee was unrepresentative in most postwar Congresses both in terms of the geographical location of its members' constituencies (they tended to be southern and western) and in terms of their general voting stance (which tended to be conservative). District of Columbia was unrepresentative in terms of its members' voting stance in most Congresses. Merchant Marine and Fisheries and Interior were unrepresentative in terms of the location of their members' constituencies (with the former overrepresenting coastal and riverine districts, the latter overrepresenting western districts).

Although these results are broadly consistent with the predictions of the partisan selection model, they are also consistent with self-selection, so they can hardly be taken as definitive. Nonetheless, we believe that one can choose between these two models. Partisan selection has in its favor not only the surface facts—appointments to the standing committees of the House are formally made by party committees—but also some key statistical evidence. In particular, in chapter 1 we show that over 40 percent of Democrats' assignment and transfer requests in the Eighty-sixth through Ninety-seventh Congresses were denied by their CC, and in chapter 7 we show that members who were more loyal to the party leadership were generally more likely to receive desirable transfers.

Self-selection, it seems to us, is only half the story. The other half, equally important, is the regulatory effort of each party's committee on committees. This effort appears both in the form of attentiveness to the loyalty of members who seek appointment to important committees and in the form of an attempt to keep committees with significant external effects more or less in line with overall sentiment in the party.

PART FIVE

Parties as Procedural Coalitions: The Scheduling Power

In the previous part we investigated one of the key structural powers of the parties—the power to appoint the members of the standing committees. We presented statistical evidence that members more loyal to the party leadership have been more likely to receive desirable committee assignments throughout the postwar era; we also showed that most contingents have been representative of the party from which they were drawn and that the exceptions are predictable.

Another key structural power is the ability to set the legislative agenda. This power is shared by the majority party leaders and the committee chairs. In chapter 9 we emphasize the degree to which competition between committees for scarce time on the floor leads to anticipation and accommodation of the wishes of the majority party leadership; we also consider the partisan implications of veto power. Chapter 10 then turns to a variety of empirical indicators of the extent to which the majority party has succeeded in controlling the agenda in the postwar era.

NINE

The Majority Party and the Legislative Agenda

The power of the Speaker of the House is the power of scheduling.

Thomas P. O'Neill

In part 1 we examined parties' efforts to structure the House in their favor through use of their power to staff committees. We presented evidence in support of our belief that parties structure committee composition to ensure fidelity to their agency relationship with committee personnel. In this chapter we model the mechanics by which the majority party in the House uses another key feature of legislative structure—the legislative agenda—to its advantage.

The legislative agenda is controlled by both the party leadership and House standing committees and subcommittees. The House has structured the delegation of authority to its committees not just to ensure that the fruits of committee specialization are in fact conveyed to the floor but also to ensure that the majority party has an advantage in setting the legislative agenda both on the floor and in committee. Thus, for example, to the scheduling power of the majority leadership on the floor corresponds the scheduling power of the chair in committee; the influence of the majority leadership (and caucus) over committee jurisdictions corresponds to the influence of the committee chair (and majority contingent) over subcommittee jurisdictions; and the majority leadership's advantage in staff resources over its minority counterparts corresponds to the (rather larger) advantage of committee majorities over committee minorities.[1]

---

1. Throughout the early and mid-1980s (at least) the sum of staff allocations to the majority leader and whip equaled the sum of staff allocations to the minority leader and whip. Nonetheless, the majority had an advantage because it also controlled the Speaker's

In this chapter we consider how the "structural advantages" con-
trived by the majority party help its committee-based and elective leaders control the legislative agenda. We focus on the power to schedule
legislation, beginning with the majority leadership's control of the floor
agenda and moving backward to the chairperson's control of the committee agenda. In section 1 we consider how a "rational" Speaker would
schedule legislation if given the unilateral power to do so. In section 2
we investigate the complications that arise when the Speaker's agenda-
control powers are subject to floor overrides. In section 3 we consider
how committee majorities' anticipation of what the Speaker wants can
influence what they report and, hence, what their chairs find profitable
to schedule. We argue in both sections 1 and 3 that there is a clear
partisan bias in the selection of bills to be considered. The result of
putting these two advantages—one at the committee stage and one at
the floor stage—together is an advantage in the construction and maintenance of intercommittee logrolls for the majority party. The "integration" of decisions made in the various committees may be a difficult
task even for the majority party, but as we argue in section 4, they have
a vast advantage over the minority in this regard. Section 5 concludes.

1. THE SPEAKER'S COLLECTIVE
   SCHEDULING PROBLEM

My two biggest competitors are the clock and the calendar. There are so many things I would like to do. . . .
The trouble is you have only so many weeks in the legislative year, and so many days in the legislative week,
so many hours in the legislative day.

James C. Wright

The Speaker, the majority leader, the members of the Rules Committee,
and the various committee and subcommittee chairs face a collective
scheduling problem:[2] which bills of the many in their respective "in
baskets" to bring formally to the attention of the larger group that they
serve (subcommittee, committee, or floor). In this section we consider

---

staff allocation, which was always the largest. At the committee level, the following figures are indicative: in 1965, 1972, 1976, and 1977 the percentage of total committee
staff positions allocated to the minority were, respectively, 11.3, 16.9, 16.7, and 16.5
(Fox and Hammond 1977, 171, table 3).

2. The leadership faces this problem in addition to the personal scheduling problem—
shared by every member of Congress—of how best to spend their time.

the Speaker's *preferences* in this regard. The question is, What would a Speaker with basic motivations like those described in chapter 5 want to do if he had full control over the House's agenda? "Full control" does not mean that the Speaker can call up any bill at any time, but rather that the majority leader and Rules Committee do what he asks, so that he can schedule his pick of the bills that have been reported from committee.[3] Such a power to select which reported bills will receive floor consideration is tantamount to a suspensory veto in that those bills not selected are at least temporarily blocked. If the Speaker persists in not scheduling them, they will not be passed at all unless the House overrules the Speaker's scheduling decisions. In this respect the Speaker (as modeled here, with a pliant Rules Committee) has a veto power similar to that attributed to committees or committee chairs.

In figuring out his best schedule, the Speaker is essentially engaged in a dynamic optimization problem. From a modeling perspective, the search literature in economics and, more generally, the literature on stochastic dynamic programming are relevant. The model becomes more complicated, as we note in section 2, once one moves from the question of what the Speaker *wants* scheduled to what he actually *gets*.

The simplest form of scheduling problem that faces the Speaker is encapsulated in the question, What next? The Speaker must decide the entire schedule for a week, a month, a session, or a Congress. Although this way of posing the scheduling problem suggests that optimal schedules consist of ordered lists of what bills to bring up, from an analytical standpoint it is more fruitful to think of optimal schedules as decision rules that tell, at any given time, what bill should be taken next. Such rules can generate schedules of the "ordered list" kind but retain the flexibility to change in light of new information.

A genre of models in which such flexible decision rules emerge are familiar in the literature on dynamic programming and stochastic control. Here we adapt such a model to the problem of legislative scheduling. (The technical details are not provided in the text;[4] instead, the model is more fully developed in appendix 2.)

The gist of the argument is that the Speaker's preferences as to what

3. The model we have in mind ignores noncontroversial bills that pass under consent procedures. It also ignores bills that pass under suspension of the rules (a procedure that the Speaker controls), although it could be adapted to include such bills. The bills that the model includes are those that go through the textbook sequence of report, calendar, special rule, and floor consideration.

4. We adapt the version of the problem given in Whittle 1982 and Roberts and Weitzman 1980. The basic results were first derived in Gittins and Jones 1974 and Gittins 1979.

legislation to schedule for floor consideration are fairly straightforward. First, he prefers not to schedule at all those bills that, from his perspective, would worsen the status quo. Second, of those bills that would improve on the status quo, he prefers—other things equal—to schedule first those that will take less time, effect a bigger improvement in the status quo if passed, and have a better chance at passing.

The model from which these conclusions follow is in some respects fairly general. But it has several shortcomings that underestimate the complexity of the scheduling problem and the value of the scheduling power.

First, the model assumes that the Speaker's preferences are separable—that is, that the benefit he derives from the passage of a particular bill does not depend on the legislative fates of any other bills. This is obviously not a general assumption. Relaxing it would introduce a new motivation to schedule a bill—the possibility that it would greatly enhance the value of some other (pending or enacted) legislation—and the conclusions reached here would no longer necessarily be true. Nonetheless, we believe that the qualitative thrust of our conclusions would not be misleading in the more general model.

A second restrictive feature of our model is the assumption that a bill's probability of progressing from one stage to another is constant over time and independent of the fates of other bills. This assumption is obviously violated in the real world: if bills b_1 and b_2 are to be voted on sequentially as parts of a logroll, then obviously the probability of passage of the second depends on the fate of the first. Relaxing the "independence" assumption would allow the model to capture the value of timing more fully. Although we think that this is an important and potentially tractable extension of the model, we do not pursue it here. The qualitative point that such an extension would elucidate is clear enough in the myriad stories of Speakers delaying legislation that they wish to pass until support for it has grown sufficiently, or speeding it if they fear an erosion of support.[5]

A third area in which the model presented in appendix 1 is limited is in its recognition of "gaming" possibilities. It is beyond the scope of this book to deal fully with these issues, but we do touch on some of them in the next two sections.

5. As former Speaker Tip O'Neill used to say, "Everything in politics is timing"; quoted in Davidson and Oleszek 1990, 311.

2. LIMITS ON THE SCHEDULING POWER

In section 1 we investigated how a rational Speaker would schedule legislation, given the unilateral ability to do so. This section considers how the base model is complicated when the Speaker's scheduling decisions can be overturned by the House as a whole; his power to schedule, in other words, is not exogenous. We consider a second complication, that in practice the Speaker shares control over the agenda with the majority leader and the Rules Committee, only in passing.

If one ignores both of these points and endows the Speaker with an unchallengeable and unilateral power to schedule, then the model that results is a rather stark (but still useful) one, similar to Shepsle's (1979) model of the committee system. Shepsle posits a variety of committees, each with an unchallengeable and unilateral ability to veto legislation (by refusing to report it out) in a given jurisdiction. He shows how such a power to veto (approximated if not attained in the textbook Congress) might affect the outcome in a spatial model of legislative activity, paying particular attention to the way in which a committee system might structurally induce stability where none existed in an "institution-free" model.

One might simply add to Shepsle's model a Speaker with the scope of power suggested above: the unilateral and unchallengeable ability to choose which committee-reported bills are considered on the floor. Such a model can be analyzed in the fashion made familiar by the spatial literature (see section 3), but not much thought is needed to see that the Speaker would "stabilize" the spatial outcome; in particular, the Speaker's ideal point would be stable because he would have the power and incentive to veto any change from it.[6] More generally, as noted above, the Speaker would be able to veto any change that made him worse off. Thus, although the Speaker certainly cannot dictate policy, he can act as an "anchor," stabilizing policy decisions that may be far away in spatial terms from the median floor member's ideal point.

6. Of course, this stability does not mean that the Speaker's "ideal point"—spatial modeling jargon for the policy package he most prefers—will inevitably be the outcome. It is just as true in this model that the ideal point of the median committee member is stable. Which of the many stable points will emerge as the outcome depends on the status quo and reversion point.

2.1 CHALLENGEABLE SCHEDULING DECISIONS

Although the model just sketched certainly suggests the scheduling power's potency and its importance in maintaining a distinctly partisan legislative outcome, its starkness gives one pause. One of the neglected questions in the literature has been how to deal with the assumption that committee vetoes are unchallengeable, in order to take account of the real-world options for neutralizing them (e.g., discharge petitions). Similarly, it would be nice if the model included some way of recognizing that there are limits to the Speaker's scheduling power. The question in each case is whether slightly weakening the veto power in the model will have only a small effect on the results derived from the starker model, or whether any weakening at all significantly erodes the veto's effect.

By way of an answer we note that two reasonable models of how vetoes operate predict that the effects of vetoes will be only slightly modified when their "strength" is slightly impaired. The two models hinge on the notions of retaliation costs and transactions costs.

Consider first the possibility of retaliation. It is often suggested in the literature that those pondering a direct challenge to a committee decision are deterred by the thought of things that the committee (especially its chair) can do in retaliation. The same argument plays out with at least equal force regarding challenges to the Speaker's decisions, since the array of individually targetable benefits and costs at the Speaker's disposal is large compared to that of most committee chairs.

The important point here is that a veto that is respected because of the threat of individual retaliation fades away slowly, not all at once, as the threat becomes less fearsome. The strength of a veto in the retaliation model can be measured simply in terms of the quantity of sanctions supporting it. An unchallengeable veto is one that is backed up by a superabundance of sanctions. If the veto's strength fades—that is, if the quantity of sanctions diminishes—then one expects the effects of the veto to fade but not to disappear all at once.[7]

---

7. A special case of the retaliation model is the retaliation in kind that is envisioned in models of reciprocity. It is often suggested that committee decisions in general (not just vetoes) are upheld because other committees fear retaliation in kind. The idea is that each committee cares most about the decisions made in its own jurisdiction and thus benefits from a general policy of reciprocal forbearance. A similar story can be told regarding the scheduling decisions of the Speaker: In each instance where the Speaker's decision does not enjoy majority support, there is some minority that benefits from the decision. If these benefited minorities tend to care more about the Speaker's favorable decisions than about the unfavorable ones, then again a policy of mutual forbearance may be mutually benefi-

Consider next the importance of transactions costs. Any majority of Congress wishing to overturn a committee's veto (or a Speaker's veto) faces a prisoner's dilemma of sorts. We assume that members of Congress do not know each other's minds costlessly. Thus, anyone in a potential overturning majority must decide whether to invest scarce time in discovering whether a majority really exists and, if one does, whether to help organize it on the floor. In both endeavors there is an incentive to free ride.

The strength of the veto in the transactions costs model corresponds to how difficult it is to detect and organize floor majorities in support of an override attempt, which in turn depends on the depth of ignorance of floor members about each other's preferences and on the institutional hoops through which any floor majority must jump in order to overturn the veto (e.g., the 218 signatures needed on a discharge petition). The unchallengeable veto model can be taken to assume an infinitely high institutional hoop; the qualitative effects of the veto fade but do not disappear as the hoop is lowered.

Formally, the notions of fear of retaliation and transactions costs can be modeled by adding individual and collective costs to the process of overriding a veto. Adding such costs modifies but does not eradicate the qualitative predictions of the original, unchallengeable veto, model (see appendix 3).

If the reader is convinced that slightly weakened vetoes lead only to slight departures from the predictions of the model in which vetoes are unchallengeable, then all that remains to do is to argue that the actual departures from this ideal are not so large as to remove any interest in the original model's implications. All we shall say in this regard is that the strength of the Speaker's veto, measured in terms either of the sanctions backing it up or of the transactions costs necessarily incurred in overturning it, seems comparable to the strength of the veto possessed by ordinary committees. So the importance of the Speaker as a "policy anchor" (at least when he has a pliant Rules Committee) seems comparable to that of individual committees.

---

cial. In this reciprocity model, the strength of the committee veto (or the Speaker's) corresponds to the number and temporal proximity of opportunities for retaliation in kind. Under certain circumstances, small changes in these variables may lead to the destruction of a cooperative equilibrium. But we do not think that retaliation in kind is the sole factor operating to support vetoes; hence, we do not see this potential discontinuity as worrisome.

2.2   SHARING THE SCHEDULING POWER

The next point to consider is that the Speaker does not exercise unilateral control over the flow of legislation to the floor. He shares control with the majority leader and the Rules Committee.

The most obvious consequence of this sharing of power is that both the majority party leadership (i.e., the Speaker in tandem with the majority leader) and the Rules Committee possess an independent power to veto. The Rules Committee can delay and sometimes effectively veto the 5–10 percent of all bills that require a special rule to be tractable on the floor. The majority leaders can influence a much wider range of bills. They can delay and effectively veto bills that receive rules because "once the Rules Committee has reported a rule, the decision to call it up is largely left to the [majority] leadership" (Robinson 1963, 35), so that "a rule . . . does not guarantee House consideration of a measure" (Clapp 1964, 348). They can also determine the fate of the many bills that seek to gain access to the floor via suspension of the rules (a procedure whose use must be sanctioned by the Speaker), unanimous consent, or special procedures.

John Nance Garner, Speaker in the Seventy-second Congress, "thought nothing of bottling up the bills of enemies or of members on the fence. If members were not loyal to 'Cactus Jack' Garner, their legislative bills were indefinitely shelved" (Peabody 1976, 46). Although most Speakers since Cactus Jack's day have had a less prickly style, postwar members such as Clem Miller have still counted the Speaker's control over scheduling as among his most important assets: "Particularly for lesser legislation (which may be the life-blood of individual congressmen) the chasm between the standing committee and the House floor is bridged with the unchallenged power of the Speaker" (C. Miller 1962, 44).[8]

Because the Rules Committee is composed of members of both parties and operates by majority rule, it may be a less reliable agent of majority party interests than is the elected leadership. This was most notoriously the case during the 1937–61 period, when a bipartisan alliance of Republicans and southern Democrats controlled the Rules Committee on many issues. Nonetheless, the Speaker had considerable influence over the Rules Committee's decisions even during those years.[9]

---

8. Peabody (1976, 44) echoes this sentiment: "The ability to help members overcome the gap between the standing committee and the floor is one of the most important resources of power available to the majority leadership."

9. As Clapp (1964, 349) notes in a book dealing with the latter part of this period, it

And the two-to-one ratio of majority- to minority-party members on the committee, coupled with the influence of the majority party leadership over appointments, has acted before and after this period to ensure that the committee is a more or less reliable arm of the leadership.

Thus, for the most part we ignore the role of the Rules Committee in the theoretical analysis that follows. This is not to say that we think the role of the Rules Committee in its heyday was unimportant; quite the contrary, we think it was crucial. But by assuming that the majority leadership faces a pliant Rules Committee, the model makes the leadership as strong as possible and lays bare the kinds of effects that a strong leadership would have. The general consequences of reintroducing an independent Rules Committee to the model will be clear enough.

3.   COMMITTEE AGENDAS AND THE SPEAKER

When you are in the majority, if you have any cohesiveness
between the committee chairmen and the leadership,
what is coming out of the mill is a program to which
you are usually committed.

Anonymous member of the House of
Representatives, 1959

In this section we consider how anticipation of the Speaker's scheduling decisions influences the decisions of committees as to which bills to report and, hence, the decisions of committee chairs as to which bills to schedule for hearings and markup. We adapt Shepsle's (1979) model to investigate these matters. The three main parts of this model are, first, a description of the policy space and members' preferences over that space; second, a description of the committee system; and third, a description of the Speaker's scheduling powers. (Although we provide a fairly complete description of the model, this is not the place to provide a full exposition or defense of the use of spatial models in legislative studies. The reader who finds the going difficult is referred to Shepsle [1979], Krehbiel [1987a], Enelow and Hinich [1984], or Ordeshook

---

was only "seldom" that a rule would be given to a bill "opposed by the leadership." Most of the troubles with the Rules Committee came not when it reported out legislation that the leadership opposed but rather when it refused to report out legislation that the leadership—or some vocal segment of the party—supported. Even here, the leadership was far from impotent. See Robinson 1963; Truman 1959, 23, 197.

[1986] for a fuller introduction to the basics of spatial modeling of committees.)

To begin with, imagine a set of w issues, with $w > 1$. On each issue it is possible to take a variety of different positions—which positions, in spatial models, one assumes can be represented by the numbers on the real line. Thus, if x_i is the real variable representing position on the ith issue, the vector $x = (x_1, \ldots, x_w)$ represents an entire policy program. The *policy space,* W, is simply the set of all possible policy programs (or all vectors corresponding to possible policy programs).[10]

The legislature consists of n ordinary legislators, indexed by the integers from 1 to n, plus the Speaker, denoted by the index 0. We assume that legislator j's preferences among the policies in W can be represented by a separable and strictly single-peaked utility function, u_j, with ideal point $z_j = (z_{j1}, \ldots, z_{jw})$. Thus, on dimension i, legislator j has a unique most-preferred position, z_{ji}, that does not depend on the policies adopted on other dimensions; and, as between any two points on dimension i that are to the same side of z_{ji}, he or she prefers the policy closer to z_{ji}.[11]

We interpret the origin in w-space as corresponding to the status quo; thus, the legislators' ideal points $\{z_j\}$ can be taken to represent their desired changes from the status quo. If w were equal to three and all three issues concerned budgetary allocations, for example, the ideal point $(100, -200, 0)$ would (assuming that the unit of expenditure is one hundred thousand dollars) correspond to the policy program that would increase expenditure on the first line item by \$100,000, decrease expenditure on the second line item by \$200,000, and hold expenditures on the third line item steady.

We also normalize the utility functions so that, for each legislator j, $u_j(0, \ldots, 0) = 0$. The impact of this is that the utility value $u_j(x)$ can be interpreted as indicating how much better off legislator j would be at x as opposed to the origin (status quo).[12]

The committee system is modeled along the lines of Shepsle 1979. Each ordinary member of the legislature belongs to one or more of k committees. The jurisdiction of the kth committee, denoted J_k, is de-

10. Here, W is assumed to be a convex subset of w-dimensional Euclidian space, with nonempty interior.
11. The meanings of *separability* and *strict single-peakedness* are explained more fully in appendix 4.
12. For more on how to interpret utility functions, and on the process of normalization, see, for example, Hamburger 1979, chap. 3.

fined as a subset of the w issue dimensions of the policy space. Committee jurisdictions may be multidimensional but do not overlap. A committee with jurisdiction over an issue dimension has the unilateral and unchallengeable right to report (or not to report) bills dealing with that dimension.

If a bill is reported from a committee, it goes onto a legislative calendar to await further scheduling. We assume that all bills are unidimensional, which is to say that they propose changes in only one dimension.[13]

The Speaker is a member of no committee but does have the unilateral and unchallengeable power to choose which of the bills reported from committee will be slated for consideration on the floor; he also decides whether a slated bill will receive a closed or an open rule. The situation is thus similar to that considered in section 1, and we assume that the Speaker's scheduling preferences are as described there. If the Speaker has scheduled a bill for floor consideration, voting is by majority rule, subject to whatever rule the Speaker has granted.

Having laid out the basic components of the model, we can now turn to the task of deducing what outcome can be expected under various circumstances. The outcome depends on how scarce time on the floor is. Accordingly, we consider two basic cases: first, when there is enough time to consider all the bills that are reported from committee; second, when there is not enough time.

3.1 WHEN TIME IS AMPLE

The outcome when time is ample can be analyzed by considering the actions of the various legislators in reverse chronological order, starting with the floor and working backward to the committees.

Suppose, then, that a bill (denoted x_i) proposing some changes on dimension i is scheduled for floor consideration by the Speaker. If the bill has an open rule, then Black's Theorem applies and the equilibrium outcome is m_i, the ideal point of the median legislator on dimension i. (If we denote the set of all legislators by $F = \{0, 1, \ldots, n\}$, then $m_i = \text{med}\{z_{ji} : i \epsilon F\}$.) If, however, the bill has been granted a closed rule,

---

13. Allowing multidimensional bills—the analog of omnibus bills in the real world—complicates the analysis considerably but does not alter fundamentally the kinds of conclusions we draw here. Thus, the assumption of unidimensionality is for the most part an expository convenience rather than a substantive restriction.

then the outcome is either x_i, if some majority on the floor prefers x_i to 0, or 0.

Because this is a model of complete information, the Speaker can perfectly forecast what the floor will do and use this information in deciding his own strategy. Thus, if the floor is known to prefer x_i to 0, the Speaker has his choice between three different outcomes: he can preserve the status quo by vetoing the bill (refusing to schedule it); he can secure m_i as the result by giving the bill an open rule; and he can secure x_i as the result by giving the bill a closed rule. If, by contrast, the floor is known not to prefer x_i to 0, then the Speaker can secure only two outcomes: the status quo (by vetoing or giving a closed rule); or m_i (by giving an open rule).

With these preliminary observations about the Speaker and the floor, we can now turn to the committee with jurisdiction over dimension i, denoted $C(i)$. The first point to make is that, in this model, it is pointless for $C(i)$ to report a bill that the floor does not prefer to 0. For, with such a bill, only two outcomes are possible: m_i (if the Speaker gives the bill an open rule), or 0 (otherwise). The first outcome could be achieved simply by reporting out m_i to begin with, the second by not reporting any bill at all. So, in essence, the members of $C(i)$ have three choices: refuse to report out any bill on dimension i; report out m_i (which is equivalent to any other bill that, foreseeably, will get an open rule from the Speaker); or report out a bill to which the Speaker will give a closed rule, and which the floor will pass under such a rule. In order for some majority of $C(i)$ to pursue the last strategy, there must exist some bill that simultaneously (1) is preferred to the status quo by some committee majority; (2) is preferred to both the status quo and to m_i by the Speaker; and (3) is preferred to the status quo by some floor majority. Let the set of all such bills on dimension i be denoted Q_i. Then the collective decision problem facing the members of $C(i)$ boils down to a choice between 0, m_i, and the points in Q_i.

The equilibrium choice of $C(i)$ depends simply on the majority-preference relation of the committee over the set of "attainable" options, $Q_i \cup \{0, m_i\}$.[14] If 0 is majority-preferred to all the other attainable options, then the committee will report no bill; if m_i is majority-preferred to all the other attainable options, then the committee will report some bill to which the Speaker will give an open rule (which one does not

14. We know this majority preference relation is well behaved (i.e., transitive) because of the separability and strict single-peakedness of individual legislators' utility functions. See Fishburn 1973, theorem 9.2.

matter); finally, if there is some point $x_i \epsilon Q_i$ that is majority-preferred to all the other attainable options, then it will be reported.[15]

Such an outcome highlights the power of both the Speaker's and the floor's veto. No bill that does not make the Speaker better off than he is at the status quo can pass, because he will either veto it or give it an open rule. No bill that does not make the floor better off can pass, because it will be amended if given an open rule and defeated if given a closed rule.

The outcome also illustrates the anticipation of the Speaker's and floor's preferences by the committee, in that as these preferences change, so do the key parameters of the committee's decision—the point m_i and the set Q_i.

Nonetheless, when time is ample, there is no competition between one committee and another for time slots on the floor. As we show in the next section, such competition increases the influence of the Speaker at the committee stage.

3.2   WHEN TIME IS SCARCE

Not all bills receive a hearing when time on the floor is scarce, even if the Speaker is disposed to grant them one. To capture this constraint in the model, we shall assume that only L bills can be considered in whatever portion of the session remains. Thus, if the number of bills reported exceeds L, not all will be scheduled.

Even though the Speaker has fewer options available under such conditions of scarcity than he does when time is ample, his position is strengthened,[16] for each committee now must compete for the scarce slots on the floor. Each knows that the Speaker will select bills in a definite order, defined by the rate of return calculated in appendix 2. Thus, each committee majority that foresees that it will not be among those given floor time has an incentive to change its bill so that it is more attractive to the Speaker and hence has a positive chance of being

15. It is not possible that 0 and some point $x_i \epsilon Q_i$ are tied in the committee's majority preference relation, because by definition Q_i is a subset of the points that are strictly majority preferred to 0 by the committee. It is possible that m_i and some point $x_i \epsilon Q_i$ are tied in the committee's majority-preference relation, but in this case there is always some other point $y_i \epsilon Q_i$ that is majority preferred to both x_i and m_i, because Q_i is an open set. If 0 and m_i are tied in the committee's majority-preference relation, then we can simply assume that the committee reports no bill.

16. The Speaker has fewer options in that any set of bills that can be scheduled when time is scarce can also be scheduled when time is ample, but not vice versa.

considered on the floor. If it can do so and still produce a bill that it prefers to the status quo, then it will have achieved a net gain.

This result can be described in greater detail with some further notation. Denote by x_i the proposal of committee $C(i)$ on issue dimension i. If $x_i = 0$, then $C(i)$ reports no bill; otherwise, it reports a bill proposing the change given by x_i's (nonzero) value. Define a *committee equilibrium* to be a set of proposals, one for each issue dimension, such that no committee majority has an incentive to change any of the proposals made by its committee, on the assumption that all other committee proposals will remain fixed.

The next step is to consider the most attractive possible bill on the ith dimension, from the Speaker's point of view, while still being worth reporting from $C(i)$'s point of view. On the one hand, if the set Q_i is null, then any bill that $C(i)$ reports will either be vetoed or given an open rule. Assuming that the Speaker prefers m_i to 0, any bill at all will be given an open rule, and m_i will be the final result. In this case, then, the highest payoff that the Speaker can be offered on the ith issue dimension by $C(i)$ is simply $W_i = u_0(m_i)$.[17] On the other hand, if the set Q_i is not null, then the committee can report a bill that both ranks higher in the committee majority-preference relation than 0 and ranks higher in the Speaker's preference relation than either 0 or m_i. Thus, if Q_i is non-null, the "best" bill that the $C(i)$ can offer the Speaker is simply the bill in Q_i that yields the highest payoff. Since any bill in Q_i will, by construction, be given a closed rule and will pass under such a rule, this highest payoff can be written $W_i = \sup\{u_0(x_i): x_i \epsilon Q_i\}$.[18]

Having identified the "highest" payoff that can be offered the Speaker on each dimension, we can turn to the highest payoff that can be offered by the kth committee while still benefiting some committee majority. This payoff is simply $W(k) = \max\{W_i: i\epsilon J_k\}$, the maximum of the highest payoffs from each dimension in the kth committee's jurisdiction. It will be convenient to renumber the committees, so that $W(1) > W(2) > \ldots > W(K)$.[19]

We can now state the main result, proven in appendix 3:

Proposition: If $L < K$, $W(L+1) > 0$, and $x = (x_1, \ldots, x_w)$ is a committee equilibrium, then $\max\{u_0(x_i): i\epsilon J_k\} \geq W(L+1)$ for all $k < L+1$.

17. Where we assume that some committee majority does in fact prefer m_i to 0. Otherwise, the committee reports no bill at all.
18. It is necessary to use the supremum here instead of the maximum because Q_i is an open set.
19. We assume strict inequalities in what follows. Weak inequalities just complicate things without altering their fundamental character.

The first two conditions in the proposition ensure that not all committees can be assured of scheduling a bill and that the top $L + 1$ committees can all report at least one bill that would be attractive to the Speaker (i.e., would improve on the status quo, from his perspective) while still being worthwhile for some committee majority. Under these conditions, the proposition declares that any committee equilibrium must be such that each of the top L committees is reporting a bill that is at least as good, from the Speaker's point of view, as the best that committee $L + 1$ can offer.

The impact of competition among committees on the final legislative outcome can be large or small. In special cases it can ensure that the Speaker's ideal point is adopted on all dimensions; in other cases it puts little constraint at all on the bills that committees report. But the general existence of this kind of incentive is fairly clear, even from the simplified model presented here.

The intriguing feature of the equilibrium when time is scarce is that, although the Speaker has fewer options, the legislative outcome is more to his liking. The reason for this result is that time constraints make the Speaker's implicit veto threat more potent. If there is plenty of time for everything, then committees can offer the Speaker take-it-or-leave-it choices, confident that he will always "take" bills that represent improvements on the status quo from his perspective, even if they are small improvements. If time is scarce, by contrast, then the Speaker has a credible (if typically implicit) threat to take only the top L bills in his ranking; committees respond accordingly, trying to ensure that their bills are among the top L, if possible.

It is true that the influence of the Speaker's preferences on committee decisions is less when the Speaker shares power with a Rules Committee whose members' opinions on policy diverge from his own, for then committees must compete to make it past both the Rules Committee and the Speaker. In the usual case, however, where the Speaker exerts considerable influence over the Rules Committee, it is his preferences that are dominant and must be correctly anticipated. Moreover, the process of anticipation does not stop at the report stage. It reaches all the way back to the decisions of chairs as to what bills to schedule for hearings and markup in committee.

3.3 THE CHAIR'S SCHEDULING DECISION

There are certainly reasons why a subcommittee or committee chair might schedule a bill for hearings, even if she believes it has no chance of passage. But usually chairs are interested in passing bills; other things equal, bills that have no chance are less attractive than those that do. Thus, committee chairs will anticipate not only what can pass muster in their committees, but also what can get a favorable rule from the Rules Committee, what is likely to be scheduled by the Speaker, and what will ultimately pass on the floor. Because two of these "gates" are controlled by the majority party leadership, the kind of legislation that an outcome-oriented committee chair will find attractive will usually be that which is palatable to the majority party's leadership. This may be true also simply because all committee chairs are members of the majority party and thus are more likely to agree with their party's leadership.[20]

4. INTERCOMMITTEE LOGROLLS

If one considers the advantages that the majority party has in controlling the agenda—both in committee and on the floor—it is not surprising that it seems to have a particular advantage in the construction and maintenance of logrolls, especially "complex" logrolls that require the cooperation of members from more than one committee. The majority party's advantage can be seen particularly clearly by considering how complex logrolls are made.

4.1 CONSTRUCTING COMPLEX LOGROLLS

Logrolls come in many sizes and shapes.[21] The simplest are those made between members of the same committee concerning their own committee's legislation. More complicated logrolls involve either members of different committees or legislation from different committees, or both. Such complex logrolls can be enacted either all at once, in an omnibus bill of some kind, or sequentially, with first one group and then another carrying out its part of the legislative bargain. Neither method of consummating a complex logroll is generally feasible, however, without the active support of the majority leadership.

Omnibus bills that include legislation touching more than one com-

20. Of course, if the Rules Committee is not an arm of the leadership, or if extramural forces—the Senate and the president—have markedly different policy views, then the process of anticipating "what will fly" is more complicated and may not produce results so beneficial to the majority party leadership in the House.

21. See Froman 1967, chap. 2.

mittee's jurisdiction can be created in two basic ways. First, such bills can be introduced just like ordinary bills, in which case the Speaker's referral power comes into play. Second, one bill can be made in order as an amendment to another by the Rules Committee—so that the omnibus is effectively made on the floor rather than in committee. In this case, of course, the Speaker's independent veto and influence over the Rules Committee independent veto comes into play. Either way, the majority leadership's support is typically crucial.

Complex logrolls that require a sequence of legislative enactments on the floor are, if anything, even more dependent on the goodwill of the majority leadership. At a minimum the leadership must agree to schedule all the pieces of the legislative bargain—and everyone must know that they have so agreed. Otherwise, whoever goes first (votes first, reports out a bill first, etc.) has no guarantee that the other side will even be given the opportunity to uphold their end of the bargain.

The leadership thus is well placed to scuttle a logrolling deal, whether it is packaged as a single omnibus bill or as a sequence of bills. This suggests that the majority leadership's cooperation is necessary, an observation that is consistent with the particular view of the role of party leaders to which we now turn.

4.2 THE MAJORITY PARTY'S LEADERS AS DEAL BROKERS

The role of the majority party's leadership in the House of Representatives has received a good deal of scholarly attention. Here we wish to emphasize its role as broker. The general view has been articulated quite explicitly in the literature:

> The party leaders' functions are to act as information clearinghouses and vote brokers. They try to ascertain the relative importance of different issues to each member and then build and maintain the party coalition by negotiating the appropriate vote trades. . . . The party in this case is an ongoing coalition built around a more or less stable set of vote trades. (Jackson 1974, 6)

> Essentially, party leadership in the House plays a broker's role between the various elements in the leadership environment. . . . At times the role of broker takes the form of acting as liaison between two or more factions. On other occasions the role calls for the active participation of the leadership in the bargaining among and between the rank and file party members, the White House, senior committee personnel, and private groups. (Eidenberg and Morey 1969, 119)

Closely allied to this notion of party leaders as brokers of (mostly intra-party) trades are the ideas that leaders are positioned at the center of their party's informational networks (for example, see Ripley 1983, 246; Truman 1959, 97; Jewell and Patterson 1977, 147) and that they are high-volume traders on their own account (for example, see Ripley 1967, 154; Peabody 1976, 63–64 n. 30).

The evidence for these stylized characterizations of the leadership's role comes from innumerable observational studies of Congress. One particularly clear and well-known case (see Ripley 1969a; Ripley 1969b; Ferejohn 1986) involves the logroll engineered between urban Democrats from the Northeast, eager to start a food stamps program, and rural Democrats from the South, eager to maintain the agricultural subsidies program. The southerners controlled the Agriculture Committee, which had jurisdiction over both programs. Their part of the deal was to report out a food stamps bill and support it on the floor. In return, the northerners were to vote to maintain agricultural subsidies. The southerners, acting first, naturally needed some assurances that the leadership would in fact allow both pieces of legislation onto the floor in a timely fashion; otherwise, the proposed exchange could not be consummated. The Democratic leaders favored the logroll and "used their control over House floor procedures to make sure that the terms of the trade were successfully fulfilled" (Ripley 1969b, 44). It was only later, after the logroll was incorporated in a regular omnibus bill reported by the Agriculture Committee, that "explicit assistance from the leadership was no longer required" (Ferejohn 1986, 251).

The facilitation by the majority leadership of logrolls of which they approve is also clear in Mayhew's more wide-ranging study of Congress in the early postwar era (Mayhew 1966). Mayhew found that the majority leadership generally supported the party's "intense" committee-based minorities in their efforts to trade with one another. The Agriculture Committee, for example, appeared to be quite powerful in its own right; "what allowed the Committee to win its victories in the period in question . . .—what indeed saved its program from decimation by the nonfarm majority in the House—was the partisan context within which it operated" (29). Mayhew cites in particular the support that the leadership lent to the committee in its efforts to get nonfarm Democrats to vote for agricultural programs, noting that debates were "punctuated with references to the mutual obligations of sections of the party to each other on matters of concern to each" (51). In marked contrast to the Democrats, the Republican leadership and nonfarm majority usually voted against the farm programs reported out by the committee, and hence against their farm members.

Mayhew found this pattern of majority leadership support and the minority leadership opposition to committee initiatives repeated across several other issue areas. Truman (1959) found a similar pattern in his study of congressional parties in the Eighty-first Congress, as did Murphy (1974) in his study of the Public Works Committee.[22]

This pattern of leadership support might be due to an ideological predilection on the part of the Republican leadership and party not to spend money (unless it is of direct benefit to their constituents). But it is also consistent with the idea that much of the major legislation reported out of committee was part of Democratic logrolls.

5. CONCLUSION

The policy advantage in a Congress is with the majority
party, for the power of the legislative majority party
is the power to organize the legislature. . . . The minority
can, of course, manipulate some victories, but they
normally take a negative form—that is, defeating
majority party legislation.

Charles O. Jones, Party and Policy-Making

In this chapter we have presented two simple models touching on the process of agenda setting in the House of Representatives. In section 1 we focused on the scheduling power of the majority party leadership and, in particular, on what their preferences in using this power would be. Assuming a leadership that is either unified or dominated by the Speaker, the model shows conditions under which leaders will schedule bills according to their expected return per unit of time needed for consideration on the floor. Thus, among those bills that the leaders would like to see passed, they will schedule those that (1) have better chances at passage; (2) have higher payoffs if passed; and (3) will take less time on the floor. Because the payoffs of the majority leadership reflect the

22. Murphy (1974, 173) notes that "there is a remarkable disparity in the perspectives of uninterested Democrats and Republicans on allocation questions. Consider, for example, the relationship between shared interests and party conflict on the Appalachian regional development legislation. In both 1965 and 1967 the Democratic majority supported the Appalachian Democrats, whereas the Republican majority . . . opposed the legislation and hence the Appalachian Republicans."

collective interests of the party (as explained in chapter 5), the leadership's scheduling preferences do too.

The second model, presented in section 3, simply adds a Speaker (standing in for a unified leadership) to Shepsle's well-known model of the committee system. Assuming that the Speaker's scheduling powers are as unchallengeable as those of the committees, the model shows two ways in which the Speaker's influence might creep back into committee deliberations, even without any explicit intervention on his part. The first way derives simply from anticipation of the Speaker's veto: if, for example, a committee chair knows that a bill that has been referred to her committee will be repugnant to the Speaker, then, other things equal, she would prefer to schedule some other bill with better prospects for being scheduled on the floor for committee deliberation. The second way in which the Speaker may influence committee deliberations derives from the competition that can arise among committees when floor time is scarce. If a committee anticipates that its bill is unlikely to be scheduled in the time remaining in the session, it can modify the bill before reporting it, agree to amendments to be included in the rule after reporting it, or in other ways sweeten the deal for the Speaker (or factions that the Speaker wants on board before proceeding). But other committees can play this game, too, and the resulting implicit competition among committees may have a fairly broad impact on the kind of bills that are reported and, hence, on the legislative agenda.[23]

23. Although in this chapter we have focused on the Speaker's scheduling power, it should be clear that the scheduling power of the committee chairs has important partisan consequences as well. If chairs have what is tantamount to a veto over legislative proposals within their committee's jurisdictions, then policy outcomes will be structurally stabilized in a fashion generally advantageous to the majority party.

TEN

Controlling the Legislative Agenda

In the introduction to this part we asked whether committees are agents of the House, of the majority party, or of no one but themselves. It is uncontroversial to say that committees are *in principle* agents of the House. It is, after all, the House that decides whether there will be any committees at all and, if so, determines their jurisdictions, staff allowances, party ratios, and everything else of consequence. The very word *committee* originally denoted a person (later, a group) to whom some charge, trust, or function had been committed.[1]

The argument arises over who exercises the power that the House undoubtedly possesses. The committee government model essentially argues that no one group or coalition is able to use this power effectively; it is so little exercised that committees might just as well be taken as autonomous. We argue, by contrast, that the most important function of the majority party is precisely to usurp the House's power to structure the committee system.

The rest of this chapter deals with three questions that naturally arise regarding our claims. First, how does the majority party use the structuring power of the House to influence the committee system? Second, what are the consequences of this structural power? Third, how does our view inform one's reading of the postwar history of the House?

---

1. In the American colonies the term *committee* was often used as a synonym for "representative." For example, the General Court of Massachusetts referred to the Continental Congress as "a meeting of committees from the several colonies" (McConachie 1898, 6).

1. THE MAJORITY PARTY AND THE COMMITTEE SYSTEM

Asking how the majority party structures the committee system entails two subsidiary questions: one about the instruments of control it uses and one about how its members can agree to their use. We consider both these questions in turn.

1.1 THE INSTRUMENTS OF CONTROL

In principle, the majority party might seek to control committees in the same way that management in other large organizations attempts to control subunits: by creating and destroying them, by assigning them tasks and giving them the resources to accomplish those tasks, by regulating their personnel, and by providing for the review and revision of their decisions. Broadly speaking, each of these techniques is used by the majority party in the House, as a brief review will show.

1.1.1 Creating and Destroying Subunits   The fundamental power of creating and destroying committees has, since the Legislative Reorganization Act of 1946, been used only sparingly in the House. In the two most important instances where this power has been used, however, it has been used to promote the interests of the majority party.

The only House standing committee to be dissolved since 1946—the Internal Security Committee—was disbanded pursuant to actions by the Democratic Steering and Policy Committee (which appointed only one member to the committee in December 1974) and the Democratic Caucus (which passed a resolution calling for the committee's dissolution on 13 January 1975). The Republicans had no real say in the matter.

Perhaps the most important committee to be dissolved in recent memory is the Joint Committee on Atomic Energy. The Democratic Caucus, during its organizational meetings after the 1976 election, voted 133–97 to eliminate the committee and redistribute its jurisdiction among five standing committees. This decision was incorporated in the proposed House rules for the Ninety-fifth Congress, which were subsequently adopted on a party-line vote. The Republicans again had no effective say in the matter.

1.1.2 Assigning Tasks and Resources   The majority party affects the tasks undertaken by committees by (re)defining their jurisdictions, by giving substantial agenda-setting power to committee chairs, by using the referral power, and by allocating staff and other resources among and within committees.

The majority party has reshuffled jurisdictional responsibilities several times since the Legislative Reorganization Act of 1946 (see, generally, Dodd and Oppenheimer 1977). In 1954, for example, a Republican majority included a provision in the Atomic Energy Act giving jurisdiction over public nuclear power projects to the Joint Committee on Atomic Energy (Green and Rosenthal 1963). A series of jurisdictional changes were made under Democratic auspices as part of the "Bolling-Hansen" reform efforts of the early 1970s. The Democratic leadership first appointed a special, bipartisan committee, chaired by Richard Bolling (D.-Mo.), to consider reform of the committee system in 1973. The Democratic Caucus then referred the committee's report to its own Committee on Organization, Study, and Review (the Hansen Committee) for a "political screening" (Davidson 1977, 49). This screening process led to the rejection of the main thrust of the Bolling proposal, but several jurisdictional changes were approved (*Congressional Quarterly Almanac* 1974, 634–41).[2] Perhaps the most dramatic change made by the Democrats was their subsequent decision (in a 146–122 caucus vote) to strip responsibility for making Democratic committee assignments from the party's contingent on Ways and Means (*Congressional Quarterly Almanac* 1975, 27–28).

Another source of influence that the majority party has over the tasks that a committee takes up arises simply because the chairs of House committees and subcommittees have been endowed with substantial agenda-setting powers and are always members of the majority party. This condition means that most of the key decisions about what each committee will and will not consider are made by senior members of the majority party. To a first-order approximation, we can model events

2. The Agriculture Committee lost jurisdiction over the nondomestic aspects of the Food for Peace program to Foreign Affairs. The Banking Committee lost jurisdiction over urban mass transit to Public Works, nursing home construction to Commerce, some international trade matters (including commodity agreements and export controls) to Foreign Affairs, and the entire jurisdiction of its Small Business Subcommittee to the Select Committee on Small Business. Commerce lost civil aviation and surface transit to Public Works, and civil aviation research and development to Science. Education and Labor lost oversight of legal services to Judiciary. Foreign Affairs lost oversight of international financial organizations to Banking. Science lost biomedical research to Commerce. And Ways and Means was stripped of responsibility over health care programs not funded by payroll taxes (to Commerce), renegotiation (to Banking), aspects of international commodity agreements and export controls (to Foreign Affairs), and revenue sharing (to Government Operations).

as if chairs had vetoes over what their panels considered.[3] The literature has focused on politically controversial uses of this veto power—that is, on cases where a chair vetoes a bill that a substantial portion of the majority party wishes to see reported to the floor. But for every such use of the veto, there are many more in which the bill vetoed is a proposal of some member of the minority party. Indeed, the attention drawn to "improper" use of the veto suggests the typical use: to weed out proposals from the minority party, along with unimportant or quack proposals, leaving only those which are innocuous or for which there is substantial support in the majority party or in the House as a whole.

In addition to setting committee jurisdictions and endowing their chairs with scheduling power, the majority party can also influence the tasks that committees take up through the referral power of the Speaker. A classic example is the 1963 Civil Rights Bill, "which was drafted somewhat differently for each chamber so that it could be referred to the Judiciary Committee in the House and the Commerce Committee in the Senate" (Oleszek 1984, 77). More recently, the majority party has made increasing use of multiple referrals, in tandem with complex rules, in order to control legislative outcomes (Bach and Smith 1988; Davidson, Oleszek, and Kephart 1988; Collie and Cooper 1989).

A final example of how the majority party influences committee agendas is the allocation of staff resources within committees. The Republicans had the good fortune of being in office when it came time to appoint the new committee staff created by the Legislative Reorganization Act of 1946. Although these staff were supposed to be selected "on a permanent basis without regard to political affiliations and solely on the basis of fitness to perform the duties of the office,"[4] contemporary observers were surprised that the Democrats effected changes in only a third of all staff positions when they regained control of the House in 1949 (cf. Kampelman 1954, 545; Kammerer 1951, 1128). The Democrats evidently continued to make changes, however: by the early 1960s the Republicans were complaining loudly about their measly share of staff, which, by one account, was about one in ten (*Congressional Quarterly Almanac* 1963, 80; *Congressional Quarterly Weekly Report,* 8 Feb. 1963, 151). But Republican complaints had only a limited impact: minority staff never constituted more than 16.9 per-

3. Of course, the strength of this veto varies by position (full committee chair or subcommittee chair) and time (pre- or postreform).
4. 60 *Stat.* 834 (1946).

cent of all committee staff over the next decade and a half.[5] By the 1980s continued Republican complaints had resulted in a more substantial improvement: one-third of partisan committee staff were allocated to the minority party.[6]

1.1.3 Regulating Subunit Personnel   The majority party decides both how many total members each committee will have and what share of this total each party will get. It has used these powers throughout the postwar era to enhance its control of key committees. The power to set the size of committees was used to "pack" the Rules Committee in 1961, for example, thereby making it more representative of the party as a whole.[7] The power to set party ratios on committees has been used to give the majority party at least 60 percent of the seats on the control committees (Appropriations, Rules, Ways and Means, and Budget) in every postwar Congress.

The majority party has also influenced committee personnel through the appointment process. This includes both a general influence exerted through the promotion of those more loyal to the leadership (see chapter 7) and more specific kinds of influence, as when the Democrats took care not to appoint members favorable to home rule to the District of Columbia Committee (Bolling 1965, 1), refurbished the Education and Labor Committee with liberals (Ripley 1967, 22), appointed members to the Public Works Committee to help vote out legislation authorizing the St. Lawrence Seaway (Murphy 1974, 171; Clapp 1964, 229–30), attempted to co-opt Boll Weevil Democrats by giving them positions on the Budget Committee (Rohde 1991, 47), and so forth.

1.1.4 Reviewing and Revising Subunit Decisions   Committee proposals must pass muster with several other bodies after they are reported. If they authorize the expenditure of money, they must be ap-

5. See Fox and Hammond 1977, 171; U.S. Congress, Joint Committee on the Organization of Congress 1965, 354; U.S. Congress, House Rept. 93–916, part 2, 1974, 358. Note that some staff were "nonpartisan"; the minority proportion of "partisan" staff would be higher.

6. Committee activity can also be influenced by the allocation of other resources. In 1947, for example, the Republican majority conferred subpoena powers on several committees in order to facilitate investigations into labor racketeering and—in the words of Adolph Sabath (D. -Ill.)—"to scare our administrative agencies into impotence" (*Congressional Quarterly Almanac* 1947, 68).

7. Many other committees have also been expanded when the majority leadership saw fit to do so, although the link to party control has rarely been as clear as it was in the case of Rules (cf. Westefield 1974).

proved by the Appropriations Committee, which has extra seats for the majority party. If they need a special rule, they must be approved by the Rules Committee, which also has extra seats for the majority party (and, since the 1970s, a particularly close relationship with the majority leadership). If they are to be scheduled advantageously, they must please the majority leadership. Finally, if they are to be sent to the Senate or president, they must be approved on the floor of the House itself—under terms and conditions that are largely set by the majority party leadership and (sometimes) the Rules Committee.

1.2 CAN THE MAJORITY PARTY ACT?

Even with all the instruments that the majority party has at its disposal to control committees, the question remains whether the members of the party can agree on their use often enough to establish any real control. In answering this question, it helps to recognize that the majority party exerts two different kinds of control. One is a kind of "automatic pilot" control: give members of the majority party significant advantages at every stage of the legislative process, and then let that process go, confident that the result will be substantially biased to the majority side of the aisle. Because this kind of control entails giving individual members of the majority party increased power and resources—more seats on powerful committees, a bigger say in setting the legislative agenda in committee or on the floor, more staff, and so forth—there is an automatic constituency for much of the structure that the party sets up (namely, the beneficiaries of that structure).

A second kind of control is active: disciplining those members or committees who have failed to produce the kind of legislative proposals of which the majority party can consistently approve. There is certainly some of this kind of control—committees are purged (e.g., HUAAC in 1949), packed (e.g., Rules in 1961), stripped of jurisdiction (e.g., Ways and Means in 1975), discharged (e.g., Ways and Means in 1954), and so forth—but the primary idea is to bias the committee system enough in the majority party's favor so that real difficulties seldom arise. Thus, active control does not appear, and does not *need* to appear, very often.

Active control in the form of sanctions may appear infrequently for a variety of reasons. Of course, the typical story in the literature is that sanctions such as violating a member's seniority or discharging a committee's bill are rare because parties are weak and committees strong.

This is one possible explanation for the paucity of sanctions, but there are many others.

We have already considered the case of seniority violations at length in chapter 2, so we focus here on discharge petitions. The main point is that, from the infrequency of successful discharge petitions alone, one cannot validly infer that committees are strong or protected by norms of reciprocity. It is just as possible that the committee, once the discharge petition was filed, took whatever actions were necessary to forestall the petition's passage—commencing hearings, say, or incorporating certain provisions in a related bill. These possibilities have not been systematically investigated in the literature, so we do not know for sure what the impact of discharge petitions has been; all we know is that few of them have actually acquired enough signatures to discharge.

The more general point is that active sanctions in any system are applied most when there is uncertainty about their application. If the balance of power between leaders and followers is well understood, then the difference between what is possible and what is not is well understood, and sanctions are incurred rarely and meted out rarely. If, by contrast, there is uncertainty about what can be got away with, then probings of the boundaries of acceptable behavior can be expected, with consequent sanctions. So the frequency of sanction may depend more on uncertainty than on centralization of power.

When the necessity for active control does appear, the majority party often seeks to lessen the potential that the party will split by putting changes in the sessional rules or other omnibus devices. Thus, for example, the twenty-one-day rule for discharging the Rules Committee was adopted in the Eighty-first Congress by incorporating it in the sessional rules, the Democratic Caucus having previously voted to bind its members to support said rules (Robinson 1963, 64). Similarly, when Representatives Herbert (D.-La.) and Rankin (D.-Miss.) were purged from HUAAC, the relevant changes were rolled together with all the other sessional appointments in a single omnibus resolution rather than going to the floor as a separate motion.

2. THE CONSEQUENCES OF STRUCTURAL POWER: THE LEGISLATIVE AGENDA

In the previous section we sketched out some of the primary tools with which the majority party might seek to influence committees and made a distinction between automatic pilot control and active control. Much of the literature concentrates on the paucity of active control by the majority party as evidence that, to borrow a phrase from Gertrude Stein, there is no there there. But this inference ignores automatic pilot control. If all of the most important agenda-setting positions are staffed by members of the majority party, then the legislative agenda will certainly be affected. It will, at the very least, be dominated by the interests of those members of the majority party endowed with scheduling power. It may even reflect some sort of collective agenda of the majority party, to the extent that the majority party leadership is influential (along the lines of the analysis in chapter 9).

Is the legislative agenda in fact dominated by the majority party? Is the set of bills making it out of committee something like a majority party agenda? How could one tell if it was? The rest of this section deals with these questions. We first consider some evidence on bill sponsorship and committee reports, noting that most bills reported from committee are sponsored by members of the majority party and supported by all or nearly all of that party's members on the committee. We then turn to some evidence concerning the reception of committee bills on the floor, noting that majority party members are much more likely than minority party members are to be "deferential" toward committee handiwork.

2.1   SPONSORSHIP AND COMMITTEE REPORTS

In this section we consider evidence bearing on two questions: Who sponsors the bills that are reported from committee? And who dissents from the majority opinion in committee reports?

To answer the first of these questions, we have randomly sampled about one hundred reported bills from four Congresses—the Eighty-second, Eighty-third, Ninety-second, and Ninety-seventh—and ascertained for each such bill the party of the member(s) who introduced it.[8] Prior to the Ninetieth Congress no more than one member could sponsor a given bill, so the difference between the majority and minority party can be given simply by the percentage of bills in the sample that were sponsored by members of the minority party. As it turns out, this

8. We chose these Congresses with an eye to catching a change in party control (the Democrat-controlled Eighty-second versus the Republican-controlled Eighty-third) and a prereform (Ninety-second) versus postreform (Ninety-seventh) contrast. We do not count delegates; indeed, we dropped from the analysis all bills sponsored solely by delegates, resident commissioners, or third-party members.

figure is 26 percent for the Eighty-second Congress (controlled by the Democrats 234–199) and 13 percent for the Eighty-third Congress (controlled by the Republicans 221–213). A loss of only thirteen seats thus reduced the Democratic sponsorship rate from 74 percent of all sample bills reported from committee to 13 percent.

After the rules change allowing more than one member to sponsor the same bill, one can no longer divide bills into just those sponsored by Democrats and those sponsored by Republicans; many bills have mixed sponsorship. In the Ninety-second Congress, for example, 22 percent of all sampled bills were sponsored solely by Republicans, 24 percent solely by Democrats, and 54 percent by both Republicans and Democrats. The analogous figures for the Ninety-seventh Congress were 12.4, 40.1, and 46.7 percent.

These figures are, of course, ambiguous. Because the bills were chosen at random, they include bills important and unimportant, partisan and nonpartisan, controversial and uncontroversial. The mere fact of sponsorship, moreover, does not tell us much about the political content of the bills involved. Nonetheless, the figures for the Eighty-second, Eighty-third, and Ninety-seventh Congresses all suggest the predominance of the majority party in the setting of the legislative agenda. This predominance was well recognized by members of Congress in the 1950s, especially concerning important legislation. As Clapp (1964, 157) put it: "In the House . . . few members succeed in getting their names on important legislation. Junior members of the House have little chance for such fame, and members of the minority party virtually none."

Another clue to the partisan coloration of committee bills is the lodging of dissenting or minority opinions with the committee report. We have investigated each of the 5,789 reports issued from committee in the Eighty-fourth, Eighty-sixth, Eighty-eighth, Ninetieth, Ninety-second, Ninety-fourth, Ninety-sixth, and Ninety-eighth Congresses, identifying all members who dissented from the majority report.[9] The percentage of reports from which at least one Democrat dissented is small: 4.4 percent on average. Not surprisingly, in view of how few reports are dissented from by any Democrat, the average percentage of committee Democrats endorsing committee reports exceeds 99 percent.

9. Members use many adjectives to describe the additional reports that they write or endorse, including *separate, additional, individual, minority,* and *dissenting.* Only the last two were counted as really "dissenting" from the majority report (and even then a small but noticeable percentage of "minority" reports do not so much dissent as provide a different perspective or different reasons for supporting the bill).

The percentage of bills on which Democrats dissent is smaller in each of the Congresses examined than the corresponding percentage for Republicans. Over all eight Congresses, Republicans dissented more than twice as frequently as Democrats (10.2 versus 4.4 percent).[10] The contrast between the parties is even greater if the number of dissidents is taken into account: when committee Republicans dissented, on average 36 percent joined the dissent; when committee Democrats dissented, on average only about 5 percent participated.

A final indication of the dominance of the majority party in committee is simply members' allocation of time. Davidson (1981b, 127) notes: "It is no accident that, according to the Obey Commission (1977), Democrats tend to spend more time in subcommittee and committee sessions, while Republicans tend to devote more time on the floor. In other words, those not in control at the committee stage find in floor debate a chance to appeal to the court of public opinion."[11]

2.2 DEFERENCE TO COMMITTEE PROPOSALS

In the previous section we showed that most bills reported from committee are sponsored by members of the majority party and come to the floor with the support of almost all of the majority party's committee contingent. In this section we investigate how committee bills are received on the floor. Our general expectation is that the set of bills making it to the floor, having already run a gauntlet of veto points guarded by important majority-party interests, will appeal to a substantial segment of the majority party.[12] The minority party, by contrast, having had less of a say in what committees consider to begin with and less of a say in what they actually report to the floor, will be less pleased.

10. We examine interesting temporal variations in these figures below.

11. The dominance of the majority party over the committee stages of legislation is also reflected in data on recorded votes in committee. Parker and Parker (1985, 40–41), who study votes over the 1973–80 period for most committees, note that "nonunanimous procedural and final-passage votes tend to be partisan in nature." Indeed, they exclude these votes from their analysis because "to include these votes . . . might strengthen the effect of partisan forces to the point that they obscure other salient influences in a committee's environment." Even after excluding these votes, Parker and Parker still find that *every* committee had a salient partisan cleavage in the period under study (249).

12. There is an important distinction to make between bills that form part of what might be called the majority party's agenda, defined here as bills that the party's leadership favors, and bills that do not form part of the party agenda. The expectation of widespread support in the majority party is even stronger for bills in the party agenda. But even bills that are not in the party agenda were typically promoted by some Democrat and mustered enough support to get through committee, so that substantial majority party support is likely.

Members of the minority party will be more likely to push amendments, call for roll calls, and in other ways show their displeasure with committee decisions.

The evidence of displeasure on which we focus here is simply voting against the position taken by a majority of committee members.[13] We have computed a series of committee support scores for each MC in each of the Eighty-fourth, Eighty-sixth, Eighty-eighth, Ninetieth, Ninety-second, Ninety-fourth, Ninety-sixth, Ninety-eighth, and Hundredth Congresses. For example, the Agriculture support scores for the Ninety-sixth Congress were calculated as follows: for all thirty-one roll call votes pertinent to bills reported out by the Agriculture Committee, the position (aye or no) adopted by the majority of the committee was identified; each member's score was then computed as the percentage of times that that member's vote agreed with the committee's position.[14] These scores tap the "deference" that each member accords to the Agriculture Committee, in that members who more frequently defer to the committee's judgment (as expressed by the majority of its members) will have higher scores. They may also tap constituency similarities, ideological similarities, and other bases of agreement between the member and the committee.

We have computed the average committee support score among two classes of member—noncommittee Democrats and noncommittee Republicans—for each committee in each of the nine Congresses in our purview. The results for all exclusive and semiexclusive committees (except Budget and Rules) are displayed graphically in figures 11–22.

We think that these figures substantiate two main points. First, noncommittee Democrats agreed with the decisions of most committees most of the time. Only four committees—Armed Services, Interstate and Foreign Commerce, Judiciary, and Post Office—ever received

13. The evidence on amendment sponsorship (Smith 1988, 148) does not show a sustained impact of reform on Republican activity. Sponsorship may not be a good measure of who is really behind an amendment, however, since Republicans can get Democrats to "shill" for them. In the postreform era, it is mostly Republicans who vote for amendments (Rohde 1990). Statistics compiled by David Rohde show that Republicans called for 60 percent of all roll calls in 1969, 68 percent of all roll calls in 1979, and 74 percent of all roll calls in 1987 (personal communication).

14. By *majority of the committee* we mean the majority of committee members, not the majority party members of the committee. If the committee was evenly split on a roll call, as has happened on rare occasions, that roll call was deleted from the analysis. A member who paired in support of a committee's position was counted as supporting it. Since the average member of Congress voted or paired in 80–90 percent of all roll calls in the Congresses considered here, not much difference is made in the results reported below if one counts unpaired absences as failure to support.

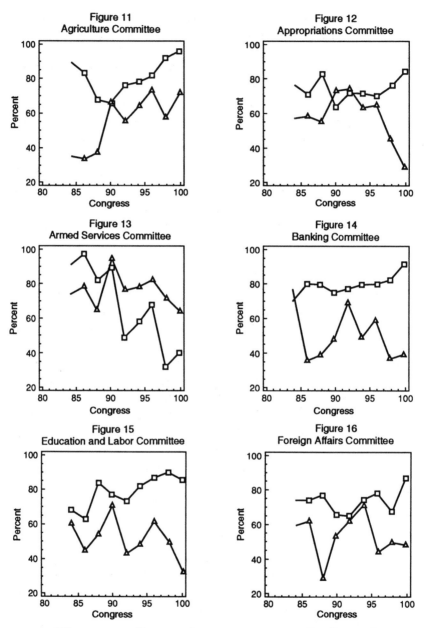

FIGURES 11–16. Committee Leadership Support Scores, by Committee

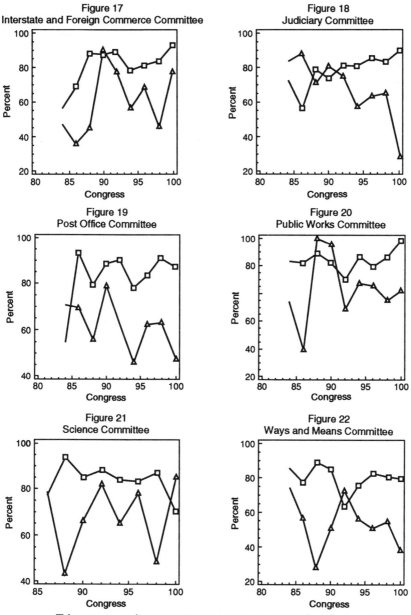

FIGURES 17–22. Committee Leadership Support Scores, by Committee

support on less than 60 percent of their decisions from the average Democrat. Moreover, averaging the Congress-by-Congress support levels (table 35) for each committee shows that support for committee decisions among noncommittee Democrats has exceeded 75 percent for almost all committees. Even the committee receiving the least support from noncommittee Democrats, HUAAC, was still supported 72 percent of the time, on average.

Second, noncommittee Democrats generally accorded committee decisions a higher level of support than did noncommittee Republicans. Two committees—Foreign Affairs and Education and Labor—never received a higher average level of support from noncommittee Republicans than from noncommittee Democrats. Five more—Agriculture, Banking, Interstate and Foreign Commerce, Post Office, and Ways and Means—received more support from Republicans than Democrats in only one of the nine Congresses (and the difference in support levels is small in each case except that of Post Office in the Eighty-fourth Congress). Three more committees—Appropriations, Public Works, and Science—received more support from Republicans than Democrats in two of the nine Congresses (with the differences in support levels being small in the case of Appropriations).[15] Finally, only two committees received more support from Republicans than Democrats in more than two of the nine Congresses—Judiciary (in three) and Armed Services (in six).

Another way to gauge the typical difference between Democratic and Republican support for a committee's decisions is to subtract the typical level of support accorded committee decisions by noncommittee Republicans from the analogous figure for noncommittee Democrats. This difference was less than 15 percentage points for only six committees—Judiciary, House Administration, Small Business, Veterans' Affairs, Armed Services, and HUAAC (table 35, column 6). The first four had differences of between 5 and 10 percentage points; the last two actually received higher levels of support, on average, from Republicans than from Democrats.

An ancillary point worth noting is that support for committee decisions among Democrats was less variable than it was among Republicans. The standard deviations given in table 35 show that the Congress-to-Congress variance in support was less among Democrats than Re-

---

15. Note that Science existed for only eight of the Congresses covered here.

TABLE 35.   AVERAGE COMMITTEE SUPPORT
SCORES, BY PARTY

Committee	Democrats		Republicans			Difference in Overall Averages
	Overall Average	Std. Dev.	Overall Average	Std. Dev.	N	
Banking	79.3	.06	50.3	.15	9	29.0
Education and Labor	79.1	.09	51.9	.12	9	27.2
Foreign Affairs	73.4	.07	53.2	.12	9	20.2
Ways and Means	79.8	.07	53.8	.14	9	26.0
Agriculture	81.5	.10	55.5	.16	9	26.0
Appropriations	74.6	.07	58.4	.14	9	16.2
Commerce	80.8	.12	60.5	.19	9	20.3
Post Office	82.4	.12	61.3	.11	9	21.1
Dist. of Columbia	77.3	.11	62.3	.20	8	15.0
Public Works	83.9	.08	63.0	.24	9	20.9
Gov. Operations	84.2	.10	66.0	.21	9	18.2
Interior	84.6	.08	66.6	.15	9	18.0
Merchant Marine	86.6	.07	67.7	.17	9	18.9
Judiciary	77.7	.10	67.9	.18	9	9.8
Science	84.1	.07	68.8	.16	8	15.3
House Admin.	81.7	.20	72.2	.27	7	9.5
Armed Services	75.6	.18	82.3	.07	9	− 6.7
Small Business	96.3	.06	86.5	.11	4	9.8
Veterans	96.7	.05	91.0	.13	9	5.7
HUAAC	72.2	.23	91.2	.08	4	− 19.0

NOTE: The analysis pertains to nine Congresses: the Eighty-fourth, Eighty-sixth, Eighty-eighth, Ninetieth, Ninety-second, Ninety-fourth, Ninety-sixth, Ninety-eighth, and Hundredth. For each of these Congresses we have computed a series of committee support scores for each member and then averaged these scores among noncommittee Democrats and noncommittee Republicans, as described in the text. The "overall averages" given in the table are (simple) averages of the Congress-by-Congress averages. The standard deviations give an indication of the extent to which average levels of support for a committee vary from Congress to Congress. Column 5 gives the number of Congresses for which average committee support scores were calculated (in some Congresses some committees did not exist, or no roll calls were taken on the committee's bills). The committees are presented in ascending order of their overall average Republican support.

publicans for every committee except Armed Services, HUAAC, and Post Office.

The data displayed in figures 11–12 and table 35 show that the typical committee receives a fairly high level of support from noncommittee Democrats and substantially more support from them than from noncommittee Republicans. Moreover, Democratic support also varies less from Congress to Congress than does Republican support.[16]

The primary exceptions to this characterization are Small Business, Veterans' Affairs, Armed Services, and HUAAC. The first two of these are service committees with client groups (small business owners and veterans) that give the Republicans considerable electoral support. Thus, the average level of support among noncommittee Republicans is very high—86.5 percent for Small Business and 91.0 percent for Veterans' Affairs. Nonetheless, the level of support among noncommittee Democrats is even higher—96.3 and 96.7 percent, respectively. Thus, although the difference in support levels between the two parties is not very large, it can hardly be maintained that these committees are doing anything that seriously displeases the majority party.

Armed Services and HUAAC are a different story, however. They are the only two committees whose decisions were consistently supported more by Republicans than by Democrats. Armed Services behaved normally enough in the first three Congresses, but starting with the Ninetieth Congress it has always received more support on the floor from the Republicans than from the Democrats. HUAAC received more support from Republicans than Democrats in every Congress for which we have data (the Eighty-sixth, Eighty-eighth, Ninetieth, and Ninety-second). Moreover, the variability of support for both Armed Services and HUAAC decisions is greater for Democrats than for Republicans, reversing the pattern seen in the other committees.

We do not think that there is any denying that these two committees have been somewhat "out of control" from the majority party's viewpoint. But the party has certainly *tried* to rein these committees in. Indeed, along with the control committees, Armed Services and HUAAC have come in for some of the most obvious attempts at restructuring and realignment.

The Democrats purged their membership on HUAAC in 1948, as described in chapter 2. After the balance of power in the party between

16. Nearly all of the differences in average levels of support pictured in figures 11–12 and reported in table 35 are significant at conventional levels of significance.

liberal and conservative began to shift decisively in the liberals' favor, HUAAC's funding was regularly cut below its requests (*Congressional Quarterly Weekly Report,* 7 Apr. 1967, 507; 22 Mar. 1968, 587; 7 May 1971, 1019; 11 Mar. 1972, 551). Proposals to abolish the committee were floated in 1969, 1971, and 1973 before finally meeting with success in 1975 (*Congressional Quarterly Weekly Report,* 21 Feb. 1969, 274; 7 May 1971, 1019; 24 Mar. 1973, 676; *Congressional Quarterly Almanac* 1975, 31).

The Armed Services Committee did not have its funding reduced, nor, of course, was it abolished. Instead, the Democratic Caucus "fired" two of its chairs—F. Edward Hebert in 1975 and C. Melvin Price in 1985—and made its displeasure with a third, Les Aspin, plain in 1987.[17]

3. THE CONSEQUENCES OF STRUCTURAL POWER: PUBLIC POLICY

If the majority party does control the legislative agenda, as suggested in the previous section, then what passes will also tend to have a partisan cast. A full recounting of how policy changes with changes in partisan control of the House is well beyond the scope of this chapter, but some of the main lines of evidence can be briefly cited.

The Republicans have controlled the House only twice in the postwar era, but in both cases the policy consequences were substantial and clear-cut. The consequences were particularly clear in the realm of fiscal policy (Cox and McCubbins 1991), spending policy (Kiewiet and McCubbins 1991), and welfare policy (Browning 1985), but, of course, they also extended to such matters as the Taft-Hartley Act.[18]

17. The other exceptions to the general characterization of committees as making decisions with which Democrats are happier than Republicans are all temporary. For example, four committees (Agriculture, Appropriations, Commerce, and Ways and Means) show a marked decline in average support from Democrats, together with a marked increase in average support from Republicans, in the Ninetieth or the Ninety-second Congress. The leadership of each of these committees was either removed or faced with a new set of incentives in the Ninety-fourth Congress: the chair of Agriculture was removed; the subcommittee chairs of the Appropriations Committee were made subject to caucus approval; the chair of one of Commerce's subcommittees was removed; and the chair of Ways and Means retired rather than be replaced. In addition, the Commerce Committee, after a large influx of new liberal members, introduced a series of important new rules (Ornstein and Rohde 1977a), and the Democratic Caucus both stripped Ways and Means of its committee assignment duties and increased its size considerably.

18. As regards expenditure, an analysis for two postwar Congresses can serve as an indication of the importance of partisan control. The midterm election of 1966 saw the majority Democrats lose 49 seats. Twelve years earlier, in the midterm election of 1954, the Democrats picked up 21 seats and moved from minority to majority status. One perspective, based loosely on a unidimensional, median voter model of spending deci-

4. COMMENTS ON THE POSTWAR HOUSE

The picture of the postwar House that this chapter and chapter 9 have painted is one in which the majority party acts as a structuring coalition, stacking the deck in its own favor—both on the floor and in committee—to create a kind of "legislative cartel" that dominates the legislative agenda. The majority party promotes its agenda-setting advantage in two basic ways: by giving its members greater power to veto legislative initiatives; and by giving its members greater power to push legislative initiatives onto the floor.

Although these powers might be thought of as two sides of the same agenda-setting coin, they are also inherently in tension: one person's power to push proposals to the floor may run up against another's power to prevent them from getting there. Such conflicts could be resolved on a case-by-case basis, of course, but it is also possible to give a general advantage either to those wishing to enact legislation or to those wishing to prevent legislation. For example, the requirement that expenditures be authorized *and* appropriated separately; the necessity for many major bills to be both reported from committee *and* given a rule by the Rules Committee; and the requirement that two-thirds vote for suspension of the rules—all these conditions improve the chances of those seeking to stop legislation relative to the chances of those seeking to pass legislation. Depending on what structural choices are made, rather different systems of agenda control can result with different consequences for internal party politics. We think the Democrats operated a system in which the power to veto was especially strong early in the postwar era, but they then redressed the balance more in favor of the power to propose with the committee reforms of the 1970s.

---

sions, would predict a significant spending decrease, *ceteris paribus,* as the number of Democrats in the House shrank by 49 from fiscal year 1967 to fiscal year 1968, and that the policy change would be large relative to any change in spending from fiscal year 1955 to fiscal year 1956 (since fewer seats changed hands). By contrast, we argue that the more important change took place in the election of 1954, when the majority in the House changed from the Republicans to the Democrats. We would expect a relatively large change in policy to accompany the turnover in partisan control in fiscal 1956, but no significant change in policy in fiscal 1968. Thus, we should expect a significant spending increase for 1955–56, but, *ceteris paribus,* no significant change in spending for 1967–68. Using data provided by Kiewiet and McCubbins (1991), we performed a difference-of-means test, looking at 45 nondefense agencies that existed during both time periods. We found a significant increase in spending in 1956, but no significant change in spending for 1968. This simple test suggests that it is quite possible to overestimate the independence of members of Congress from party.

The Democrats had a clear factional division between South and North even before World War II. This division meant that the cost to the party of unwanted positive action was high: there were many possible proposals that could split the party. Thus, throughout most of the postwar era the Democratic system of agenda control was one in which the power to veto was strong relative to the power to propose; bills had to run a gauntlet of veto points, and both wings of the party were well represented at most of them. The party thereby set the probability of one kind of error—party-splitting positive action—to a low value.

Lowering the probability of this type of error, however, raised the probability of another kind of partisan "error": the failure to act on issues that one wing of the party wished to pursue. This failure was most evident, of course, in the various and well documented instances in which the South exercised its veto over northern liberal proposals. The South's agenda was primarily to conserve its own way of life (especially regarding race relations), and so it is not surprising that northern vetoes of southern initiatives should have been so much less frequent.

Nonetheless, the North did get something out of the system. The Republicans would have pushed plenty of proposals to the floor if they could, but these proposals were blocked by the North's veto. Attention did not attach to these vetoes, however, because it was not news that the minority party's legislative agenda was being thwarted in committee; that was to be expected.

As the southern wing of the party became smaller and more liberal, however, the dominance of veto power over proposal power became less sensible. More members of the party were willing to lessen the veto power of the committee chairs and redress the balance in favor of proposal power. The Subcommittee Bill of Rights has been viewed chiefly as a decentralization of power in the House; we view it as redressing the balance between veto and proposal power in favor of the latter by increasing the number of subunits with proposal power.

The basic logic is simple. When there are only twenty-odd committee chairs with the staff resources and the scheduling power necessary to legislate, the total number of proposals seriously pursued will be limited by the time, energy, and interests of the sitting chairs.[19] When subcommittees are given fixed jurisdictions (with automatic referral of bills),

19. As Rohde (1991, 21) notes: "On many [prereform] committees the members had no access to staff without the chairman's permission. This made it more difficult to formulate legislative alternatives to bill provisions favored by the chair."

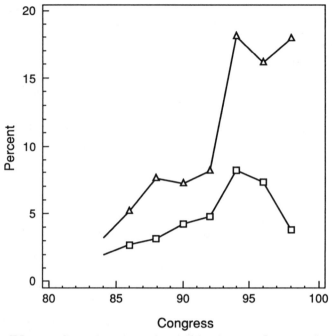

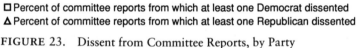

□ Percent of committee reports from which at least one Democrat dissented
△ Percent of committee reports from which at least one Republican dissented

FIGURE 23.   Dissent from Committee Reports, by Party

the right to hold hearings and to mark up legislation, and independent
staff allocations, then the number of members with the ability actively
to pursue their legislative interests goes up considerably. If, in addition,
rules are adopted requiring that subcommittee ratios must be at least as
favorable to the majority party as those in the full committee (with
regard to Commerce, for example, see Ornstein and Rohde 1977b, 218),
then the majority party's advantage in numbers will be larger at the
subcommittee than committee stage, and larger in committee than on
the floor.

   What were the consequences of this restructuring of the committee
system by the majority party? First, the unhappiness of Republican
committee members with their own committees' proposals (as measured by their willingness to file dissenting opinions with the committee
report) increased sharply (figure 23). This increase was to be expected
since the veto screen through which the legislation had to pass no longer
included both a northern and a southern veto, but just a northern one.

   Second, floor reception of committee bills became rockier, with many more amendments offered. Current explanations of this increase in amending activity point to the inexperience of subcommittee chairs relative to full committee chairs (they were simply less adept at anticipating what would fly on the floor) and to the increased "independence" of members in the new, decentralized House. We view the increase in amendments as a consequence of the majority party's "opening the spigot" to legislation. The prefloor screening process was less tough, and the southern veto in the Rules Committee was largely removed, so that more proposals made it to the floor with which committee Republicans were unhappy. Republicans who were unhappy in committee carried the fight onto the floor: an increasing proportion of the roll call votes demanded on the floor were demanded by Republicans,[20] and an increasing proportion of amendments on domestic initiatives were pushed by Republicans (Rohde 1990a, 15).

20. Again, Science existed for only eight of the Congresses covered here.

Conclusion

American political scientists have had a long and stormy relationship with political parties. If we date the formation of a self-conscious discipline from the founding of the American Political Science Association (APSA) in 1903, then it is clear that the profession's initial attitude was decidedly negative—born of Progressive opposition to machine politics, a fascination with "scientific" administration, and such influential antiparty tracts as Mosei Ostrogorski's *Democracy and the Organization of Political Parties* (1902). As early as the middle of the century, however, the profession had reconsidered the value of parties—a reconsideration given corporate expression with the publication of APSA's *Toward a More Responsible Two-Party System* in 1950. Whereas the organization had once sought to exorcise the demons of partisanship at the local level through civil service exams, nonpartisan elections, and other reforms, the post–New Deal APSA sought ways of bolstering party, taking it as axiomatic that "popular government in a nation of more than 150 million people requires political parties which provide the electorate with a proper range of choice between alternatives of action" (APSA 1950, 15). The authors of the APSA report feared that, without reform to strengthen the leadership of the congressional parties, Congress would be immobilized, interest groups empowered (19–20, 34), "excessive responsibility" shifted to the president (14), and voters prompted to turn their backs on the parties in favor of a congeries of independent candidates or, worse, "extremist parties . . . each fanatically bent on imposing on the country its particular panacea" (14).

Many of the fears voiced by the authors of the 1950 report have become recurrent themes in the literature. Lowi's (1979) *End of Liberalism,* for example, see the development of interest group power and congressional inaction culminating in radical change in the conduct of public affairs. Indeed, as Lowi puts it, "during the decade of the 1960s the United States had a crisis of public authority and died" (271); a new public philosophy, embodied in the "Second Republic," began to govern affairs: "The new public philosophy embraced the shift from Congress-centered to executive-centered government. . . . Congress was redefined as a useful collection of minorities and then belittled further by the idea that Congress was only one part of a long policy-making process within which organized minorities had rightful access for purposes of informal and formal participation" (275). Public policy in Lowi's Second Republic came not "from voter preferences or congressional enactments but from a process of tripartite bargaining between the specialized administrators, relevant members of Congress, and the representatives of self-selected organized interests" (xii).

This book has sought to deal with several of the problems presented by this view of congressional death and dismemberment by iron triangle (or its more understated versions in the committee government model). We concentrate here on just two problems.

First, viewing committees as autonomous agents underemphasizes the importance of systemic structure. Behavioralist scholars have quite naturally focused their research on observable actions; because most of the observable work of Congress is conducted in committee, this focus has led to a concentration on committees and subcommittees, too often ignoring the incentives created by the House's rules of procedure.

A preliminary to all committee action is the setting up of the committee system itself, embodying a certain set of rules and incentives. Although it is widely accepted that congressional parties achieve consistently high levels of cohesion on procedural votes, especially those that set up the structure of the House, this cohesion is not generally seen as incompatible with committee government. We, by contrast, view it as clearly incompatible. There are too many ways in which the majority party can influence the committee system to speak of autonomy in any but a rhetorical sense.

A second problem with the committee government view is that it does not really help us to understand the full range of postwar developments in Congress. Consider the example of the reforms of the 1970s. The most natural explanation of the reforms from the committee government viewpoint was that they simply continued the process of decentralization of power down to the subcommittee level. But such a view of the reforms ignores the whole range of party-building measures that Rohde (1991), among others, has so carefully described. And it ignores also the high levels of party cohesion achieved in the 1980s (comparable to those achieved in the era of strong Speakers). If one believes that parties were *not* particularly consequential in the 1980s, one must explain a lot of evidence on other grounds. If one believes that parties *were* consequential in the 1980s, but also that we had a system of committee government in the prereform era, then one has some questions of origin to answer: Did the autonomous committees decide to re-create parties? Did parties, like Lazarus, rise from the dead?

We prefer to think that the parties never died and that we have had a version of "party government," in the House at least, throughout the postwar period. At the electoral level there continue to be national, partisan tides in congressional elections—tides to which strategic politicians both respond and contribute (Jacobson and Kernell 1990). These tides represent a common component in the electoral fates of members of the same party. Ignoring this common component, as researchers generally view MCs as doing, would lead not just to a lack of collective responsibility as described by Lowi (1979) or Fiorina (1977) but also to a kind of electoral inefficiency (as described in chapter 5). We argue that MCs recognize the collective reputations that tie them together; although much of their time is spent in pursuit of their own parochial electoral interests, they nonetheless support partisan institutions that both regulate the amount and mitigate the external electoral effects of self-serving behavior.

Within the House, representatives have another reason to create and maintain partisan institutions—so that policy deals can be more efficiently struck, policed, and incorporated in law. It is well known that games involving the division of a pie are theoretically unstable when decisions are made by majority rule: any proposed division (say, 50 percent to A and 50 percent to B, with nothing for C) can be overturned by another (say, nothing for A, 55 percent for B, and 45 percent for C). The same kind of instability also affects decisions involving public goods— that is the central lesson of the famous spatial instability theorems (Plott 1967; McKelvey and Wendell 1976; Schofield 1980). Thus, from a theoretical perspective congressional decisions are always susceptible to overturning. Hence, deal making, or trade in legislative support, is discouraged.

Influential researchers (Shepsle 1979; Shepsle and Weingast 1981; Weingast and Marshall 1988) have argued that "structure"—in particular the committee system—is key to understanding why decisions in Congress are not forever overturned by shifting majorities. We share this emphasis on structure but view the key actors as not the committees, but the parties.

In our view, congressional parties are a species of legislative cartel. These cartels usurp the rule-making power of the House in order to endow their members with differential power (e.g., the power of committee chairs) and to facilitate and stabilize legislative trades that benefit their members.[1] Most of the cartel's efforts are centered on securing control of the legislative agenda for its members. This book has focused on various aspects of these efforts to control the agenda.

With our view of parties, of course, there is no need to ask whether the autonomous committees decided to create parties in the 1970s or whether parties rose from the dead. The prereform era of legislative stalemate emerges as a natural consequence of the divisions in the majority party and subsequent decisions about how to structure the agenda-setting power: both the South and the North had an effective veto in either the Rules Committee or the leadership, or both. The reforms themselves are predictable consequences of the shrinkage and liberalization of the southern wing of the party, which induced a different view of the appropriate role of agenda power, one in which the power to propose was spread to a substantially larger number of party members.

1. Legislative cartels, like other cartels, are potentially unstable because their members face incentives to free ride and renege on agreements. But parties have an advantage over many other cartels in that they can adopt rules that bind all groups smaller than a House majority (and impede even House majorities). It is through these rules, which dictate the structure of the legislative process, that legislative coalitions achieve a measure of stability and longevity.

Uncompensated Seniority Violations, Eightieth Through Hundredth Congresses

Eightieth: None.

Eighty-first: None.

Eighty-second: Christian A. Herter (R.-Mass.), a prominent member of the liberal northeastern wing of the Republican party, had served on the Rules Committee in the Eightieth and Eighty-first Congresses. During the second session of the Eighty-first Congress, he was one of twenty-one House Republicans to dissent publicly from minority leader Joseph Martin's "GOP '50 Plan," a campaign platform for Republicans in the off-year elections (see *New York Times,* 12 Jan. 1950 and 4 July 1950). He also voted with the liberal Democrats on Rules on the issue of reporting out a bill creating a Fair Employment Practice Commission and actively promoted liberal labor and tax legislation (see *Congressional Quarterly Almanac* 1950, 375–79; *New York Times,* 13 Mar. 1950). Herter was not reappointed to Rules at the beginning of the Eighty-second Congress, taking instead the eleventh-ranking position on Foreign Affairs. He would have moved up a notch in seniority, to third out of four, had he been reappointed in the Eighty-second.

Eighty-third through Eighty-seventh: None.

Eighty-eighth: James C. Auchincloss (R.-N.J.) was ranking minority member on both the Public Works and District of Columbia committees in the Eighty-sixth and Eighty-seventh Congresses. In the Eighty-eighth, his last Congress, he retained his position on Public Works but was ranked second on District of Columbia. As noted in the *Washington Post* (15 Jan. 1963), Auchincloss announced that he was stepping down as ranking minority member of District of Columbia "because of the press of other duties." Several things might be noted in connection with Auchincloss's step down. First, there was discontent with his lack of aggressiveness in pushing for greater minority staffing; and the same year that he stepped down, a leader of the fight for better staffing (Frederick Schwengel of Iowa) was appointed to the committee. Second, Auchincloss was clearly identified with the liberal northeastern wing of the party. Third, his support of the Republican leadership had steadily declined from the Eighty-sixth to Eighty-eighth Congresses: he was around the third quartile in terms of leadership support in the Eighty-sixth Congress, near the median in the Eighty-seventh, and in the bottom fourth by the Eighty-eighth. We found no direct evidence, however, that any of this is relevant to his relinquishing of his position.

Eighty-ninth: (1) Peter H. B. Frelinghuysen (R.-N.J.) resigned his ranking minority position on Education and Labor without taking on any new assignment. He stated at the time that "he wished to give more attention to his Foreign Affairs Committee duties" (*Congressional Quarterly Weekly Report,* 22 Jan. 1965, 109). Frelinghuysen was relatively junior on Foreign Affairs and never became ranking member. His leadership support scores were generally quite low. In the Eighty-eighth, the Congress before his resignation, he supported the Republican leaders on 66.2 percent of all leadership opposition votes, putting him in the bottom 10 percent of Republicans in terms of loyalty. What is interesting about Frelinghuysen's case is the series of actions taking place before he announced his resignation. On 4 January 1965 the House Republican Conference elected a new minority leader, Gerald R. Ford of Michigan, rebuffing incumbent leader Charles Halleck. Eight days later Ford announced his support for Frelinghuysen's bid to unseat Leslie Arends as minority whip. On 14 January, the day on which the vote for whip was to be held, the conference first adopted a new rule prohibiting a member from serving simultaneously as ranking member on a standing committee and in a leadership position. Had Frelinghuysen won, he would therefore have had to relinquish his position on Education and Labor. In the event, he lost—and still relinquished the position.

(2) The Democratic Caucus voted to demote John Bell Williams to the lowest seniority ranking on both committees on which he served (District of Columbia and Commerce) as punishment for having supported Republican presidential nominee Barry Goldwater in 1964.

(3) The Democratic Caucus voted to demote Albert Watson to the lowest-ranking position on his committees, also for having supported Goldwater in 1964.

Ninetieth: (1) A motion to restore John Bell Williams's seniority on Commerce was defeated, and Williams was given no committee assignments.

(2) The Democratic Caucus voted to demote Adam Clayton Powell, moving him from the chair to the second position on Education and Labor. The action was prompted by Powell's failure to pay fines levied by the New York courts.

Ninety-first: The Democratic Caucus voted to strip John R. Rarick of his seniority on the Agriculture Committee in retaliation for his support of George Wallace's 1968 presidential candidacy.

Ninety-second: Rarick continued to serve below other members with fewer terms of consecutive service on Agriculture.

Ninety-third: Rarick continued to serve below other members with fewer terms of consecutive service on Agriculture.

Ninety-fourth: (1) The Democratic Caucus voted to remove Wright Patman as chair of Banking and Currency and to install in his stead Henry S. Reuss. Reuss had less seniority than did two others on the committee—Leonor Kretzer Sullivan and William A. Barrett—so, all told, three members had their seniority violated.

(2) The Democratic Caucus voted to remove F. Edward Hebert as chair of Armed Services and to install in his stead the second-ranking member, C. Melvin Price.

(3) The Democratic Caucus voted to remove William R. Poage as chair of Agriculture and to install in his stead the second-ranking member, Thomas S. Foley.

(4) Wilbur Mills "voluntarily" stepped down as chair of Ways and Means and assumed the second-ranking position on the committee. Mills, involved in a scandal over his alcoholism and sexual exploits, was not compensated for giving up the chair and probably would have been removed by the caucus had he not stepped down.

(5) John Jarman was elected as a Democrat to the Eighty-second through Ninety-fourth Congresses. At the beginning of the Ninety-fourth Congress, however, he changed his party affiliation and became a Republican. The Republicans gave him the third-ranking spot on Science

and Astronautics, a committee on which he had never before served, thereby violating the seniority of seven Republicans on the committee.

Ninety-fifth: William R. Poage continued to serve on the Agriculture committee in the second-ranking position behind Thomas S. Foley, who had fewer terms of continuous service.

Ninety-sixth: Charles C. Diggs, Jr., was chair of the District of Columbia Committee in the Ninety-third, Ninety-fourth, and Ninety-fifth Congresses. In the Ninety-sixth he decided not to seek reappointment as chair, taking the second spot instead. Diggs, involved in a bribery scandal, was not compensated for giving up the chair and probably would have been removed by the caucus had he not stepped down.

Ninety-seventh: Raymond F. Lederer was elected to the Ninety-fifth, Ninety-sixth, and Ninety-seventh Congresses and served on Ways and Means in the Ninety-fifth and Ninety-sixth. Lederer was the only member of Congress to be reelected after being indicted in the FBI sting operation known as Abscam. He was convicted at the beginning of the Ninety-seventh Congress, on 9 January 1981. The Republicans planned to propose removing Lederer from the Ways and Means Committee had the Democrats followed tradition and reappointed him. Such a proposal would have forced Democrats either to vote against their leadership's committee nominations or to vote for a convicted felon. The Democrats got wind of the Republican plan, however, and voted to remove Lederer from Ways and Means. He received no compensating committee assignment (indeed, he was not appointed to any committee) and resigned 29 April 1981.

Ninety-eighth: None.

Ninety-ninth: The Democratic Caucus voted to vault Les Aspin over six more senior colleagues to the chairmanship of Armed Services.

Hundredth: Aspin came back to regain the chairmanship of Armed Services after first losing his retention vote as chair, again serving over six more senior colleagues.

A Model of the Speaker's Scheduling Preferences

A Speaker must decide which of a finite set of bills, $B = \{1, \ldots, B\}$, to schedule in a finite amount of time. We think of the set B as containing all bills reported from standing and conference committees as of a given time. B could be given a time subscript to emphasize that it changes over time as new bills are reported, but we dispense with that notational clutter here. Each bill is in a certain "state" describing its floor progress: some have not yet received any consideration, some have been read a first time, some have been sent to conference, and so forth. The possible states in which a bill might be are indexed by the integers $1, \ldots, S$.

This is a discrete time model, meaning that time is thought of as divided into a sequence of discrete periods. In any given period exactly one of the B bills must be selected for further development.[1] If bill b is selected and is in state s, a "reward" R_{bs} is collected (which can be zero or negative) and bill b makes a transition from state s to state u with probability P_{bsu}.[2] Thus, for example, if bill b is in state 1 and the states

---

1. Thus, "package" votes—in which a single vote serves to pass a whole collection of bills—are not allowed in this model. This stricture does not mean that the model disallows omnibus bills, which have been packaged before the legislation reaches the floor.

2. That the reward depends only on the bill and its state is perhaps the most restrictive feature of the current model, as it says that the payoff to taking up one bill does not depend on the developmental stage of any other bill. That the transition probabilities also depend only on the bill and its state is similarly restrictive; among other things, it means that the model admits of no reason for the Speaker to delay a bill until there is sufficient support for it, one of the most obvious uses of the scheduling power. This particular restriction could probably be removed. We have not done so because it makes the model more unwieldy and also because we focus on the use of the scheduling power to veto bills.

are numbered consecutively (higher numbers meaning more advanced stages of development), then b may have a probability P_{b11} of failing to advance, a probability P_{b12} of advancing one stage, a probability P_{b13} of advancing two stages, and so forth. All probabilities can be thought of as the Speaker's subjective estimates, taking into account whatever information is available to him at the time.

A discount factor, d_{bs}, is applied to future returns. This discounting can be interpreted as reflecting the amount of floor time that bill b (in state s) will need before any transition can be decided on, with the consequent delay of all other bills. Delay is important not just because payoffs are deferred but also because enough delay—past the end of the session—can be fatal.

The problem of selecting which bill to schedule next can be posed in a dynamic programming format. Let the "condition" of the legislative agenda as a whole be given by the vector $C = (s_1, \ldots, s_B)$—which is simply a listing of the current state of all the bills on the calendar (s_b denotes bill b's current state). Let $V(C)$ represent the discounted expected value to the Speaker of following an optimal scheduling policy from the current time on, when the condition of the legislative agenda is C. For each possible condition C, the valuation function V must satisfy the fundamental recursive relation

$$V(C) = \max_b \{R_{bs} + d_{bs}\Sigma P_{bsu} V(C-b,u)\}$$

where the summation is taken over $u = 1, \ldots, S$ and $C-b,u$ is a vector equal to C, except in the bth component, where it equals u. In words, the value of an optimal scheduling policy starting at condition C must equal the immediate payoff from some bill b (the one that the schedule starts with) plus the appropriately discounted value of following an optimal policy thereafter, in light of what happens with the first bill.

A special case of the model sketched above is all that we need here. Instead of considering the full range of potential "states" in which a bill might be, we consider just three: not yet considered on the floor ($=1$); passed unamended ($=2$); and rejected beyond resurrection ($=3$). If a bill is in state 1 (not yet considered), then the "reward" for taking it up, R_{b1}, is zero (which can be interpreted as implying that there are no intrinsic rewards from the act of considering a bill).[3] The probabilities

3. Of course, the general model of which this is a special case allows positive or negative values of R_{b1}.

of transition from state 1 are $P_{b11} = 0$; $P_{b12} = P_b$; and $P_{b13} = 1 - P_b$. Thus, a bill considered for the first time is always resolved one way or another, up or down, and P_b is simply the "probability of bill b passing, if it is considered."

If a bill is rejected (with probability $1 - P_b$), the Speaker gets no increment to his utility because the status quo has not been changed.[4] If a bill is passed (with probability P_b), the Speaker gets a "reward," R_b.[5]

All told, then, the present special case is one in which the Speaker must choose from among a finite set of unconsidered bills the one to be considered next. Whatever bill is chosen will be voted up or down at the end of its period of consideration on the floor. If the chosen bill is voted up, the Speaker receives a utility increment, R_b; if the bill is voted down, he receives nothing. Bills can differ in their probability of passage (P_b), in the amount of time they are likely to take (indicated by the discount factor d_b), and in the utility increment that the Speaker receives should they pass.

As it turns out, the optimal scheduling rule in this special case is very simple. At any given time the Speaker should choose to schedule next the bill with the highest value of the following "internal rate of return":

$$W_b = d_b P_b R_b / (1 - d_b)$$

The numerator of W_b simply gives the discounted expected value of considering bill b; the denominator is a measure of how long bill b is likely to take (the longer it will take, the smaller is the discount factor on future payoffs, hence the larger the denominator). Thus, W_b can be interpreted as a measure of the *increment to discounted expected value*

4. This occurrence is represented formally in the model as follows: Once a bill has reached state 3 (rejected), it can, formally, be taken up again. On doing so, however, the Speaker gets a "reward" of $R_{b3} = 0$, transits to the same state with probability 1 ($P_{b33} = 1$), and incurs no new discount ($d_{b3} = 1$). Thus, there is no incentive whatever to take up a rejected bill, although the opportunity exists formally in the model.

5. This occurrence is represented formally in the model as follows: Once a bill has reached state 2 (passed), it can, formally, be taken up again. On doing so, the Speaker gets a "reward" of $R_{b2} = R_b$, transits to state 3 (which can now be interpreted as the state of not just "rejected" but also "fully processed" bills) with probability 1 ($P_{b23} = 1$), and incurs no new discount ($d_{b2} = 1$). Thus, there is every incentive to take up a passed bill, if $R_b > 0$. The model is formally identical to one in which the reward from passage comes automatically at the end of the first period. Of course, if $R_b < 0$, then the Speaker will want to avoid taking up state 2 bills, so we need to add a proviso that "any bill in state 2 must be taken up immediately on reaching that state." The only reason for these formalistic oddities is the generality of the multi-armed bandit model. In order to apply to a large array of specific applications, the notation adopted turns out to be convenient.

that bill b *yields per unit of time that it takes up on the floor*—and the optimal scheduling rule dictates taking up bills in order of this ratio.[6]

SOME IMPLICATIONS OF OPTIMAL SCHEDULING

The model developed above suggests two basic conclusions about how a Speaker with unilateral scheduling power would exercise that power. First, bills that made the Speaker worse off would not be scheduled at all; thus, unless the Speaker's scheduling decisions could be overturned, such bills would be effectively vetoed. Second, those bills that made the Speaker better off would be taken in a definite order, according to their "internal rate of return," W_b.

Some useful comparative statics relations follow straightforwardly from consideration of the formula for the internal rate of return. The partial derivatives of W_b with respect to d_b, P_b, and R_b are all positive, assuming that the bill is desirable (i.e., $R_b > 0$).[7] Thus, other things equal, a desirable bill has a higher internal rate of return and, hence, a greater likelihood of being scheduled, (1) the less time on the floor it is likely to take (the larger is d_b); (2) the higher its probability of passage (P_b); and (3) the higher its expected payoff to the Speaker, if passed (R_b).[8] Bills that are undesirable ($R_b < 0$), by contrast, have negative returns and so will not be scheduled at all if the Speaker can avoid it.[9]

6. Essentially the same conclusion is reached in a continuous time model in which each bill is characterized not by a discount factor but by an amount of time needed on the floor, and the Speaker must schedule subject to a total time constraint. Moreover, the more general model outlined above also yields similar conclusions under a variety of conditions; see Whittle 1982, vol. 1, chap. 14.

7. The partial derivatives of W_b with respect to d_b, P_b, and R_b are, respectively, $P_b R_b / (1 - d_b)^2$, $d_b P_b / (1 - d_b)$, and $d_b P_b / (1 - d_b)$. All three are strictly positive if $0 < d_b < 1$, $R_b > 0$, and $P_b > 0$.

8. These comparative statics relations hold up in more general versions of the model than the special case elaborated here. The interested reader should refer to Whittle 1982 for a survey of more general results.

9. If the Speaker cannot avoid it, then he is more likely to schedule such bills the more time they take, the less likely they are to pass, and the lower the absolute value of their payoffs to the Speaker.

Unchallengeable and Challengeable Vetoes

We consider a simplified version of the model of legislative politics outlined in section 3 of chapter 9. There are n ordinary members of the legislature, indexed by the integers from 1 to n, plus a Speaker, indexed by 0. Each member i has a Euclidian utility function u_i defined over a one-dimensional policy space, with ideal point z_i. The median floor member's ideal point is denoted by F.

Some subset of the ordinary members belong to a committee, the median ideal point of which is denoted C. This committee has the sole right to initiate bills.

If the committee decides to report a bill, it goes onto a calendar to await further processing. The Speaker, with ideal point $z_0 = S$, has the right to remove bills from the calendar and schedule them for floor votes. If a bill makes it to the floor, it is considered under an open rule.

To say that the Speaker's veto is "unchallengeable" or "challengeable" in the current model can be construed as follows. Suppose that the Speaker's decision not to schedule a bill can be overridden at a collective cost of c. That is, if legislator i contributes c_i to the overriding effort, and the sum of c_i over all i exceeds c, then the bill can be scheduled over the Speaker's objections; otherwise not. Then a veto is "unchallengeable" if c is so large that no bill would be worth the costs of overriding the Speaker's veto, whereas a veto is "challengeable" if some bills are important enough to make veto overrides collectively profitable.

The policy consequences of unchallengeable vetoes, challengeable ve-

TABLE 36.   SPATIAL EQUILIBRIA UNDER
ALTERNATIVE VETO SPECIFICATIONS

Case	No Veto	Veto Specification Challengeable Veto	Unchallengeable Veto
$SQ < S$	F	If (O then F; else as in column 3	SQ or F (whichever is closer to S)
$S < SQ < F$	F	If (O then F; else as in column 3	SQ
$F < SQ < C$	SQ	SQ	SQ
$C < SQ$	SQ or F (whichever is closer to C)	SQ or F (whichever is closer to C)	SQ or F (whichever is closer to C)

NOTE: The table pertains to the case where $S < F < C$. Entries describe the equilibrium outcome under the conditions specified by the row and column variables.

toes, and no vetoes at all are easily analyzed and are presented in tabular form in table 36 for the particular case when $S < F < C$ (other cases can be similarly analyzed). To illustrate how this table was compiled, consider the entry in the top row, middle column. The top row corresponds to cases where SQ, the status quo–reversion point (the point that would obtain if no bill were passed), is less than S. The middle column corresponds to the challengeable veto case. The condition (O) referred to is as follows, where the summation is taken over the set of all i such that $u_i(F) > u_i(SQ)$:

$$\text{Condition (O): } \Sigma[(z_i - SQ)^2 - (z_i - F)^2] > c.$$

If condition (O) is satisfied, then the total "voters' surplus" from passing F rather than SQ exceeds c, the collective costs that must be borne to override the Speaker's veto. There is, of course, no guarantee that collective action will be undertaken just because it would be beneficial if it were. We nonetheless assume that whenever condition (O) is met, any veto is overridden; this illustrates the lower bound on the strength of the challengeable veto.

The entry in the top middle cell can then be interpreted as follows. If condition (O) is satisfied, the Speaker's veto (if any) is overridden, the bill is reported, and the final outcome is just F, the floor median. (The committee does report a bill in this case because it prefers F to SQ.) If condition (O) is not satisfied, then the Speaker can veto any bill that the committee reports with success. Thus, if SQ is closer to S than is F, the Speaker will veto and SQ will result; but if F is closer to S, the Speaker will not veto the committee's bill, and the final outcome will again be F. The other cells can be similarly interpreted.

The point of table 36 is simply to demonstrate that the challengeable veto case is truly intermediate between the no veto and unchallengeable veto cases. This circumstance is illustrated by the second row. One can see that, for any positive c, no matter how small, there is some $SQ < F$ such that condition (O) is not satisfied. Therefore, even a weak challengeable veto can "anchor" policy to some extent, achieving policy outcomes that are not attainable in the no veto case. And as the value of c increases, the range of points for which condition (O) is not satisfied grows continuously, eventually extending beyond S and on toward negative infinity.

The Scheduling Power

In this appendix we expand on the model of legislative politics outlined in chapter 9, section 3. The set of all members is denoted by F, for floor, and is divided into the ordinary members, indexed by the integers from 1 to n, plus a Speaker, indexed by 0. Each member j has a separable and strictly single-peaked utility function u_j defined over a w-dimensional policy space, W, with ideal point z_j. Separability means that the utility function's value at a point x in W can be expressed as follows:

$$u_j(x) = \Sigma u_{ji}(x_i)$$

where the summation is over $i = 1, \ldots, w$. Thus, the contribution to utility of each component x_i does not depend on the value of other components. Strict single-peakedness is equivalent to strict quasi concavity and means that, for any two points x and y such that $u_j(x) > u_j(y)$, and any real number t between 0 and 1, $u_j(tx + (1-t)y) > u_j(y)$.

The policy space W is assumed to be convex and to have a nonempty interior. We normalize the problem so that (1) the origin in w-space corresponds to the status quo; and (2) $u_j(0, \ldots, 0) = 0$ for all j. This second normalization can be performed simply by subtracting the value at the origin of the "original" utility function; that is, if U_j represents legislator j's preferences, then so does u_j, where $u_j(x) = U_j(x) - U_j(0, \ldots, 0)$. Thus, the utility values can be interpreted as indicating how much better off a member would be at x as opposed to the origin (status quo).

Each ordinary member of the legislature belongs to one or more of K committees. Each committee has a jurisdiction, defined as a subset of the dimensions in w-space, and has the exclusive right to initiate legislation in its jurisdiction. We denote committee k's jurisdiction by J_k. We take K to be less than w, so that some or all committees may have multidimensional jurisdictions. There is, however, no overlap in committee jurisdictions. We denote by $C(i)$ the committee with jurisdiction over issue dimension i.

If a committee decides to report a bill, it goes onto a calendar to await further processing. The Speaker has the sole right to remove bills from the calendars and schedule them for floor votes. He can also decide whether to give closed or open rules to those bills that he does allow onto the floor. Time on the floor is scarce in the sense that only L bills can be processed in a session.

Let $x = (x_1, \ldots, x_w)$ be the vector of changes in each dimension proposed by the committees of jurisdiction (with $x_i = 0$ indicating that the committee decided to propose no change and hence reported no bill). We assume that each bill concerns only a single dimension. The number of bills reported to the calendars is thus $B(x) = \#\{i: x_i \text{ differs from } 0\}$, where $\#T$ is the number of elements in the set T.

For any two points y_i and v_i on the ith dimension, and any subset T of F, let $n_T(y_i, v_i) = \#\{j \epsilon T: uj(y_i) > uj(v_i)\}$ be the number of legislators in T who prefer y_i to v_i. For any subset T of F, and any point y_i on the ith dimension, let $P_i(T, y_i) = \{v_i: n_T(v_i, y_i) > \#T/2\}$ be the set of points on the ith dimension that some majority of T prefers to y_i. Let $m_i = \text{med}\{z_{ji}: j\epsilon F\}$ be the median ideal point on the ith dimension.

Although it is not essential to do so, the analysis is greatly simplified if we make the following three assumptions:

Assumption 1: m_i differs from 0 for all i.

Assumption 2: If the Speaker is indifferent between a bill x_i and m_i, then he will give the bill an open rule.

Assumption 3: A committee will report a bill if and only if it would give a positive payoff, contingent on the Speaker scheduling it.

The first assumption confines the analysis to those cases where the status quo on each dimension differs from the floor median; the second allows us to determine unambiguously when the Speaker will grant open and closed rules; the third is useful in dealing with situations in which a committee is indifferent between reporting out some bill and reporting out no bill.

Given these assumptions and notation, we can identify the conditions under which a committee will and will not report a bill:

Lemma 1: Committee $C(i)$ will report no bill on dimension i (i.e., will set $x_i = 0$) if $P_i(0) = P_i(C(i),0) \cap P_i(\{0\},0) \cap P_i(F,0)$ is null.

Proof: If $P_i(0)$ is null, then there is no point on dimension i that is simultaneously (1) preferred by some majority on committee $C(i)$ to 0; (2) preferred by the Speaker to 0; and (3) preferred by some majority on the floor to 0. Thus, if committee $C(i)$ reports a bill x_i that it prefers to the status quo, it knows that nothing good can come of it. If the Speaker vetoes the bill, then no change is made, and the committee's payoff is zero. If the Speaker lets the bill onto the floor under an open rule, it must be because he prefers m_i to 0 (and to x_i); but then, since by definition of m_i (and assumption 1) there is some floor majority that prefers m_i to 0, it must be that the committee does not prefer m_i to 0, and its payoff is nonpositive. If the Speaker lets the bill onto the floor under a closed rule, it must be because he prefers x_i to 0 (and to m_i); but then, since the committee by assumption prefers x_i to 0, it must be that the floor does not prefer x_i to 0—so the bill will not pass, and the committee again gets a payoff of zero. Thus, if $P_i(0)$ is null, the committee cannot find a bill that would, if scheduled, yield a positive expected utility increment, and it therefore (by assumption 3) reports no bill at all. QED.

Lemma 2: The subset of bills in $P_i(0)$ to which the Speaker will give a closed rule, if he schedules them at all, is $Q_i = P_i(0) \cap P_i(\{0\},m_i)$.

Proof: If the Speaker gives an open rule to a bill x_i, then the final outcome will be m_i. If he gives a closed rule, then, since $x_i \epsilon P_i(0)$, the final outcome will be x_i. Thus, if the Speaker prefers m_i to x_i, he gives an open rule, while if he prefers x_i to m_i, he gives a closed rule. If he is indifferent between m_i and x_i, he gives an open rule by assumption 2. QED.

Lemma 3: If the Speaker likes m_i at least as much as y_i for all $y_i \epsilon P_i(0)$, and m_i is not an element of $P_i(0)$, then committee $C(i)$ will report no bill.

Proof: Given the hypothesis, we know from lemma 2 that the Speaker will give any bill in $P_i(0)$ an open rule. The final outcome will therefore be m_i, for any bill in $P_i(0)$. Since the floor prefers m_i to 0 (recall the assumption that m_i differs from 0) and the Speaker does, too (by hypothesis and transitivity), if the committee prefers m_i to 0, then $m_i \epsilon P_i(0)$, a contradiction of the hypothesis. So it must be that committee $C(i)$ prefers 0 to m_i, or is indifferent. Thus, it will not report a bill. QED.

Having shown two conditions under which a committee will not report a bill, we now turn to a condition under which it will. This condition is just the negation of the union of the hypotheses of the first two lemmas.

Lemma 4: If either (1) $P_i(0)$ is not null and there is some $y_i \epsilon P_i(0)$ that the Speaker prefers to m_i; or (2) $m_i \epsilon P_i(0)$; then committee $C(i)$ will report a bill.

Proof: Hypothesis (1) says that $P_i(0)$ is not null and that there is some $y_i \epsilon P_i(0)$ such that the Speaker prefers y_i to m_i. Thus, Q_i is not null.

If the committee reports a bill in Q_i, then by definition the Speaker will give it a closed rule and it will pass, yielding a positive payoff to the committee, contingent on the Speaker scheduling the bill. Thus, by assumption 2 the committee will report some bill.

If hypothesis (2) holds, on the other hand, then the bill $x_i = m_i$ will pass and yield a positive payoff to the committee, contingent on the Speaker scheduling it. Hence, again, the committee will report some bill. QED.

We can now indicate the most attractive possible bill on the ith dimension that $C(i)$ could report, from the Speaker's point of view, while still being worth reporting from the committee's point of view. In what follows, we assume that all bills take the same amount of time.

Define W_i as the "best" payoff that the Speaker can get from the ith dimension, subject to the constraint that some majority on $C(i)$ gets a positive payoff. If Q_i is not null, then $W_i = \sup\{u_0(x_i): x_i \epsilon Q_i\}$. (This can be seen as follows: We know from lemma 2 that the Speaker will give any $x_i \epsilon Q_i$ a closed rule, if he schedules it at all, and that it will then pass. Thus, the Speaker's payoff from scheduling any $x_i \epsilon Q_i$ is $u_0(x_i)$. Since the Speaker by definition prefers any bill in Q_i to m_i, his best payoff in this case is the supremum of the set of payoffs from bills in Q_i.) If Q_i is null but $m_i \epsilon P_i(0)$, then $W_i = u_0(m_i)$. (We know in this case that $P_i(0)$ is not null, so that the committee will report some bill. Whatever bill it is, however, it will be given an open rule, since Q_i is null, and so the final outcome will be m_i. Thus, the Speaker's largest payoff in this case is simply $u_0(m_i)$.) Finally, if neither of the first two conditions holds, then committee $C(i)$ will report no bill on the ith dimension and the Speaker's best payoff will be zero; so $W_i = 0$.

The best bill that the kth committee can report, from the Speaker's viewpoint, while still being worth reporting from the committee's viewpoint, is $W(k) = \max\{W_i: i\epsilon J_k\}$. Renumber the committees, if necessary, so that $W(1) > \ldots > W(K)$. (We assume strict inequality in what follows; weak inequalities just complicate the analysis without changing its fundamental character.)

Definition: A vector $x = (x_1, \ldots, x_w)$ is a committee equilibrium if and only if there is no committee majority that could make itself better off by reporting a different set of bills from its committee's jurisdiction.

Lemma 5: If $L < K$, $W(L+1) > 0$, and $x = (x_1, \ldots, x_w)$ is a committee equilibrium, then the Speaker schedules L bills for floor consideration.

Proof: Suppose that $W(L+1) > 0$ and the Speaker schedules fewer than L bills for floor consideration. Then there must exist a $k < L+1$ such that none of committee k's bills is considered; hence, committee k receives a zero payoff. But since $W(k) > W(L+1) > 0$, committee k could report a bill that the Speaker would schedule and would yield a positive payoff to some committee majority. Hence, x cannot be an equilibrium, a contradiction. QED.

Proposition 1: If $L < K$, $W(L+1) > 0$, and $x = (x_1, \ldots, x_w)$ is such that $\max\{u_0(x_i): i\epsilon J_k\} < W(L+1)$ for some $k < L+1$, then x is not an equilibrium.

Proof: Since $L < K$ and $W(L+1) > 0$, we know that the Speaker schedules L bills, from lemma 5. There are two cases to consider.

First, the L committees whose bills are scheduled by the Speaker are $1, \ldots, L$. In this case committee $L+1$ gets a payoff of zero, but it could get a positive payoff—since $W(L+1) > \max\{u_0(x_i): i\epsilon J_k\}$ for some $k < L+1$ by hypothesis.

Second, one of the first L committees—say k—is not scheduled by the Speaker. In this case, committee k gets a payoff of zero, but it could get a positive payoff—since $W(k) > W(L+1)$ for all $k < L+1$.

Thus, in either case, some committee has an incentive to change its bill. So x is not an equilibrium. QED.

References

Abram, Michael, and Joseph Cooper.
1968   "The Rise of Seniority in the House of Representatives." *Polity*
            1:52–85.
Achen, Christopher H.
1982   *Interpreting and Using Regression.* Beverly Hills: Sage.
Alchian, Arman A.
1950   "Uncertainty, Evolution, and Economic Theory." *Journal of
            Political Economy* 59:211–21.
Alchian, Arman A., and Harold Demsetz.
1972   "Production, Information Costs, and Economic Organization."
            American Economic Review 62:777–95.
Aldrich, John.
1988   "Modeling the Party-in-the-Legislature." Paper presented at the
            annual meeting of the American Political Science Association,
            Washington, D.C.
American Political Science Association, Committee on Political Parties.
1950   *Toward a More Responsible Party System: A Report.* New York:
            Rinehart.
Arnold, R. Douglas.
1979   *Congress and the Bureaucracy: A Theory of Influence.* New
            Haven: Yale University Press.
1990   *The Logic of Congressional Action.* New Haven: Yale Univer-
            sity Press.
Aumann, Robert J.
1981   "Survey of Repeated Games." In *Essays in Game Theory
            and Mathematical Economics in Honor of Oskar Morgenstern,*
            by Robert J. Aumann et al. Mannheim: Bibliographisches In-
            stitut.

Axelrod, Robert.
1981   "The Emergence of Cooperation Among Egoists." *American Political Science Review* 75:306–18.
1984   *The Evolution of Cooperation.* New York: Basic Books.
Bach, Stanley, and Steven S. Smith.
1988   *Managing Uncertainty in the House of Representatives: Adaptation and Innovation in Special Rules.* Washington, D.C.: Brookings Institution.
Banks, Jeffrey S., and Joel Sobel.
1987   "Equilibrium Selection in Signaling Games." *Econometrica* 55:647–61.
Barry, John M.
1989   *The Ambition and the Power.* New York: Viking.
Bartels, Larry.
1985   "Alternative Misspecifications in Simultaneous Equation Models." *Political Methodology* 11:181–99.
Bates, Robert H.
1987   "*Contra* Contractarianism: Some Reflections on the New Institutionalism." Working Paper No. 1, John M. Olin Program in Normative Political Economy, Duke University, Durham, N.C.
Baumol, W.
1962   "On the Theory of Expansion of the Firm." *American Economic Review* 52:1078–87.
Baylis, Thomas A.
1989   *Governing by Committee: Collegial Leadership in Advanced Societies.* Albany: State University of New York Press.
Blalock, Hubert M., Jr.
1979   *Social Statistics.* 2d ed. New York: McGraw-Hill.
Bloom, Howard S., and H. Douglas Price.
1975   "Voter Response to Short-run Economic Conditions: The Asymmetric Effects of Prosperity and Recession." *American Political Science Review* 69:1240–54.
Bolling, Richard.
1965   *Defeating the Leadership Nominee in the House Democratic Caucus.* Indianapolis: Bobbs-Merrill.
1974   "Committees in the House." *American Academy of Political Science, Annals* 411 (Jan. 1974):1–14.
Brady, David W.
1973   *Congressional Voting in a Partisan Era: A Study of the McKinley Houses and a Comparison to the Modern House of Representatives.* Lawrence: University Press of Kansas.
Brady, David W., and Charles S. Bullock III.
1983   "Party and Factional Organization in Legislatures." *American Journal of Political Science* 8:599–654.
Brady, David W., Joseph Cooper, and Patricia A. Hurley.
1979   "The Decline of Party in the U.S. House of Representatives, 1887–1968." *Legislative Studies Quarterly* 4:381–407.

Browning, Robert X.
1985   "Presidents, Congress, and Policy Outcomes: U.S. Social Wel-
            fare Expenditures, 1949–77." *American Journal of Political
            Science* 29:197–216.
Bullock, Charles S., III.
1971   "The Influence of State Party Delegations on House Committee
            Assignments." *Midwest Journal of Political Science* 15:525–46.
1973   "Committee Transfers in the United States House of Represen-
            tatives." *Journal of Politics* 35:85–120.
1976   "Motivations for U.S. Congressional Committee Preferences:
            Freshmen of the 92nd Congress." *Legislative Studies Quarterly*
            1:201–12.
Bullock, Charles S., III, and John Sprague.
1969   "Research Note on the Committee Reassignments of Southern
            Democratic Congressmen." *Journal of Politics* 31:493–512.
Bullock, Kari, and John Baden.
1977   "Communes and the Logic of the Commons." In *Managing the
            Commons,* ed. Garrett Hardin and John Baden. San Francisco:
            W. H. Freeman.
Burke, Edmund.
1975   "On the Present Discontent" (1770). In *Edmund Burke on
            Government, Politics, and Society,* ed. B. W. Hill. Hassocks,
            Eng.: Harvester.
Calvert, Randall L.
1985   "The Value of Biased Information: A Rational Choice Model of
            Political Advice." *Journal of Politics* 47:530–55.
1988   "Coordination and Power: The Foundations of Leadership among
            Rational Legislators." Paper presented at the Hoover Institution
            Conference on Legislative Institutions, Practices and Behavior,
            Stanford University, Palo Alto.
Calvert, Randall L., and John Ferejohn.
1983   "Coattail Voting in Recent Presidential Elections." *American
            Political Science Review* 77:407–19.
Campbell, Angus, Philip E. Converse, Warren E. Miller, and Donald E. Stokes.
1976   *The American Voter.* [1960] Chicago: University of Chicago
            Press.
Cater, Douglass.
1964   *Power in Washington.* New York: Random House.
Cheung, Frederick Hok-Ming.
1983   "From Military Aristocracy to Imperial Bureaucracy: Patterns
            of Consolidation in Two Medieval Empires." Ph.D. diss., Uni-
            versity of California, Santa Barbara.
Claggett, William, William Flanigan, and Nancy Zingale.
1984   "Nationalization of the American Electorate." *American Polit-
            ical Science Review* 78:77–91.
Clapp, Charles L.
1964   *The Congressman: His Work as He Sees It.* Garden City, N.Y.:
            Doubleday.

Clark, Joseph.
　1964　　　*Congress—The Sapless Branch.* New York: Harper.
Clubb, Jerome M., and Sandra Traugott.
　1977　　　"Partisan Cleavage and Cohesion in the House of Representa-
　　　　　　tives, 1861–1974." *Journal of Interdisciplinary History* 7:375–
　　　　　　402.
Cochrane, Willard Wesley.
　1958　　　*Farm Prices, Myth and Reality.* Minneapolis: University of
　　　　　　Minnesota Press.
Cohen, Linda, and Roger Noll.
　1991　　　*The Technology Pork Barrel.* Washington, D.C.: Brookings In-
　　　　　　stitution.
Collie, Melissa P.
　1984　　　"Legislative Voting Behavior." *Legislative Studies Quarterly* 9:3–
　　　　　　50.
　1988a　　"The Rise of Coalition Politics: Voting in the U.S. House, 1933–
　　　　　　1980." *Legislative Studies Quarterly* 13:321–42.
　1988b　　"Universalism and the Parties in the U.S. House of Representa-
　　　　　　tives, 1921–80." *American Journal of Political Science* 32:865–
　　　　　　83.
Collie, Melissa P., and David W. Brady.
　1985　　　"The Decline of Partisan Voting Coalitions in the House of
　　　　　　Representatives." In *Congress Reconsidered,* 3d ed., ed. Law-
　　　　　　rence D. Dodd and Bruce I. Oppenheimer. Washington, D.C.:
　　　　　　Congressional Quarterly Press.
Collie, Melissa P., and Joseph Cooper.
　1989　　　"Multiple Referral and the 'New' Committee System in the House
　　　　　　of Representatives." In *Congress Reconsidered,* 4th ed., ed.
　　　　　　Lawrence C. Dodd and Bruce I. Oppenheimer. Washington, D.C.:
　　　　　　Congressional Quarterly Press.
Cook, Timothy E.
　1983　　　"The Policy Impact of the Committee Assignment Process in the
　　　　　　House." *Journal of Politics* 45:1027–36.
Cooper, Joseph.
　1970　　　*The Origins of the Standing Committees and the Development
　　　　　　of the Modern House.* Houston: Rice University.
Cooper, Joseph, and David W. Brady.
　1981　　　"Institutional Context and Leadership Style: The House from
　　　　　　Cannon to Rayburn." *American Political Science Review* 75:411–
　　　　　　25.
Cooper, Joseph, David W. Brady, and Patricia A. Hurley.
　1977　　　"The Electoral Basis of Party Voting: Patterns and Trends in the
　　　　　　U.S. House of Representatives." In *The Impact of the Electoral
　　　　　　Process,* ed. Louis Maisel and Joseph Cooper. Beverly Hills: Sage.
Cox, Gary W.
　1987　　　"The Uncovered Set and the Core." *American Journal of Polit-
　　　　　　ical Science* 31:408–22.

| 1989 | "Undominated Candidate Strategies under Alternative Voting Rules." *Mathematical Computer Modelling* 12:451–59. |

Cox, Gary W., and Mathew D. McCubbins.

| 1991 | "Divided Control of Fiscal Policy." In *The Politics of Divided Government,* ed. Gary W. Cox and Samuel Kernell. Boulder: Westview. |

Cox, Gary W., Mathew D. McCubbins, and Thomas Schwartz.

| N.d. | "The Theory of Legislative Parties." In preparation. |

Crotty, William J.

| 1984 | *American Parties in Decline.* 2d ed. Boston: Little, Brown. |

Davidson, Roger H.

1974	"Representation and Congressional Committees." *Annals of the American Academy of Political and Social Science* 441:48–62.
1977	"Breaking Up Those 'Cozy Triangles': An Impossible Dream?" In *Legislative Reform and Public Policy,* ed. Susan Welch and John G. Peters. New York: Praeger.
1981a	"Congressional Leaders as Agents of Change." In *Understanding Congressional Leadership,* ed. Frank H. Mackaman. Washington, D.C.: Congressional Quarterly Press.
1981b	"Subcommittee Government: New Channels for Policy Making." In *The New Congress,* ed. Thomas E. Mann and Norman J. Ornstein. Washington, D.C.: American Enterprise Institute.

Davidson, Roger H., and Walter J. Oleszek.

| 1977 | *Congress Against Itself.* Bloomington: Indiana University Press. |
| 1990 | *Congress and Its Members.* 3d ed. Washington, D.C.: Congressional Quarterly Press. |

Davidson, Roger H., Walter J. Oleszek, and Thomas Kephart.

| 1988 | "One Bill, Many Committees: Multiple Referrals in the U.S. House of Representatives." *Legislative Studies Quarterly* 13:3–28. |

Dodd, Lawrence C., and Bruce I. Oppenheimer.

| 1977. | "The House in Transition." In *Congress Reconsidered,* ed. Lawrence C. Dodd and Bruce I. Oppenheimer. New York: Praeger. |
| 1989. | "Consolidating Power in the House: The Rise of a New Oligarchy." In *Congress Reconsidered,* 4th ed., ed. Lawrence C. Dodd and Bruce I. Oppenheimer. Washington, D.C.: Congressional Quarterly Press. |

Downs, Anthony.

| 1957. | *An Economic Theory of Democracy.* New York: Harper. |

Duverger, Maurice.

| 1954 | *Political Parties: Their Organization and Activity in the Modern State.* New York: Wiley. |

Eidenberg, Eugene, and Roy D. Morey.

| 1969 | *An Act of Congress: The Legislative Process and the Making of Education Policy.* New York: Norton. |

Enelow, James M., and Melvin J. Hinich.
1984   *The Spatial Theory of Voting: An Introduction.* Cambridge: Cambridge University Press.

Fama, Eugene.
1980   "Agency Problems and the Theory of the Firm." *Journal of Political Economy* 88:288–307.

Farrell, Joseph.
1987   "Cheap Talk, Coordination, and Entry." *Rand Journal of Economics* 18:34–39.

Fenno, Richard F.
1962   "The House Appropriations Committee as a Political System: The Problem of Integration." *American Political Science Review* 56:310–24.

1966   *The Power of the Purse.* Boston: Little, Brown.

1973   *Congressmen in Committees.* Boston: Little, Brown.

1978   *Home Style: House Members in Their Districts.* Boston: Little, Brown.

Ferejohn, John.
1974   *Pork Barrel Politics: Rivers and Harbors Legislation, 1947–1968.* Stanford: Stanford University Press.

1986   "Logrolling in an Institutional Context: A Case Study of Food Stamp Legislation." In *Congress and Policy Change*, ed. Gerald C. Wright, Leroy N. Rieselback, and Lawrence C. Dodd. New York: Agathon Press.

Fiorina, Morris P.
1974   *Representatives, Roll Calls, and Constituencies.* Lexington, Mass.: Lexington Books.

1977   *Congress: Keystone of the Washington Establishment.* New Haven: Yale University Press.

Fiorina, Morris, and Roger Noll.
1979   "Majority Rule Models and Legislative Elections." *Journal of Politics* 41:1081–1104.

Fishburn, Peter C.
1973   *The Theory of Social Choice.* Princeton: Princeton University Press.

Fowler, Linda.
1982   "How Interest Groups Select Issues for Rating Voting Records of Members of the U.S. Congress." *Legislative Studies Quarterly* 3:401–14.

Fox, Harrison W., Jr., and Susan Webb Hammond.
1977   *Congressional Staffs: The Invisible Force in American Lawmaking.* New York: Free Press.

Freeman, John Leiper.
1955   *The Political Process: Executive Bureau–Legislative Committee Relations.* New York: Random House.

Friedman, Sally.
N.d.   "Committee Assignments of Women and Blacks in Congress: 1964–1990." Unpublished paper, SUNY-Albany.

Frohlich, Norman, and Joe A. Oppenheimer.
1978   *Modern Political Economy.* Englewood Cliffs, N.J.: Prentice-Hall.
Frohlich, Norman, Joe A. Oppenheimer, and Oran R. Young.
1971   *Political Leadership and Collective Goods.* Princeton: Princeton University Press.
Froman, Lewis A., Jr.
1967   *The Congressional Process: Strategies, Rules, and Procedures.* Boston: Little, Brown.
Froman, Lewis A., Jr., and Randall B. Ripley.
1965   "Conditions for Party Leadership: The Case of the House Democrats." *American Political Science Review* 59:52–63.
Gauthier, David P.
1969   *The Logic of Leviathan: The Moral and Political Theory of Thomas Hobbes.* Oxford: Clarendon Press.
Geddes, Barbara.
1991   "A Game Theoretic Model of Reform in Latin American Democracies." *American Political Science Review* 85:371–92.
Gertzog, Irwin N.
1976   "The Routinization of Committee Assignments in the U.S. House of Representatives." *American Journal of Political Science* 20:693–712.
Gilligan, Thomas W., and Keith Krehbiel.
1987   "Collective Decision-Making and Standing Committees: An Informal Rationale for Restrictive Amendment Procedures." *Journal of Law, Economics, and Organization* 3:287–335.
1989   "Collective Choice Without Procedural Commitment." In *Models of Strategic Choice in Politics,* ed. Peter C. Ordeshook. Ann Arbor: University of Michigan Press.
1990   "Organization of Informative Committees by a Rational Legislature." *American Journal of Political Science* 34:531–64.
Gittins, John C.
1979   "Bandit Processes and Dynamic Allocation Indices." *Journal of the Royal Statistical Society,* series B 41:148–64.
Gittins, John C., and D. M. Jones.
1974   "A Dynamic Allocation Index for the Sequential Design of Experiments." In *Progress in Statistics,* ed. J. Gani. Amsterdam: North Holland.
Goodwin, George.
1959   "The Seniority System in Congress." *American Political Science Review* 53:412–36.
1970   *The Little Legislatures.* Amherst: University of Massachusetts Press.
Goss, Carol F.
1972   "Military Committee Membership and Defense-Related Benefits in the House of Representatives." *Western Political Quarterly* 25:215–33.

Green, Harold, and Alan Rosenthal.
1963   *Government of the Atom: The Integration of Powers.* New York: Atherton Press.

Grier, Kevin B.
N.d.   "Congressional Preference and Federal Reserve Policy." Photocopy, George Mason University, Fairfax, Va.

Griffith, Ernest S.
1961   *Congress, Its Contemporary Role.* 3d ed. New York: New York University Press.

Hall, Richard L.
1989   "Committee Decision Making in the Postreform Congress." In *Congress Reconsidered,* 4th ed., ed. Lawrence D. Dodd and Bruce I. Oppenheimer. Washington, D.C.: Congressional Quarterly Press.

Hall, Richard L., and Bernard Grofman.
1990   "The Committee Assignment Process and the Conditional Nature of Committee Bias." *American Political Science Review* 84:1149–66.

Hamburger, Henry.
1979   *Games as Models of Social Phenomena.* San Francisco: W. H. Freeman.

Hardin, Russell.
1982   *Collective Action.* Baltimore: Johns Hopkins University Press.
1991   "Hobbesian Political Order." *Political Theory* 19:156–80.

Harsanyi, John C., and Reinhard Selten.
1988   *A General Theory of Equilibrium Selection in Games.* Cambridge: MIT Press.

Hayek, Friedrich A. von.
1960   *The Constitution of Liberty.* Chicago: University of Chicago Press.

Hinckley, Barbara.
1971   *The Seniority System in Congress.* Bloomington: Indiana University Press.
1976   "Seniority 1975: Old Theories Confront New Facts." *British Journal of Political Science* 6:383–99.
1983   *Stability and Change in Congress.* 3d ed. New York: Harper and Row.

Hirschman, Albert O.
1977   *The Passions and the Interests: Political Arguments for Capitalism before Its Triumph.* Princeton: Princeton University Press.

Hogg, Robert V., and Allen T. Craig.
1978   *Introduction to Mathematical Statistics.* 4th ed. New York: Macmillan.

Holmström, Bengt.
1982   "Moral Hazard in Teams." *Bell Journal of Economics* 13:324–40.

Jackson, John Edgar.
1974   *Constituencies and Leaders in Congress: Their Effects on Senate Voting Behavior.* Cambridge: Harvard University Press.

Jacobson, Gary C.
1989   "Strategic Politicians and the Dynamics of U.S. House Elections, 1946–86." *American Political Science Review* 83:773–93.

1990   "Divided Government, Strategic Politicians, and the 1990 Congressional Elections." Paper presented at the annual meeting of the Midwest Political Science Association, Chicago.

Jacobson, Gary C., and Samuel Kernell.
1981   *Strategy and Choice in Congressional Elections.* New Haven: Yale University Press.

1983   *Strategy and Choice in Congressional Elections.* 2d ed. New Haven: Yale University Press.

1990   "National Forces in the 1986 House Elections." *Legislative Studies Quarterly* 15:65–87.

Jenkins, Peter.
1988   *Mrs. Thatcher's Revolution: The Ending of the Socialist Era.* Cambridge: Harvard University Press.

Jensen, Michael C., and William H. Meckling.
1976   "Theory of the Firm: Managerial Behavior, Agency Costs and Ownership Structure." *Journal of Financial Economics* 3:305–60.

Jewell, Malcolm, and Chi-Hung Chiu.
1974   "Membership Movement and Committee Attractiveness in the U.S. House of Representatives, 1963–1971." *American Journal of Political Science* 18:433–41.

Jewell, Malcolm, and Samuel C. Patterson.
1977   *The Legislative Process in the United States.* 3d ed. New York: Random House.

Jones, Charles O.
1961   "Representation in Congress: The Case of the House Agriculture Committee." *American Political Science Review* 55:358–67.

1964   *Party and Policy-Making: The House Republican Policy Committee.* New Brunswick: Rutgers University Press.

1969   "The Agriculture Committee and the Problem of Representation." In *New Perspectives on the House of Representatives,* ed. Robert L. Peabody and Nelson W. Polsby. Chicago: Rand McNally.

1977   *An Introduction to the Study of Public Policy.* 2d ed. North Scituate, Mass.: Duxbury Press.

Kalai, Ehud, and Dov Samet.
1982   "Persistent Equilibria in Strategic Games." Unpublished paper, Northwestern University.

Kammerer, Gladys M.
1951   "The Record of Congress in Committee Staffing." *American Political Science Review* 45:1126–36.
Kampelman, Max M.
1954   "The Legislative Bureaucracy: Its Response to Political Change, 1953." *Journal of Politics* 16:539–50.
Kavka, Gregory S.
1987   *Moral Paradoxes of Nuclear Deterrence.* Cambridge: Cambridge University Press.
Kawato, Sadafumi.
1987   "Nationalization and Partisan Realignment in Congressional Elections." *American Political Science Review* 81:1235–50.
Kernell, Samuel.
1991   "Facing an Opposition Congress: The President's Strategic Circumstance." In *The Politics of Divided Government,* ed. Gary Cox and Samuel Kernell. Boulder: Westview.
Kiewiet, D. Roderick, and Mathew D. McCubbins.
1991   *The Logic of Delegation: Congressional Parties and the Appropriations Process.* Chicago: University of Chicago Press.
Koford, Kenneth J.
1989   "Dimensions in Congressional Voting." *American Political Science Review* 83:949–62.
Kramer, Gerald.
1971   "Short-Term Fluctuations in U.S. Voting Behavior, 1896–1964." *American Political Science Review* 65:131–43.
1983   "Electoral Politics in the Zero-Sum Society." Social Science Working Paper No. 472, Division of the Humanities and Social Sciences, California Institute of Technology, Pasadena.
Krehbiel, Keith.
1987a   "Sophisticated Committees and Structure-Induced Equilibria in Congress." In *Congress: Structure and Policy,* ed. Mathew D. McCubbins and Terry Sullivan. Cambridge: Cambridge University Press.
1987b   "Why Are Congressional Committees Powerful?" *American Political Science Review* 81:929–35.
1990   "Are Congressional Committees Composed of Preference Outliers?" *American Political Science Review* 84:149–63.
1991   *Information and Legislative Organization.* Ann Arbor: University of Michigan Press.
Kreps, David M.
1990   "Corporate Culture and Economic Theory." In *Perspectives on Positive Political Economy,* ed. James E. Alt and Kenneth A. Shepsle. Cambridge: Cambridge University Press.
Kreps, David M., and Robert Wilson.
1982   "Sequential Equilibria." *Econometrica* 50:863–94.
LaPalombara, Joseph, and Myron Weiner.
1966   "The Origin and Development of Political Parties." In *Political*

Parties and Political Development, ed. Joseph LaPalombara and Myron Weiner. Princeton: Princeton University Press.

Lijphart, Arend.
1984   *Democracies: Patterns of Majoritarian and Consensus Government in Twenty-one Countries.* New Haven: Yale University Press.

Lowi, Theodore J.
1972   "Four Systems of Policy, Politics, and Choice." *Public Administration Review,* July–Aug., 298–310.
1979   *The End of Liberalism: The Second Republic of the United States.* New York: Norton.

McConachie, Lauros G.
1898   *Congressional Committees.* New York: Thomas Y. Crowell.

McConnell, Grant.
1966   *Private Power and American Democracy.* New York: Vintage Books, Random House.

McCubbins, Mathew D.
1985   "The Legislative Design of Regulatory Structure." *American Journal of Political Science* 29:721–48.

McCubbins, Mathew D., and Thomas Schwartz.
1988   "Congress, the Courts, and Public Policy: Consequences of the One Man, One Vote Rule." *American Journal of Political Science* 32:388–415.

McKelvey, Richard D.
1976   "Intransitivities in Multidimensional Voting Models and Some Implications for Agenda Control." *Journal of Economic Theory* 12:472–82.
1979   "General Conditions for Global Intransitivities in Formal Voting Models." *Econometrica* 47:1085–1112.
1986   "Covering, Dominance, and Institution-Free Properties of Social Choice." *American Journal of Political Science* 30:283–314.

McKelvey, Richard D., and R. E. Wendell.
1976   "Voting Equilibria in Multidimensional Choice Spaces." *Mathematics of Operations Research* 1:144–58.

Maddala, G. S.
1977   *Econometrics.* New York: McGraw-Hill.
1988   *Introduction to Econometrics.* New York: Macmillan.

Manley, John F.
1970   *The Politics of Finance: The House Committee on Ways and Means.* Boston: Little, Brown.

Marwell, Gerald.
1967   "Party, Region and the Dimensions of Conflict in the House of Representatives, 1949–1954." *American Political Science Review* 61:380–99.

Masters, Nicholas A.
1961   "Committee Assignments in the House of Representatives." *American Political Science Review* 55:345–57.

Matthews, Donald R.
1960   *U.S. Senators and Their World*. New York: Random House.
Mayhew, David.
1966   *Party Loyalty among Congressmen*. Cambridge: Harvard University Press.
1974   *The Electoral Connection*. New Haven: Yale University Press.
Miller, Clem.
1962   *Member of the House: Letters of a Congressman*. Ed. John W. Baker. New York: Scribner.
Miller, Gary J.
1987   "Administrative Dilemmas: The Role of Political Leadership." Political Economy Working Paper, School of Business and Center in Political Economy, Washington University, St. Louis.
Miller, Nicholas R.
1980   "A New Solution Set for Tournaments and Majority Voting." *American Journal of Political Science* 24:769–803.
Mirrlees, James.
1976   "The Optimal Structure of Incentives and Authority Within an Organization." *Bell Journal of Economics* 7:105–31.
Munger, Frank J., and Richard F. Fenno, Jr.
1962   *National Politics and Federal Aid to Education*. Syracuse: Syracuse University Press.
Munger, Michael C.
1988   "Allocation of Desirable Committee Assignments: Extended Queues Versus Committee Expansion." *American Journal of Political Science* 32:317–44.
Murphy, James T.
1974   "Political Parties and the Porkbarrel: Party Conflict and Cooperation in House Public Works Committee Decision-Making." *American Political Science Review* 68:169–86.
Ogul, Morris.
1976   *Congress Oversees the Bureaucracy*. Pittsburgh: University of Pittsburgh Press.
Oleszek, Walter J.
1984   *Congressional Procedures and the Policy Process*. Washington, D.C.: Congressional Quarterly Press.
Olson, Mancur.
1965   *The Logic of Collective Action*. Cambridge: Harvard University Press.
Oppenheimer, Bruce I.
1977   "The Rules Committee: New Arm of Leadership in a Decentralized House." In *Congress Reconsidered*, ed. Lawrence C. Dodd and Bruce I. Oppenheimer. New York: Praeger.
Ordeshook, Peter C.
1986   *Game Theory and Political Theory: An Introduction*. Cambridge: Cambridge University Press.
Ornstein, Norman J., and David W. Rohde.
1977a   "Revolt from Within: Congressional Change, Legislative Policy

and the House Commerce Committee." In *Legislative Reform and Public Policy,* ed. John G. Peters and Susan Welch. New York: Praeger.

1977b "Shifting Forces, Changing Rules, and Political Outcomes: The Impact of Congressional Change on Four House Committees." In *New Perspectives on the House of Representatives,* 3d ed., ed. Robert Peabody and Nelson Polsby. Chicago: Rand Mc-Nally.

Ostrogorski, Mosei.

1902 *Democracy and the Organization of Political Parties.* Trans. Frederick Clarke. New York: Macmillan.

Palazzolo, Dan.

1989 "The Speaker's Relationship with the House Budget Committee: Assessing the Effect of Contextual Change and Individual Leader Discretion on a 'Leadership Committee.'" Paper presented at the annual meeting of the Midwest Political Science Association, Chicago.

Panebianco, Angelo.

1988 *Political Parties: Organization and Power.* Trans. Marc Silver. Cambridge: Cambridge University Press.

Parker, Glenn, and Suzanne L. Parker.

1985 *Factions in House Committees.* Knoxville: University of Tennessee Press.

Peabody, Robert.

1976 *Leadership in Congress: Stability, Succession, and Change.* Boston: Little, Brown.

Perkins, Lynette P.

1980 "Influences of Members' Goals on Their Committee Behavior: The U.S. House Judiciary Committee." *Legislative Studies Quarterly* 5:373–92.

Plott, Charles R.

1967 "A Notion of Equilibrium and Its Possibility under Majority Rule." *American Economic Review* 57:787–806.

Polsby, Nelson W., Miriam Gallaher, and Barry Rundquist.

1969 "The Growth of the Seniority System in the House of Representatives." *American Political Science Review* 62:148–68.

Poole, Keith T., and Howard Rosenthal.

1985 "A Spatial Model for Legislative Roll Call Analysis." *American Journal of Political Science* 29:357–84.

Ray, Bruce A.

1980a "Federal Spending and the Selection of Committee Assignments in the U.S. House of Representatives." *American Journal of Political Science* 24:494–510.

1980b "The Responsiveness of the U.S. Congressional Armed Service Committees to Their Parent Bodies." *Legislative Studies Quarterly* 5:501–15.

Riker, William H.

1980 "Implications from the Disequilibrium of Majority Rule for the

Study of Institutions." *American Political Science Review* 74:432–46.

Ripley, Randall B.
1967   *Party Leaders in the House of Representatives.* Washington, D.C.: Brookings Institution.
1969a   "Legislative Bargaining and the Food Stamp Act, 1964." In *Congress and Urban Problems,* ed. Frederic Cleveland. Washington, D.C.: Brookings Institution.
1969b   *Majority Party Leadership in Congress.* Boston: Little, Brown.
1983   *Congress: Process and Policy.* 3d ed. New York: Norton.

Ripley, Randall B., and Grace A. Franklin.
1984   *Congress, the Bureaucracy, and Public Policy.* 3d ed. Homewood, Ill.: Dorsey Press.

Ritchie, Robert C.
1986   *Pirates: Myths and Realities.* Minneapolis: James Ford Bell Library, University of Minnesota.

Roberts, K. W. S., and M. L. Weitzman.
1980   "On a General Approach to Search and Information Gathering." Economics Working Paper 263, Massachusetts Institute of Technology, Cambridge.

Robinson, James.
1963   *The House Rules Committee.* Indianapolis: Bobbs-Merrill.

Rohde, David W.
1988   "Variations in Partisanship in the House of Representatives, 1953–1988: Southern Democrats, Realignment, and Agenda Change." Paper presented at the annual meeting of the American Political Science Association, Washington, D.C.
1989   "Democratic Party Leadership, Agenda Control, and the Resurgence of Partisanship in the House." Paper presented at the annual meeting of the American Political Science Association, Atlanta.
1990a   "Agenda Change and Partisan Resurgence in the House of Representatives." Paper presented at "Back to the Future: The United States Congress in the Twenty-first Century," Carl Albert Center, University of Oklahoma, Norman, 11–14 Apr.
1990b   " 'The Reports of My Death Are Greatly Exaggerated': Parties and Party Voting in the House of Representatives." In *Changing Perspectives on Congress,* ed. Glenn R. Parker. Knoxville: University of Tennessee Press.
1991   *Parties and Leaders in the Postreform House.* Chicago: University of Chicago Press.

Rohde, David, and Kenneth A. Shepsle.
1973   "Democratic Committee Assignments in the House of Representatives: Strategic Aspects of a Social Choice Process." *American Political Science Review* 67:889–905.

Salisbury, Robert H.
1969   "An Exchange Theory of Interest Groups." *Midwest Journal of Political Science* 13:1–32.

Schattschneider, Elmer Eric.
1935   *Politics, Pressures, and the Tariff: A Study of Free Private Enterprise in Pressure Politics, as Shown in the 1929–1930 Revision of the Tariff.* New York: Prentice-Hall.
1942   *Party Government.* New York: Farrar and Rinehart.
Schelling, Thomas C.
1978   *Micromotives and Macrobehavior.* New York: Norton.
Schick, Allen.
1980   *Congress and Money: Budgeting, Spending, and Taxing.* Washington, D.C.: Urban Institute.
Schlesinger, Joseph.
1966   *Ambition and Politics: Political Careers in the United States.* Chicago: Rand McNally.
1985   "The New American Political Party." *American Political Science Review* 79:1152–69.
Schofield, Norman.
1980   "Generic Properties of Simple Bergson-Samuelson Welfare Functions." *Journal of Mathematical Economics* 7:175–92.
Schwartz, Thomas.
1986   *The Logic of Collective Choice.* New York: Columbia University Press.
Selten, Reinhard.
1975   "Reexamination of the Perfectness Concept for Equilibrium Points in Extensive Games." *International Journal of Game Theory* 4:25–55.
Shannon, Wayne.
1968   *Party, Constituency, and Congressional Voting.* Baton Rouge: Louisiana State University Press.
Shepsle, Kenneth.
1978   *The Giant Jigsaw Puzzle.* Chicago: University of Chicago Press.
1979   "Institutional Arrangements and Equilibrium in Multidimensional Voting Models." *American Journal of Political Science* 23:27–59. Rpt. in *Congress: Structure and Policy,* ed. Mathew D. McCubbins and Terry Sullivan. Cambridge: Cambridge University Press, 1987.
1989   "Studying Institutions: Some Lessons from the Rational Choice Approach." *Journal of Theoretical Politics* 1:131–47.
1990   "The Changing Textbook Congress: Equilibrium Congressional Institutions and Behavior." In *American Political Institutions and the Problems of Our Time,* ed. John E. Chubb and Paul E. Peterson. Washington, D.C.: Brookings Institution.
Shepsle, Kenneth, and Barry R. Weingast.
1981   "Structure-Induced Equilibrium and Legislative Choice." *Public Choice* 37:509–19.
1984   "Legislative Politics and Budget Outcomes." In *Federal Budget Policy in the 1980s,* ed. Gregory B. Mills and John L. Palmer. Washington, D.C.: Urban Institute.

1987a   "The Institutional Foundations of Committee Power." *American Political Science Review* 81:85–104.

1987b   "Reflections on Committee Power." *American Political Science Review* 81:935–45.

Sinclair, Barbara.

1983   *Majority Leadership in the U.S. House.* Baltimore: Johns Hopkins Press.

1989   "House Majority Party Leadership in the Late 1980s." In *Congress Reconsidered*, 4th ed., ed. Lawrence C. Dodd and Bruce I. Oppenheimer. Washington, D.C.: Congressional Quarterly Press.

Smith, Steven S.

1988   "An Essay on Sequence, Position, Goals, and Committee Power." *Legislative Studies Quarterly* 8:151–77.

Smith, Steven S., and Christopher J. Deering.

1984   *Committees in Congress.* Washington, D.C.: Congressional Quarterly Press.

1990   *Committees in Congress.* 2d ed. Washington, D.C.: Congressional Quarterly Press.

Smith, Steven S., and Bruce A. Ray.

1983   "The Impact of Congressional Reform: House Democratic Committee Assignments." *Congress and the Presidency* 10:219–40.

Stokes, Donald.

1965   "A Variance Components Model of Political Effects." In *Mathematical Applications in Political Science,* ed. John M. Claunch. Dallas: Southern Methodist University Press.

1967   "Parties and the Nationalization of Electoral Forces." In *The American Party Systems: Stages of Political Development,* ed. William N. Chambers and Walter D. Burnham. New York: Oxford University Press.

Sugden, Robert.

1986   *The Economics of Rights, Cooperation, and Welfare.* Oxford: Basil Blackwell.

Taylor, Michael.

1976   *Anarchy and Cooperation.* London: Wiley.

1987   *The Possibility of Cooperation.* Cambridge: Cambridge University Press.

Thompson, Margaret Susan, and Joel Silbey.

1984   "Research on Nineteenth Century Legislatures: Present Contours and Future Directions." *Legislative Studies Quarterly* 9:319–50.

Thurow, Lester.

1980   *The Zero-Sum Society: Distribution and the Possibilities for Economic Change.* New York: Basic Books.

Tirole, Jean.

1988   *The Theory of Industrial Organization.* Cambridge: MIT Press.

Truman, David B.

1959   *The Congressional Party.* New York: Wiley.

Tufte, Edward R.
1975   "Determinants of the Outcomes of Midterm Congressional
            Elections." *American Political Science Review* 69:812–26.
Turner, Julius.
1951   *Party and Constituency.* Baltimore: Johns Hopkins Press.
Turner, Julius, and Edward V. Schneier.
1970   *Party and Constituency: Pressures on Congress.* Rev. ed. Balti-
            more: Johns Hopkins Press.
U.S. Congress. House. Select Committee on Committees.
1974   *Final Report, Committee Reform Amendments of 1974* (The
            Bolling Committee Report). 93d Cong., 2d sess. H. Rept. 93–
            916.
U.S. Congress. Joint Committee on the Organization of Congress.
1965   *Hearings,* Part 3. 89th Cong., 1st sess. Washington, D.C.: Gov-
            ernment Printing Office.
Uslaner, Eric M.
1974   *Congressional Committee Assignments.* Beverly Hills: Sage.
Waldman, Sidney.
1980   "Majority Leadership in the House of Representatives." *Politi-
            cal Science Quarterly* 95:373–93.
Wattenberg, Martin.
1984   *The Decline of American Political Parties, 1952–80.* Cam-
            bridge: Harvard University Press.
Watts, Ross L., and Jerold L. Zimmerman.
1983   "Agency Problems, Auditing, and the Theory of the Firm: Some
            Evidence." *Journal of Law and Economics* 26:613–33.
Weingast, Barry R.
1979   "A Rational Choice Perspective on Congressional Norms."
            American Journal of Political Science 23:245–62.
1989   "Floor Behavior in Congress: Committee Power under the Open
            Rule." *American Political Science Review* 83:795–815.
Weingast, Barry R., and William Marshall.
1988   "The Industrial Organization of Congress." *Journal of Political
            Economy* 96:132–63.
Weingast, Barry R., and Mark Moran.
1983   "Bureaucratic Discretion or Congressional Control? Regulatory
            Policymaking by the Federal Trade Commission." *Journal of
            Political Economy* 91:775–800.
Westefield, Louis P.
1974   "Majority Party Leadership and the Committee System in the
            House of Representatives." *American Political Science Review*
            68:1593–1604.
Whittle, Peter.
1982   *Optimization over Time: Dynamic Programming and Stochas-
            tic Control.* New York: Wiley.
Williamson, Oliver E.
1967   "Hierarchical Control and Optimum Firm Size." *Journal of Po-
            litical Economy* 73:123–38.

1975   *Markets and Hierarchies: Analysis and Antitrust Implications.*
            New York: Free Press.
Wilson, Woodrow.
    1885   *Congressional Government.* Boston: Houghton Mifflin.
Yoder, Edwin M.
    1990   "The Party's Over, So Responsible Politics Called It a Day."
            Washington Post Weekly, Nov.

Author Index

Abram, Michael, 46, 49
Achen, Christopher H., 180
Alchian, Arman A., 83n, 85, 91, 92, 94, 97, 98, 103
Aldrich, John, 7n, 134
Arnold, R. Douglas, 62n, 197, 198
Aumann, Robert J., 101n
Axelrod, Robert, 99

Bach, Stanley, 256
Baden, John, 101
Banks, Jeffrey S., 102
Barry, John M., 54
Bartels, Larry, 178
Bates, Robert H., 86
Baumol, W., 104n
Baylis, Thomas A., 105
Blalock, Hubert M., Jr., 212
Bloom, Howard S., 122
Bolling, Richard, 193n, 196n, 257
Brady, David W., 3, 6, 10, 45, 139–141, 143, 156
Browning, Robert X., 269
Bullock, Charles S., III, 3n, 4, 27, 34n, 42, 43, 167n, 201
Bullock, Kari, 101
Burke, Edmund, 107
Burnham, Walter Dean, 109

Calvert, Randall L., 102, 109
Campbell, Angus, 110
Cater, Douglass, 13, 19n

Cheung, Frederick Hok-Ming, 90
Chiu, Chi-Hung, 34n
Claggett, William, 112
Clapp, Charles L., 42n, 52, 240, 257, 261
Clark, Joseph, 56
Clubb, Jerome M., 139, 140, 143, 144, 146
Cochrane, Willard Wesley, 194
Cohen, Linda, 193
Collie, Melissa P., 3, 139, 142–144, 147, 191n, 256
Converse, Philip E., 110
Cook, Timothy E., 22, 23, 34n
Cooper, Joseph, 6, 10, 45, 46, 49, 139–141, 143, 156, 159, 160n, 191n, 256
Cox, Gary W., 129, 130, 134, 269
Craig, Allen T., 73n
Crotty, William J., 3

Davidson, Roger H., 3, 19n, 23, 69, 195, 196, 236n, 255, 256, 262
Deering, Christopher J., 22–24, 27, 30, 34, 40, 42, 62, 64, 65, 163n, 224
Demsetz, Harold, 85, 91, 92, 94, 97, 98, 103
Dodd, Lawrence C., 13, 19, 20n, 42, 53
Downs, Anthony, 107, 108n
Duverger, Maurice, 107

Enelow, James M., 241

Fama, Eugene, 105n
Farrell, Joseph, 88

Fenno, Richard F., 4, 10, 11, 24, 27, 38, 42, 43, 62, 64, 65, 70, 71, 156n, 159, 161n, 182n, 196
Ferejohn, John, 109, 156, 192, 250
Fiorina, Morris P., 6n, 24, 110, 124, 156, 277
Fishburn, Peter C., 244n
Flanigan, William, 112
Fowler, Linda, 63
Fox, Harrison W., Jr., 234n, 257n
Franklin, Grace A., 19n
Freeman, John Leiper, 19n
Friedman, Sally, 43, 201
Frohlich, Norman, 91, 92, 99n, 103
Froman, Lewis A., Jr., 248n

Gallaher, Miriam, 46–49, 52n, 53, 54, 59n
Gauthier, David P., 91, 93
Gertzog, Irwin N., 12, 21–23, 31, 32n, 40–42, 163n
Gilligan, Thomas W., 6, 23n, 160
Gittins, John C., 235n
Goodwin, George, 22, 34n, 62, 64, 65, 70, 71, 164
Goss, Carol F., 62n, 198
Green, Harold, 255
Grier, Kevin B., 23n
Griffith, Ernest S., 19n
Grofman, Bernard, 74n, 203n, 212

Hall, Richard L., 62n, 74n, 203n, 212
Hamburger, Henry, 242n
Hammond, Susan Webb, 234n, 257n
Hardin, Russell, 94n, 101, 131
Hayek, Friedrich A. von, 83
Hinckley, Barbara, 45, 53, 55, 56, 59, 70, 71, 163n, 165
Hinich, Melvin J., 241
Hirschman, Albert O., 93, 104
Hobbes, Thomas, 14, 83, 85, 91, 93, 95n, 104, 106, 131
Hogg, Robert V., 73n
Holmström, Bengt, 95–99, 106
Huitt, Ralph, 8n
Hurley, Patricia, 6, 139–141, 143, 156

Jackson, John Edgar, 249
Jacobson, Gary C., 111, 112, 117, 120, 172n, 277
Jenkins, Peter, 132
Jensen, Michael C., 105
Jewell, Malcolm, 34n, 250
Jones, Charles O., 4, 6, 8, 19n, 62n, 251
Jones, D. M., 235n

Kalai, Ehud, 102
Kammerer, Gladys M., 256

Kavka, Gregory S., 90n, 91, 93, 102
Kawato, Sadafumi, 112, 113n
Kephart, Thomas, 256
Kernell, Samuel, 111, 120, 122, 172n, 277
Kiewiet, D. Roderick, 3, 42, 43, 61n, 103n, 161n, 201, 212, 227, 269, 270n
Koford, Kenneth J., 72n
Kramer, Gerald, 121, 122, 127
Krehbiel, Keith, 6, 23n, 69–71, 160, 212, 219, 241
Kreps, David M., 100, 102, 105

LaPalombara, Joseph, 107
Lijphart, Arend, 105
Lowi, Theodore J., 19n, 276, 277

McConachie, Lauros G., 253n
McConnell, Grant, 19n
McCubbins, Mathew D., 3, 42, 43, 58, 61n, 103n, 134, 161n, 194, 197n, 201, 212, 228, 269, 270n
McKelvey, Richard D., 5, 129, 130, 277
Maddala, G. S., 178, 179n
Manley, John F., 62n, 164, 165
Marshall, William, 6, 219, 278
Marwell, Gerald, 139
Masters, Nicholas A., 20, 22, 24, 42n, 164, 166, 170
Matthews, Donald R., 139
Mayhew, David., 6, 94, 109, 121, 122n, 147n, 189, 250, 251
Meckling, William H., 105
Miller, Clem, 1, 61n, 240
Miller, Gary J., 96
Miller, Nicholas R., 129, 130
Miller, Warren, E., 110
Mirrlees, James, 98
Moran, Mark, 23n, 278
Munger, Frank J., 196
Munger, Michael C., 34n
Murphy, James T., 192, 251, 257

Nelson, Garrison, 27n, 69n
Noll, Roger, 124, 193

Ogul, Morris, 62n, 195n, 196n
Oleszek, Walter J., 19n, 23, 236n, 256
Olson, Mancur, 91, 93, 99n, 123, 133, 135
Oppenheimer, Bruce I., 13, 19, 20n, 42, 53, 91, 92, 99n, 103
Ordeshook, Peter C., 241
Ornstein, Norman J., 21n, 62n, 193n, 194, 269n, 272
Ostrogorski, Mosei, 275

Palazzolo, Dan, 61n
Panebianco, Angelo, 107n
Parker, Glenn, 262n
Parker, Suzanne L., 262n
Patterson, Samuel C., 250
Peabody, Robert, 132, 240, 250
Perkins, Lynette P., 195n
Plott, Charles R., 5, 277
Polsby, Nelson W., 46–49, 52n, 53, 54, 59n
Poole, Keith T., 69n, 72, 206

Ray, Bruce A., 22–24, 26, 27, 62n 166, 167, 169, 172, 180
Riker, William H., 6
Ripley, Randall, 4n, 6, 11, 19n, 51, 156, 161n, 167n, 250, 257
Ritchie, Robert C., 104
Roberts, K. W. S., 235n
Robinson, James, 62n, 159, 167n, 240, 241n, 259
Rohde, David W., 3, 5, 6, 21n, 24, 25n, 26n, 48n, 62n, 134, 137, 140, 141, 150, 155, 163n, 166, 167, 171, 193n, 194, 257, 263n, 269n, 271n, 272, 273, 277
Rosenthal, Alan, 255
Rosenthal, Howard, 72, 206
Rundquist, Barry, 46–49, 52n, 53, 54, 59n

Salisbury, Robert H., 91
Sament, Dov, 102
Schattschneider, Elmer Eric, 19n, 107
Schelling, Thomas C., 90n, 105
Schick, Allen, 61n
Schlesinger, Joseph, 105n, 109, 140n
Schofield, Norman, 5, 129, 277
Schneier, Edward V., 139, 155
Schwartz, Thomas, 129, 134, 194, 197n
Selten, Reinhard, 102
Shannon, Wayne, 155
Shepsle, Kenneth A., 3, 6, 11n, 12, 19–22, 23n, 24–26, 30–32, 34, 38, 40,
41, 42n, 61n, 160, 163n, 165–169, 172, 177, 180, 188, 201, 237, 241, 242, 252, 278
Silbey, Joel, 139
Sinclair, Barbara, 4n, 13
Smith, Steven S., 22–24, 27, 30, 34, 38, 40–42, 62, 64, 65, 163n, 166, 167, 169, 172, 177, 180, 224, 256, 263n
Sprague, John, 34n
Stokes, Donald, E., 110, 112
Sugden, Robert, 99n

Taylor, Michael, 86, 90n, 93, 94n, 99
Thompson, Margaret Susan, 139
Thurow, Lester, 6n
Tirole, Jean, 92n
Traugott, Sandra, 139, 140, 143, 144, 146
Truman, David B., 6, 9, 139, 155, 241n, 250, 251
Tufte, Edward R., 122
Turner, Julius, 139, 155

Uslaner, Eric M., 8n

Waldman, Sidney, 168, 169
Wattenberg, Martin, 3, 109
Watts, Ross L., 105
Weiner, Myron, 107
Weingast, Barry, 3, 6, 11n, 12, 19n, 23n, 160, 219, 278
Weitzman, M. L., 235n
Wendell, R. E., 277
Westefield, Louis P., 22, 257n
Whittle, Peter, 235n, 286n
Williamson, Oliver E., 92n, 104n
Wilson, Robert, 102
Wilson, Woodrow, 9, 10

Yoder, Edwin M., 6n
Young, Oran R., 91

Zimmerman, Jerold L., 105
Zingale, Nancy, 112

Subject Index

AFL-CIO and Committee on Political Education (COPE), 67, 68, 72n, 196, 199, 219

Agency, delegation and: and central authority, 86, 90, 93, 94, 97–99, 102–105; credible threats, 51, 99, 100, 102, 104, 156, 238, 247; selective incentives, 91–93, 99n, 103; and standardization problem, 87. *See also* Committees, as agents; Entrepreneurs, political and economic; Executive agencies; Games and game theory; Leadership; Theory of the firm

Agenda, 251; committee, 241, 256; control of, 235, 237, 248, 255, 271; legislative, 5, 15, 157, 161, 231, 233–235, 237, 248, 251–253, 255, 258–261, 268–271, 278, 283, 284; minority party, 150, 271; North and South, 271; party, 145–153, 155–157, 260, 262n; political, 196

Agents. *See* Agency, delegation and; Committees, as agents

Agricultural policy, 194, 220n; and subsidies and logrolls, 156, 250

Agriculture Committee, 12, 20n, 24–29, 36, 39, 52, 61n, 62, 64, 69, 70, 75–77, 79–81, 183n, 194, 198, 200, 203–205, 206n, 208–210, 212, 214–218, 220, 223, 224, 229, 250, 255n, 263, 264, 266, 267, 269n, 281, 282

Albert, Carl, 156, 169, 281

American Federation of State, County, and Municipal Employees (AFSCME), 63, 72n

American Political Science Association (APSA), 9, 275

American Security Council (ASC), 63, 66, 72n, 79, 219

Americans for Constitutional Action (ACA), 63, 68, 72n, 73, 74, 76, 78n, 203n, 206n

Americans for Democratic Action (ADA), 62, 63, 72n, 74, 75, 78n, 79, 203–207, 212, 213, 219, 224

Appointments and assignments, 8, 13, 18, 21–23, 44, 58, 69n, 159, 161, 163–172, 175, 182, 183, 185–191, 194, 200, 202, 207n, 225n, 229, 231, 241, 255, 257, 259; of committee staff, 256, 262, 263, 272, 273; to control committees, 38, 164–166, 201; of freshmen, 15, 23, 25–34, 38–44, 52, 164, 183–186; history and process of, 3, 12–13, 18, 20–22, 40, 43, 50–51, 58, 225, 269n; and member requests or interests, 12, 18, 21–27, 30–34, 38–44, 52, 60, 126, 164, 166, 168n, 169, 170n, 172, 173, 176–178, 180, 182–184, 186, 188, 194, 229; minority party, 28, 29, 198; norms of appointing women, minorities, and members of state delegations, 42, 43; and representativeness, 60, 61, 188, 198–201, 224, 228, 231; and seniority, 18, 45–47,

49–51, 52–53, 279–282; and southerners, 184. *See also* Committees;
Leadership, member loyalty to; Republicans; Self-selection; Transfers;
Vacancies on committees
Appropriations Committee, 20, 28–30,
34, 36, 38, 39, 42, 43, 51, 52, 61, 70,
75–77, 80, 81, 145, 146, 159, 161,
164, 165, 177, 190, 192, 198, 200,
201, 204, 205, 207–218, 222, 223,
225, 228, 257, 258, 264, 266, 267,
269n
Armed Services Committee, 20n, 24–26,
28, 29, 36, 39, 62, 69, 70, 74–78, 80,
81, 183n, 185, 196–198, 200, 203–
205, 206n, 208–210, 212, 214–219,
221n, 222, 223, 228, 263, 264, 266–
269, 281, 282
Aspin, Les, 269, 282
Assignments. *See* Appointments and assignments
Auchincloss, James C., 49, 50n, 52, 279,
280
Automatic pilot, 8, 258–260

Bandit model. *See* Dynamic programming
Bankhead, William B., 151
Banking and Currency Committee, 12,
20n, 24–29, 36, 39, 64, 70, 74–78,
80, 81, 183n, 196, 198, 200, 203–
205, 208–210, 212, 214–218, 223,
228, 255n, 264, 266, 267, 281
Battle of the sexes. *See* Games and game
theory, battle of the sexes
Bolling, Richard, 195, 255
British parties and politics, 5, 9, 90n,
104n, 132, 133, 142n; whip and open
votes, 144
Broker. *See* Leadership, as broker
Budget balancing, and Holmström's
model, 95–97
Budget Committee, 20n, 28n, 35n, 36n,
61n, 172, 192, 203, 257, 263
Bureaucracy and bureaucrats, 17, 85,
194
Bush, Alvin Ray, 52n

Cannon, Joseph (Boss), 3, 21, 58, 163,
170, 201n. *See also* "Czar Rule"
Cartel. *See* Legislative cartel
Caucus, 49, 58, 126, 163, 165, 198, 212,
233; Black, 43, 195; Democratic, 3,
21, 45, 54n, 55, 56, 59, 131, 218,
254, 255, 259, 269, 280–282; Wom-
en's, 43
Central authority. *See* Agency, delegation

and: and central authority; Entrepre-
neurs, political and economic; Leadership; Speaker
Chairs. *See* Committee chairs
Chenoweth, J. Edgar, 52, 53
Civil rights, 112, 150, 153, 155, 157,
195, 196n, 256
Civil service exams, 257
Closed rule, 160, 243–246, 291–293
Coelho, Tony, 115
Collective action problems. *See* Collective
goals and interests; Games and game
theory
Collective benefits. *See* Goods, public and
private; Legislation, collective benefit
legislation
Collective goals and interests: of coalition partners, 58; versus individual
goals, 93, 94, 96, 108, 132, 133, 260,
277; and policy, 155. *See also* Committees, goals and interests of; Games
and game theory; Leadership, goals
of; Parties, general goals of; Legislators, general goals of; Speaker
Collective goods. *See* Goods, public and
private
Colmer, William, 56
Commerce Committee, 20n, 25, 26n,
28–30, 36, 39, 52n, 74–77, 80, 81,
183n, 185, 192, 198, 200, 204–210,
213–218, 221, 223, 255n, 256, 263,
265–267, 269n, 272, 280, 281
Committee chairs, 10, 19, 50, 51, 54n,
58, 91, 92, 123, 125, 133n, 238, 241,
255, 256, 269, 271, 272, 278, 281,
282; referral power, 255; and scheduling power, 8, 161n, 231, 233–235,
247, 248, 252; and seniority, 13, 18,
45–49, 53, 55; and southerners, 56,
57, 59, 234, 241, 248, 252, 269. *See
also* Leadership; Speaker; Subcommittee; *specific committee names*
Committee equilibrium, 247, 294; definition, 246
Committee government, 1–3, 5, 8–11,
14, 19, 45, 60, 82, 83, 159, 276, 277.
See also Subgovernments
Committee on Committees (CC), 3, 21–
23, 30, 32–35, 42, 43, 49- 51, 55,
56, 58, 60, 163–68, 177, 180, 182n,
183, 185, 188, 189, 191, 198, 200–
202, 224, 228, 229
Committee on Political Education
(COPE). *See* AFL-CIO and Committee on Political Education (COPE)
Committee reports and sponsorship. *See*
Legislation, sponsorship of

Committees: as agents, 8, 19, 159, 160n, 233, 240, 253, 276; assigning tasks to, 254–257; autonomy of, 8–10, 12–14, 17, 18, 20n, 21, 45, 47, 49, 57–61, 83, 159–161, 253, 276–278; control of, 1, 4, 8, 17, 18, 20, 43, 47, 51, 53, 58, 161, 254–259, 268; creating and destroying, 254, 271; deference and reciprocity, 10, 11, 13, 61, 67n, 79, 82, 160n, 223, 238n, 239n, 259, 260, 262, 263; extramural effects, 199, 200; goals and interests of, 67, 79, 82, 159; jurisdictions of, 8, 10–13, 17–19, 25–27, 44, 164, 188–203, 212, 213, 218, 219, 222, 223, 233, 237, 238, 242–244, 246, 249, 250, 252n, 253–256, 258, 271, 291, 294; regulating personnel, 257, 258; standing, 1, 3, 4n, 8n, 10, 17, 28n, 35n, 45, 51, 159, 170n, 188–90, 229, 231, 233, 240, 254, 280, 283; support scores of, 263, 264, 265, 267. See also Agenda, committee; Agency; Appointments and assignments; Committee chairs; Control committees; Exclusive committees; Nonexclusive committees; Representativeness of committees; Semiexclusive committees; Seniority; Staff; Subgovernments; specific committee names
Congressional Budget and Impoundment Control Act, 161n
Congressional Directory, 27
Congressional Quarterly, 27, 50, 57, 166–168, 255–257, 269, 279, 280
Constituents, 1, 121, 129, 263; interests of, 12, 18, 21, 23–27, 43, 44, 60, 62, 91, 121, 130, 134, 188–190, 193, 194, 196, 202, 229, 251; Labour party activists, 132; and reelection, 111, 134, 156. See also Voters
Consumer Federation of America, 72n
Contract theory, 85, 94, 97, 99, 103, 106, 108
Control committees, 20, 38, 61, 78, 226–228, 257, 268; assignments to, 164–166, 169–177, 182–186; non-control, 40, 174, 183–185. See also Appropriations Committee; Budget Committee; Exclusive committees; Nonexclusive committees; Rules Committee; Semiexclusive committees; Ways and Means Committee; specific committee names
Corrupt Practices Act, 90n
"Czar Rule," 19, 46. See also Cannon, Joseph (Boss)

Democratic Caucus. See Caucus
Democratic Study Group, 48
Democrats: interest group ratings, 63, 67, 68, 206n; Northern and Southern, 50, 56, 57, 59, 62, 69, 78, 117–119, 150, 151, 153–157, 171, 173, 179, 183–185, 195, 196, 201, 224, 229, 240, 250, 270–273, 278–280; rural and urban, 12, 156, 194, 197, 198, 250. See also Committees; Incentives, of majority; Interest groups, and measures of ideology; Parties; Vetoes, of majority party; Leadership
Diggs, Charles C. Jr., 282
Discharge petitions, 11n, 161n, 238, 239, 259
Discrete time model, 283
District of Columbia, Committee on, 20n, 28–30, 33, 36, 38, 39, 49, 64, 70, 195, 198, 200, 203, 218, 223, 229, 257, 267, 279, 280, 282
Dynamic programming, 235, 284, 285

Economic organization. See Organization, economic
Economist, 194n
Education and Labor Committee, 20n, 24–26, 28–30, 32, 33, 36, 39, 51, 62, 64, 69, 70, 74–78, 80, 81, 196, 198–200, 203–205, 208–210, 212, 214–219, 223, 228, 255n, 257, 264, 266, 267, 280, 281
Elections. See Constituents; Parties; Reelection
Electoral inefficiency, 122–126, 134, 277
Electoral tides, 109, 112, 115–122, 277
Entrepreneurs, 14, 83, 85, 91–93, 97, 104, 106. See also Agency; Theory of the firm, monitoring
Exclusive committees, 20, 22, 25, 34, 37, 38, 146, 164, 165, 169, 172, 263, 291. See also Control committees; Nonexclusive committees; Semiexclusive committees; specific committee names
Executive agencies, 12, 19, 58, 257n, 270n

Fair Employment Practice Commission, 50, 279
Federal spending and outlays, 26, 161n, 192, 194, 221, 269, 270
Federalist, The, 103
Floor coalitions. See Parties as coalitions, floor
Floor leader, 146, 148n, 151, 152
Foley, Thomas S., 281, 282
Food for Peace program, 255n

Food stamps, 156, 250

Foreign Affairs Committee, 20n, 25, 26, 28, 29, 36, 39, 50, 64, 69, 70, 74–78, 80, 81, 196, 198, 200, 203–205, 207–210, 214–218, 223, 228, 255, 264, 266, 267, 279, 280

Free-rider problem, 106, 125, 134, 156, 239, 278. *See also* Games and game theory

Freshmen: large class of, 55; southern, 185. *See also* Appointments and assignments, of freshmen; Republicans, freshmen

Games and game theory, 86–89, 100–102, 122, 130, 131, 135, 202, 252, 277; battle of the sexes, 86n, 88n, 94n; Chinese river boat pullers, 90, 92, 98; collective action problems, 14, 83–99, 102–106, 123–125, 134, 135, 137, 288; folk theorem, 86n, 101; group punishment, 102; majority Condorcet procedures, 131; Nash equilibria, 86–90, 95, 96, 101, 102; Pareto efficiency, 86–88, 95, 96, 98, 99n, 103; prisoner's dilemma, 86, 89–93, 94n, 96, 99–102, 104, 131, 239; retaliation, 99, 100, 102, 106, 238, 239; standardization game, 86–89, 102; tit-for-tat strategy, 99. *See also* Agency, and central authority; Collective goals and interests; Entrepreneurs; Free-rider problem; Organization, economic

Garner, John Nance, 240

Gingrich, Newt, 120

Goldwater, Barry, 56, 280, 281

Goods, public and private, 95, 99, 101, 102, 104, 108, 123, 277; and collective benefits, 87, 88, 90, 91, 103, 105, 123–125, 130, 134; particularistic benefits, 125, 134, 189, 196n, 221, 222

GOP '50 Plan. *See* Martin, Joseph

Government Operations Committee, 20n, 28, 29, 36, 39, 52, 64, 70, 74–78, 80, 81, 193, 194, 198, 200, 203–206, 207–210, 212, 213–218, 223, 255n, 267

Great Britain. *See* British parties and politics

Hansen Committee, 255

Hebert, F. Edward, 50, 51, 53, 259, 269, 281

Herter, Christian A., 50, 52, 279

Hobbes, Thomas, 14, 83, 85, 91, 93, 95, 104, 106, 131

House Administration Committee, 20n, 28–30, 33, 36, 38, 39, 46n, 193, 194, 198, 200, 207, 218, 223, 266, 267

House Directory, 69

House Journal, 27, 69

House of Commons, 133. *See also* British parties and politics

House reforms, 83n; of 1960s and 1970s, 3–5, 21–23, 169, 172, 175, 176, 179, 200, 255, 256n, 260n, 270, 271n, 276–278; early twentieth-century, 19; post-New Deal era, 275–278; and Republicans, 263n

House Un-American Activities Committee (HUAAC), 20, 28, 29, 36, 50, 51, 64, 70, 192, 203, 258, 259, 266–268

Ideal points: defined, 237n; of the electorate, 130; of leadership, 202n; of legislators, 237, 242, 243, 287, 290, 291; of the Speaker, 237, 247, 287. *See also* Spatial modelling

Incentives: of CC, 198; of central agent, 92, 93, 103, 104, 133; and collective action, 96, 98, 99, 101, 106; of committee members, 200; of interest groups, 63; of kings, 104; of majority, 245–247, 269n, 276, 294; of party leaders, 125, 134, 159; of Speaker, 128, 130, 237, 285n; of workers 95, 98, 99. *See also* Free-rider problem; Legislators; Speaker, preferences of

Incumbents, 33, 109, 111, 113, 115–117, 118, 120, 122, 131; incumbency advantage of 3, 115n, 132

Index of likeness, 220

Interest groups, 12, 19, 62, 112, 123, 194, 195, 275; and measures of ideology, 63, 67, 68, 72, 73, 79, 206, 219, 220, 224, 276. *See also* Nominal Three-step Estimation procedure (NOMINATE); *specific groups*

Interest-seeking hypothesis, 24, 26, 27, 43, 44, 60. *See also* Constituents, interests of

Interior Committee, 20n, 24–26, 28, 29, 36, 39, 52n, 62, 64, 74–78, 80, 81, 194, 195, 198, 200, 203–205, 208–210, 212, 214–218, 223, 224, 229, 267

Internal Security Committee, 254

Interstate and Foreign Commerce Committee. *See* Commerce Committee

Iron triangles, 19, 67, 160, 276. *See also* Subgovernments

Jarman, John, 281
Joint Committee on Atomic Energy, 254, 255
Joint Committee on the Organization of Congress, 257
Judiciary Committee, 25, 28, 29, 36, 39, 52, 62n, 65, 74–78, 80, 81, 105, 195, 198, 200, 203–205, 207–210, 214–218, 223, 228, 255, 256, 263, 265–267
Jurisdiction. *See* Committees, jurisdictions of

Krueger, Otto, 52, 53

Labour Party, 132. *See also* British parties and politics
Leadership, 102, as broker, 249–251; of cartel, 2, 3; Democratic, 91, 94, 255; goals of, 15, 22, 125, 132–35, 159, 187, 198, 231, 251, 252, 258, 260, 262n, 269n, 271; influence on legislation, 164, 248; and logrolls, 248, 249; member loyalty to, 14, 22, 23, 42, 43, 170n, 184; and parliamentary system, 5; of party, 4–6, 9, 14, 48n, 49–53, 94, 104, 125–135, 137, 139, 147n, 153–157, 161, 163–172, 174–176, 178–187, 229, 231, 233, 240, 257, 275, 280; and power over members and committees, 13, 19–23, 38, 46, 47, 58, 156, 163–167, 188–90, 241, 259, 260; Republican, 154, 280; and support scores, 50, 52, 74, 147, 149, 150, 152–155, 168, 263, 280. *See also* Agency, and central authority; Agenda, legislative; Agenda, party; Appointments and assignments; Collective goals and interests; Committee on Committees (CC); Entrepreneurs; Games and game theory; Legislators, general goals and interests of; Party leadership votes; Rules Committee; Speaker, scheduling power; Ways and Means Committee
League of Conservation Voters (LCV), 62, 72n, 79
Lederer, Raymond F., 282
Legislation: and consequences of structural power, 269, 270, 276, 277, 287–290; collective benefit legislation, 124, 125, 134; control by individuals, 52, 57, 58, 248, 261, 270; policy expertise, 12, 61; impact on parties, 111, 122–125, 164, 190, 198; policy inefficiencies, 134; policy making, 2, 4, 8, 19, 61, 79, 82, 83, 133, 143, 156, 160, 164, 201, 202, 237, 239, 240, 251, 252n, 257, 261,

271–273, 291; and member preferences, 7, 18, 23, 62, 108, 109, 111, 121, 123, 128–131, 135, 155, 189, 190, 213n, 242, 247, 248n; sponsorship of, 260–263, 272; stages of, 4, 262n; and subgovernments, 17–21, 23, 61, 67, 276. *See also* Committees, jurisdictions of; Spatial modelling; Scheduling power
Legislative agenda. *See* Agenda, legislative
Legislative cartel, 2, 17, 85, 270, 278
Legislative party. *See* Parties, legislative
Legislative Reorganization Act: of 1970, 4n; of 1946, 20n, 254–256
Legislators: advertising and credit claiming, 125, 189, 190; general goals and interests of, 6, 20, 55, 58, 79, 91, 108, 187–189, 191, 193, 195n, 196, 198–200, 276; and rational choice theory, 7; strategic incentives of, 2, 33, 123, 126, 182n, 239, 245–247, 278n, 294. *See also* Collective goals and interests; Constituents; Leadership; Reelection; Representativeness of committees; Self-selection; Speaker, position of, as a goal; Subgovernments
Logroll, 20, 67n, 156, 236; and collective action, 124, 125, 134; Democratic, 94; intercommittee, 61, 79, 82, 221, 234, 248–251; intracommittee, 222, 223; intraparty, 157
Loyalty. *See* Appointments and assignments; Leadership, member loyalty to; Parties, and support scores; Transfers

McCormack, James, 156, 169
Maclean's, 100n
Madison, James, 103
Martin, Joseph, 50, 279
Members of Congress. *See* Legislators; Incumbents
Merchant Marine and Fisheries Committee, 28–30, 33, 34, 36, 37n, 38, 39, 52n, 62, 65, 70, 74–77, 80, 81, 195, 198, 200, 203–205, 208–210, 212, 214–218, 223, 224, 229, 267
Miller, A. L., 52n
Miller, Clem, 1, 240
Mills, Wilbur, 160, 281
Minority party. *See* Republicans
Mondale, Walter, 112n
Multiple referrals, 191n, 256

Nash equilibria. *See* Games and game theory

National Conservative Coalition (NCC). See *National Journal*

National Education Association (NEA), 63, 72n

National Farmer's Union (NFU), 68, 72n

National Journal, 68, 72, 74, 77, 206

National Security Index. *See* American Security Council

National Taxpayers Union (NTU), 68, 72n

New York Times, 50n, 51, 56n, 151n, 279

Nominal Three-step Estimation procedure (NOMINATE), 72, 73, 78–81, 206–211, 212, 213–219, 222, 224, 225

Nonexclusive committees, 20n, 25, 37, 38, 79, 165, 169, 170, 172, 174, 175. *See also* Exclusive committees; Semiexclusive committees; *specific committee names*

Obey Commission, 262

Official Conduct Committee. *See* Standards of Official Conduct Committee

Omnibus bills and resolutions, 193, 243, 248–250, 259, 283

O'Neill, Thomas P. (Tip), 233, 236n

Open rule, 243–246, 287, 291–293

Open votes, 144

Organization, economic, 85, 92, 94, 95, 97, 104n, 235; multiperiod contracts, 99, 106. *See also* Entrepreneurs; Theory of the firm

Pareto efficiency. *See* Games and game theory, Pareto efficiency

Parliamentary systems, 5, 9, 57, 104, 107, 132, 133

Particularistic benefits. *See* Goods, public and private, particularistic benefits

Parties: cohesion, 3, 4, 108, 137, 139–145, 147, 149–151, 155- 157, 276, 277; general goals of, 2, 107–109, 121–127, 131, 132–135, 182, 187, 191, 202, 240, 251n, 252, 254, 262; goal of seat maximization, 189, 190, 198, 228; homogeneity, 7, 67, 137, 155, 156; legislative, 14, 85, 104, 107, 108, 112n, 132; organization, 3, 83, 156; strength, 4, 5, 9, 14, 109, 110, 137, 140–145, 153, 155, 156, 262n, 275; structural powers of, 2–4, 8, 9, 17, 92, 107, 141, 161, 163, 189, 231, 233, 234, 253, 254, 258, 259, 269, 270, 276, 278; and support scores, 147, 149, 166–168, 170, 171, 179, 183, 185; as unitary actors, 6, 7, 8n, 14, 108. *See also* Agenda, party; Collective goals and interests; Interest groups, and measures of ideology; Leadership; Parties as coalitions; Party government; Party platform; Party record; Party voting; Party voting cues; Party whip organization

Parties as coalitions, 108n, 249, 270; floor, 4, 5, 14, 137; procedural, 3–8, 14, 159, 231

Party government, 1, 3, 8, 9, 160, 277; conditional, 5, 137, 155; limited, 14

Party identification, 3, 110

Party leadership. *See* Leadership

Party leadership's position, 145, 146, 200

Party leadership votes, 139, 145, 146, 148n, 152–155, 170

Party platform, 6, 50, 112, 130, 279

Party record, 110–112, 120, 121, 123

Party swing, 113, 115–119, 121, 122

Party unity score. *See* Parties, and support scores

Party voting, 3, 137, 139–147, 149–151, 168

Party voting cues, 3n, 140, 145

Party whip organization, 144–146, 149, 151, 170, 233

Pascal's wager, 98

Patman, Wright, 281

Pennington, William, 134n

Peterson, J. Hardin, 50, 51

Platform. *See* Party platform

Poage, William R., 281, 282

Policy. *See* Legislation

Post Office and Civil Service Committee, 20n, 28–30, 33, 34, 36, 38, 39, 61, 62n, 65, 71, 74–77, 80, 81, 193, 198, 200, 204, 205, 207–210, 213–218, 223, 263, 265–267

President, 3, 46n, 58, 258; support of, 46, 50, 55, 56, 59, 109, 280, 281; influence of, 9, 248, 275; and impact on elections, 111, 121, 122; party of, 112n, 126; veto of, 153

Price, C. Melvin, 269, 281

Prisoner's dilemma. *See* Games and game theory, prisoner's dilemma

Procedural coalitions. *See* Parties as coalitions, procedural

Progressive ambition, 105n

Protracted seat control, 43

Public goods. *See* Goods, public and private

Public Policy. *See* Legislation

Public Works Committee, 12, 20n, 25–29, 36, 39, 49, 52n, 74–77, 80, 81, 183n, 190, 192, 198, 200, 203–210, 213–217, 223, 224, 251, 255n, 257, 265–267, 279

Rankin, John E., 50, 51, 53, 259
Rarick, John R., 281
Rational choice theory, 5, 7, 8, 83, 85, 86, 87, 93, 101, 109, 123, 126, 234, 237
Rayburn, Sam, 10–13, 45–47, 50, 58, 169
Reagan, Ronald, 112n, 155
Reciprocity. *See* Committees, deference and reciprocity
Reelection, 7, 83, 108–112, 116–118, 120, 122–130, 192, 198, 202, 225n; of leadership, 128–130, 132–134; as reason for assignments, 27. *See also* Constituents, and reelection
Referral power: *See* Speaker; Committee chairs
Reforms of the House, *See* House, reforms
Representativeness of committees, 12, 17, 18, 26, 42–44, 59–62, 69–83, 187–191, 198–225, 228, 229, 231, 257, 276; among coalition partners, 58; regional, 58, 59, 61, 62, 64, 65, 69, 72, 73, 78, 79, 224; and southerners, 56, 117, 118, 150, 271. *See also* Appointments and assignments, representativeness; Committees, jurisdictions of; Republicans; Retirement; Subcommittee
Republicans, 123, 132, 143, 149, 151, 154, 202n, 251n, 255, 256, 260n, 261, 264, 265, 267, 269, 270, 272; alliance with southern Democrats, 240; and appointments, 21, 27, 28, 51, 163, 168, 172, 201, 202n, 206; constituencies, 91, 121, 156, 190, 250; freshmen, 27–29; and interest group ratings, 63, 66–68, 203, 206, 207, 213n; loyalty among, 50, 52, 53, 67, 142, 143, 147, 151, 152, 155, 170, 171, 176, 185, 186, 251, 262, 263, 266, 268; and minority status, 125–128, 133, 233, 234, 241, 251, 254, 256, 257, 260–262, 271–273, 269n, 270n; progressive, 19; and representativeness, 43, 205, 206n, 210, 211, 213, 216–218, 225, 228; retirement rates, 120, 134; and seniority violations, 46, 49, 54, 55, 279–82; and vote swings, 113–115, 117, 118. *See also* Agenda, party; Appointments and assignments; Leadership; Party leadership votes; Transfers
Reputation: of firms, 100; of laborers, 102; of managers, 105; of parties and legislators, 123, 129, 190, 277
Retaliation Model. *See* Games and game theory, retaliation

Retirement: benefits, 105; and committee vacancies, 172; of incumbents, 115, 269; rates, 120, 125, 126, 134; and representativeness, 202; and reputation, 100
Roll call votes, 3, 4, 14, 62, 67, 68, 72, 73, 139–147, 149, 151, 152, 155, 170, 182, 203, 219–223, 263, 273. *See also* Agenda, party; Party leadership votes
Rostenkowski, Daniel, 54n, 91, 123, 133n
Rules Committee, 20, 28, 29, 34, 36, 39, 50–52, 56–58, 61, 62n, 65, 75–77, 80, 81, 159, 164, 165, 167, 177, 190, 192, 198, 200, 201, 204–210, 213–217, 219n, 223, 225–228, 234, 235, 237, 239–241, 247–249, 257–259, 263, 267, 270, 273, 278, 279

Sabath, Adolph, 257n
St. Lawrence Seaway, 257
Scheduling power, 8, 161, 190, 231, 233, 234, 247–249, 251, 252, 256, 258, 260, 271; with ample time, 243–245; with scarce time, 245–247. *See also* Speaker, scheduling power
Science Committee, 20n, 27–30, 33, 36, 37n, 38, 39, 71, 74–77, 80, 81, 193, 198, 200, 204, 205, 207–210, 213–217, 223, 255n, 265–267, 273n, 281
Self-selection, 13, 18–23, 40, 43, 44, 60, 159, 163, 167, 186, 188–190, 194, 222n, 228, 229, 276. *See also* Appointments and assignments; Iron triangles; Subgovernments
Semiexclusive committees, 20n, 25, 30n, 37, 38, 79, 165, 169, 170n, 172, 174, 175, 263. *See also* Exclusive committees; Nonexclusive committees; *specific committee names*
Senate, 50, 161, 167, 195, 196, 248, 256, 258
Seniority: system, 3, 13, 17, 18, 42, 133, 170, 171, 174, 183, 186, 200, 255, 258; violations, 45–59, 259, 279–282; comparison to academic tenure, 47, 159. *See also* Appointments and assignments; Committee chairs; Republicans
Small Business Committee, 20n, 28n, 36n, 172, 192, 203, 255n, 266, 268
Smith, Howard W., 57, 58
Southern Democrats. *See* Agenda, North and South; Appointments and assignments, and southerners; Committee chairs, and southerners; Democrats; Freshmen, southern; Representative-

ness of committees, and southerners; Republicans, alliance with southern Democrats

Spatial modelling, 5, 6, 7n, 67n, 72, 108n, 129, 202, 237, 241, 242; instability, 5, 6, 125, 129–131, 277. *See also* Ideal points

Speaker, 21, 134, 251; and appointment power, 22, 58; election of, 4; limits to scheduling power, 237–241; as policy anchor, 237, 239, 289; position of, as a goal, 91, 125, 126, 130; preferences of, 126–129, 132, 134n, 165, 235–237, 285n; referral power of, 249, 256; role of, 131, 132, 163, 164, 252; scheduling power, 8, 233, 234–238, 241–248, 252, 283–287, 290–294; strength, 3, 19, 48, 156, 159, 169, 201n, 239, 277; veto of, 235, 237–240, 244–249, 252, 283n, 286–289. *See also* Agency, and central authority; Collective goals and interests; Ideal points; Incentives; Leadership

Spending. *See* Federal spending and outlays

Sponsorship of bills and amendments. *See* Legislation, sponsorship of

Staff: of campaigns, 3n; and party ratio, 161; of committees, 233, 234n, 253, 255–258, 271, 280

Standards of Official Conduct Committee, 20n, 28n, 35n, 36n, 71, 172, 192

Steering and Policy Committee, 3, 21, 23, 165, 166, 254

Stein, Gertrude, 260

Subcommittee, 1, 27, 194n, 262, 269, 276; and agenda control, 233, 255; autonomy of, 10, 20; Bill of Rights, 271; chairs of, 48, 234, 247, 256, 272; changing status of, 3, 10, 13, 20n, 277; relation to committees, 233; and representativeness, 12; subcommittee government, 1, 3, 9. *See also* Iron triangles; Subgovernments

Subgovernments, 17, 19–21, 60, 61, 67, 73, 74, 78, 79, 160; definition, 12. *See also* Committees; Iron triangles; Representativeness of committees; Self-selection

Taft-Hartley Act, 196, 269

Tax legislation, 50, 221, 279; and health care, 255; and monarchs, 93, 103; 1986 Tax Reform act, 91, 123, 133n; "tax and spend," 190, 206

Taylor, Dean P., 52n

Thatcher, Margaret, 134

Theory of the firm, 14, 83, 85, 91–100, 104n, 106, 108; managers, 55, 94, 98, 104n, 105, 106, 254; monitoring, 91–93, 97–100, 103, 105, 106. *See also* Agency, and central authority; Entrepreneurs; Incentives, of central agents; Incentives, of workers

Thurmond, Strom, 46n, 50

Tragedy of the commons, 195n

Transfers, 35n; accommodation of, 14, 33–40, 43; as compensation 52; leader influence over, 58, 182, 183, 186, 229; and loyalty, 40, 164, 166–179, 184, 186, 222n; Republican, 175, 176; requests, 25, 27, 33, 39, 177, 180–183, 229. *See also* Appointments and assignments; Vacancies

Transition Rules, 91, 123, 133, 221

Uncovered set, 130, 131

United Auto Workers, (UAW), 62, 67, 68, 72

United Kingdom. *See* British parties and politics

Universal votes, 142–144

Vacancies, 33–35, 38, 39, 42, 171–173, 175n, 179, 182, 201, 212, 228. *See also* Appointments and assignments; Transfers

Veterans' Affairs Committee, 26–30, 33, 36, 38, 39, 51, 71, 74- 77, 80, 81, 193, 198, 200, 203–210, 212–218, 222–224, 228, 266–268

Vetoes: challengeable and unchallengeable, 238, 239, 287–289; of committee chairs, 252n, 256; of committees, 10, 237–240; and Democrats in postwar era, 270, 271; expost, 11n, 160; of floor, 245; of majority party, 15, 231, 240, 248, 262, 270; of North and South, 56–58, 271, 273, 278; presidential, 153; of speaker, 235, 237–240, 244, 245–247, 249, 252, 283n, 286, 292

Voters: and collective goods, 123, 125, 129; in England, 89; and evaluations of parties, 110, 111, 121, 275; median voter model, 269; as reelection constituency, 156, 189; and straight-party ballots, 3; utility of, 130, 276; voters' surplus, 288. *See also* Constituents; Party identification; Roll call votes; Voting

Vote swing. *See* Electoral tides

Voting cues. *See* Party voting cues

Voting, and economic conditions, 111, 121, 122. *See also* Party identification; Roll call votes; Voters

Washington Post, 49, 120, 280
Watson, Albert, 46, 56, 281
Ways and Means Committee, 20, 21, 28,
   29, 32, 34, 36, 38, 39, 44, 51, 54n,
   61, 62n, 65, 75–77, 80, 81, 91, 92,
   123, 130, 133n, 160, 164, 165, 177,
   192, 198, 200, 201, 204–210, 213–
   217, 221, 223, 225, 226–228, 255,
   257, 258, 265–266, 267, 269n, 281,
   282

Whip organizations. *See* Parties, whip or-
   ganizations
Whip votes. *See* British parties and poli-
   tics; Party leadership votes; Party
   whip organization
Williams, John Bell, 46, 56, 280, 281
Wilson, Woodrow, 9, 10
Wood, John S., 51
Wright, James C., 54n, 120, 234

Compositor: Maple-Vail Book Mfg. Group
Text: 10/13 Sabon
Display: Sabon
Printer: Maple-Vail Book Mfg. Group
Binder: Maple-Vail Book Mfg. Group